Red Hat® Linux® Fedora™ Desktop For Dummies®

by Susan Douglas and Korry Douglas

Wiley Publishing, Inc.

Red Hat® Linux® Fedora™ Desktop For Dummies®

Published by
Wiley Publishing, Inc.
111 River Street
Hoboken, NJ 07030-5774

Published by Wiley Publishing, Inc., Indianapolis, Indiana

Published simultaneously in Canada

For general information on our other products and services or to obtain technical support, please contact our Customer Care Department within the U.S. at 800-762-2974, outside the U.S. at 317-572-3993, or fax 317-572-4002.

Wiley also publishes its books in a variety of electronic formats. Some content that appears in print may not be available in electronic books.

Library of Congress Control Number: 2003114460

Part number: 0555013219

Manufactured in the United States of America

10 9 8 7 6 5 4 3

1B/RZ/RR/QT/IN

About the Authors

Susan Douglas is the CEO of Conjectrix, Inc., a software consulting firm specializing in database and security related issues. **Korry Douglas** is the Director of Research and Development for Appx Software. They are the coauthors of *PostgreSQL* (Sam's, 2003).

Susan and Korry enjoy life on a farm in rural Virginia where they raise horses and other small livestock. They telecommute to have more time to spend with their 200 or so animal friends . . . and occasionally, Gracie, the neighbor's pit bull (who comes over to hide during lightning storms).

Authors' Acknowledgments

We would like to thank the staff of Wiley Publishing who have been helpful every step of the way. The guidance and direction of Terri Varveris and Nicole Sholly has been invaluable, and the support of the folks in the media department has also been great. Big thanks go to Paul Sery, for finding time in his busy schedule to tech edit for us — we appreciate it.

Thanks also to all the developers who have made Linux a fun and useful operating system. Without them, life just wouldn't be the same.

Publisher's Acknowledgments

We're proud of this book; please send us your comments through our online registration form located at `www.dummies.com/register/`.

Some of the people who helped bring this book to market include the following:

Acquisitions, Editorial, and Media Development

Project Editor: Nicole Sholly

Acquisitions Editor: Terri Varveris

Senior Copy Editor: Barry Childs-Helton

Technical Editor: Paul Sery

Editorial Manager: Kevin Kirschner

Permissions Editor: Laura Moss

Media Development Specialist: Travis Silvers

Media Development Manager: Laura VanWinkle

Media Development Supervisor: Richard Graves

Editorial Assistant: Amanda Foxworth

Production

Project Coordinator: Erin Smith

Layout and Graphics: Michael Kruzil

Proofreaders: Laura Albert, Carl William Pierce, TECHBOOKS Production Services

---

Publishing and Editorial for Technology Dummies

Richard Swadley, Vice President and Executive Group Publisher

Andy Cummings, Vice President and Publisher

Mary C. Corder, Editorial Director

Publishing for Consumer Dummies

Diane Graves Steele, Vice President and Publisher

Joyce Pepple, Acquisitions Director

Composition Services

Gerry Fahey, Vice President of Production Services

Debbie Stailey, Director of Composition Services

Table of Contents

Introduction

This book is a guide to some of the cooler features of Red Hat Linux. The big book included in this kit (*Red Hat Linux Fedora For Dummies*) shows you how to install and configure Red Hat Linux, how to connect your computer to the Internet, and how to get some real work done. And we show you how to play. Along the way, we also show you a few productivity tools and introduce you to the KDE desktop.

About This Book

Historians tell us that, in ancient times, computer users were shackled to an archaic data entry device called the *command-line*. Recently, we've discovered that, although the command-line was originally thought to control the computer, it in fact controlled the user. The Dark Ages ended with the appearance of the graphical user interface.

Today's theological debate concerns which desktop environment you should use with your Linux computer. The two opposing factions are KDE (the K Desktop Environment) and GNOME (GNU Network Model Environment). In this book, we talk about KDE. The KDE desktop is a bundle of graphical tools, some of which are shared with the GNOME environment and some exclusive to KDE. We discuss some of each. With this book, you can

- Use the KDE productivity tools
- Take pictures with a digital camera and share them with friends
- Play games
- Watch a DVD or streaming video
- Listen to a music CD or streaming audio
- Live a Linux life in a Windows world

Note: At press time, Red Hat renamed its Linux product the Fedora Project. Throughout the course of this book, we refer to the product as Red Hat Linux or simply as Red Hat. You'll probably see the product referred to as the Fedora Project in the news, on the Web, and elsewhere, but you can rest assured that the different terms, as used in this book, are referring to the same product.

Conventions Used in This Book

This book focuses on the KDE desktop, so most of the programs that we show you are graphical in nature (as opposed to "graphic in nature" — that's something completely different). There are a few programs that just don't have a graphical user interface, and you have to resort to typing in commands.

When it comes time to type in a command, we show you the text that you have to enter in **bold**. Some commands, like `if`, would look pretty strange in the middle of a sentence if we didn't call special attention to them somehow, so they show up in `monofont`.

Simple keystrokes are . . . simple. (When we say "press the Enter key," you press the Enter key.) Some keystroke sequences are less simple, such as Ctrl+Alt+Backspace — when you see one of these, you press all three keys (Ctrl, Alt, and Backspace) at the same time.

When we want you to open an item in a menu, we write something like "choose File⇨Open". When you see that, open the File menu on the main menu and then choose Open. In some cases, we refer to the KMenu (down at the bottom of your desktop) or the pop-up menu (which appears when you right-click something). Unless we tell you otherwise, all menu choices come from the main menu.

What You're Not to Read

We've arranged this book so that you can skip over entire chapters if you don't need the information right now. If you don't need to know how to run Windows software in Linux, just skip that chapter; you won't be missing any information critical to other chapters. If you don't want to play games, ignore the gaming chapters (or just tell your co-workers that you skipped the games section; we won't tell). You can also skip over the sidebars and any paragraphs marked with a Technical Stuff icon, but you may find them interesting or at least entertaining.

Foolish Assumptions

It's not always advisable to make assumptions, but we've made some nonetheless: We assume you have a computer and that you've followed the instructions in the big book about loading Red Hat Linux on your computer, and are thrilled with the newfound speed and power that you've achieved. Congratulations!

We also assume that you want more . . . more games, more fun, more tunes, more productivity. And we assume you know the basics: You know where a

CD goes, you know how to use a mouse and keyboard. The simple stuff. This isn't quantum physics; just follow the bouncing book. . . .

How This Book Is Organized

Most of the books in the *For Dummies* series are longer than this one and are divided into four or five parts. We've done things a little differently, so we could squeeze in as much content as possible. Here's a rundown of each chapter:

Chapter 1: The first chapter is all about the KDE desktop. Find your way around the desktop, the Kicker panel, the KDE menu, and Konqueror (the KDE browser/file manager). You also find out how to add shortcuts to your desktop and adjust your personal preferences.

Chapter 2: KDE comes with a ton of productivity tools. In this chapter, you'll find everything from a simple calculator to an overachieving clipboard to a full-featured personal information manager (address book, e-mail, and organizer). We show you how to use each tool and how the tools all work together.

Chapter 3: Like listening to music while you work? How about watching a movie while you fill in your tax returns? (Okay, maybe that's not such a good idea.) Chapter 3 shows you how to use multimedia applications with Red Hat Linux.

Chapter 4: Remember that scene in *The Shining* where Jack Nicholson is typing and typing and typing? `All work and no play makes Jack a dull boy.` Take a break and play some games.

Chapter 5: Full-featured digital cameras are finally affordable and they work great with Red Hat Linux. In this chapter, we show you how to connect your camera to your computer and how to copy pictures to your hard drive.

Chapter 6: If you use more than one computer, you'll love remote desktops. Remote desktop software lets you see one computer's desktop from another. You can sit in front of your favorite monitor, mouse, and keyboard and connect to another desktop in another room or in another country. In this chapter, we show you how to install two (actually two and a half) remote desktop programs and how to use them.

Chapter 7: Wine goes well with Red Hat Linux. A good glass of Pinot Noir can mellow out those kernel-tuning sessions. If you're a programmer, you know the value of a good shot of . . . no not that kind of wine. We're talking about Wine — a tool that lets you run (many) Windows programs in Linux. The big book that comes with this kit shows you how to download and install Wine; we show you the easy way to manage Wine and what to do when your Wine goes bad.

Chapter 8: Webmin (and its trusty sidekick, Usermin) make it easy to manage your Linux computer. In this chapter, you discover the joy of system administration. Well, at least you find out that it's not as bad as it was in the old days. Webmin lets you manage your computer (or another computer) from the comfort of a Web browser. We also show you how to install and use Usermin and how to watch what your computer is doing.

Appendix: In this appendix is a list of all the software we've included on the companion CD-ROM (cool games, cool tools, and a couple of e-books). We tell you what kind of hardware you need to run each package, and we give you a one-liner that describes how to install the package. Some packages require a bit more work to install, which we cover in detail in the corresponding chapter.

Icons Used in This Book

Following the time-honored tradition of the *For Dummies* series, we use a few special-purpose icons to help you find useful information.

We use the Remember icon to point out things that you'll want to squirrel away for later use.

The Tip icons can turn you into a power-user. A tip helps you get something done in a smarter and faster way.

There's a reason that this icon looks like a bomb. Pay attention to the warnings and you'll get the benefit of our scars of experience without the trauma.

You may have noticed that there were two authors for this book. One of us wears a propeller; the other has good fashion sense. We throw in a Technical Stuff icon whenever one of us gets carried away with geek-speak.

Where to Go from Here

Everywhere! Linux is an open-source project. That means that there are thousands of programmers out there working on programs that are near and dear to them. Chances are, if you don't find what you need in this book, it's out there on the Web.

Of course, the DVD and companion CD include a lot of cool tools (and fun games). Pull up a comfortable chair, boot your computer, and pick up a good book (oh, you've already got one). Have fun!

Chapter 1

KDE and Red Hat Linux: Environmentally Friendly

In This Chapter

- Celebrating the clean desktop, a sign of a sick mind
- Customizing your desktop — make yourself at home

When you first log in to Red Hat Linux, you see the KDE desktop. The desktop is a place where you can drop frequently used applications, documents, and tools. In this chapter, we show you around the KDE desktop and then, because the KDE desktop is highly customizable, we also show you how to tailor your desktop to your needs.

Finding Your Way Around the Desktop

Along the left side of the screen (see Figure 1-1), you see a set of useful tools. The top icon (the one that looks like a trashcan) *is* a trashcan: drop things in there and they disappear. If you have a disk in your computer's floppy drive, you can double-click the floppy-drive icon to see the contents of the disk. Double-click the Home icon to view the contents of your home directory. The Start Here icon opens a window that lets you browse the applications installed on your computer, adjust personal preferences, or carry out system-management tasks.

At the bottom of your screen is the Kicker. In the following sections, we take you on a guided tour of the Kicker, starting with that funny-looking hat on the left.

Figure 1-1: The KDE Desktop.

If your desktop doesn't look like Figure 1-1, you may be using the GNOME desktop instead of the KDE desktop. (In particular, if you see a red fedora hat in the bottom-left corner of the screen, you're using GNOME.) If you want to switch from GNOME to KDE (don't worry, you can change your mind later), click the Red Hat Menu, then choose System Settings⇨More System Settings⇨ Desktop Switching Tool. Choose KDE, click OK, and then log out and back in again (to log out, click the Red Hat Menu and choose Logout). If you can't find the Desktop Switching Tool, you probably haven't installed KDE. That's easy to fix; just open the Red Hat Menu, choose System Settings⇨Add/ Remove Applications. When the application list appears, click the Install button next to KDE Desktop Environment.

The KDE menu

At the left end of the Kicker panel, you should see a button that looks like a letter 'K' with a funky artistic gear behind it. Click that button and you see the KDE Menu (which we call the KMenu). A snapshot of the KMenu is shown in Figure 1-2.

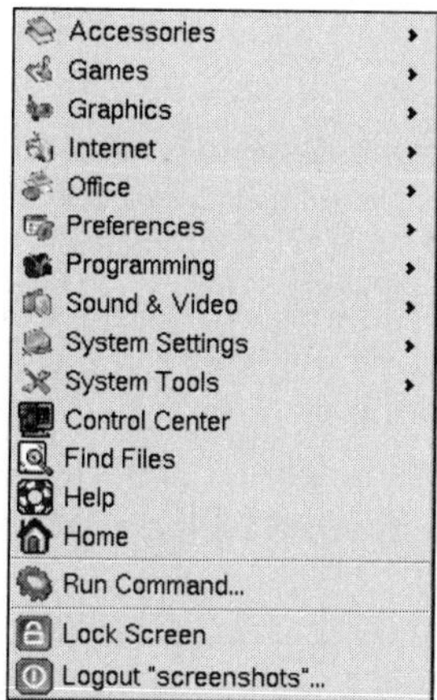

Figure 1-2: The KMenu.

Any item that has a little black arrow to the right of the name has a *submenu* (another menu hidden in there). To open a submenu, just click the name and then hover your mouse pointer over the item for a moment. Here's a quick list of the items you see on the KMenu:

- **Accessories:** On this submenu, you can find handy little tools like the clipboard viewer, printer manager, and scientific calculator.
- **Games:** This is where the fun stuff lives — don't spend *too* much time here.
- **Graphics:** Here's where you find tools (viewers and editors) for working with image files; the scanner and digital-camera tools also live in this menu.
- **Internet:** You can find Web browsers, e-mail tools, and an instant messaging tool in the Internet submenu.
- **Office:** The Office submenu contains the Open Office suite of tools; if you need a word processor, spreadsheet, or diagramming tool, this is the place to go.
- **Preferences:** Use the Preferences submenu to custom tailor your personal preferences (we show you more details of this process a little later in this chapter).
- **Programming:** If you chose the Workstation option when you installed Red Hat Linux, the Programming submenu contains a few handy programming tools; if you chose the Desktop option, you won't see the Programming submenu.

- **Sound & Video:** Want to play music or burn a CD? This is the place for you.
- **System Settings:** Use the System Settings submenu to add and remove software, change passwords, and adjust your mouse and keyboard settings.
- **System Tools:** The System Tools submenu is another collection of tools you can use to control the hardware on your system; you'll also find the Red Hat Network update-monitoring tool here.
- **Control Center:** The KDE Control Center lets you customize KDE components (you can also change hardware and networking settings from the Control Center).
- **Find Files:** A typical Red Hat Linux system starts out with over 140,000 files; Find Files makes it easy (well, *easier* anyway) to find the files you need.
- **Help:** This is a great starting point if you're looking for online documentation about your Red Hat Linux system.
- **Home:** Click the Home button to open the Konqueror Web browser (and file manager), which then opens to your home directory.
- **Run Command:** The Run Command button gives you an easy way to execute a Linux command without opening a terminal window.
- **Lock Screen:** If you're going to be away from your computer for a while, you might want to lock the screen so nobody else can mess with your system (you'll have to enter your password to unlock the screen when you get back).
- **Log Out:** Be sure to log out when you're finished; otherwise, anybody can walk up to your system and use your own personal account (to send embarrassing e-mail in your name).

If you're confused about which tools appear on the System Settings submenu, the System Tools submenu, and the Control Center, don't worry; we don't see a pattern either (somewhere there's a guy running around with a propeller on his head — we're hoping he can explain it to us).

Kickin' with the Kicker

At the bottom of your screen, you see the Kicker. If you haven't already modified your Kicker, you should see the KMenu on the left, an icon for the Mozilla Web browser, an icon for the Evolution e-mail client, and then a group of icons that launch the OpenOffice.org applications. Figure 1-3 shows the Kicker.

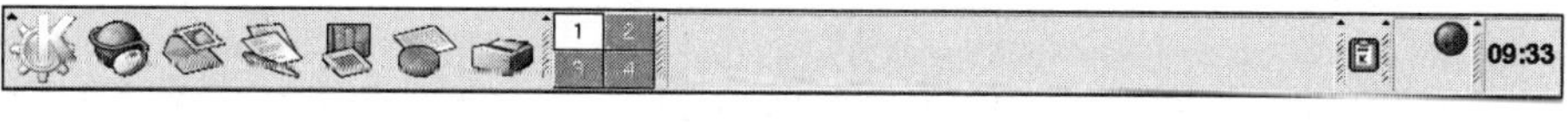

Figure 1-3: The Red Hat Linux Kicker.

To the right of the printer icon, you see the *pager*. KDE gives you one physical desktop and any number of virtual desktops and the pager lets you move from desktop to desktop.

To the right of the pager, you see the Taskbar applet (an *applet* is like a mini-application — it doesn't do much, but what it does, it does well). The Taskbar holds one button for each program that you run. Each button is labeled with the name of program (plus a little extra information, depending on the program). You can switch from one running program to another running program if you click the corresponding button in the Taskbar.

At the right end of the Kicker, you see the clipboard application (called Klipper), the Red Hat up2date throbber, and the clock. Click the clipboard to view its contents; click the clock to see a calendar. The up2date throbber keeps your system up to date with any critical patches distributed by Red Hat.

Conquering Konqueror

Konqueror is one of the most powerful tools on your desktop. Konqueror is a Web browser, a graphical file manager, an image viewer, a document viewer, and an application launcher all rolled into one easy-to-use package. To start Konqueror, just double-click the Home icon on your desktop (refer to Figure 1-1) and Konqueror displays the contents of your home directory (as in Figure 1-4).

The KDE file manager

To use Konqueror as a graphical file manager, just open a directory: press Alt+O to move your cursor to the Location field, type in the name of a directory, and press the Enter key. Konqueror makes it easy to work with files and directories. Click a directory and Konqueror opens that directory. Click a file and Konqueror tries to do something useful with that file. That probably sounds a bit vague, doesn't it? Well, Konqueror works differently depending on the file type. For example, if you double-click a program, Konqueror runs that program. If you double-click an image file (a PNG, GIF or JPEG file), Konqueror displays the image. Double-click an archive (a `.tar` or `.gzip` file, for example) and Konqueror opens the archive so that you can poke around inside it. When Konqueror doesn't know what to do with a file, it asks you to decide.

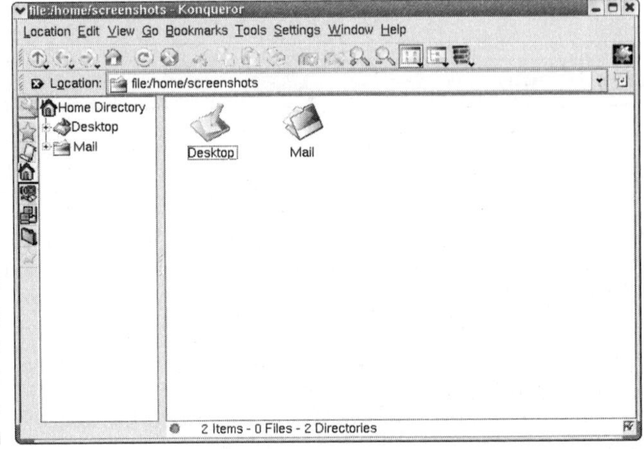

Figure 1-4: The Konqueror Application.

You can also right-click a file to choose an action from a pop-up menu (again, your choices vary by file type). To copy (or move) a file to your desktop, just drag it from the Konqueror window onto the desktop; when you drop it, you can choose to copy, move, or link the file to the desktop. You can drag files (or, for that matter, complete directory trees) from place to place without using the desktop as a middleman — but you must have two Konqueror views open first.

You can open a new Konqueror window by choosing Location⇨New Window, but Konqueror has a much cooler feature to impress your Windows-savvy friends: Choose Window⇨Split View Left/Right and Konqueror splits your window into two views (vertically). Choose Window⇨Split View Top/Bottom and Konqueror splits your window into two views (horizontally). You can have as many views open as you like. So here's the easiest way to copy something from one location to another:

1. **Navigate to the file that you want to copy or move.**
2. **Split your Konqueror window either horizontally or vertically.**
3. **Navigate to your target location (that is, where you want to copy *to*).**
4. **Drag the file from one view to the other.**

You can copy or move an entire directory tree simply by dragging the folder from one view to another.

Konquering the Web

Konqueror is a very capable Web browser. To open a Web page, enter a URL in the Location field and press the Enter key. For example, to view the KDE Web site, try the following:

1. **Open Konqueror and press Alt+O to move your cursor to the Location field.**
2. **Type** www.kde.org **and press Enter (or click the Go button to the right of the Location field).**

In a few moments, you should see the KDE Web site. To jump to another page on the KDE site, just click one of the links — Konqueror shows you the new page in place of the old one. What if you want to view two pages at once? Konqueror gives you three different ways to view multiple pages:

- Right-click a link and choose Open in New Window; Konqueror opens a second window to display the new page.
- Split your Konqueror window (Window➪Split View Left/Right or Window➪Split View Top/Bottom) and drag a link to the other window.
- Right-click a link and choose Open in New Tab.

Split views are handy when you want to see two (or more) Web pages side by side. Tabbed viewing is nice when you want to switch between two or more Web sites quickly but need more screen real estate than you would get using split views.

Konqueror gives you three quick ways to jump to Web sites that you visit frequently:

- **History:** The history list keeps track of all the sites you've visited.
- **Bookmarks:** A *bookmark* is a shortcut that *you* create so you can get back to an interesting location.
- **Web Shortcuts:** A *Web shortcut* is a (very) short name for a much longer URL.

The easiest way to work with your history list or bookmark list is to use the *navigation panel*, which lives on the left edge of the Konqueror window. If you can't see the navigation panel, press the F9 key to open it (press F9 again to close it). From top to bottom, the navigation panel buttons take you to these handy places:

- The Navigation Panel configuration options (click the Multiple Views option to open multiple windows in the navigation panel)
- Your bookmark list (click an entry to jump to that page)
- Your history list (click an entry to jump to that page)
- Your home directory (also known as `$HOME`)

- Useful Web sites (in this case, *useful* is defined by the KDE authors)
- The root directory (also known as "/")
- Services (a handy way to see the devices on your system, the computers on your local network, and the printers on your local network)

To make the navigation panel smaller, just double-click any of those buttons (double-click again to expand the navigation panel). To close the Navigation Panel completely, click Window⇨Show Navigation Panel.

Web shortcuts are abbreviations for longer URLs. For example, if you want to do a Google search for the phrase *1812 Overture*, move your cursor to the Location field, type in `gg: "1812 Overture"` (remember to include the quotation marks), and press the Enter key. The "`gg:`" part is a shortcut for a Google search and the `"1812 Overture"` part is a search phrase. Most of the predefined Web shortcuts are wired to search engines. To see a complete list of Web shortcuts, choose Settings⇨Configure Konqueror⇨Web Shortcuts.

Tailoring Your Desktop

The KDE desktop was designed to work in the same way that a real desktop works; it's a place to keep things that you need to find quickly and easily. You can drop frequently used documents (and Web addresses) on the desktop, and you can also keep useful tools on your desktop.

Adding shortcuts to the desktop

A shortcut is just what it sounds like — a quick way to get somewhere you want to be. Creating a shortcut is easy. Follow these steps to create a desktop shortcut that takes you to the KDE Web site:

1. **Right-click in an empty area of your desktop and choose Create New⇨ Link to Location (URL).**
2. **When the pop-up window appears, type** `KDE Web Site` **in the File Name field.**
3. **Type** `http://www.kde.org` **in the URL field.**
4. **Click OK.**

That's it! Your desktop now contains a shortcut labeled `KDE Web Site`. If you click that shortcut, Konqueror opens, showing you the home page for KDE.

The icon that KDE assigned to this shortcut isn't very intuitive. You can change the icon like this:

1. **Right-click the shortcut and choose Properties from the pop-up menu that appears.**
2. **Click the picture that looks like a blank page (that's the default icon) and choose a new icon from the list that KDE displays.**

   Click the Devices button to choose an icon from another category (you can choose from action icons, application icons, device icons, file-system icons, and mimetype icons). Click the Other button to see more choices.
3. **When you've made your choice, click OK to close the Icon Chooser.**
4. **Click OK to close the Properties dialog box.**

Tailoring your configuration

You can custom tailor KDE panels and menus to fit your own personal style. By using the KDE Control Module, you can change the placement and size of the panels and the appearance of the icons on your panel.

Panel configuration

To open the KDE Control Module, right-click the Kicker panel and choose Configure Panel. The KDE Control Module opens with the Layout menu selected and Arrangement tab open (see Figure 1-5).

The Control Module features three menus altogether:

- **Layout menu:** This menu features three tabs — Arrangement, Hiding, and Menus — that you can use to affect how the panel looks on your screen.

  On the *Arrangement tab* (refer to Figure 1-5), you can control the placement and size of the panel (remember to click Apply to see your changes right away):

  - **Move the panel:** Click one of the placement boxes shown in the position grid to move the panel. If you choose to make your panel narrower than the entire screen width, the left/right positioning affects placement.
  - **Lengthen or shorten the panel:** Below the position window, you see a slider tool; this makes the panel shorter or longer. If you want to adjust the panel length, move the slider or adjust the percentage of the screen devoted to the panel.
  - **Change panel icon height:** To select your icon height, use the radio buttons in the Size box. Choose from preset sizes that range from tiny to large, or select Custom to set the icon size as a specific number of pixels.

The *Hiding tab* features options to hide panels when not in use, or to create panel hiding buttons (little arrows on the ends of the panel that you click to hide or bring back the panel when you need it). It might seem like you are hiding the handiest part of the screen by doing this, but if screen real estate gets tight, this can free up a bit of space.

The *Menus tab* is where you go to configure the appearance of the KMenu. You can also access the KDE Menu Editor (to add and remove menu items) via the Edit KMenu button located near the middle of the screen — we get to that in a moment, in the section "Menu configuration."

- **Appearance menu:** Click the Appearance button if you want to change the colors of the panel buttons and background. You can also enable or disable tooltips from this window.
- **Taskbar menu:** Configure the taskbar from this menu. You can change the appearance of the taskbar and you can define what happens when you click a mouse button on the taskbar. (Of course, we've never actually met anyone geeky enough to *need* this configuration window.)

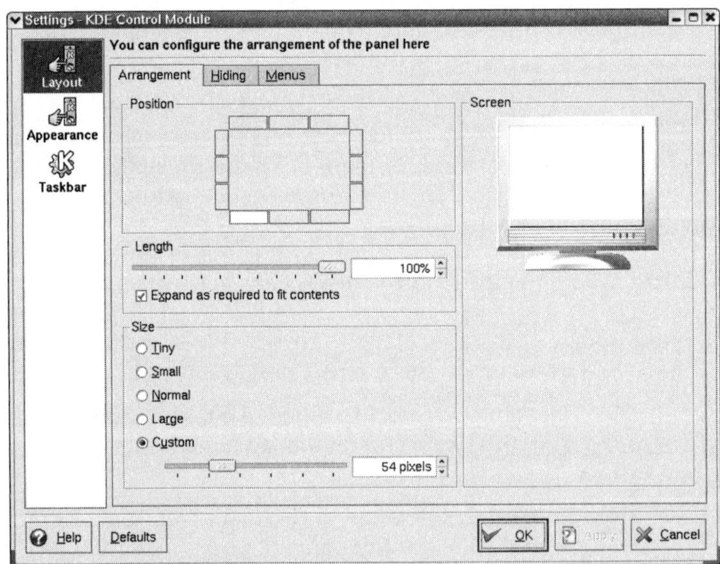

Figure 1-5: The KDE Control Module dialog box.

Adding applications to a panel

When you know you'll be using an application often, adding a launcher for that application to the panel is a real timesaver. To add an application icon to the panel:

1. **Right-click a blank space on the panel and then click Add on the pop-up menu that appears.**
2. **Click the Application button.**

   A pull-out menu that looks suspiciously similar to the Main Menu appears.
3. **Find your application on the menu and click the application's name or icon.**

   Like magic, an icon for your program appears on the panel. Just double-click the new icon, and the program starts.

Menu configuration

Menu customization starts with a visit to the KDE Menu Editor, where you can rearrange the icons to a more logical order, or create a *favorites* submenu sorted by project, preference or . . . really, any way you like them sorted. Open the menu configuration options by right-clicking the KMenu and choosing Menu Editor. The KDE Menu Editor appears, as shown in Figure 1-6. To move an item from one submenu to another, just drag it to the new location.

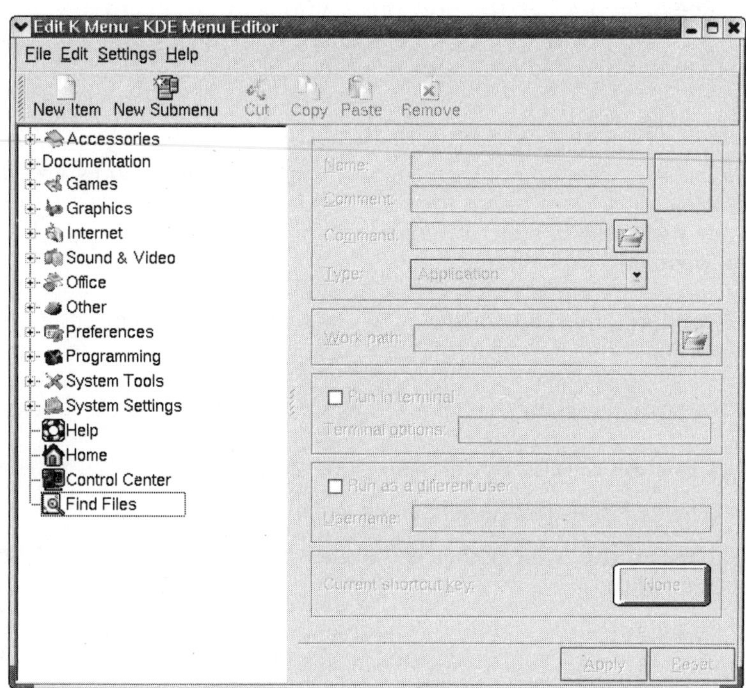

Figure 1-6: The KDE Menu Editor.

If you need a new submenu to hold project-related applications, or just want a custom menu for games and media, that's easy to do too. To create a new submenu, open the KDE Menu Editor and then follow these steps:

1. **Click the white space below the menu tree (just to be sure that any tree items are deselected).**
2. **Select the New Submenu icon — it's the second one from the left on the toolbar.**
3. **Enter a name for the new submenu, and click OK.**

   You find the new submenu at the top of the menu tree. When you finish, the menu items appear in alphabetical order, but for now it's at the top. Now the fun begins. . . .
4. **Click the submenus to find things that you're interested in, and drag and drop the applications you want into your favorites menu.**

Setting your preferences

If you've been through the previous sections of this chapter, you're probably noticing a trend here — you can rearrange and set personal preferences for most anything in Red Hat Linux.

Themes (for those of you with Sensitive Skins)

A *theme* is a collection of icons, mouse cursors, colors, and sometimes sounds that are coordinated to set the look and feel of your desktop or browser. People with time to spare often create themes and post them on the Web for busy people to download.

KDE comes prepackaged with a few themes; visit `www.kdelook.org` for lots of downloadables tailored to fit the KDE desktop.

Setting a theme is often referred to as *skinning*. To skin your desktop:

1. **Click the KMenu button and then choose Control Center.**

   The KDE Control Center opens as shown in Figure 1-7.
2. **Expand the Appearance & Themes menu and then click Theme Manager.**

   In the resulting window, you have the option to choose from prebuilt packages of icons, backgrounds, borders, and wallpapers that give your desktop the look of that theme.

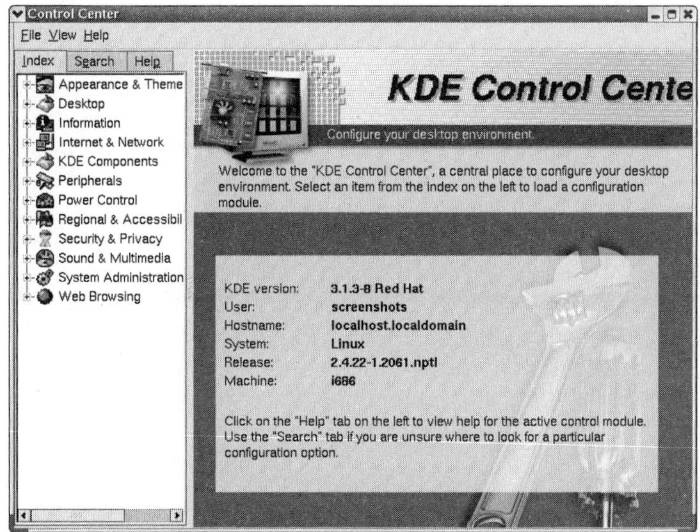

Figure 1-7: The KDE Control Center.

3. **Click a theme name to highlight it.**

   A preview of the look and feel appears in the box to the right.

4. **When you find a theme you like, click the Apply button.**

If you aren't finding any themes that suit your taste and/or lifestyle, you can customize your KDE desktop with your own preferences.

Stylizing your icons

You can change the group of icons used by KDE to a style that suits your liking. Set your Icon Theme by following these steps:

1. **Open the Control Center (as described in the preceding section).**
2. **Expand Appearances & Themes and then click Icons.**

   A window opens, offering a list of themes — click a theme name to see the icons associated with that theme displayed at the top of the window.

3. **After choosing a theme for your desktop icons, click the Apply button in the lower-right corner.**

   The screen repaints, and your new icons are displayed.

If you choose an icon set other than the default (Bluecurve), your KMenu will likely change its appearance — we still refer to it as the KMenu even though it may not have a 'K' on it.

Making your font preferences known

Use the KDE Control Center to set your font preferences as well. Open the KDE Control Center, expand Appearances & Themes, and then click Fonts.

The window that opens has a list of the font groups with a Choose button out to the right. The groups are pretty much what they sound like — the Taskbar font shows up on the Taskbar, the Menu font is used to paint menus, and so on. To change a given font, follow these steps:

1. **Click the Choose button to the right of the font you want to change.**

   The Select Font dialog box opens, as shown in Figure 1-8. This box contains the attribute information for the font you've chosen to modify. Play with the font type, size, and styles (you can make it Bold or Italic too), until you find one you like.

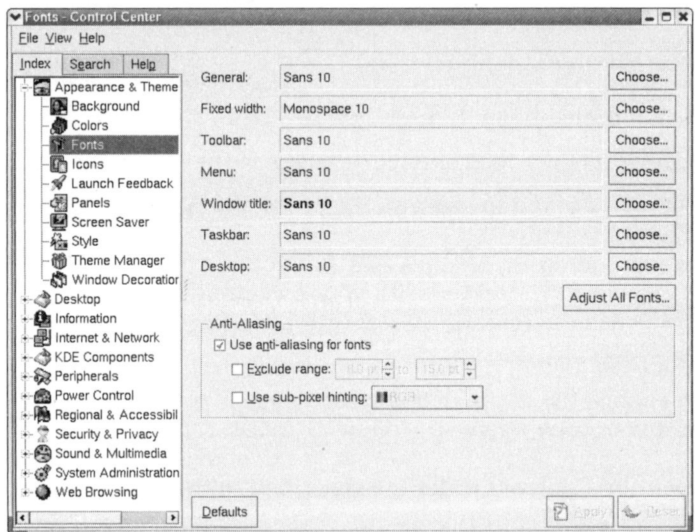

Figure 1-8: The Select Font dialog box.

2. **Click OK to apply the newly chosen font to your screen.**

We can never resist trying it, but we should tell you that Dingbats and Symbols can be a bear to read.

Choosing colors of desktop features

You can also set desktop colors using the KDE Control Center menu. Open the KDE Control Center and expand Appearances & Themes and then click Colors. The window in the top half of the display has samples of the various places on your screen that you can change the colors of.

To change the color of the Active Window Titlebar (just an example), follow these steps:

1. **Click the color bar for the Active Window.**
2. **Within the Widget Color box, click the color bar to open the Select Color dialog box.**
3. **Point and Click the new color you want for the titlebar.**
4. **Click OK, and the changes are reflected in the sample box at the top.**
5. **When you've created your new color scheme, click Apply.**

The same basic steps work to change the colors on any of the items shown in the sample box. You can also choose items to modify with the pull-down menu. If you're not in a creative mood, you might want to choose from the series of preset color patterns shown in the Color Scheme box; just click to preview the color, and then choose Apply to apply the changes.

Changing the background colors

In the KDE Control Center, you can also set background colors for your desktop. Choose Main Menu➪Control Center➪Appearances & Themes➪Background. The window that opens has a preview desktop in the right corner, the desktop name you're modifying in the left corner, and your choices for wallpaper and color on tabs across the bottom.

You can choose a common background for all your desktops, but it's handy (or just plain entertaining) to have a different wallpaper or color pattern for each. To set individual backgrounds, be sure the Common Backgrounds box is not selected.

Click a desktop to make it active. Then choose from among the tabs at the bottom of the window to customize colors, gradient fills, and wallpapers.

Be sure the `No Wallpaper` option is selected if you want to use background colors and gradients — the wallpaper option overrides the color screens.

Setting up your screen saver

A screen saver is a program that kicks in when your desktop is inactive for a while. KDE comes with a number of cute screen savers that you can choose from. Choose Main Menu➪Control Center➪Appearances & Themes➪Screen Savers to customize your screen saver. Consider these issues when you set up your screen saver:

- Do you want the screen saver to start automatically? If so, check the Start Screensaver Automatically box, and enter a delay (in minutes) in the After text box.
- Do you want to require a password when you wake up the screensaver? If so, mark the Require Password to Stop Screensaver check box.
- Last, but most important, what screen saver do you want to display? This can range from a blank screen to any number of screen savers that you can download. A great place to look for screen savers is `www.kdelook.org`. After downloading and installing your screen saver, preview it by clicking the test button. (Move your mouse to stop the test when you've seen enough.)

Screen savers are often adjustable — you can change how many widgets show up on the screen and how fast they move (use the Setup button below the list of screen savers). Point, click, and have fun. Just don't forget to apply any changes you want to keep.

Chapter 2

Using KDE Productivity Tools to Your Advantage

In This Chapter

- Talking KDE into recognizing your removable media
- Grabbing stuff with Klipper — a talented and versatile clipboard
- Looking smart with KDict
- Putting away your slide rule and opening up KCalc
- Tracking your time with KAlarm and KArm
- Keeping track of (ahem) *stuff* with KNotes and KJots
- Getting (really) organized with the KDE organizers
- Snagging news, news, and more news (KNode and KNewsTicker)
- Chatting with your buddies

KDE is more than just a desktop. When you install KDE on your Red Hat Linux system, you're installing a whole suite of desktop productivity tools (KDE calls these tools "accessories"). Many of its accessories stand alone. KCalc, for example, is a sophisticated desktop calculator. Other accessories (such as KOrganizer and KAddressBook) cooperate with each other to make your desktop feel completely integrated.

When you're comfortable with the KDE accessories, you can use them to do all sorts of things you may not have thought about doing before. The KDE accessories can help you prioritize your work; organize your time; and stay informed about the world outside your door.

Running Autorun

The Autorun tool is, in effect, a "CD-ROM mounter for the lazy user." (If you can relate to that, think about raising your hand.) Autorun isn't very visible; it just sits in the background and watches your CD drive for you, and it's useful if you want KDE to automatically fire up the CD Player whenever you insert an audio CD into your CD drive. By default, Autorun examines your CD (or DVD) drive once each second to see whether you've inserted any useful media. If you do insert an audio disc, Autorun starts the CD player (kscd). If you insert a data CD, Autorun mounts the disc on the /mnt/cdrom file system. To enable Autorun, open the KMenu and choose Accessories⇨Autorun. (Autorun doesn't show you anything that tells you that it's running, but it's there in the background somewhere.)

Before you can access the information on a data CD, you have to *mount* the file system contained on that CD over the top of a directory. After you've mounted a CD, the content of that CD is accessible within the directory that you chose as a mount point. The usual place to mount removable media is in the /mnt directory. You typically mount a data CD over the /mnt/cdrom directory. The /mnt/floppy directory is where the data from your removable medium (in this case a floppy-disk drive) would appear. Autorun automatically mounts the CD drive for you, so you don't have to remember a complex command.

In a typical Linux system, only the *superuser* (a user account named root) is allowed to mount whole file systems (a security feature that keeps nasty people from loading harmful media into your system). If you trust your physical environment (that is, if you know that nasty people can't get their hands on your CD drive), you may want to relax that restriction so that mere mortals can change CDs. To do so, just follow these steps:

1. **Log in as user** root **(or use the** su **command to give yourself superuser privileges).**
2. **Open the file** /etc/fstab **in your favorite editor (**kate **or** kedit **will do).**
3. **Find the line that controls access to your CD drive (it's usually the line that starts with "**/dev/cdrom**").**

   It may not be obvious, but each line in /etc/fstab contains six columns:

   - The device name (/dev/cdrom).
   - The name of the mount point (/mnt/cdrom).
   - The file-system type (udf,iso9660).
   - The fourth column is the one you want to change — it should contain a comma-separated list of options such as noauto,owner,kudzu,ro.
   - The sixth column is used by the backup utility and some system maintenance programs. Don't mess with this column.

4. **Add the string "`,user`" to the third column so that it looks like this:**

```
noauto,owner,kudzu,ro,user
```

5. **Now save your changes and close your editor.**

   After making this change, you can play music CDs or mount data CDs without having to give the superuser password each time.

Autorun has a lot of capabilities that aren't enabled on a typical Linux distribution: You can run a program automatically each time a CD is inserted — or each time a CD is ejected — and you can even change the name of the CD player that starts when you insert a music CD.

For a complete list of Autorun options, enter the command `autorun -help` at a command-line prompt. If you want to change your Autorun options, edit the "`Exec=`" entry in your `$HOME/.kde/Autostart/Autorun.desktop` file.

Klipping with the Clipboard

The basic *clipboard* application for Red Hat Linux is a temporary container for items that you cut, copy, and paste. When you cut or copy something, it goes to the clipboard. When you paste, you get back whatever you most recently added to the clipboard. (If you're an experienced Windows user, you're already familiar with the notion of a clipboard.) If you've never used KDE's clipboard tool (Klipper), you ain't seen nothin' yet. It's really amazing to see what the crew at KDE added to the basic clipboard.

The cut, copy, and paste operations in most KDE applications work pretty much the way you would expect. Highlight the text that you want to copy and press Ctrl+C to copy (or Ctrl+X to cut) and then use Ctrl+V to paste from the clipboard. You can also use the old Windows shortcuts — Ctrl+Insert to copy, Shift+Delete to cut, and Shift+Insert to paste.

In most applications, you can select a range of text by using the mouse. Just click (and hold) the left mouse button on the starting character and drag the mouse to highlight the text that you want to copy or cut. Unlike the Windows Clipboard, Klipper puts the text that you select on the clipboard as soon as you release the mouse button. That's about all you can do with the standard clipboard. Pretty simple so far.

Normally, the clipboard is invisible, but you can view its contents by pressing Ctrl+Alt+V. The first thing you might notice is that Klipper doesn't just hold the last object that you cut or copied; instead, it keeps a history of your clipboard operations. Press the Esc key to close the Klipper window.

So what can you do with such a clipboard *history stack*? When you cut or copy, you put things onto the top of a stack. When you paste, you paste whatever is on the top of the stack. With Klipper, you can also rearrange the history stack in case what you need isn't at the top. To rearrange your clipboard history, follow these steps:

1. **Press Ctrl+Alt+V to see your history stack.**
2. **Click an item to move it to the top of the stack.**

   You can also change the selection using the up- and down-arrow keys; press Enter when you've highlighted your choice.

Whenever you paste, you paste the topmost item on the Klipper stack.

Klipper has one more trick up its sleeve — and this one's pretty cool. Press Ctrl+Alt+V again to open the Klipper window. If you don't see a check mark next to the line that says `Actions Enabled`, press Alt+Ctrl+X to tell Klipper that you want to enable actions. Now copy the following text to your clipboard:

```
mailto:wishlist@microsoft.com
```

If things go well, a small window should pop up close to the task bar at the bottom of your screen (if that doesn't happen, press Ctrl+Alt+R).

What just happened? Klipper recognized a *pattern* on the clipboard and triggered an *action* associated with that pattern. In this case, Klipper noticed that you copied a string that started with `mailto:` — and Klipper knows that when you copy (or cut) something that starts with `mailto:`, it should offer you the chance to send an e-mail. Klipper recognizes a number of patterns straight out of the box:

- Copy a string that starts with `ftp://` and Klipper offers to start an FTP session for you (using Konqueror, Mozilla, or Netscape).
- Copy a complete pathname that ends with `.jpg` and Klipper offers to fire up a picture viewer (`.jpg` files are usually JPEG photos).
- Copy a complete pathname that ends with `.txt` and Klipper offers to open that file with a text editor.

You can add your own patterns and actions to the Klipper, but it's not for the faint of heart. For more details, see the online KDE Help Center (open the KMenu and choose Help).

KDict — Dictionary, Thesaurus, CIA Fact Book

Using the KDict accessory is like stuffing the reference section of your local library onto your desktop. When you open KDict, you see a window that looks suspiciously similar to a Web browser (in fact, you need an Internet connection to use KDict), as shown in Figure 2-1. You can find KDict in the Accessories section of the KMenu.

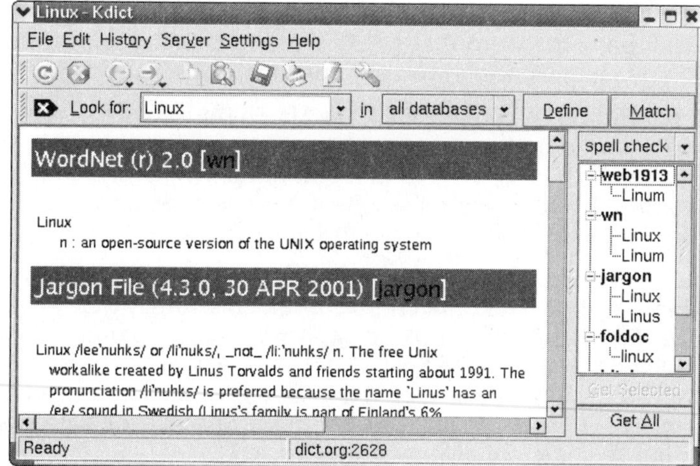

Figure 2-1: The KDict window.

Time to explore the parts of KDict:

- **Look For text box:** Underneath the toolbar is a Look For text box where you can type a word or phrase to search for; press Enter and KDict connects to a dictionary server and searches for a definition of the word that you entered. The results show up in the large window below the text box.

  A *dictionary server* is a host out on the Internet that provides a dictionary lookup service for programs like KDict. When you install KDict on your system (and that usually happens when you install KDE), it assumes you want to use the public dictionary server at `www.dict.org`, where you can also choose other dictionary servers to fit your needs. If you find a server more suitable to your work habits, tell KDict to use that server by clicking the Configure KDict toolbar button and then typing the server name into the `Hostname` field.

Sometimes your search results contain hyperlinks. If you click a hyperlink, KDict searches for the definition of that word or phrase. This feature is handy for following a trail of synonyms and antonyms.

- **All Databases button:** Immediately following the Look For field, you see an All Databases button. If you click that button, you probably won't see any choices other than All Databases. If you find that you use KDict frequently, you may want to group databases into meaningful database sets (that's what the next-to-last toolbar button does), such as *foldoc and jargon* for computer-related terms. When you have defined a few database sets, the All Databases button lets you choose which database set you want to query.
- **Define button:** When you click the Define button, KDict searches for the definition of the word that you entered (this is the same thing that happens when you enter a word and press the Enter key).
- **Match Button:** When you click the Match button, KDict searches for words *similar* to the word that you entered and displays the possible matches in the tree view to the right of the results window. You may be surprised by some match results — for example, trying to match the word Linux winds up with hits for *Linux*, *Linus*, and *Linum*.
- **Spell Check button:** This button controls the type of match that KDict performs. By default, Match uses a search strategy that works well for *spell checking* (that is, looking up words when you don't know the exact spelling). If you click the Spell Check button, you can choose other search strategies (such as *exact*, *prefix*, *substring*, *regular expression*, or even *soundex similarity*). Play around with the Spell Check button a little to try out the different search strategies.
- **Get Selected and Get All buttons:** Below the Spell Check button is a tree of match results. Click the one that you want and click the Get Selected button to see that definition in the main results window, or click the Get All button to retrieve all the definitions.

If you find that you use KDict frequently, why not add KDict to your KDE panel for easy access? See the KDict online help for more information.

Kalculating with KCalc

The scientific calculator packaged with KDE is more talented than your average desktop calculator. You can personalize KCalc to fit your needs. If you need Trig functions, KCalc can handle it. If you need statistical functions, KCalc can help. If you need to do math in a numbering system other than the usual decimal, KCalc understands hexadecimal, octal, and binary (you can even do extremely geeky things like left-shifting, *and*-ing, and modulo-ing). You can even cut, copy, and paste values using the clipboard. To start KCalc, open the KMenu, then choose Accessories➪Scientific Calculator. Figure 2-2 shows the KCalc accessory.

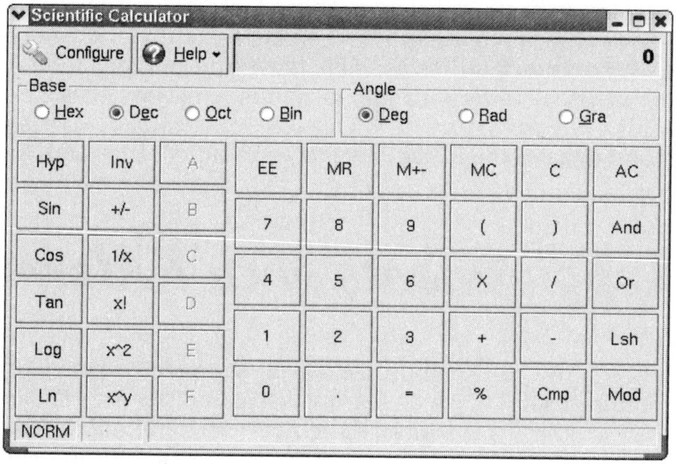

Figure 2-2: KCalc.

The following bullets highlight the various parts of KCalc and describe how some of its functions work:

- **The Configure button:** One click opens a dialog box where you can customize precision, fonts, and colors. You can also choose between a layout specialized for trigonometric work and a layout tailored for statistical work.
- **Standard math functions:** Use KCalc in the same way you would use any other calculator: Just type in the numbers you want to work with, separate them with operators (such as +, ×, and –), and click (the virtual equivalent of pressing) the equals-sign key to see the result. If you want to call a function (such as the Sine function), just enter the operand value and click the button that corresponds to that function.
- **Angle area:** If you're entering angle values, you can choose between degrees, radians, or gradians (1/400th of a circle). You can convert between angular units of measurement by entering a value in one unit, and then choosing the unit you'd like to convert to.
- **Base area:** The Hex, Dec, Oct, and Bin buttons switch between base-16 (hexadecimal), base-10 (decimal), base-8 (octal), and base-2 (binary) numbering systems. If you need those buttons, you already know what to do with them.

- **Single key accelerators:** These are shortcuts that KCalc knows. For example, the Enter key also acts like the Equal-sign button. You can find a complete list of shortcuts in the online help text (Help➪KCalc Handbook).
- **Interactivity with Klipper:** This is a particularly handy feature of KCalc. Click the display to copy the current value to the clipboard. Right-click the display to paste from the clipboard into KCalc (if you don't have a numeric value on your clipboard, KCalc pretends that you pasted a zero). KCalc also features a *results stack*. You can recall the result of previous calculations with the up- and down-arrow keys.

Go ahead and poke at the KCalc buttons — you can't break anything.

Keeping Appointments with KAlarm

Using the KAlarm accessory is kind of like arranging for a wake-up call in a high-tech hotel. You can set multiple alarms at specific times and ask KAlarm to do something useful when an alarm is triggered. To start KAlarm, open the KMenu, then choose Accessories➪More Accessories➪KAlarm. To create a new alarm, choose Actions➪Menu from the KAlarm menu bar. You should see a dialog box similar to the one in Figure 2-3, showing the Alarm tab.

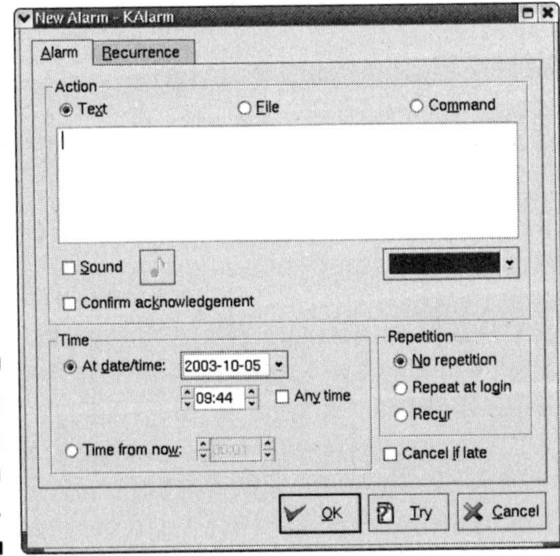

Figure 2-3: Adding a new alarm in KAlarm.

This dialog box is split into two parts: The Time area (bottom) where you schedule the alarm, and the Action area (top) where you tell KAlarm what to do when the alarm is triggered. Take a look at the bottom set of controls:

- **At date/time:** Use this button to enter the exact date and time that you want the alarm to fire.
- **Time from now:** Click this button and you can type in an interval such as 02:45 (meaning the alarm should fire 2 hours and 45 minutes from the time you set it).
- **Repetition:** To the right of the Time controls, KAlarm gives you a chance to define the repetition type for this alarm. Your options are
  - *No Repetition:* A one-time alarm fires at the designated time, and only then.
  - *Repeat at login option:* The alarm is triggered each time you log in. In this case, the date/time that you specify controls when the alarm stops triggering, not when it starts.
  - *Recur:* Schedules a recurring alarm. When you create a recurring alarm, go to the Recurrence tab of the dialog box to tell KAlarm how often you want the alarm to recur (every hour, every day, every week, and so on). You can also tell KAlarm when to *stop* firing a recurring alarm on this tab.
- **The OK, Try, and Cancel buttons:** Click OK when you're finished defining your alarm or click Cancel to call the whole thing off. Click Try if you want to test out your alarm without having to wait for the timer to expire (kind of handy just to make sure you've got the action defined properly).

The three radio buttons across the top are the most important items in the Action area:

- **Text:** Select this button to create a text alarm (that is, just a simple pop-up message).
- **File:** Select File if you want to display the contents of a given file when the alarm goes off.
- **Command:** This button lets you execute a command at the appropriate time.

What happens when an alarm is fired? That's pretty much up to you. You can have KAlarm display a textual message in a pop-up window (see Figure 2-4), display the contents of a file (looks similar to Figure 2-4 except that the pop-up displays the contents of the file), or execute a Linux command. A command alarm simply executes a command. If the command creates a window, you'll see that command pop up on your desktop; if not, the command executes silently.

Be aware that when you ask KAlarm to schedule a command, KAlarm does *not* create a window for that command. For example, if you want to schedule the `top` command to display the CPU usage pattern for your system, you can't just enter a command name of `top`. If you do that, `top` does in fact execute, but you won't be able to see it. Instead, you can tell KAlarm to execute the command `konsole -e top`; this way, KAlarm creates a shell window (the konsole) and then `top` runs within that window. If you want to run a command that exits as soon as it completes (unlike `top`, which runs until you interrupt it), you should include the `-noclose` flag. For example, to schedule the `who` command, you should tell KAlarm to execute the following command:

```
konsole -noclose -e who
```

Figure 2-4: An alarm fired by KAlarm.

Tracking Your Time with KArm

The KArm accessory gives you a handy way to keep track of how much time you spend working on projects. With KArm, you can quickly create a whole forest of tasks and subtasks (and sub-subtasks, and sub-sub-subtasks. . . .). Start KArm by opening the KMenu and then choosing Accessories⇨More Accessories⇨KArm. When you start working on a task (or subtask), fire up KArm, select the task you're working on, and press *S* to start the timer (the Escape key stops the timer).

To create a new top-level task, do the following:

1. **With the KArm accessory up and running, press Ctrl+N or click the third toolbar icon from the left (it looks like a blank sheet of paper).**
2. **Enter a task name in the field provided.**

   This name should be something that you can easily recognize as a project. For example, if you happen to be a consultant (or a lawyer), you might create a top-level task for each of your clients.
3. **If you've already spent some time on this task, you can use the Edit Absolute or Edit Relative controls to enter a starting value.**

   If you don't enter a starting value, KArm assumes that you haven't spent any time on this task and the timer starts at zero.
4. **Click the OK button.**

Voilà! You have a new task. If you press the S key (or click the leftmost toolbar button), KArm starts accumulating time for that task. KArm continues to credit time to this task until you close the application or click the Stop button (in the toolbar). When you close KArm, it saves the time accumulated for each task and subtask that you have created. The next time you open KArm, you can just click a task and tell KArm to start accumulating time for that task.

If you double-click a running task, it stops accumulating time. If you double-click a stopped task, it starts accumulating time.

You can also create *subtasks* — subordinate parts of parent tasks. For example, in Figure 2-5, you see two top-level tasks (`Earn a living` and `Play with dogs`). Underneath the *Play with dogs* task, you see four subtasks, each corresponding to one of our four lovable mutts. If I select the *MoDean* task and click the Start button, KArm starts accumulating time for *two* tasks (the *MoDean* task and the *Play with dogs* task). Why? Because when you spend time on a subtask, you are spending time on the parent as well (if I wrestle with MoDean, I'm also playing with the dogs).

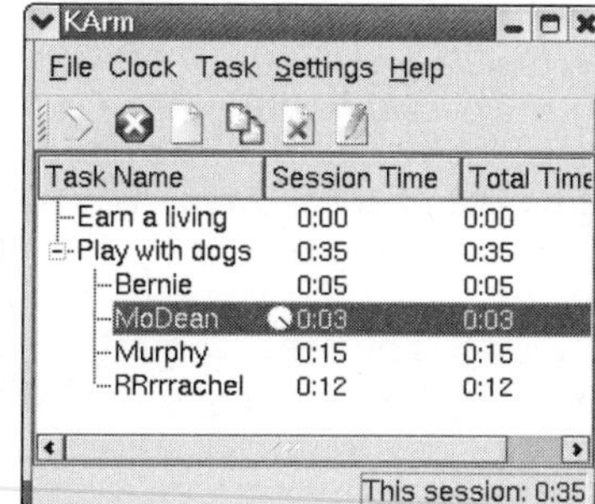

Figure 2-5: Tasks and subtasks in KArm.

To create a subtask, do the following:

1. **Select the parent task and press Ctrl+N.**

   Or you can click the fourth toolbar icon from the left (this one looks like a stack of blank pages).

2. **Fill in the blanks just like you're creating a top-level task, and then click OK.**

Now that you know how to get information into KArm, how do you get the information back out again? Simply choose File➪Print. The standard KDE print dialog box appears, and you can print a simple report that shows all tasks and subtasks, and the amount of time spent on each one.

Keeping KNotes

KNotes is a very simple tool. You use KNotes to create little sticky notes on your desktop. When you fire up KNotes, a small icon appears on your taskbar.

Right-click that icon and you should see a menu that you can use to create new notes or to configure KNotes. When you start the KNotes accessory (open the KMenu and then choose Accessories➪More Accessories➪KNotes), a small window appears on your desktop and the text cursor moves to that window, waiting for you to type in a message. A typical KNote looks like Figure 2-6.

Figure 2-6: A KNote.

There are two active parts to a KNotes window. Click the message text to change the message (right-click the message text if you want to see some standard shortcuts like Cut, Paste, and Undo). Click the title bar of the KNote window to mail or print the note, rename the note, create a new note (or delete the current one), or set your KNotes preferences.

If KNotes was running the last time you logged out, it automatically starts the next time you log in to KDE. In other words, when you log out of KDE, make sure you've arranged your desktop the way you want it to look the next time you log in.

KJotting Things Down

The KJots accessory is a tool that lets you organize notes into more meaningful (and usually lengthier) collections called *books*. Each KJots book has a name (of your choosing) and is divided into pages. You can create as many books as you like, each book can contain an unlimited number of pages, and each page can contain as much (or as little) text as you like.

You'll find KJots on the KMenu, in the Accessories➪More Accessories area. The first time you run KJots, it asks you to create a new book (all you have to do is choose a name for the book — you know, `MyBook`, `War and Peace`, the usual). You can always create a new book later by choosing File➪New Book, or by pressing Ctrl+N. When you have created a new book, you can start typing on page one. While you are editing a page, the usual edit shortcuts (such as Cut, Copy, Paste, and Find) should work. If you want to start a new page, just click the leftmost toolbar icon (the one that looks like a blank sheet of paper) or press Ctrl+Shift+N.

To move from page to page, you can use any of the following methods:

- Choose Go⇨Previous Page, press the Page Up key, or click the Previous Page toolbar button to move to the previous page.
- Choose Go⇨Next Page, press the Page Down key, or click the Next Page toolbar button to move to the next page.
- Choose Go⇨Go to Page, press Ctrl+L, or click the Go To Page toolbar button to choose a new page from a list of pages.

Figure 2-7 shows a snapshot of the KJots window. Below the main editing window is a Hotlist area. The three buttons in the Hotlist area correspond to the books that you use most frequently. You can add a book to the Hotlist by selecting that book (from the Books menu) and choosing Hotlist⇨Add Current Book to Hotlist. After you've added a few books to the Hotlist, you can switch to another book by clicking the corresponding button.

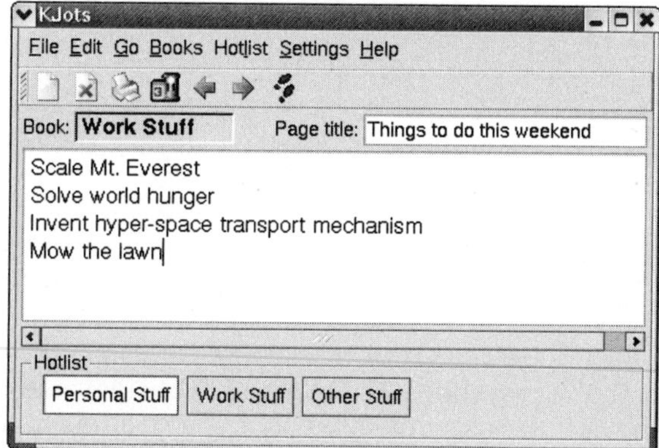

Figure 2-7: The KJots application.

KJots books are stored underneath your home directory in a subdirectory named `$HOME/.kde/share/apps/kjots`. If you look in that location, you'll see one file per KJots book. Notice that these files are not encrypted in any way, so you may not want to keep a personal diary in KJots.

As does any good application, KJots lets you get your data back out again. To print the current book, choose File⇨Print. You can also export the current book (or just the current page) to a flat ASCII file of your choice by choosing File⇨Save Book to ASCII File or File⇨Save Page to ASCII File menu options.

KAddressBook, KMail, and KOrganizer

The KMail, KAddressBook, and KOrganizer tools all work together to create a personal information manager (PIM). As you can probably guess, KMail is an e-mail client, KAddressBook is a sophisticated address book, and KOrganizer is a calendar/scheduling tool.

KAddressBook

To start KAddressBook, open the KMenu, then choose Accessories⇨More Accessories⇨Address Manager. Figure 2-8 shows the main KAddressBook window. Immediately below the toolbar you see a scrolling list of the entries you have added to your address book. If you click one of the column headers (Given Name, Family Name, E-mail Address, or Role), the list is sorted by that column (click again and the ordering is reversed). You can add a new entry by pressing Ctrl+N, choosing File⇨New Contact, or by clicking the New Contact button on the toolbar (click the button that looks like a blank sheet of paper).

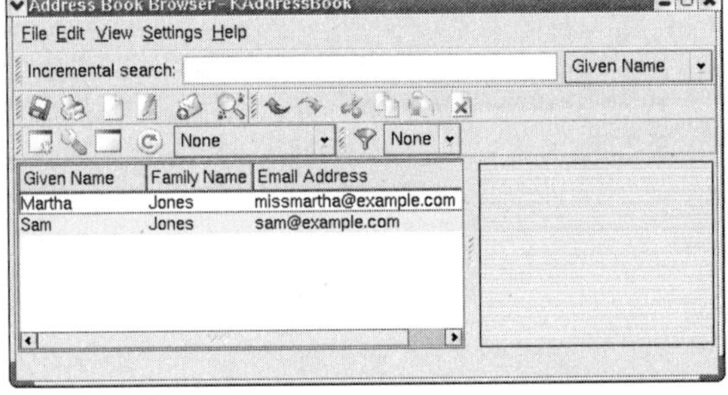

Figure 2-8: The KAddress Book accessory.

When you add a new entry (or when you modify an existing entry), a dialog box appears, similar to the one shown in Figure 2-9. This dialog box might look a bit intimidating at first; just remember that you don't have to fill in all the blanks. If you want to use KAddressBook along with KMail, the two most important bits of information are the Name and E-mail address.

KAddressBook is a feature-rich application — you can keep lots of information for each contact in your address book. To see an example, click the Name button. You should see a dialog box where you can enter a prefix (Mr., Mrs., Dr., or one of your own invention), a given (or first) name, additional names, family (or last) name, suffix (such as Jr. or Sr.), phone number, street address, Web address, and Instant Messaging (IM) address.

Notice the two None buttons in Figure 2-8. Use the left None button to devote some screen real estate to the contact editor or the distribution-list editor. (The other None button lets you apply a *filter* to the list of names in your address book — you can create a new filter from the Settings⇨Edit Filters menu.) A *distribution list* is just a handy nickname for a group of contacts. Creating a new distribution list is a bit tricky. Try the following:

1. **With the Distribution Lists window open, click the New List button.**
2. **When prompted, enter a name for the new list (something like *bad-jokes-list*) and click OK.**

3. **Now move your mouse back to the scrolling list of contacts, click the one you want, and drag it down to the distribution list.**

That's it! It's not difficult to build a distribution list, but `KAddressBook` doesn't have a Add This Contact to My Distribution List button, so you have to use the drag-and-drop trick instead.

Remember, you can click a column header to sort the contacts by that column and you can drag and drop the column headers to change the left-to-right ordering of the columns themselves.

KAddressBook is a handy tool all by itself, but it's priceless when you combine it with KDE's e-mail client.

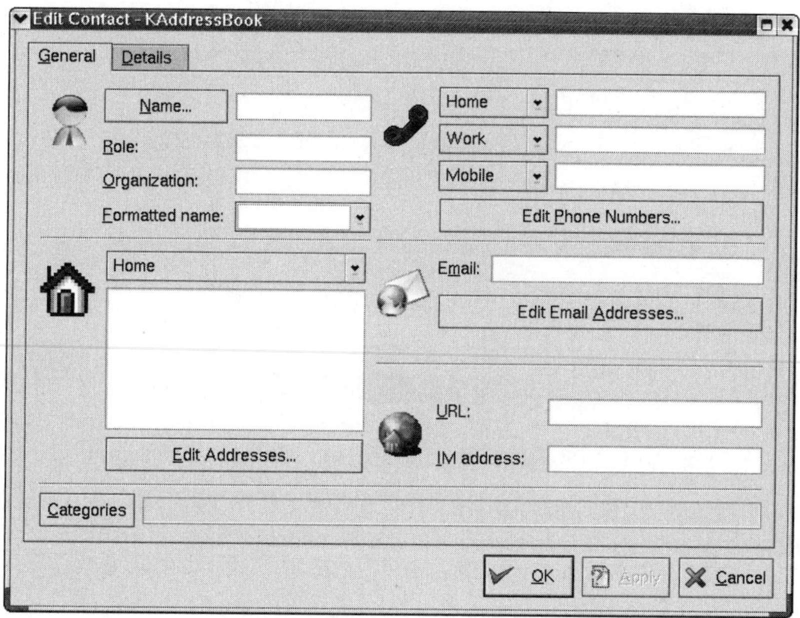

Figure 2-9: Adding a new contact in KAddress Book.

KMail

KMail is an e-mail client that you use to compose, send, and receive e-mail. To run KMail, open the KMenu and choose Internet⇨More Internet Applications⇨KMail. When you fire up KMail, you see a window similar to Figure 2-10.

Before you can use KMail, you must have an e-mail account; this is usually provided by your ISP (Internet service provider), but you can also find free e-mail servers on the Web. Your ISP or e-mail provider gives you the information you'll need to connect KMail to your ISP's mail server. You'll need the following nuggets of knowledge before you can *send* e-mail:

- The SMTP host name
- The SMTP port number
- Your login name and password for the SMTP server
- Any special authentication instructions

You also need the following information before you can *receive* e-mail:

- The type of e-mail server (POP3 or IMAP)
- The POP3 or IMAP port number
- Your login name and password for the server
- Any special authentication and encryption instructions

When you have all that information, you can give it to KMail by choosing Settings⇨Configure KMail, and then clicking the Network button.

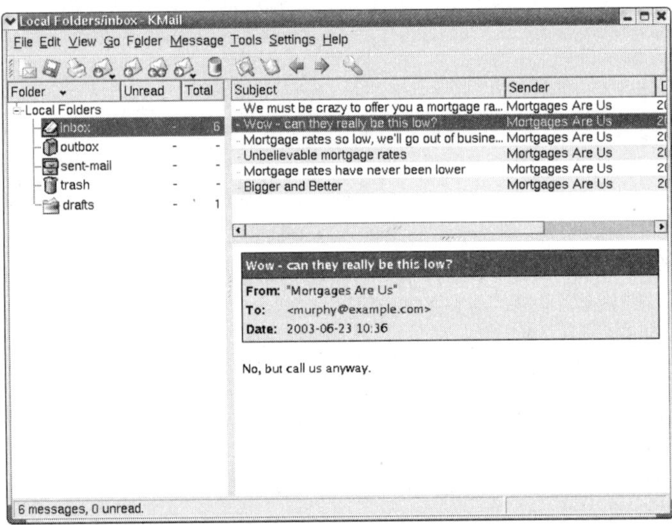

Figure 2-10: KMail main window.

Finding your way around the main KMail window

Notice that the main KMail window (refer to Figure 2-10) is divided into three panes. In the left pane, you see a list of *folders*. A folder is simply a place where e-mail messages hang out until you put them somewhere else. KMail automatically creates the folders you see in Figure 2-10 the first time you run the program; you can create new folders by right-clicking Local Folders and selecting New Folder (or by choosing Folder⇨New Folder from the menu bar).

In the top-right pane of the main KMail window, you see the list of e-mail messages in the active folder. Here are a few things you can do with the message list:

- Click a message to display it in the bottom-right pane.
- Double-click a message to view the complete message in its own window.
- Click a column header to sort by that column (click again to sort the messages in reverse order).
- Grab the horizontal scrollbar (underneath the top-right pane) and pull it to the right to see more information about each message.
- Change the left-to-right column ordering by dragging a column header to a new location.

The bottom-right pane displays the contents of the message that is currently selected.

Filtering your messages

KMail sports a powerful message-filtering package. You can create filters to do any of the following

- Bounce the message back to the sender (see following steps)
- Forward the message to another recipient
- Move the message to another folder
- Execute a command against the message
- Check for a specific sender
- Check for offensive words or phrases in the subject line (you have to tell KMail *which* words and phrases you find offensive)
- Check for offensive words or phrases in the body of the e-mail
- Filter by message size

If you look closely at Figure 2-10, you'll notice that we receive a lot of unsolicited offers from helpful salespeople around the Web — and we bet that you do, too. A nice feature of KMail is that you can create filters to help weed out messages that you don't particularly care to see. Follow these steps to create a filter that weeds out all those incredibly useful and welcome mortgage offers from this particular sender:

1. **Right-click an offending message in the top rightmost pane.**
2. **When the pop-up menu appears, choose Create Filter⇨Filter on From.**
3. **In the Filter Rules dialog box (Figure 2-11), click the Move to Folder button, choose Bounce from the pop-up menu that appears, and then click OK.**

   Now, whenever you receive an e-mail from this sender, it's rejected (it *bounces* back to the sender with a reply stating that the original message was undeliverable).

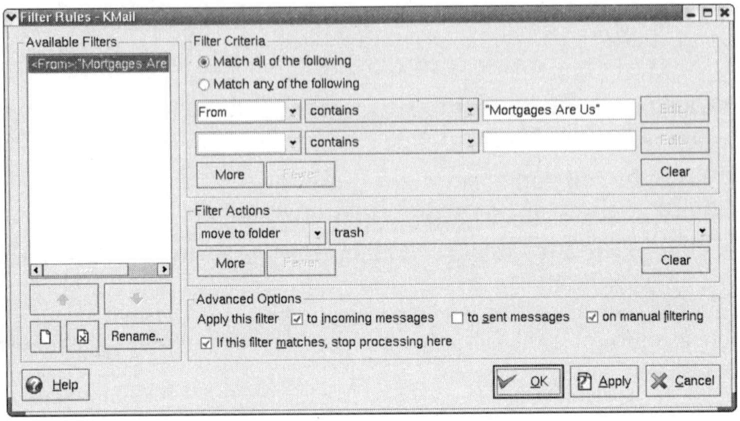

Figure 2-11: Creating a new filter with KMail.

Sending mail

So far, we've talked about receiving e-mail messages. At some point, you're going to want to *send* a message with KMail. Composing and sending an e-mail message is easy. Click the leftmost toolbar button (the one that looks like a blank sheet of paper with an envelope on top), and then press Ctrl+N or choose Message➪New Message from the menu bar. KMail opens a smallish window (see Figure 2-12) where you can enter recipient names (in the To field), a subject line, and the body of your message.

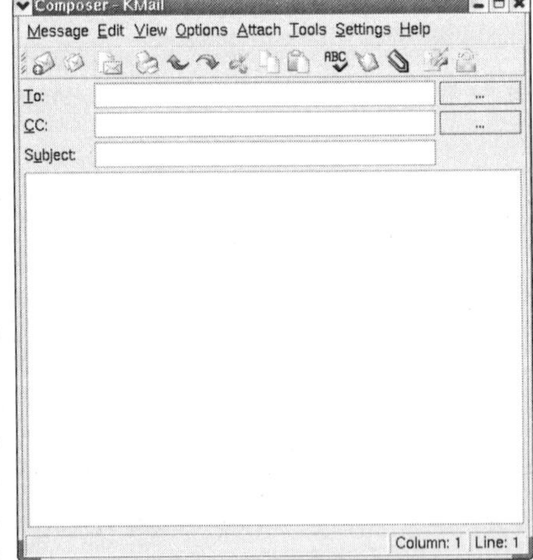

Figure 2-12: Composing a new message in KMail.

KMail lets you address mail in the usual three ways: To, CC, and BCC.

If you don't see the BCC field when you're composing a message, choose View⇨BCC (or View⇨All Fields) from the menu bar.

To the right of the To, CC, and BCC fields are three buttons. Click one of those buttons and you can choose a recipient from your KAddressBook address book — very handy.

When you're finished composing your e-mail, you can send it on its way by clicking the leftmost button on the toolbar, pressing Ctrl+Enter, or choosing Message⇨Send from the menu bar. (If you close an outbound e-mail without clicking the Send button, KMail asks whether you want to save the message in the Drafts folder.)

KOrganizer

The KOrganizer accessory is the third member (along with KMail and KAddressBook) of KDE's PIM triumvirate. KOrganizer is primarily a scheduling tool that you can use to manage your own schedule and coordinate with other KOrganizer users.

You can start KOrganizer by choosing KMenu⇨Accessories⇨More Accessories⇨KOrganizer. The first time you run KOrganizer, you should see a window that looks similar to Figure 2-13. There's a lot going in this window. On the left side you see a calendar displaying the current month (the current day has a box around it). The right half of main KOrganize's window can morph into many different views. The default view (shown in Figure 2-13) is the Day view. In the Day view, you see your schedule for the day on an hour-by-hour basis.

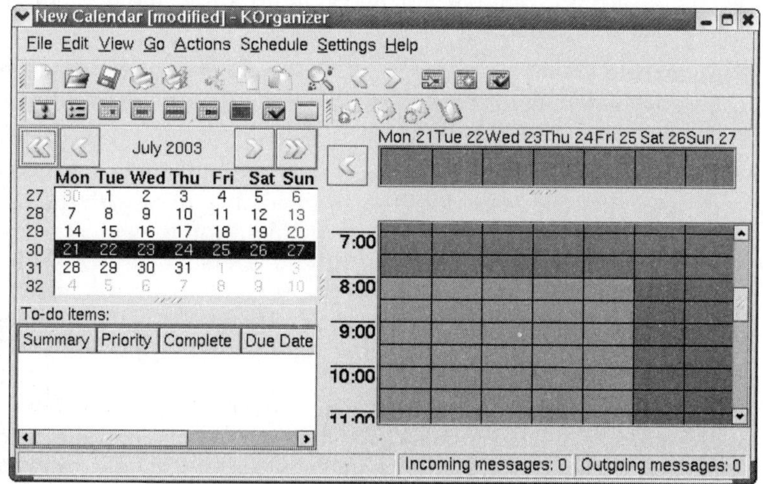

Figure 2-13: The main KOrganizer window.

To see events scheduled on a different day, just click that date in the calendar display (on the left). You can choose from any of the following views:

- **Day:** View your schedule for any given day.
- **Next 3 Days:** View your schedule for the next 3 days (or for any 3 consecutive days).
- **Work Week:** View your schedule for any given work week.
- **Week:** View your schedule for any given week.
- **Month:** View your schedule one month at a time.
- **What's Next:** View the next few items on your schedule.
- **List:** View your schedule as a simple list (rather than a cutesy looking day organizer).
- **To Do List:** View your To Do entries (more on To Do lists in a moment).
- **Journal:** View your journal entries for any given day (a journal is sort of like a diary — just a collection of notes that you want to attach to a particular day).

You can change the Next 3 Days view to Next 9 Days, Next 2 days, or any value you like by navigating to Settings⇨Configure KOrganizer⇨Views. You can also change the hour at which your workday begins.

Here are your options for scheduling events and coordinating with others:

- **New event:** To schedule a new event, choose Actions⇨New Event from the menu bar (or click the New Event button on the toolbar). The event editor gives you tons of options, most of which you can ignore for now. The most important parts of an event are the Summary, Start Date/Time, and End Date/Time.
- **Recurring event:** If you are scheduling a recurring event (a meeting every Monday morning for example), check the Recurring Event box and click the Recurrence tab to tell KOrganizer how often to reschedule your event.
- **Coordinating events:** If you want to coordinate an event with other people, click the Attendees tab and add attendees with the button labeled New. KOrganize can send an invitation to each attendee on your behalf (just be sure to enter the attendee's e-mail address). To send the invitations, finish defining the event, then choose Schedule⇨Request. KOrganizer drafts an e-mail for you (addressed to all attendees); when you're happy with the e-mail, just send it on its way.

If you've poked around on the menus in KOrganizer, you may have noticed that you can schedule events and To-Do items. What's the difference? An event is an interval of time (that is, an event has a start date and an end date). A To-Do has an end date (such as "I need to get the oil changed by next Thursday"). An event can recur; a To-Do cannot. To-Do's show up in the To-Do list view, events don't. Other than that, To-Do's and events behave the same.

Reading Newsgroups with KNode

A *newsgroup* is a public forum where anyone can contribute to a discussion (or start a new discussion). Newsgroups usually have names such as `alt.glassblowing`, `rec.equestrian`, or `redhat.general`. The leading part of the name is used to group newsgroups into broad categories (`comp.` for computer-related discussions, `rec.` for recreational newsgroups, `alt.` for alternative issues, and so on).

Before you can read (or post a message to) a newsgroup, you must have an account on a news server. Your ISP (Internet service provider) probably offers a news service.

To connect KNode to your service provider, you need the name of the news server (that is, the host name). Some news providers also require a username and password. When you have that information, fire up KNode: just open the KMenu and choose Internet➪More Internet Applications➪KNode. The first time you run KNode, the Preferences dialog box appears, as shown in Figure 2-14.

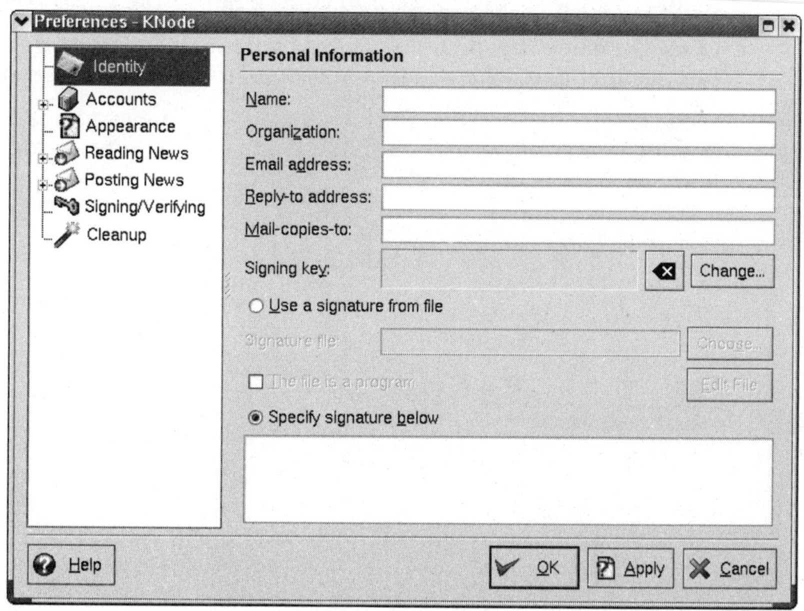

Figure 2-14: KNode preferences.

The following steps show how to connect KNode to your service provider and then subscribe to newsgroups:

1. **Leave all the Personal Information text boxes blank for now and click Accounts in the left pane.**

   We strongly suggest leaving the personal information empty in KNode until you've poked around for a while. You should assume that any information that you put into KNode is viewable by everyone else on the Web. There's no better way to invite unsolicited e-mail than to post a newsgroup message from your real e-mail address.

2. **Click the News button and an (empty) list of Newsgroup Servers appears.**

3. **Click the New button (no *s*) and then fill in the blanks in the Server Signup dialog box.**

   The Name field is for your own use, so you can just make up a name (the name of your ISP is probably a good choice); enter the host name that your ISP gave you in the Server field. If your ISP gave you a login name and password for the news server, check the Server Requires Authentication check box and enter the username and password.

4. **Click OK to close the Server Signup dialog box, and then click OK again to close the Preferences dialog box.**

   At this point, you should be back at the main KNode window and your news server should be listed in the left pane.

5. **Right-click the server name and choose Subscribe to Newsgroups.**

6. **Click Yes when KNode tells you that you don't have any groups for this account and asks whether you want to fetch a current list.**

   When KNode has finished downloading a list of newsgroups from your provider, you should see the Subscribe to Newsgroups dialog box shown in Figure 2-15.

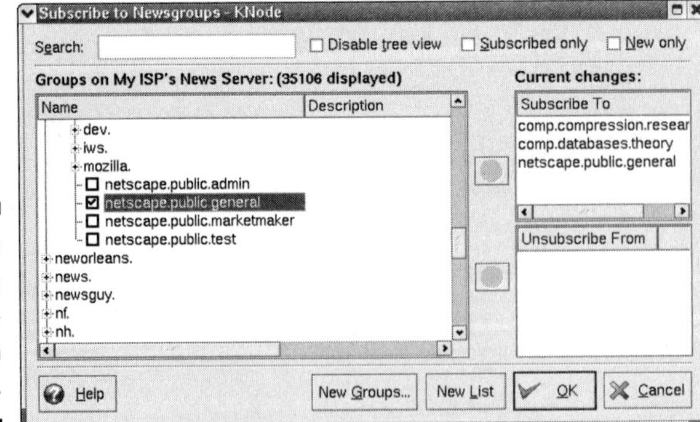

Figure 2-15: Subscribing to newsgroups with KNode.

Posting to a newsgroup

There is a complex set of online ethics when it comes to posting a message (or a reply) to a newsgroup. For example, unless specifically invited to send e-mail, you should never reply to a post except by posting a follow-up message to the newsgroup. Messages that you post should be appropriate to the newsgroup that you post to. We recommend that you lurk for a while before you post a message. Find out the rules by watching what others do and seeing how readers respond to different posting styles.

When you're reasonably sure that you want to start a new discussion (or reply to an existing one), go to the Preferences dialog box by choosing Settings➪Configure KNode and fill in your personal information. To start a new discussion, select the group you want to post to and choose Article➪Post to Newsgroup. To reply to an existing message, select the message and choose Article➪Followup to Newsgroup.

Now you can scroll through the list of newsgroups (on the left) and subscribe to the ones you are interested in (just double-click to subscribe). When you subscribe to a newsgroup, you aren't really sending any information to the server; you're just telling KNode that you want to peruse the messages in that group.

There are a lot of newsgroups out there. Our ISP serves up over 35,000 newsgroups! You can always come back to this window to subscribe to (or unsubscribe from) other newsgroups later. Just choose Account➪Subscribe to Newsgroups from the menu bar. When you've selected the newsgroup that you want, click OK and you're back to the main KNode window. To browse through the messages in a newsgroup, just click the newsgroup name. After a short delay, you should see a list of subjects currently being discussed in that group. If a plus sign appears to the left of a subject, that topic is *threaded*, meaning that one or more readers have posted a reply to that topic. Click the plus sign to see the replies. To read a message, just click it (right-click a message to see your other options).

Watching the Headlines with KNewsTicker

If you want to know what's happening in the world around you (and you have an Internet connection), KNewsTicker is the ticket. The KNewsTicker accessory looks sort of like one of those old-fashioned stock tickers (the kind that spit out a stream of narrow paper tape). KNewsTicker scrolls through a stream of news headlines. Where do the headlines come from? That's pretty much up to you. Straight out of the box, KNewsTicker gathers headlines from the following news sources:

- **KDE Dot News:** This is a news feed dedicated to all things KDE.
- **Slashdot:** Self-described as "News for Nerds — Stuff that matters."
- **LWN.net:** This is the source for Linux news (well, one of them anyway).
- **kuro5hin.org:** With a name pronounced "corrosion," this group offers news about technology and culture.

If you want to see more, er, traditional news, you can tell KNewsTicker to connect to news sources such as CNN, HotWired, or eFilmCritic.

When you see a headline that captures your interest, click the headline and KNewsTicker opens your favorite Web browser and points it to the full story.

Most people embed the KNewsTicker in the Kicker panel (see Chapter 1 for more about the Kicker), but you can also run KNewsTicker in its own window. Just open the KMenu and choose Internet➪More Internet Applications➪KNewsTicker. Figure 2-16 shows a KNewsTicker running in its own window:

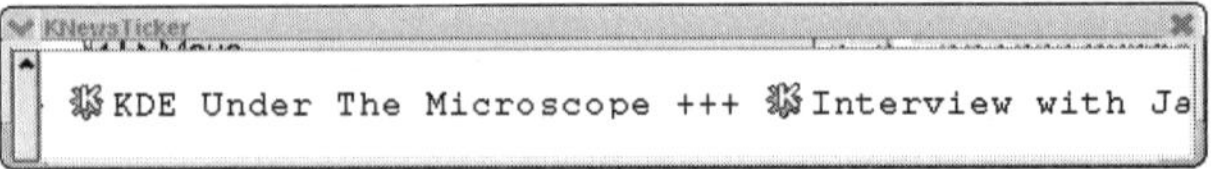

Figure 2-16: KNews-Ticker.

Whether you embed KNewsTicker in the KDE panel or in its own window, click the little up arrow at the left end of the window to open the configuration menu. From there, you can choose alternate news feeds, create news filters, and tell KNewsTicker to scroll headlines up, down, left, or right.

Instant Messaging

If you've watched TV at all within the last few years, you've heard of instant messaging. What is instant messaging? Instant messaging gives you a way to hold an online conversation with friends (or strangers, but we won't go there). Each participant in your conversation must run an instant messaging (IM) client. KDE's IM client is called Kit. You can find Kit in the Internet➪More Internet Applications section of the KMenu.

Before you can use IM to chat with your friends, you have to create an account on a messaging server. Most people use AOL and Kit is happy to talk to AOL on your behalf. The first time you fire up Kit, it asks whether you'd like to create an AOL account; choose Yes and your Web browser pops up at the AOL signup site. When you complete the signup process, do the following:

1. **Minimize your Web browser window so that you can see Kit again.**
2. **Type in a Profile name and click OK.**

   You can use any name you like here (nobody else will know if you want to call yourself Commander Magnificent).
3. **Enter the screen name and password that you obtained from AOL (other people will know you by your screen name).**
4. **Mark the Save Password check box if you want Kit to remember your password for you.**

   If you tell Kit to save your password, you should know that the password is not encrypted — and anybody that can get to your home directory can find your password.

   At this point, you're nearly ready to converse with your buddies. The only thing left to do is to tell Kit who your buddies are.
5. **Click the words Buddy List in the tree view on the left.**
6. **Click the Add button (under the word Groups) and make up a name for your buddy list (you can create multiple buddy lists so each one has a name) and then click OK.**
7. **Now click the Add button (under Group Members) and enter the screen name of your first buddy (you have to know the screen name for each buddy that you want to converse with) and then click OK.**
8. **Repeat Steps 6 and 7 to add as many buddies as you like.**
9. **When you're finished, click OK.**

Let's face it, there are a lot of strange people lurking around on the Web. Unless you specify otherwise, anyone on the Web can try to open a conversation with you. You may want to tell Kit to ignore invitations from anyone not on your buddy list. Choose Settings➪Configure Kit➪Permissions and set up a Permit list for yourself.

That's it! You're ready to instant message. You're sitting at a (mostly) blank screen now. To announce your presence to the world, click the Offline button (way down at the bottom of the window) and choose Online from the pop-up menu that appears. After a few seconds, you should see a list of your buddies, along with an indication of which ones are online, which ones are offline, and which ones are online but currently away from their desks.

To start a conversation with one of your buddies:

1. **Double-click the name of the person you want to chat with (choose someone who's actually online).**

   Kit opens a new chat window. Your text cursor appears in a small window at the bottom of the chat window. You can use that window to compose your thoughts.

2. **Type your message and press Enter when you're done.**

   The message is sent to the IM client that your buddy is running. If your buddy is feeling conversational, you receive a reply in a few moments and you can continue to carry on your conversation.

3. **When you're finished (say goodbye first), just close the chat window and change your status from Online to Offline (or Away).**

Kit has a lot of extra features. See the online help text (Help⇨Kit Handbook) for more information.

Chapter 3

Multimedia Madness

In This Chapter

- Listening to RealPlayer audio streams
- Using RealPlayer to watch TV
- XMMS — the X Multimedia System
- Watching DVDs with MPlayer

The multimedia tools in Red Hat Linux let you listen to recorded and streaming audio, or watch recorded and streaming video. In this chapter, we walk you through using RealPlayer for streaming audio and video (as in live, from the Internet radio and TV), and using MPlayer to watch DVDs. We also introduce you to the world of XMMS — the X Multimedia System. XMMS lets you play streaming and recorded audio in different formats and use plug-ins to improve sound quality.

RealPlayer

RealPlayer is a program that works with Red Hat Linux to play streaming audio and video files. The Web is full of sites that offer RealPlayer-compatible news and entertainment files. After you install RealPlayer media player, Red Hat Linux uses RealPlayer to play streaming audio and video sources that you find on the Web, and you can also use it to watch TV!

To install RealPlayer, follow these steps:

1. **Insert the companion CD.**
2. **Open a terminal window and give yourself superuser privileges with the `su` command.**
3. **Fire up the Red Hat package manager with the following command:**

```
rpm -Uhv rp8*
```

The Red Hat package manager begins the installation process. After a *long* delay, the Mime Type and Plugin Configuration dialog box appears (Figure 3-1), giving you a chance to associate RealPlayer-compatible audio and video streams with RealPlayer.

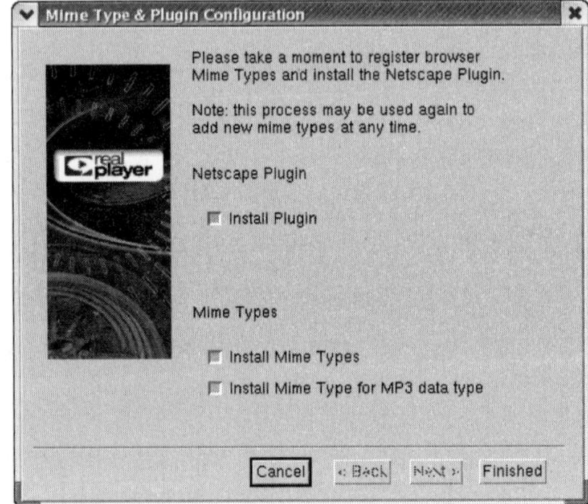

Figure 3-1: RealPlayer One - Mime Configuration.

4. **Accept the default values.**

   Many KDE and GNOME applications know how to play audio and video streams using RealPlayer.

5. **Click Finished to continue to the next window.**
6. **Click Next to finish.**

   We know, that's a strange sequence, but we didn't write that code.

7. **Click OK.**

   You're greeted with the RealPlayer registration window shown in Figure 3-2.

8. **Complete the registration.**

   Fill in your e-mail address, country of residence, and postal code. Mark the Inform Me of Updates and Events check box if you want to receive e-mail from the RealPlayer entertainment team whenever an interesting concert (or other broadcast) is scheduled.

9. **Click Next to continue.**

   Choose your connection speed (or at least a connection speed that's close to your actual network connection speed).

10. Click Finished.

At this point, the RealPlayer window wakes up (it's been lurking in the background) and plays an audio introduction to let you know that everything worked.

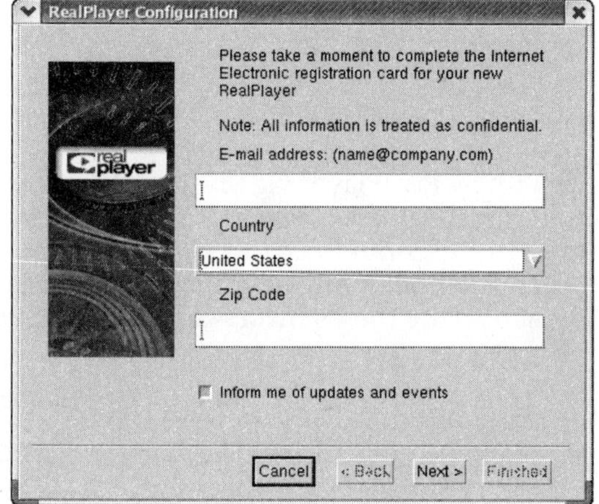

Figure 3-2: RealPlayer One registration window.

Of course you can use RealPlayer to listen to music and news online. But did you know that you can watch streaming video with RealPlayer? Well you can. To find a video stream to watch in RealPlayer, follow these steps:

1. **Open Mozilla and go to** `www.c-span.org`**.**

   C-Span is the public-affairs network that broadcasts Congressional meetings and programming on political issues. A collection of video archives (labeled Latest Video and Most Watched Video) appears, from which you can choose a topic that interests you.

2. **Just select a topic and then click okay to play the video.**

   After a short delay, RealPlayer appears and attempts to connect to the C-SPAN streamer. You may see a couple of other windows appear before RealPlayer — the first is asking you what you want to do with the content that you selected. The second window that may appear is the Mozilla download manager; you can just ignore that window or close it if it gets in your way.

Here are a few Web sites that feature Linux/RealPlayer-friendly video broadcasts:

- `http://tv4all.com`: A directory listing over 700 (!!!) television stations that broadcast live and archived video from around the world; the links in blue are RealPlayer compatible.
- `www.c-span.org`: Live and archived coverage of United States Senate and House proceedings, conferences, and other political features.
- `www.bbc.co.uk`: Live and archived news from the BBC (BBC News 24); you can also watch feeds from the House of Lords or House of Commons (BBC Parliament).
- `www.courttv.com/video`: Coverage of trials and court proceedings.

If you find that Mozilla won't play RealPlayer videos, it may be that you have RealPlayer installed, but not the RealPlayer plug-in. To see your plug-ins, open Mozilla and surf to `about:plug-ins` (no `http` or `www` here). If you don't see a plug-in named `rpnp.so`, then you don't have your plug-in installed in the right place. That's easy to fix; just execute the following commands while you're logged in as the superuser:

1. **Type the following command:**

   ```
   dirname $(rpm -ql RealPlayer | grep RealPlayer8/rpnp.so)
   ```

   This command displays the location of the `rpnp.so` file (that's the RealPlayer plug-in). Make a note of this pathname.

2. **Type the following command:**

   ```
   dirname $(rpm -ql mozilla | grep nullplugin)
   ```

   This time you should see the location of the Mozilla plug-in directory — probably something like `/usr/lib/mozilla-1.4/plugins/`. Make a note of this pathname; you'll need it in the next step.

3. **Copy the `rpnp.so` file from Step 1 to the directory found in Step 2.**

   For example, if the command in Step 1 tells you that `rpnp.so` is located at `/usr/lib/RealPlayer8/rpnp.so` and Step 2 tells you that Mozilla looks for plug-ins in `/usr/lib/mozilla-1.4/plug-ins/` you would execute the following command:

   ```
   cp /usr/lib/RealPlayer8/rpnp.so /usr/lib/mozilla-1.4/plugins
   ```

4. **Start Mozilla again.**

   If Mozilla is already running, shut it down and start it again to force it to load the new plug-in.

5. **Browse to `about:plug-ins` again.**

   You should see the `rpnp.so` plug-in listed.

XMMS: Customizing Your Listening Environment

XMMS is the X (as in *cross-platform*) Multimedia System, an open-source and full-featured alternative to RealPlayer. XMMS is an expert at playing music (and other audio sources like news and audio books). When you run XMMS the first time (to do so, open the K Menu and choose Sound & Video⇨Audio Player), the window shown in Figure 3-3 appears.

Figure 3-3: XMMS.

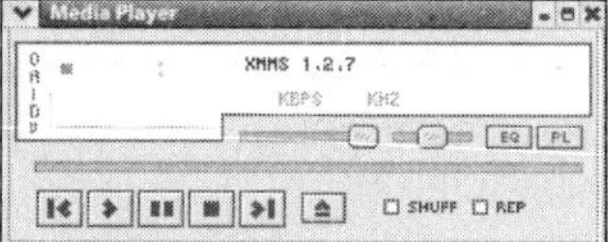

Straight out of the box, XMMS knows how to play a variety of audio formats including audio CD, Ogg Vorbis, and `.wav` (wave) files. Red Hat software has disabled the MP3 player built into their version of XMMS (apparently for patent-related distribution issues). If you want to play MP3 audio files (or audio streams) with XMMS, you can uninstall the Red Hat version (using the command `rpm -e xmms`) and download a new copy from `www.xmms.org`.

The XMMS player was designed to be small and unobtrusive, but that can also make it difficult to see. On the left edge of the XMMS window (refer to Figure 3-3) are four buttons stacked vertically and labeled O, A, I, D, and V. Click D to double the size of the XMMS window (click D again to shrink it to its original size).

Using the XMMS equalizer

Speakers (and headphones) don't reproduce sound without some distortion. You can use the XMMS equalizer to adjust the quality of your sound to match your speakers with your own personal listening preferences. To open the equalizer, press Alt+G or right-click the XMMS window and choose Graphical EQ from the pop-up menu; the equalizer window appears (Figure 3-4).

To change the shape of the sound you hear from XMMS, click the On button (in the equalizer window) and then drag the sliders up and down to increase (up) or decrease (down) the volume of each frequency range. Most headphones could use a bit more bass — so drag the sliders on the right end of the equalizer up to increase the bass. If you're listening to spoken-word broadcasts (news, talk, or audio books), you might want to increase the treble a bit.

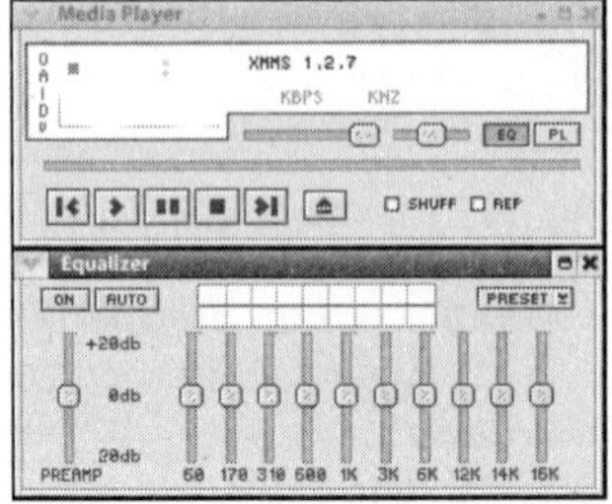

Figure 3-4: The XMMS graphic equalizer.

When you find a shape that you like, you can save the equalizer settings under a name of your choosing. Just click the Preset button, choose Save⇨Preset, then enter a name for your preset (something like Rock, Classical, or News/Headphones) and click OK. To load a preset shape later, click Preset⇨Load⇨Preset, select the one you want, and click OK.

Plugging in plug-ins

One of the really cool features of XMMS is that it knows how to incorporate plug-ins. There are (roughly) five types of plug-ins that XMMS can deal with:

- **General plug-ins:** Used to control XMMS in some way, with a joystick or infrared remote control for example.
- **Input plug-ins:** You can add input plug-ins to your copy of XMMS to play other media types like AC3, Midi, AAC, even Nintendo and Sega soundtracks!
- **Output plug-ins:** An output plug-in lets you send audio somewhere other than your speakers — use an output plug-in to convert an audio stream from one format to another (from MP3 to Ogg Vorbis, for example).
- **Sound-enhancing plug-ins:** These plug-ins add depth to an audio track (usually by simulating the sound characteristics of a large room).
- **Visualization plug-ins:** XMMS can synchronize a '60s-style light show with whatever you're listening to. Some of these can be quite beautiful; some are just plain weird.

XMMS comes preinstalled with a number of plug-ins. To see your XMMS plug-ins, make sure that your XMMS window has the keyboard focus and press Ctrl+P and the Preferences dialog box appears (as in Figure 3-5). Notice the six tabs along the top. Click the Audio I/O Plugins tab to see which input and output plug-ins are currently installed.

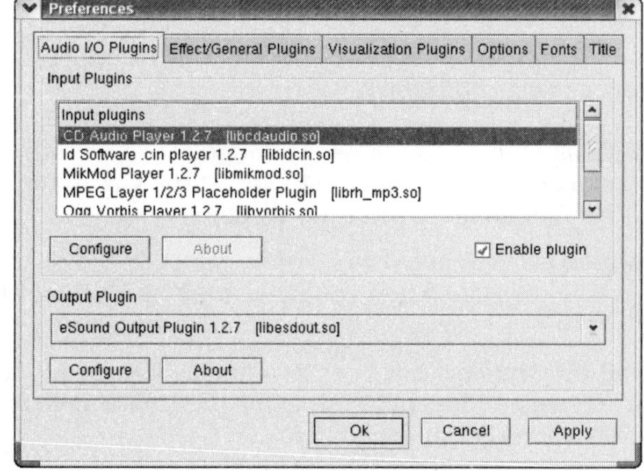

Figure 3-5: The XMMS Preference Editor.

Media types (input plug-ins and output plug-ins)

With XMMS, you can enable any number of input plug-ins, but you can only choose one output plug-in at a time. Why? Each input plug-in is designed to decode a specific type of media (CD Audio, Ogg Vorbis, MP3, and so on) and XMMS chooses the appropriate plug-in whenever you play an audio stream. An output plug-in, on the other hand, is designed to convert the incoming audio bits into another format — you have to tell XMMS which output plug-in to use (it can't figure that out by itself).

By default, XMMS sends the output stream to your sound card (and from there to your speakers or headphones). There are three popular sound card driver packages distributed with Linux: aRts, eSound, and OSS. If you don't hear anything when you play an audio stream with XMMS, try one of the other output plug-ins. Choose the Disk Writer plug-in to record sound to your hard drive. The Disk Writer plug-in channels audio bits into a WAV file in your home directory (click the Configure button in the Preferences window to choose a different directory). You can't use Disk Writer to record audio coming from an audio CD; XMMS doesn't actually process the sound coming from the CD, it just controls the CD player itself.

If you find an audio stream in a format not supported by your XMMS plug-ins, you can probably find a *decoder* (also called an *input plug-in*) at `www.xmms.org`. Just download the one that you need and install it according to the instructions at the Web site. Most plug-ins are distributed in source-code form — we recommend restricting your search to binary or RPM plug-ins unless you're comfortable compiling packages from source code.

Sound processing

XMMS (as distributed with Red Hat Linux) comes with sound-enhancement plug-ins (also known as *effect plug-ins*):

- **Echo plug-in:** This plug-in simulates the sound characteristics of a large room by adding echo; click Configure to adjust the size of the room (that is, the echo delay), feedback, and echo volume.
- **Extra stereo plug-in:** Increases the stereo separation of the sound stream; especially pleasant when you're wearing headphones (use this plug-in to avoid the "orchestra in the cranium" syndrome).
- **Voice removal plug-in:** For those of you who like Karaoke (you know who you are and we don't want to), you can use this plug-in to remove the vocals from a song (or at least try to).

You can download and install more sound processing plug-ins from the XMMS Web site (`www.xmms.org`).

Visualization

You've probably noticed that the XMMS player displays a *spectrum analyzer* (a jumpy bar graph that changes in response to the audio stream) while playing music . If you click the spectrum analyzer, you can change it into an oscilloscope display, or turn it off altogether.

The XMMS visualization system can also display a synchronized light show in a separate window (or even in full-screen mode). To enable one of the built in visualizers, press Ctrl+P, and then, on the choose the Visualization Plugins tab, enable the plug-in you'd like to see. Now go start some music and watch the light show.

The XMMS Web site lists a number of visualization plug-ins and some of them are really fun. One that we particularly like is GDancer — GDancer displays an animated character on your desktop that wiggles and gyrates to the music. To install GDancer, follow these steps:

1. **Open your Web browser and go to `www.xmms.org`.**
2. **Find the Plug-ins page and jump to Visualization plug-ins.**
3. **Find the GDancer plug-in and click the rpm link.**

   The RPM package downloads to your computer.
4. **Save the file where you can find it again easily.**

   Your home directory is a good choice.
5. **When the download completes, log in as the superuser and install the RPM file using the following command:**

   ```
   rpm -Uhv gdancer*.rpm
   ```

6. **Restart XMMS (that is, shut it down and restart it).**
7. **On the Visualization Plug-ins tab in the Preferences window (press Ctrl+P to open this window), choose GDancer plug-in and then mark the Enable Plugin check box.**

At this point, a picture of the Space Ghost cartoon character appears on your desktop, ready to tango — start some music and enjoy the show. Right-click the dancer to make changes to it. The GDancer Web site (`http://figz.com/gdancer`) has a whole list of downloadable characters ready to dance around your desktop (try the sunglasses-wearing penguin).

Skinning XMMS

The overall appearance of the default XMMS window isn't very exciting (it's compact, but not particularly pretty). XMMS is a *skinnable* application — you can change its entire look and feel by laying a new skin (or theme) over the top of it. Red Hat's version of XMMS comes with two skins. The default skin (Bluecurve-xmms) is designed to fit well into the overall style of Red Hat's Bluecurve desktop theme. The other skin — "(none)" — is rather dark and hard to see. Press Alt+S to see which skins you have installed.

You can find a huge collection of skins at the XMMS Web site — just click the Skins link. Browse around until you find a skin you'd like to try out, and then follow these steps to install it:

1. **Click the download link (underneath the preview picture).**
2. **Save the skin somewhere you can find it.**

   A directory such as `/tmp` or your home directory are good choices.
3. **When the download completes, move the skin to the following directory:**

   ```
   /usr/share/xmms/Skins
   ```
4. **If you don't have XMMS running already, start it.**
5. **Click the XMMS title bar to give XMMS the keyboard focus.**
6. **In the Skin Selector window (press Ctrl+S to open it), choose the skin you want and then click Close.**

That's it. You should see XMMS in a whole new way. In Figure 3-6, for example, notice the dancing penguin that comes from the GDancer plug-in.

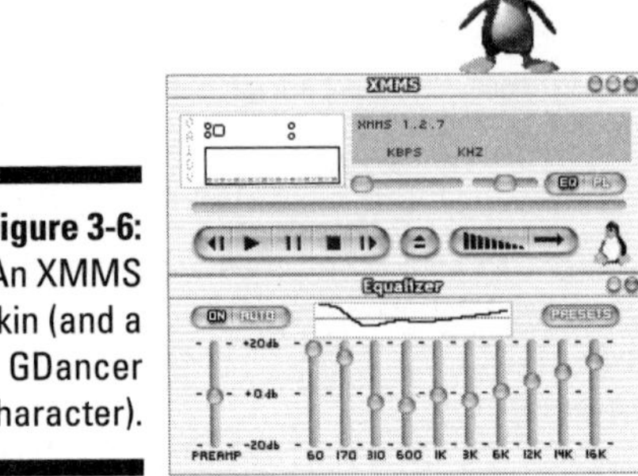

Figure 3-6: An XMMS skin (and a GDancer character).

MPlayer: Movies on Your Desktop

These days, most personal computers include a DVD drive (often in combination with a CD-ROM or CD/RW drive). The MPlayer video player lets you play DVD (or DivX, VCD, RealPlayer, and so on) movies on your Red Hat Linux desktop.

Finding your DVD drive

Before you can play a DVD with MPlayer, you have to find the name of your DVD drive. The easiest way to find the correct device name is to use the Red Hat hardware browser:

1. **Click the KMenu button on the Kicker and then choose System Tools⇨Hardware Browser.**
2. **If prompted, enter the superuser password.**

   After a short delay, the hardware browser appears, as shown in Figure 3-7.
3. **Select CD-ROM Drives (on the left side of the window).**
4. **Write down the device name from the Device Information box.**

   In Figure 3-7, for example, our DVD device is named `/dev/scd0`.

When you have the device name for your DVD drive, you *could* just tell MPlayer how to find your drive, but a name like `/dev/scd0` isn't very meaningful to people. Instead, you can create a second, more meaningful name for your DVD device. MPlayer assumes that your DVD drive is named `/dev/dvd` — well, okay, that's a pretty meaningful name, so we'll use that. To create an *alias* (a more convenient name, known technically as a *symbolic link*) for your DVD device, follow these steps:

1. **Open a terminal window on your desktop and use the** `su` **command to give yourself superuser privileges.**

   To do so, type **su**, press `Enter`, and enter the superuser password when prompted.

2. **Enter the following command that uses the device name you wrote down from the previous steps.**

   In this case, we've used `/dev/sdc0` so the command looks like this:

   ```
   ln -s /dev/scd0 /dev/dvd
   ```

3. **While you have superuser privileges, adjust the permissions for your DVD device with the following command:**

   ```
   chmod a+rw /dev/dvd
   ```

4. **Close the terminal window to finish.**

At this point, you're nearly ready to watch a movie. MPlayer may or may not be installed on your system, depending on which packages you selected during the installation process. Open the KMenu and choose Sound & Video➪More Sound & Video Applications. If you don't see MPlayer on this menu, you must install it before you can go any further. We've included a copy of MPlayer on the companion disk.

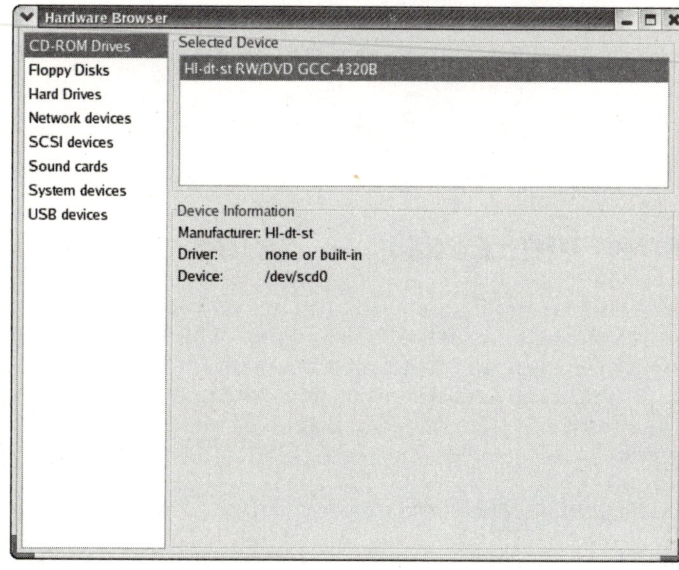

Figure 3-7: The Red Hat Hardware Browser.

All set? Place a DVD in the drive, open the K Menu, and choose Sound & Video➪More Sound & Video Applications➪MPlayer. An MPlayer window opens. The upper window (Figure 3-8) is where your movie plays; the lower window works like a remote control. To play a DVD, right-click anywhere on the lower window and then choose Open➪Play DVD.

Figure 3-8: MPlayer.

MPlayer makeover — skins

Like most graphical applications that run in Red Hat Linux, MPlayer is skinnable — you can change the look and feel of MPlayer by choosing a different skin. The easiest way to select a new skin (MPlayer only comes with one) is to download an assortment of skins all at once, and browse the selections on your own machine. You can find an RPM package at the following Web address:

```
ftp.freshrpms.net/pub/freshrpms/redhat/9/mplayer-skins/
```

Just click the mplayer-skins-1.3-fr1.noarch.rpm link and save that file to your home directory. When the download completes, install the package like this:

1. **Open a terminal window on your desktop and use the `su` command to give yourself superuser privileges.**
2. **Type the following command:**

```
rpm -Uhv mplayer-skins*.rpm
```

3. **Delete the RPM file now (you're done with it), like this:**

```
rm mplayer-skins*.rpm
```

4. **Close the terminal window.**
5. **If MPlayer is not already running, start it.**
6. **Right-click anywhere in the remote-control window and choose Skin Browser from the pop-up menu.**
7. **Click a skin name to preview that skin; when you find one you like, click OK.**

   We like the *classic* skin shown in Figure 3-9.

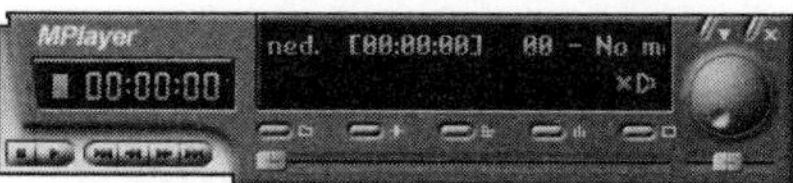

Figure 3-9: A classic.

Speed things up with direct rendering

In a normal (dedicated) DVD player, the processor doesn't have anything to do other than play your movie. When you play a DVD using MPlayer, however, your computer is decoding the video bits stored on the disc, translating them into a meaningful image, and rendering the image — while running your favorite spreadsheet, compiler, or game at the same time. That's a lot of work, and unless you have a very well configured PC, video quality may suffer. MPlayer has a few tricks up its (virtual) sleeve that may help. If you notice that the picture looks a bit jumpy or the sound quality just isn't right, try this:

1. **Right-click in either MPlayer window and choose Preferences from the pop-up menu.**

   The Preferences dialog box appears (Figure 3-10).
2. **On the Video tab, mark the Enable Direct Rendering check box.**
3. **Stop and restart your movie.**

   You don't have to shut down the player itself, you just have to start the movie playing again.

4. **If the restart doesn't help, open the Preferences dialog box again, uncheck the Direct Rendering check box, and then check Enable Double Buffering.**

5. **Stop and restart your movie.**

   If that still doesn't help, you may be out of luck, but go ahead and try some of the other drivers listed on the Video tab.

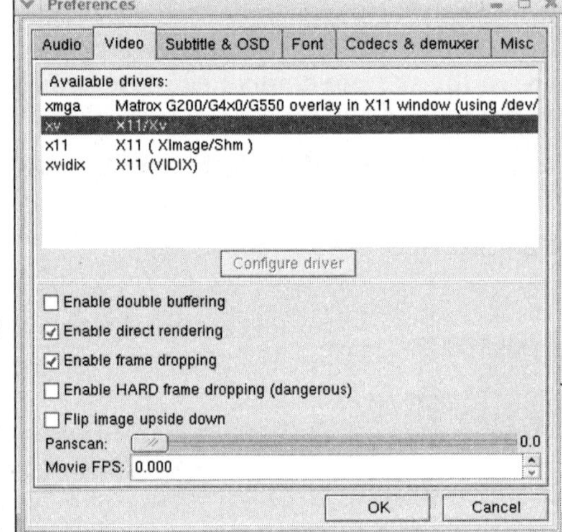

Figure 3-10: Configuring MPlayer Video preferences.

Chapter 4

Gaming on Red Hat Linux

In This Chapter

- Playing with the KDE game collection
- Racking up points with MAME — the arcade emulator
- Skulking around in Enemy Territory
- Racing with the zippy penguins

All work and no play . . . you know the expression. Red Hat agrees! Red Hat Linux not only comes with a great selection of games that are ready to play when you install Linux, but there are tons of games (and lots of them are freebies) to download from the Web. In this chapter, we show you the games that come with KDE and delve into arcade games of the past (with XMAME). We also introduce network-enabled games that you can play interactively across the Internet, and then we enter Enemy Territory.

The KDE Game Collection

KDE comes with a number of games. Some (well, okay, *most*) are based on well-known arcade or board games. We find the games (KMahjongg and Tuxracer in particular) to be a great way to spend a whole mess of time that we really should be spending on something more productive. Here is a rundown of all the games included in the KDE game collection.

Arcade games

- **KAsteroids:** In this classic video game, fly your spaceship, shoot the asteroids, shoot more asteroids, shoot a few more, and reincarnate yourself every 30 seconds or so.
- **KBounce:** Construct walls to trap the little bouncing balls; as you get better, KBounce pelts you with more balls.
- **KFouleggs:** A strange name for a Tetris clone (a *really* strange name).

- **KSirtet, KSmiletris:** Two more Tetris clones.
- **KSnakerace:** Feed the snakes, they get bigger.
- **KSpaceDuel:** Deal with gravity, space mines, solar power, energy levels, rotation, and flying bullets, all while trying not to fall into the sun (tough and addictive).
- **KTron:** Ride your lightcycle, avoid the walls, and avoid your opponent.

Board games

- **KBackgammon:** Play the classic backgammon game against your computer, against another player, or online.
- **KBattleship:** Sink your enemy's ships by shooting until you find them.
- **KBlackbox:** A challenging logic game where you guess the location of balls within a black box (hence the name) by observing the deflection of laser beams.
- **Kenolaba:** A clone of the board game Abalone; play against the computer or against an opponent (even an opponent on another computer).
- **KReversi:** Outflank your opponent to gain control of the most squares and you win (a fun strategy game that takes a long time to master).
- **KMahjongg:** An addictive tile-matching game that can entertain you for hours.
- **Shishen-Sho:** A tile-matching game similar to Mahjongg, but with a different set of rules.
- **KWin4:** A two-player game (or you against the computer); get four in a row while trying to block your opponent.
- **KTuberling:** Paste a pair of eyeballs on a potato, or a silly hat on a penguin (just like Mr. Potato Head). For some reason, KTuberling doesn't appear on any of the KDE menus. If you want to try it, open the KMenu, choose Run Command, and then type **ktuberling** in the pop-up window that appears.

Card games

- **KPatience:** A collection of fifteen different solitaire games; choose your game, choose your card deck, choose your background, and start playing.
- **KPoker:** Start out with $100 to wager; end up without a shirt on your back.
- **Lieutnant Skat:** This game is similar to the meld phase of a Pinochle game (if you don't play Pinochle, that sounds silly, so just try the game).

Strategy games

- **KJumpingcube:** The more dots you have, the more likely you'll win (read the manual for this one).
- **KMines:** An addictive logic game where you detect mines in a minefield without blowing yourself up.
- **KSokoban:** Push crates around a virtual warehouse without trapping yourself (either it's not as easy as it looks, or we're really bad at playing simple games).
- **Kolor Lines:** Move the colored marbles into a line of five and they disappear; sounds simple, but gets harder as you go.
- **Konquest:** A multiplayer game of interplanetary conquest (multiplayer only).
- **Same Game:** Click a colored marble to remove that marble and all adjacent marbles of the same color — objective: get rid of all the marbles.

MAME: The Arcade Emulator

Remember those great old arcade games at the pizza parlor? PacMan, Spy Hunter, Rally X? A dedicated team of hackers (apparently with *way* too much free time) has decided to resurrect those noisy plywood boxes with joysticks, CRTs, and coin slots. The MAME (Multi Arcade Machine Emulator) project emulates the hardware inside of a video game machine.

Just like you have a CPU inside your computer (most likely an Intel Pentium of some generation), a video game has a CPU inside of it. Programs that you run on your computer must be built (or compiled) to work with your particular type of CPU. When you run a program such as Konqueror, your CPU is executing the instructions contained in the Konqueror executable. You can add a new program to your computer by loading from removable media (like a CD-ROM), or by downloading from the Web. (An arcade machine is not as versatile as your computer.) The only way you can add a new program to an arcade machine is to replace a set of chips inside of the cabinet. The chip that you replace is called a ROM (or Read Only Memory). Each ROM works with a single type of CPU (and there are a *lot* of CPU types out there). MAME emulates the hardware inside of the video game cabinet; it emulates the CPU, the sound system, the input devices (joysticks, guns, buttons, steering wheels, and so on); it even emulates the coin slot.

MAME doesn't do much of anything all by itself. It doesn't do much good to emulate a computer that doesn't have a program to run. To use MAME (that is, to play a game), you must have a bit-by-bit copy of the ROM that holds the game you want to play. You can freely download MAME from the Web, but where do you get a ROM pack? That's a little trickier. Legally speaking (but we're not lawyers), the only way you can (legally) obtain a ROM pack for a commercial game is to buy an arcade game. Having said that, a quick Web search for "MAME ROM" returns a *lot* of hits. In fact, you can find *legal* ROM packs if you look hard enough. Some game vendors have adjusted their copyrights on older games to give them a second life. The XMame package includes three free ROM packs.

The version of MAME that runs on Linux is called XMame and it comes in two or three different flavors: X11, SDL, or OpenGL. The X11 version should run on most systems, but the SDL and OpenGL flavors might give you better performance if your hardware supports hardware-based video acceleration. To install the X11 version, do the following:

1. **Log in as user** `root` **(or use the** `su` **command to change your effective user ID).**
2. **Insert the companion disk and wait for it to mount on the** `/mnt/cdrom` **directory.**
3. **Move to the RPMS directory using the following command:** `cd /mnt/cdrom/RPMS`.
4. **Install the alsa-lib RPM with this command:**

   ```
   rpm -Uhv alsa-lib*.rpm
   alsa-lib is a sound library required by XMame.
   ```

5. **Install the XMame packages with the following command:**

   ```
   rpm -Uhv xmame*
   ```

If you want to try the SDL or OpenGL versions, you can find them at `http://x.mame.net`.

The XMame package comes with three free arcade games: Gridlee, Polyplay, and Robby Roto. To play a game, run the program xmame and include the game name at the end of the command line. For example, to play Gridlee, run the command: `xmame gridlee`. Xmame is a pretty verbose program; it generates a lot of text in your terminal emulator window, most of which you can ignore. If everything works, a small window appears on your screen telling you about the game. Follow the directions on the screen and Gridlee starts running in "attract a player" mode, waiting for you to drop a coin or two in the slot (see Figure 4-1).

Go ahead, drop a few quarters in the slot and start playing. If you can't find the coin slot on your computer (*don't* put a coin in the CD-ROM drive — but you knew that), just press the 5 key instead: one press to (virtually) insert one quarter, two presses to insert two quarters, and so on. If you want a two-player game, press the 6 key to insert coins in the right-hand coin slot. When you've inserted a coin or two, press 1 to start a single-player game and 2 to start a two-player game.

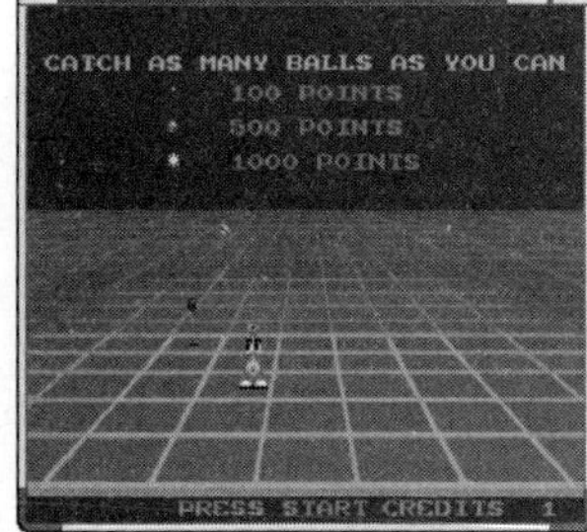

Figure 4-1: Gridlee running in XMame.

Your computer doesn't have the controls (joysticks, steering wheels, light guns, coin slots, and so on) that an arcade game usually requires, so controlling the game can be a bit tricky. When the game has started, press the Tab key to bring up a menu that let's you map the keyboard (or view the current keymap). Use the Up- and Down-arrow keys to move around in this menu; select Input (general) to see your keymap.

You can see that pressing the 'P' key will Pause your game; the UP, DOWN, LEFT, and RIGHT keys move you around within the game, and, if you scroll down a bit, you'll see that the LSHIFT (left-shift) key and *Z* key correspond to buttons that were present in the real-life Gridlee game cabinet. That means you use the left-shift key and the Z key to fire.

Play a few games with XMame — stay legal. If you find games that you like, see if you can find a legal version of the ROM pack (maybe the manufacturer has placed the game in the public domain), or buy the game from your friendly neighborhood game vendor.

Shooting Up Bad Guys in Enemy Territory

Enemy Territory is a free game in which you play the part of an Allied or Axis soldier fighting the enemy in World War II. Enemy Territory (or *ET*) is a multiplayer, online game — you must have a network connection if you want to play this game. You typically connect to an ET server somewhere out on the Web, but you can host a game yourself if you want to play with a group of friends (or co-workers) on your local network.

Downloading ET

Due to licensing restrictions, we couldn't include Enemy Territory on the companion CD; you'll have to download it from the Web. Fortunately, being an *extremely* popular game, it's very easy to find. Start your favorite Web browser, go to Google, and then search for a file named `et-linux-2.55.x86.run`. When you've found a download site (at last count, we found 233 different sites), save the file to your hard drive and follow this procedure:

1. **Log in as user `root` (or use the `su` command to change your effective user ID).**
2. **Using the `cd` command, move to the directory where you saved the download file.**
3. **Execute the following command:**

   ```
   ./et-linux-2.55.x86.run
   ```

   This command checks the installable package to make sure it hasn't been damaged, then prompts you to acknowledge two license agreements (one for Enemy Territory and one for Punkbuster, an anticheating feature).
4. **Next, the installer gives you a chance to change installation options (you can choose the default values here). Click `Begin Install` to proceed.**
5. **When the installation process completes, click Start to play the game.**

The first time you run ET, you have to create a *profile* (that is, an identity) for yourself:

1. **Click the Player Alias field and type in a name for yourself.**

   Be imaginative here, this is your chance to be Commander El Supremo, or Doctor Destruction, or whatever your dark, evil fantasy demands.
2. **Increase brightness as needed.**

   We recommend moving the control from the default of 1.3 to 2.0 — ET tends to be dim.
3. **Click Unselected (next to Connection) to choose your approximate network connection speed.**
4. **Click Enable Punkbuster if you plan to play against online opponents.**

   Most servers don't allow cheaters; Punkbuster prevents cheating.
5. **Click Create to finish.**

You're almost ready to play. Now you have to decide whether you want to play against online opponents hosted at another Web site or host a game yourself. We recommend that you start out by hosting a game yourself so that you can get familiar with the game controls and graphics before you put yourself in the field of fire. To host your own game, follow these steps:

1. **From ET's main menu, click Host Game.**
2. **Choose a Game Type:**
    - **Campaign:** Complete a series of missions in the Central Europe campaign or the North Africa campaign.
    - **Last Man Standing:** Fight against all other players, last player wins.
    - **Single-Map Objective:** Fight a single battle in the Central Europe or North Africa campaign.
    - **Stopwatch:** Complete your mission as quickly as possible, then switch sides to try to better your opponents time.
3. **Choose your battle or campaign.**
4. **Click Start Server.**

After a short delay, you're ready to join the battle.

Playing ET

You start out as a spectator (meaning that you can walk around, but you can't shoot anything). To become a combatant, press the *L* key to open the Limbo Menu (we don't know what that name means either). A complex screen appears, which includes a map (you'll probably want to come back here often) and a set of controls on the right.

About halfway down this screen, you should see a U.S. flag, a *Castle Wolfenstein* flag, and an eyeball. Click the U.S. flag to join the Allies or the Wolfenstein flag to join the Axis. Below the flags are a row of five icons (a helmet, a white cross, a wrench, and so on). Click one of those icons to become a Soldier, a Medic, an Engineer, a Field Ops Agent, or a Covert Ops Agent. When you play ET online, you'll want to build a team that includes each class of character. For now, just pick Engineer and then click OK.

You're in the fight! Use your mouse to look up, down, left, and right. Press the *W* key to walk forward and the *S* key to move back. You can sidestep using the *A* and *D* keys. To fire your weapon, press the left mouse button. To change weapons (you start out with a rifle or machine gun, depending on the type of soldier you selected), press the *1* key to select your first weapon, the *2* key to select your second weapon, and so on. Be careful — if you drop a grenade, you'd better get away quick.

Walk around for a while and get used to the controls; fire your weapon, switch weapons to try them all so that you know what each can do. You'll be amazed by how rich the graphics are in this game.

Here are a few hints:

- An **Engineer** can construct things, repair vehicles, defuse mines, and blow things up with dynamite.
- A **Medic** can revive his teammates and heal them with health packs; a medic can't do much else, so he's best paired with other team members.
- A **Field Ops agent** can call in air strikes (!!!), use artillery, and hand out ammunition.
- A **Covert Ops agent** can open locked doors, detect landmines and command centers, use smoke grenades, and steal enemy uniforms.
- A **Soldier** doesn't have any special skills, but is very useful to have in your teams; soldiers have the *cool* weapons like flamethrowers and mortars.

Going online

After you've wandered around for a while, it's time to go online and hook up with some team members. Press the Escape key a few times until you find yourself at the main menu, and then click Play Online. ET connects (over the network) to a game server directory, and then tries connections to each game server. When a game server responds, it shows up on the list of servers. You'll see a short descriptive name for each server, the ping time for each server, and a set of icons that tell you a little about the features of that game server.

The *ping time* is important — a low ping time means you'll see good responsiveness while playing a game on that server. A high ping time makes it harder to play because other players can sneak up on you while you're waiting for network traffic to clear. In fact, most game servers won't let you play if your ping time is over (about) 500.

If the icon set (at the right end of a server) includes a padlock, you aren't able to connect to that server without having a password; you can avoid those.

When you've found a game you'd like to join, click the server name to select it and then click the Join Game button (at the bottom of the screen). After a short delay, you'll be accepted into the game and you can choose a team (Allied or Axis) and class (Soldier, Medic, and so on). Click OK and watch out for grenades.

Tuxracing: Good Clean Fun with Penguins

If you're not in a combative mood, or you have little ones to entertain, Tuxracer (see Figure 4-2) definitely deserves a good look. This is the most fun you can have with a penguin in the privacy of your own home.

Figure 4-2: Tuxracer.

The goal is simple — slalom to the finish line in the best time, eating all the fish you can on the way down. An assortment or courses is included (some are pretty tough), and with some practice, you'll find yourself doing flips and spins and getting great (virtual) airtime.

To start Tuxracer:

1. **Choose Red Hat Menu⇨Games⇨More Games⇨Tuxracer.**

   This brings up the opening screen.

2. **Press any key to start.**
3. **Click Practice.**

   This brings up the course-configuration screen.

To the right of the course name, you see up and down arrows. Click the arrows to scroll through the list of courses. As you scroll through the courses, a picture and short description of each course is displayed. Below the arrow keys you see four buttons:

- The first button controls lighting — is it sunny, overcast, or nighttime?
- The second button controls the wind speed — this affects your airtime in jumps.
- The snowfall button doesn't work yet. (They're working on it. . . .)
- The button with an M on it reverses the course to its mirror image.

The arrow keys on your keypad control left and right, and the up and down keys control speed — up to go faster, down to drag your flippers. Hold down the E key to build up energy for airtime. When the energy builds up, Tux the Penguin jumps. If you release the E just before the crest of a hill, you actually gain a bit of airtime.

After you've practiced a bit, you may want to enter an event. You advance through different events by meeting qualifying times.

Copy Tuxracer to your Kicker: Just navigate to the game in the main menu and drag it to a blank place in the Kicker (see Chapter 1 for more about the Kicker). Then, when you want to play, just double-click!

Chapter 5

Say Cheese! Using Digital Cameras with Red Hat Linux

In This Chapter

- Making the camera/computer connection with gtkam
- Mounting the camera as a file system
- Sharing your photos via e-mail
- A quick introduction to the GIMP

Today's digital cameras are the perfect accessory for Red Hat Linux. Digital is definitely the way to go — no film, no developing costs, and especially no long wait to find out that you *really* want to retake that last picture. Red Hat Linux comes with some great graphics software that makes digital photography just that much more fun. In this chapter, we share some suggestions about buying a Linux-friendly digital camera, and how to use it with Red Hat Linux. You find out about new ways to use Linux applications to store, edit, and share your photos with friends, family, and the Web.

Selecting and Connecting a USB Camera

Keep life simple — buy a camera that's Linux-friendly. How do you know which cameras work well with Red Hat Linux? Go surfing.

gtkam is a program that lets you (easily) copy images from your digital camera into your Linux computer. Visit `www.gphoto.org` for a list of cameras supported by the most recent version of gtkam. Print out the list and take it shopping with you. The only problem here is that new camera models replace old models at a rate that would make your head spin; you may not be able to find the exact model listed.

A digital camera doesn't have to be expensive to offer built-in features and flexibility that make it easier to take photos and manage digital libraries. On-screen menus, extra storage, and transfer-protocol choices give you a lot of options. When you purchase a digital camera, be sure to consider the following:

- **Compatibility:** How can you be sure a camera will work on your Red Hat Linux machine without hitting the Web? To find out exactly which cameras are supported by *your* version of gtkam, do the following:

  1. **Choose Main Menu⇨Graphics⇨Digital Camera Tool.**

     This opens an application named gtkam.

  2. **Choose Camera⇨Add Camera.**

     In the Model drop-down list, you can see which cameras are compatible.

  3. **Spend a little time shopping online, and compare your research to the list provided by gtkam.**

- **Transfer protocol:** The most common transfer protocols are PTP (Photo Transfer Protocol) or USB Mass Storage. Some really clever cameras support both.

  Some manufacturers use proprietary protocols — avoid them like the plague unless you're *really* comfortable with the manufacturer and their software (often, these don't run on Linux).

  USB Mass Storage cameras store photos just like disk drives store files. To copy photos from the camera to your computer, you just mount the camera as if it were a disk drive (you can even copy pictures *into* the camera). Other devices (like portable MP3 players) also use the USB Mass Storage protocol.

  PTP, on the other hand, is designed specifically for digital cameras. PTP requires special software that recognizes when a camera is attached to the USB port. The software copies photos from the camera, usually with a user-friendly interface.

- **Image format:** Choose a camera that can store photos in a common form such as a JPEG file.

- **Video:** Many digital cameras can shoot video as well as still photos. Most cameras that support video will save the videos in AVI form. You can play AVI files with MPlayer, as shown in Figure 5-1.

- **Resolution:** These days, photo resolution is measured in mega-pixels (that's *millions* of pixels) — the more mega-pixels, the better the picture quality.

- **Storage capacity:** How many pictures can you store in the camera? Remember that most cameras support multiple resolutions and high-resolution photos use more memory than low-resolution photos. Look for a camera that lets you expand storage capacity with plug-in memory modules.
- **Hardware interface:** If you're buying a camera to work with a Linux computer, stick with USB. Some USB cameras can hook directly to a printer or a docking station.

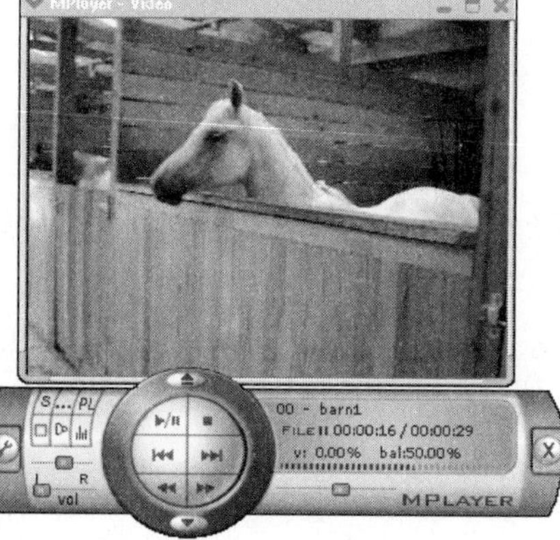

Figure 5-1: MPlayer playing video shot with a digital camera.

Camera prices range from $50 to $4,000 and up. The high end and the low end of the spectrum are usually a bit risky. Obviously, on the low end, you're giving up quality, features, and compatibility. High-end cameras feature top-notch resolution, mega-memory, great speed, and lots of optional lenses and accessories. If you can afford a high-end camera, great. Otherwise, the mid-range cameras are usually the safest, with good features, reliable manufacturers, good warranties, and enough consumers buying them to ensure they'll be supported for a while.

Introducing Your Camera to Red Hat Linux

So you've got your digital camera, you've got a Linux-based computer, now what? If your camera came with software specifically designed for Red Hat Linux, skip this section and consult your documentation. If not, there are two ways that you can make your camera and computer work together: gtkam or the USB Mass Storage driver. Both methods work reasonably well. gtkam is a bit friendlier, but the USB Mass Storage driver is much more powerful. We start with the friendly method first.

Using gtkam to talk to your camera

Without going hip deep into the details of specific camera models (they vary so much from brand to brand), here's the scoop on what to do when you get your new camera:

1. Unpack it carefully, keeping track of warranties, booklets, wrist strap, and so on. Keep a close eye on the cables — they're important.
2. Install the batteries.
3. Consult the manual that came with the camera for instructions about powering on the camera and taking photos.

Now the fun starts! Cats, dogs, children, neighbors — no one is safe. When you've collected some photos that you'd like to load onto your computer, follow these steps:

1. **Connect the camera to the computer via the USB cable that came with the camera.**

   A USB cable is small, with a rectangular connector that will plug into the USB port on your computer. Thinking optimistically, the manufacturer included a cable that has a USB connector on one end and a camera connector on the other end.

2. **Choose KMenu⇨Graphics⇨Digital Camera Tool.**

   The main screen for gtkam opens.

3. **Choose Camera⇨Add Camera.**

   The Select Camera dialog box opens, as shown in Figure 5-2.

4. **Click the Detect button so that gtkam can identify your camera.**

   If auto-detect fails, scroll through the list of camera models and select your camera type from the list.

5. **Click OK.**

If your camera is going to have a problem with gtkam, this is when you find out about it. If a Bad Parameters window appears with an error message that reads `Could not initialize camera`, your camera is *not* gtkam compatible (today). If this happens, click Close and then click Cancel. All is not lost: check out the "Finding the device name with Red Hat Linux" section, later in this chapter. Hopefully, you can mount the camera as a drive.

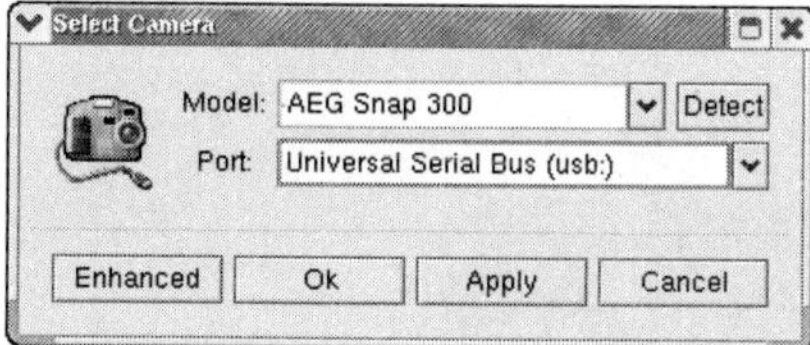

Figure 5-2: The Select Camera dialog box.

Using gtkam to retrieve and store photos

If everything went well and gtkam recognizes your camera, you can use gtkam to retrieve and store your photographs. gtkam doesn't really do much more than that, but it does give you an easy way to browse through the pictures you've taken and decide which ones to keep.

If gtkam recognizes your camera, a camera icon will appear in the left side of the window, along with a description of the camera (something like *USB PTP Class Camera*). This icon occupies the top of the directory tree that represents the file structure inside your camera. As you browse through the directory, you may find things that are not photos — don't mess with those. To retrieve your pictures, follow these steps:

1. **Click the Camera icon to open the directory tree.**
2. **Click the subdirectory you want to open.**

   Several subdirectories appear (which ones they are varies with the make of your camera).
3. **Browse around until you find the subdirectory that holds your photos (you'll probably see JPG files in that subdirectory).**

   Depending on the make of your camera, old directories may persist even after the images have been deleted. If you see several directories, the last directory in the list is usually where the current photos will be. To the right of the directory name, you should see a count of the number of items in that directory. Look for a directory populated with photos.
4. **Select the directory containing the photos.**

   Like magic, your photos appear in thumbnail form in the right side of the screen, as shown in Figure 5-3.

Now you can use gtkam to scroll through the photos, decide what to keep, and where to store them.

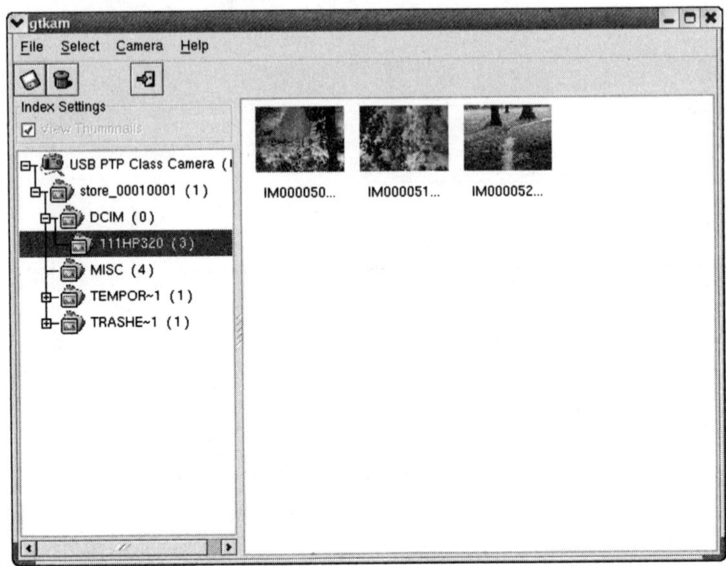

Figure 5-3: gtkam retrieving photos.

To save a photo, follow these steps:

1. **Right-click the photo and choose Save from the pop-up menu.**

   A Save dialog box opens, as shown in Figure 5-4.

2. **Create a directory to store your photos in:**

   a. **Click the Create Dir button in the upper-left corner of the window.**

   b. **Enter a directory name (we chose** `photos`**), and click Create.**

   Your new directory now appears in the list.

3. **Double-click your directory to open it and then click OK to save your photos.**

   With a little luck, your photos are on their way to your new directory.

gtkam can be a bit rough around the edges and a little inconsistent from machine to machine. You may have to tinker a bit, but at least it's an easy interface to use.

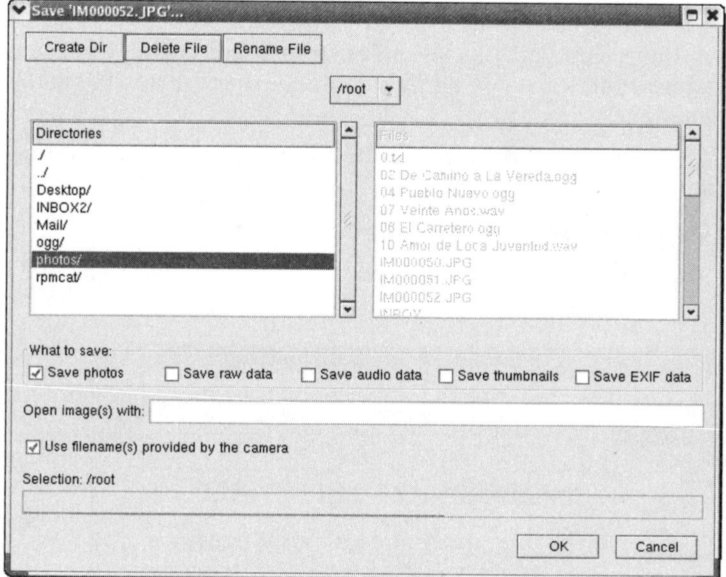

Figure 5-4: The gtkam Save dialog box.

Finding the device name with Red Hat Linux

If you've inherited someone's USB digital camera (and it's not on gtkam's list), or if gtkam just won't cooperate, there is still a good chance that Red Hat Linux can talk to your camera. This is where camera features can make all the difference in the world — if you can mount the camera as a USB Mass Storage device rather than a PTP-only device, you have a huge advantage. Try the following steps:

1. **Make sure that your camera is powered on and connected to a USB port (one on either end of the cable).**

   If your camera lets you choose between PTP and USB Mass Storage, be sure to choose the USB Mass Storage option.

2. **Open a terminal window and use the `su` command to give yourself superuser privileges.**

3. **Enter the following (admittedly cryptic) command at the command prompt:**

   ```
   insmod usb-storage
   ```

4. **Press Enter.**

   At this point, you may see an error message telling you that a module named `usb-storage` already exists — that's okay. Just ignore the message.

5. **Click the Red Hat menu (in the Kicker panel at the bottom of your screen).**

6. **Choose System Tools➪Hardware Browser.**

   After a short delay, a dialog box that looks similar to Figure 5-5 appears.

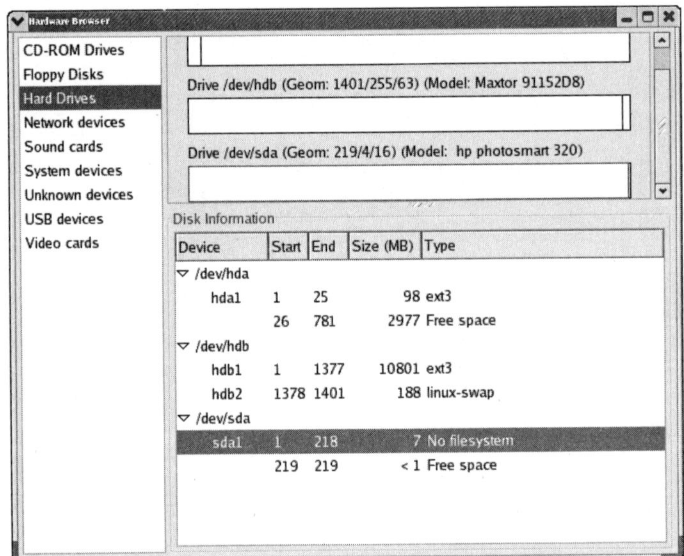

Figure 5-5: The Red Hat Hardware Browser.

7. **Click Hard Drives (in the left column).**

   The Hardware Browser displays all hard drives on your system.

   Linux treats a USB Mass Storage device as if it were a hard drive.

8. **Find the drive that matches your camera.**

   In Figure 5-5, you see that *our* HP PhotoSmart 320 camera shows a drive named `/dev/sda`. The file system inside the camera is found on `/dev/sda1`. Make note of the file system's name (you want the name with the trailing digit; that is `/dev/sda1`, not `/dev/sda`).

9. **Go back to the terminal window (you should still have superuser privileges) and type in the following command:**

   ```
   mkdir /camera
   ```

   This command creates a *mount point* for the camera's file system.

10. **Now mount the camera file system on the mount point, as follows:**

```
mount /dev/sda1 /camera
```

Of course, you should use the device name you found in Step 8 instead of `/dev/sda1`.

11. **Close your terminal window, and you're finished!**

You can now access the memory inside your camera as if it were a directory on a hard drive. To the computer, it looks just like another drive, but this drive has photo files on it. To view and manipulate the camera contents with Konqueror, drag files from the `/camera` directory onto your desktop, or into an e-mail message. Use Kuickshow (on the Red Hat Menu, choose Graphics⇨More Graphics Applications⇨Kuickshow) to watch a slideshow composed of the pictures in the `/camera` directory.

Sharing Your Photos

Now that you have photos, share them! You can e-mail them to friends and family, add them to Web sites, even use a photo as your desktop background. There is a lot of software available for organizing and altering photos, and much of it is open source (that is, free). Some places on the Web worth investigating are

- `www.sourcforge.net`: This is *the* place to find open-source software.
- `www.kde.org`: The official KDE Web site.
- `www.marginalhacks.com`: This site distributes a nice, theme-able photo album program for Linux.

E-mailing your new photo to friends and relatives is simple with Red Hat Linux. In a few easy steps, Grandma can be looking at those new photos of Junior — in minutes.

Just open KMail (this doesn't work with Evolution), address and compose your note, and drag the photo you want to share into the main body of the text — Linux attaches the photo for you. Click the Send button and it's on its way!

Don't forget that large photos and AVIs are really just large files and can tie up quite a bit of time and bandwidth in the process of leaving your mailbox and arriving in your friend's mailbox. Some e-mail services will even reject large files. If you're really careless with oversized files, you can alienate friends. A better way to share really large files might be via CD.

Using the GIMP to Enhance and Embellish Photos

The GIMP (GNU Image Manipulation Program) is a great tool for manipulating photos. It's a very complex tool; entire books are devoted to using the GIMP, so we aren't going to cover it in any depth. Just a quick foot in the door:

1. **Click the Red Hat Menu and choose⇨Graphics⇨The GIMP.**

   This opens several windows of tools to use with your photo.

2. **From the GIMP window, choose Files⇨Open.**

   The Load Image window opens.

3. **Navigate to your file in the Load Image window, and then click OK to open.**

   A new window opens, displaying your photo.

4. **In this window, use the tools included in the GIMP to crop, label, color, or distort your photo.**

Montages, collages, and transforming techniques are also possible with the GIMP's help.

This is where we leave you in the good hands of the help text and other authors. GIMP is a powerful tool, and while the online help text is a bit technical, it's well done. The official site for the GIMP is `www.gimp.org`.

Okay — we'll give you one tip about the GIMP: Most applications open multiple windows within a single workspace. GIMP opens windows all over your desktop. You can't use the File menu on the main GIMP window to save your changes. Instead, right-click your picture to open a pull-down menu with familiar options (such as Save and Mail Image).

Chapter 6

Remote Desktops — Almost as Good as Being There

In This Chapter

- Using VNC to view remote desktops
- Exposing yourself with VNC
- Connecting with KDE's Remote Desktop Connection
- Using `tsclient` with `rdesktop` to access Windows servers

The whole concept of a *remote desktop* might seem a bit odd at first, but it's a great way to access multiple computers at the same time. You can read e-mail in one window, edit a document on a second computer in another window, and browse the Web on a third machine in yet another window. Your entire network can be a click away — with each computer ready to use in its own window. You have desktop access to all the utilities and resources that a remote machine has to offer, without worrying about incompatible operating systems or hardware.

In this chapter, you see three tools that give you remote-desktop capabilities: VNC, `rdesktop`, and the KDE Remote Desktop Connection tool (`krdc`). Each tool has its advantages; be sure to pick the tool that most closely matches your needs.

VNC Server: Sneaking a Peek at Other Desktops

VNC works across a local network or across the Internet. When VNC is running within a network, it doesn't matter what operating system you're running — you can get to any desktop that's running a VNC server. You can open a window for your Windows or Mac machine from Linux and vice versa. Figure 6-1 shows a local Linux desktop viewing three remote desktops: one Windows desktop and two Red Hat Linux desktops.

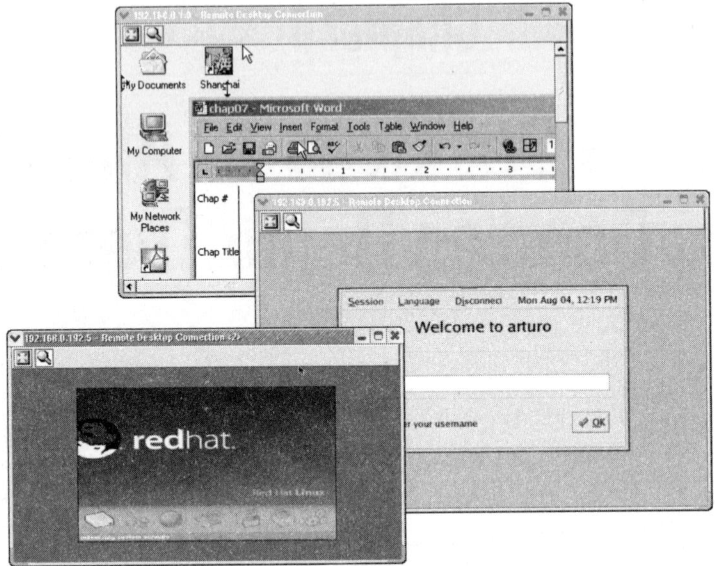

Figure 6-1: Multiple desktops open with VNC.

Installing the VNC Viewer

Every VNC connection has two parts: a VNC viewer and a VNC server. The VNC *viewer* lets you view some other desktop. The VNC *server* exposes a desktop to other viewers. If you want to view a remote desktop, install the viewer. If you want to expose your desktop to others, install the server. If you want to do both, install the viewer and the server. Just remember that you need a viewer on one computer and a server on another.

If you're using KDE

The nice people at KDE have made your life easier (well, this part of it, at least) by including a VNC-compatible viewer and a fantastic interface program. If you have time, drop them a thank-you note — it's one of the nicest things they could do for you. You still need to install the server software on the other end of your desktop connection, but the viewer end is already good to go. If you need to set up a server, go expose yourself (so to speak). If you already have a server available, you're ready to log in.

If you're not using KDE

You won't be left out in the cold, but you do need to do a few things to get a viewer connection running on your desktop. To install the VNC viewer:

1. **Insert the Red Hat Linux DVD.**
2. **Open a terminal window and give yourself superuser privileges with the** `su` **command (enter the superuser password if prompted).**

3. **Mount the CD device with the following command:**

```
mount /dev/cdrom /mnt/cdrom
```

4. **Fire up the Red Hat package manager, like this:**

```
rpm -Uhv /mnt/cdrom/RedHat/RPMS/vnc-3*.rpm
```

That's all you have to do to install the VNC viewer. If you already have a VNC server running on another machine, skip ahead to "VNC viewing made simple with KDE" section. If not, you have to create one, and that's coming right up.

Exposing yourself with VNC Server

The VNC viewer lets you interact with a remote desktop. The remote desktop needs to be running the server software to be viewed by the VNC viewer software.

If you want to view a Windows desktop, Unix desktop, or Macintosh desktop, you need the appropriate server software; the Linux VNC server can only be used on a Linux computer. You can download server software for other operating systems from `www.realvnc.com`.

To install VNC server on a Red Hat Linux machine:

1. **Insert the Red Hat Linux DVD.**
2. **Open a terminal window and give yourself superuser privileges with the `su` command (enter the superuser password if prompted).**
3. **Mount the CD device with the following command:**

```
mount /dev/cdrom /mnt/cdrom
```

4. **Fire up the Red Hat package manager, like this:**

```
rpm -Uhv /mnt/cdrom/RedHat/RPMS/vnc-server*.rpm
```

The quickest and easiest way to start your VNC Server from the terminal window on a Linux machine is to follow these steps:

1. **Type in the command `vncserver -depth 24 :1` and press Enter.**

   The `-depth 24` part tells VNC to use 24-bit color (that's 16 million colors) and the `:1` part is your display number; choose a number higher than 0.

2. **VNC Server prompts you for two passwords.**

   The first is the password that the remote user must enter in order to connect to the new desktop. The second is a *view-only* password; using the view-only password, the remote user can see the new desktop but can't do anything to it. (We usually skip the view-only password.)

After a few buzzes, clicks, and whirs, the VNC server should tell you that a new desktop is eagerly awaiting a user on display number 1.

VNC viewing made simple with KDE

KDE comes complete with a fully installed Remote Desktop Connection tool (`krdc` for short) that's compatible with VNC servers. To connect to a remote VNC desktop using `krdc`, follow these steps:

1. **Open the KMenu and choose Internet⇨More Internet Applications⇨Remote Desktop Connection.**

   The Remote Desktop Connection window opens, asking you for a Remote desktop name and Connection type.

   - Enter the name (or IP address) of the computer that you want to view, followed by a colon and a display number. If you are connecting to a remote Windows desktop, the display number is always `0` (for example, `192.168.0.1:0`). If you're connecting to a Linux (or other Unix) desktop, you have to get the display number from whoever configured the VNC server.
   - Choose the connection type that best describes the network between you and the VNC server. On low-speed connections, `krdc` tries to compress the bits streaming across the network — the display doesn't look quite as nice, but at least you get a reasonably snappy response.

2. **Enter the requested information, and click Connect.**

   A new window opens, prompting you for a password.

3. **Enter the password, and then click OK.**

   A much larger window opens, displaying the desktop of the machine you've just logged in to.

Now you can use the remote desktop as if you were actually sitting in front of that computer. If you move *your* mouse, the pointer moves on the remote desktop. If you press a key (while the VNC viewer has the keyboard focus), the other desktop responds as if you pressed that key on the remote keyboard. Whoever is sitting in front of the VNC server sees the mouse pointer move around as you move your mouse — and (of course) you see the mouse pointer move around if the *other* user's mouse moves.

There are a few cool features about this viewer. You know you can grab the lower-right corner of a window and stretch it to resize, but in most viewers, you can only see as much of the desktop as fits within the window; you have to use scrollbars to see other parts of the desktop. Thankfully, `krdc` has a scaling button. Click the magnifying glass in the upper-left corner, and the entire desktop squeezes into the window.

The little blue button with red arrows is the full-screen button. Click it, and the remote desktop expands to fill the entire screen. It leaves a toolbar across the top of the window, so you still have a way back to your other desktop.

Using VNC to view a Windows desktop

Before you can connect to a Windows desktop that's already running VNC Server, you need two pieces of information: the host name (or IP address) of the VNC server you want to connect to, and the VNC server password. To view the remote desktop, do the following:

1. **Open the K menu and choose Accessories➪More Accessories➪VNC Viewer.**

   A small window appears, prompting you for the name of the VNC server.

2. **Enter the IP address or host name of the server you want to connect to, and then press Enter.**

   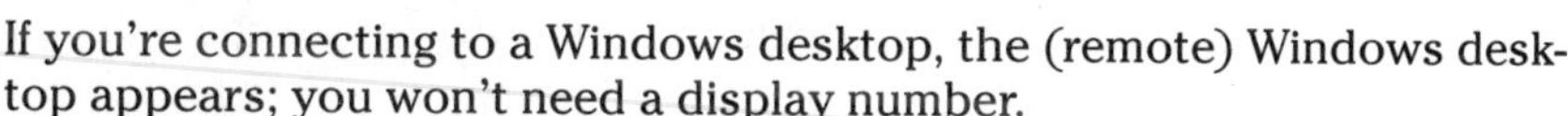

   If you're connecting to a Windows desktop, the (remote) Windows desktop appears; you won't need a display number.

   The server name window closes and another window appears, asking for a password.

3. **Type in the server password.**

   If you're planning to log in from across the Internet (say, to a friend's machine), get the correct password before you try to connect.

4. **When you're finished, log out of Windows and close the VNC window.**

One thing that you'll probably notice about VNC is that you can't drag objects between the VNC viewer window and your own desktop — that just doesn't work. You're able to cut and paste with some Linux applications, but not with others. Just pretend that cut, copy, and paste doesn't work at all — and you'll be pleasantly surprised when it does.

If you have a busy screen saver enabled on the remote desktop, we recommend turning it off while using VNC. Some screen savers can take whole *minutes* (a cyber-eternity) to come back to life over a VNC connection.

Using VNC to view a Linux desktop

When you connect to a VNC server running on a Windows host, you see a *copy* of the physical desktop — your mouse and keyboard are connected to that desktop. When you connect to a VNC server running on a Linux host, the behavior is quite different. When VNC server runs on a Linux computer, it creates a whole new session. When you connect to a Linux virtual desktop, you're not sharing the desktop with someone else — it's all yours.

To connect to a VNC desktop running on a Linux (or Unix) host, you need the following:

- The host name or IP address of the VNC server.
- The *display* number — in most cases, the display number is 1, but the administrator on the other Linux host may want you to use a different number if he (or she) is running multiple desktops.
- The VNC server password.

When you have all that, it's time to connect:

1. **Open the KMenu and choose Accessories⇨More Accessories⇨ VNC Viewer.**

   A small window appears, prompting you for the name of the VNC server.

2. **Enter the host name or IP address of the server you want to connect to and press Enter.**

   If you're using a display number other than 1, you should add a colon and the display number to the end of the server name (if you leave the colon and display number off, VNC assumes you want to connect to display number 1). For example, if the remote Linux computer is named `arturo` and you are connecting to display number two, enter `arturo:2`.

   The server name window closes and another window appears, asking for a password.

3. **Enter the password defined for the VNC server.**

   This may or may not be the same password that you would use if you were sitting in front of the other computer.

   If all goes well, you should see a brand-new *remote* desktop in a window on your *local* desktop.

4. **Do whatever you need to do; when you're finished, just close the VNC viewer window.**

   Your desktop stays there, up and running, until you connect again.

The Red Hat Throbber

In the lower-right corner of your Red Hat Linux desktop, you may see a little red circle with an exclamation point in it. The Red Hat *throbber* is there to alert you that software updates are available for your system. The throbber can be very helpful, but it also sucks up network bandwidth pretty badly when you're using VNC. You can get your bandwidth back by turning off the throbber, like this:

1. **Right-click the throbber.**
2. **Click Configure.**

   The Red Hat Network Notification Tool dialog box opens.
3. **Click Forward.**
4. **Click the Remove from Panel button.**

Other animations (such as `xeyes` and `fish`) can slow your VNC connections too.

rdesktop client for Windows Terminal Server

If you're connecting to a remote Windows desktop, you have a choice to make. You can install VNC server on *any* version of Windows, but if your Windows computer can handle it, you'll get better performance using `rdesktop`. The following versions of Windows are `rdesktop` friendly:

- Windows NT Terminal Server edition
- Windows 2000 Terminal Server edition
- Windows XP Professional
- Windows Server 2003

`rdesktop` is similar to VNC viewer — it lets you control a remote Windows desktop, just like VNC, but it performs better than VNC if your system can use it. The `rdesktop` tool isn't very flashy so Red Hat Linux includes a nice-looking wrapper called `tsclient` — which doesn't do anything useful all by itself. It manages connection information, but uses `rdesktop` or VNC to get the real work done.

Installing tsclient and rdesktop on a Red Hat Linux system

To install `tsclient` and `rdesktop`, follow these steps:

1. **Insert the Red Hat Linux DVD.**
2. **Open a terminal window and give yourself superuser privileges with the** `su` **command.**
3. **Mount the DVD with the following command:**

```
mount /dev/cdrom /mnt/cdrom
```

4. **Start the Red Hat Package Manager by typing**

```
rpm -Uvh /mnt/cdrom/RedHat/RPMS/tsclient*.rpm
```

   You've just installed `tsclient`. In Step 5, you install `rdesktop`.

5. **To install** `rdesktop`**, type in the following command:**

```
rpm -Uvh /mnt/cdrom/RedHat/RPMS/rdesktop*.rpm
```

That's it — `rdesktop` and `tsclient` are easy to install and there's no configuration work required, at least on the Linux side.

Preparing your Windows server

Before you can use `rdesktop` (and/or `tsclient`), you have to make a couple of quick changes to your Windows host:

- If the server is running Windows XP, open My Computer and double-click Properties. Then choose the Remote tab, and check the Allow Users to Connect Remotely box.
- If the server is running Windows NT Terminal Server or Windows 2000 Terminal Server, choose Start⇨Settings⇨Control Panel⇨Services. Right-click Terminal Services, and then click Start.

Opening a quick connection with tsclient

To run `tsclient`, just follow these steps:

1. **Open a terminal window.**
2. **Type** `tsclient` **and press Enter.**

   A terminal server client window opens, asking for the address of your Windows server.

3. **Enter the host name (or IP address) of your Windows server and click Connect.**

   A new window opens, displaying the desktop of the Windows Server machine.

When you use VNC viewer to view a remote Windows desktop, you are sharing the remote desktop (anything that you do on your copy of the desktop can be seen by someone sitting in front of the Windows computer that you are connected to).

Customizing your tsclient configuration

`tsclient` can remember connections options (such as host names, color depths, and screen sizes) for you. You can save an entire set of connection options under a name of your choosing. To do so, you create a connection profile — like this:

1. **Open a terminal window, type** tsclient **and press Enter.**
2. **Click More.**

   A dialog box opens.
3. **Fill in the computer name, username, and password and click Save As.**

   The Save As window appears.
4. **Choose a name for your connection profile and click OK.**

If you've installed the VNC viewer, `tsclient` can manage VNC connections for you as well. To create a VNC profile, just add a colon and the VNC display number to the end of the computer name you type in.

If you frequently connect to multiple servers, create a named profile for each one. While you have the Terminal Server Client dialog box open, poke around in the configuration tabs to see what your options are. Here's a short description of each tab:

- **General:** Lets you choose a computer, (remote) username and password, and a domain name. Leave the domain name blank unless you're connecting to a Windows host that is a member of a domain.

  Use the General tab to save named profiles and to open them again later.
- **Display:** Allows you to set the size of the server window. You can accept the default screen size, choose a custom size, or start in full screen mode. You can also choose a *color depth* — 24-bit color looks nice, but takes more network bandwidth; 8-bit color is much faster, but it can distort images that appear on the remote desktop.
- **Local Resources:** Allows you to change keyboard layouts. If you specify keyboard language, the remote desktop pretends that you are using that keyboard layout.

To see a list of valid keyboard layout codes, open the K menu and choose Regional and Accessibility⇨Keyboard Layout.

- **Programs:** Use this tab to automatically start a program on the Windows machine when you log in. If you always check your e-mail on a remote Windows desktop, you might as well have `tsclient` fire up Outlook Express on your behalf.
- **Performance:** This tab has a few tricks that give you a snappier response time if you have a slow network connection to the server:

  The Enable Bitmap Caching option tells `rdesktop` to save icons and small pictures on your local machine to avoid sending them across the network more than once.

  The Do Not Send Motion Events option reduces the amount of visual feedback from the mouse to your desktop — the mouse still works, but you see only the start- and end-points when you drag something on the remote desktops; you don't see the animation in between.

  The last option on the Performance tab isn't really a performance option. By default, the `rdesktop` window (created by `tsclient`) grabs all the keystrokes you type and sends them to the Windows desktop. For example, when you press Alt+F4, you don't close `rdesktop`; instead, you close an application on the Windows desktop. Check the Enable Window Manager's Key Binding box if you want window-manager shortcut keys to take effect on your local desktop instead of the remote Windows desktop.

To see your window-manager shortcut keys, open the KMenu and choose Regional and Accessibility⇨Keyboard Shortcuts.

Chapter 7

Fine Wine: Running Windows Applications on Red Hat Linux

In This Chapter

- What's so great about Wine?
- Making a more potent Wine
- Troubleshooting Wine

Living in a Linux world is great — tons of free software running in a flexible environment that you have complete control over, no huge corporation demanding that you conform, and if you don't like the way something is done, you can rewrite it yourself.

Now back to reality. You still want to use programs designed for Microsoft Windows. A dual-boot computer is one way to satisfy that urge — boot into Linux for your everyday work or boot into Windows when you need it. But shutting down your Linux session and rebooting into Windows is a hassle. You can use a remote-desktop tool to access a Windows computer from your Linux desktop (see Chapter 6), but that means you have to *own* a Windows computer. What you really need is a way to run Windows applications *within* Linux. That's what Wine does for you. With Wine, you can use familiar Windows favorites without sacrificing the power of working in a Linux environment.

Wine Certainly Has Its Advantages

Wine offers several advantages over a dual-boot machine:

- Wine requires less disk space than a dual-boot approach.
- You use Windows software from the comfort of a Linux environment.
- You have the freedom to use Linux tools and Windows programs at the same time. You don't have to reboot to get to the software you need.
- And, of course, the price is certainly right.

Winemaking 101

Before going much further, you should know a few things about how Wine works. Wine is *not* a Windows emulator (in fact, that's what the acronym *Wine* stands for). Microsoft Windows is not a huge monolithic program; it's a *runtime environment* for an application — a collection of functions within which the application can behave consistently. These functions (called the Win32 API) are grouped together into libraries called DLLs (dynamic link libraries). When a Win32-compatible application (such as Excel or Internet Explorer) wants the operating system to do something useful (say, read a character from the keyboard or write some data to a file), it calls a function within one of these DLLs. Wine brings those same Win32 functions and DLLs to Linux. When you run a Windows application in the Wine environment, it still calls the same Win32 function to write data to a file, but this time, that function is provided by Wine instead of by Microsoft.

A remote desktop is the perfect tool when you need it, but you *do* sacrifice speed when you use one. There is also the little matter of needing to own an extra machine *and* the networking equipment required to set up a completely separate environment for Windows. It also takes up twice the space, twice the electricity, and requires more than twice the system administration (the network doesn't just take care of itself — all those nasty security issues and stuff). Wine is sounding better and better.

Wine brings to the table (sorry) some big advantages. With Wine, you can share Linux resources like the klipboard. You can use Wine with Samba to access Windows-hosted data across a network. You can use Wine to play games that were originally designed for Windows.

Chapter 14 of the big book has complete instructions that show you how to download and install Wine — we're not going to cover that twice. Instead, we're jumping right into Wine.

Configuring Wine for Your System

Wine is *not* a complete implementation of the Windows runtime environment (that is, the Wine authors haven't had the time to rewrite every function in the Win32 API). Wine does come with over 140 DLLs (dynamic link libraries), and many Windows applications run quite nicely with just that subset.

More complex programs need more DLLs. How do you get those DLLs? You have to have a (properly licensed) Windows installation accessible from your Linux environment. If you have that *and* a dual-boot machine to run it all on, then you have two ways to make Windows DLLs available to Wine:

- You can mount the Windows partition as a Linux file system, and tell Wine to find the required files there.
- You can copy the required DLLs to your Linux file system.

You may be thinking that you can use Samba to mount a remote Windows installation as a local file system. Then you can tell Wine to look at the *network share* (that's what Samba calls a remote file system) to find required files. Don't do it — that method violates your license agreement with Microsoft.

Wine stores configuration information under your home directory, in a subdirectory named `.wine/config`. You can edit the configuration file with a normal text editor, but it's a bit intimidating. Instead, we recommend that you use a configuration utility named `winsetuptk`.

To install `winesetuptk`, follow these steps:

1. **Open a terminal window and give yourself superuser privileges with the `su` command.**
2. **Insert the companion CD and mount it with the following command:**

   ```
   mount /dev/cdrom /mnt/cdrom
   ```

3. **Use the Red Hat package manager to install the RPM package:**

   ```
   rpm -Uhv /mnt/cdrom/winesetuptk*.rpm
   ```

4. **When the installer completes its task, type** exit **to relinquish your superuser privileges.**

Wine stores configuration information in your home directory — it's important to run `winesetuptk` under your user ID so that the configuration files end up in the right directory.

Now run the `winesetuptk` program as follows:

1. **In the terminal window, type** winesetuptk **and press Enter.**

   A window similar to Figure 7-1 appears.

Figure 7-1: The WineSetup Tk window.

2. **Click Next to make** `winesetuptk` **create a configuration file in your home directory.**

   `winsetuptk` performs a quick scan of the file systems mounted on your computer. If you've mounted a Windows partition, `winesetuptk` arranges for Wine to use the DLLs (and other utility programs) in that partition.

   You must have the Windows partition listed in the `/etc/fstab` file or `winesetuptk` won't find it.

   If you don't have a Windows partition, `winesetuptk` creates a *skeleton* directory tree that has the same layout as a typical Windows installation (the skeleton is hidden in a subdirectory named `~/.wine/fake_windows`).

3. **Click Next and the window shown in Figure 7-2 appears.**

4. **If** `winesetuptk` **finds your Windows partition, you're finished; just click Next, then click Finish. If not . . .**

   If you don't have a Windows partition, here's where the real work starts. Each button on the left side of the window (Look & Feel, Window Mode, Drives, Paths, and so on) opens a new window where you can adjust configuration options. The two most important windows are the Drives window and the Paths window. When you see those windows on-screen, go to Step 5.

5. **Click Drives and you should see a window similar to Figure 7-3.**

   The Drives configuration window lets you map Window drive names onto Linux directories. In Figure 7-3, you see six drive letters listed (A, C, D, X, Y, and Z). When you run a Windows application in the Wine environment, the program will think that you have these six drives installed on your computer.

- If a Windows application looks at drive `X:`, it sees any files that you have in the `/tmp` directory.
- If the Windows application creates a new file named `C:\Documents\resume.doc`, it shows up looking like this:

```
/home/waldo/.wine/fake_windows/Documents/resume.doc
```

- In most cases, `winsetuptk` does a good job of figuring out how to map drive letters, but adjust them here if you need to.

Figure 7-2: The WineSetup Tk options window.

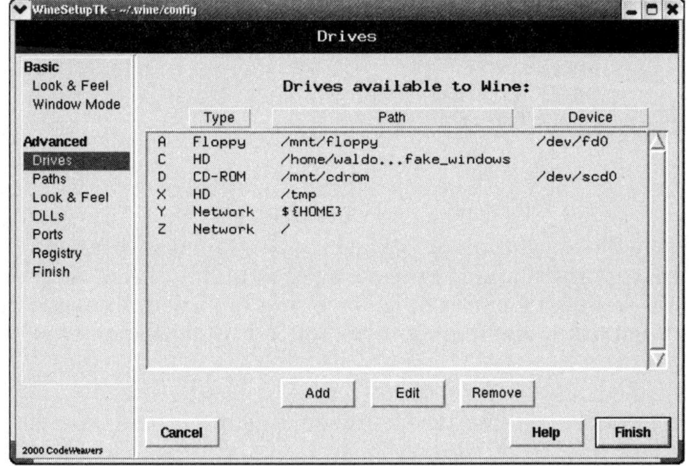

Figure 7-3: The WineSetup Tk Drives window.

6. **When you're satisfied with the drive mappings, click Paths to bring up the window shown in Figure 7-4.**

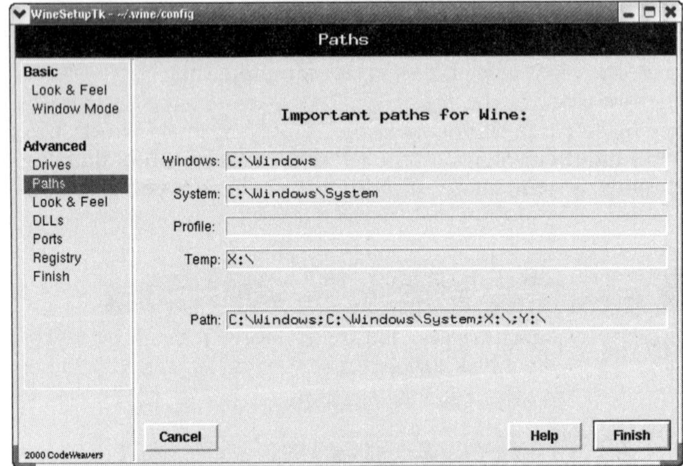

Figure 7-4: The WineSetup Tk Paths window.

This window tells Wine where to find things on your computer. Don't change too much here unless you have a really good reason.

The one entry you may want to change here is the last one: `Path`. If you try to run a Windows program without specifying a complete path (that is, if you type in something like `wine wordpad.exe`), Wine searches each directory listed in `Path`, in left-to-right order, until it finds the program. If you've stored Windows applications somewhere other than in the directories listed in `Path`, you may want to add those directory names to the `Path`.

When Wine Goes Bad . . .

A few years ago, the Paul Masson winery ran an ad campaign that made famous the phrase "We will sell no wine before its time." The authors of Wine have taken a different approach. Wine is not a finished product, but enough pieces are working that many people already find it useful. After you have Wine configured and you can run simple programs like Notepad and WordPad, you may want to try running more complex programs such as those in Microsoft Office.

In our experience, installing the software is generally the hard part. If you're using a Windows-less version of Wine (that is, you are not sharing a Windows partition), your best bet is to search through the compatibility database at the Wine Web site (`http://appdb.winehq.com`). If you *are* sharing a Windows partition (that is, you have a dual-boot computer), install Windows applications in Windows, and *then* use them from Linux — you'll have much better luck that way.

When you run a Windows application in Linux, Wine produces a ton of messages. Some look like errors, some look like warnings, some look like Klingon. You can ignore most of the messages if things seem to be working. If you have trouble trying to run a Windows program, try running Wine from a terminal window (instead of choosing Wine from a menu or the Kicker), you'll see all those mysterious Wine messages and one of them might give you a clue about what went wrong. If you can't make sense of the error messages, try searching for the text of the message with your favorite Web search engine (such as Google).

Some combinations of Linux and Wine versions don't play well together. If you can't seem to get anything to run with Wine, try typing in the following commands:

```
export LD_ASSUME_KERNEL=2.2.5
wine notepad.exe
```

If that works for you, follow these steps to create a shell script that does the nasty work for you:

1. **Open a terminal window and give yourself superuser privileges with the `su` command.**
2. **Use KWrite (or your favorite editor) to create a file named `/usr/local/bin/rum`, like this:**

   ```
   kwrite /usr/local/bin/rum
   ```

3. **Add the following text to the new file:**

   ```
   #!/bin/bash
   export LD_ASSUME_KERNEL=2.2.5
   wine $*
   ```

4. **Save your work, close your editor, and change permissions on the new file by issuing the following command:**

   ```
   chmod a+x /usr/local/bin/rum
   ```

Now, instead of running `wine`, you can run `rum`. (Sorry about that. Some programmers love puns.) For example, `rum notepad.exe`. The `rum` script defines the required environment variable (`LD_ASSUME_KERNEL`) and then invokes Wine for you.

Chapter 8

Webmin and Usermin: Managing Your System with a Web Browser

In This Chapter

- Installing Webmin on your Red Hat Linux computer
- Finding your way around Webmin
- Breaking through your firewall with Webmin
- Installing and running Usermin
- Supervising your system with Usermin
- Stopping runaway programs

As recently as a few years ago, operating systems other than Windows were seldom found in homes and small businesses. Now that Linux is becoming more popular in the home and small business environment, you have the same administrative duties as the big companies. Along comes Webmin and its trusty sidekick, Usermin.

Throughout this book, we give you tool after tool; with every new tool has come the responsibility of maintaining a secure and up-to-date system. With the possible exception of Tuxracer (see Chapter 4), nearly every application you use needs occasional care and feeding. Webmin — a graphical interface that makes administration understandable for all — can help. You use Webmin to perform system administration tasks. Usermin, on the other hand, is a tool that helps you perform day-to-day user tasks.

What Does Webmin Do?

Webmin is a graphical interface for Linux administrators. To put it simply, Webmin lets you use your favorite Web browser to manage your computer. Just install Webmin and connect to the Web server running on your own computer. Of course, if your computer is exposed to the Web, you can also manage your computer from another site (more on that later).

If you don't have Webmin, you're stuck with the command line. You have to *know* which commands to use and how to use them. With Webmin, you find the tool that you want (they're all categorized for you and clearly labeled) and fill in the blanks. You don't have to remember the command name, and you don't have to remember all the obscure command-line options.

So what can Webmin do for you? With Webmin you can

- Manage user information and passwords.
- Upload and download multiple files — either interactively, or in the background at a scheduled time.
- Burn CDs (audio, data, or mixed).
- Create and edit disk partitions.
- Create, mount, and unmount file systems.
- Back up the data on your computer.
- Restore data from a backup.
- Configure an Apache Web server.
- Manage a MySQL or PostgreSQL database.
- Custom configure boot-time tasks.
- Install and view Perl modules. (Perl is a scripting language, known affectionately as "the duct tape of the Internet.")
- Manage an SSH Server — (SSH is used for secure remote logins).
- Create and edit Samba file and print shares.

Webmin can also do a lot of things that we haven't listed. The list actually goes on and on. You can extend Webmin by plugging in new modules. First, though, you have to install Webmin.

Installing Webmin

Webmin runs on many different kinds of computers; different flavors of Linux, Unix, even Mac OS X. When you install Webmin, the installer program tries to discover which operating system you're using, and it custom tailors configuration files to match your system. At the time we're writing this, Webmin hasn't been upgraded specifically for Red Hat Linux version 10. That's not a big problem because Webmin works fine if you tell it that you're running Red Hat Linux version 9. (Yes, we're asking you to tell a small fib here; you're really running Red Hat 10.)

To install Webmin, follow these steps:

1. **Insert the companion CD, open a terminal window, and then give yourself superuser privileges with the** `su` **command.**
2. **Mount the CD with the command** `mount /dev/cdrom /mnt/cdrom`.
3. **Create a new directory named** `/usr/webmin` **and move there with the command:**

   ```
   mkdir /usr/webmin ; cd /usr/webmin
   ```
4. **Then unzip the Webmin package with this command:**

   ```
   tar -zxvf /mnt/cdrom/webmin*gz
   ```
5. **Type** `cd webmin*` **to move to the new Webmin subdirectory.**
6. **Run the setup program with this command:**

   ```
   ./setup.sh
   ```

   Webmin whirs a bit and starts a setup program that asks you a few questions about where you want it to store your files.
7. **You can accept the defaults for the directory-related questions.**
8. **When the setup program asks for your operating system version, choose Red Hat 10 if it's available; otherwise, choose Red Hat 9.**

   You're prompted for a username and password.
9. **Follow the usual rules and make it something you'll remember, but something other people aren't likely to figure out.**

   The Webmin administrative account has superuser privileges on your computer. If you give the administrative password to a friend, he'll be able to do anything he wants to your computer.
10. **Finish answering the questions (choose the defaults if you're not sure what to do), and you're ready to go.**

Using Webmin

Webmin can help you with most of the system administration tasks that you'll ever need to carry out. To use Webmin, simply open a browser (Mozilla, Konqueror, Galeon, or whichever browser you prefer) and connect to your computer on port 10000. Most computers know that their own network address is 127.0.0.1 (that is, the IP address 127.0.0.1 always refers to the local host, never to another computer). So, you can start using Webmin like this:

1. **Start your favorite Web browser, type in the URL** 127.0.0.1:10000**, and then press Enter.**
2. **Type in a username and password when prompted.**

   If this is the first time you've connected to Webmin on this server, you have to use the username and password you assigned when you installed Webmin; see the previous section (The default administrative user name is `admin`; you have to remember the password yourself.)

At this point, you should see the Webmin starter page in your browser (Figure 8-1). From here, you can start using Webmin.

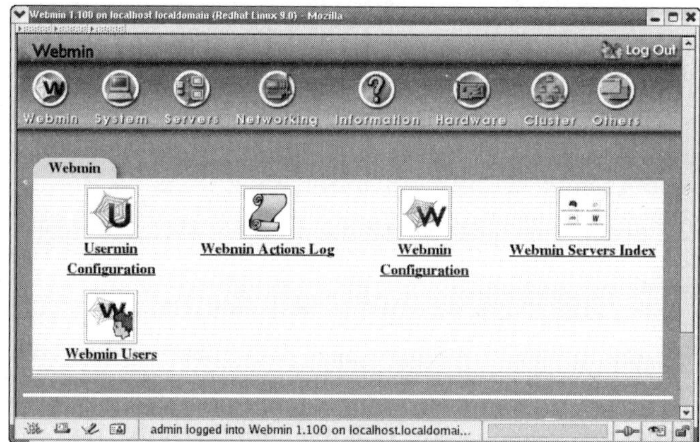

Figure 8-1: The Webmin start page.

Webmin is extendible — you can easily download and install new modules without leaving Webmin. Webmin gives you more than 70 standard modules when you install it, but the Webmin Web site (`www.webmin.com`) lists more than 150 third-party modules. Browse through the third-party modules, and you'll probably find an administrative helper that will make your life easier.

Adding an alternate Webmin user

Webmin's administrative user account (`admin`) holds superuser privileges on your computer; anyone who knows your administrative password can tango all over your system. You can create alternative, lesser-privileged user accounts to hand out to your friends or co-workers. When you create a Webmin user account, you choose which modules each user can see. Here's how to create a new Webmin user account that can only access your MySQL database (if you have one) and the CD-ROM burner on your computer:

1. **Log into Webmin using your administrative username and password.**
2. **Click the Webmin Users icon (refer to Figure 8-1).**
3. **Scroll down and click Create a New Webmin User. (It's not quite at the bottom of the page, but pretty close.)**

   The next page that you see is a bit complex looking, but don't be intimidated; you only need to fill in a few items.
4. **Start with the Username and then press Tab to move to the Password box — you have three choices here:**
   - *Set to:* Make up a password and type it in the next box on the page.
   - *Unix authentication:* This user has to type in his Linux password to log into Webmin.
   - *No password accepted:* This account is disabled (that is, you won't be able to log into this account until a Webmin administrator changes the password).
5. **Scroll down to the Modules section and mark the CD Burner and the MySQL Database Server check boxes.**

   If you want this user to have other privileges, just click the corresponding check boxes.
6. **Click Save.**

You've just created a Webmin user with limited privileges. Of course, you can choose a different set of authorized modules to suit your needs.

We recommend that you create at least one lesser-privileged Webmin user. Give that user only the privileges that you need in your day-to-day work. Use the new account rather than an administrative account whenever you can. Remember — you can't accidentally break something if you don't have enough privileges to change it. If you need to do something that requires more privileges, log in as an administrator, do your work, and then log back out.

Managing your firewall with Webmin

One of the nice things about Webmin is that a Web browser provides the entire user interface. That means that you can use a Web browser at your office to manage a (Linux) computer at your home. Or you can use a Web browser at home to manage a computer at your office. Or you can manage your computer from the road if you're traveling. Just fire up a Web browser and connect.

If you've locked your computer down nice and tight, you'll need to punch a small hole in your firewall so that Webmin traffic can get in and out of your computer. Fortunately, Webmin includes a firewall module (pretty handy, huh?).

If you chose the "no firewall" option when you installed Red Hat Linux, you don't have a firewall, so you can skip this next section. If you already have a firewall in place, follow these steps to open your network to Webmin traffic:

1. **Open your favorite Web browser and log into your Webmin server as an administrative user (or at least as a user who holds the Linux Firewall privilege).**
2. **Click the Networking icon (at the top of the page) and then click Linux Firewall.**
3. **When the next page appears, scroll down to the Chain RH-Lokkit-0-50-INPUT area.**

   Your firewall chain may have a different name; look for the word Chain at the start of the line.

   At the right side of the page is an Add column; each row has a small arrow pointing up and a small arrow pointing down. You click the up arrow to add a new rule *before* that row; click the down arrow to add a new rule *after* that row.
4. **You want the new firewall rule to be the first one in the chain, so click the first up arrow.**
5. **On the Add Rule page, type a comment in the Rule Comment text box (something like** Webmin ports**).**
6. **Next to Action to Take, click Accept (that tells the firewall to accept the packets that you're about to define).**
7. **Scroll down to the Network protocol and change** `<Ignored> TCP` **to** `Equals TCP` **(Webmin uses the TCP protocol).**
8. **In the next section of this page, set the Destination TCP or UDP Port to Equals 10000 (Webmin communicates on TCP port 10000).**
9. **Scroll to the bottom of the page and click Create.**

   When the Linux Firewall page reappears, the new rule appears at the top of the list (it should read something like `Accept ... If protocol is TCP and source and destinations parts are 10000`).
10. **Scroll to the bottom of the page and click Apply Configuration.**

Now you can use Webmin to manage your computer from other locations — all you'll need is a Web browser.

How Useful Is Usermin?

Before the days of the graphical user interface, all computing was done through an on-screen command line. Then, programmers started making menus, which were friendlier to the user, but left you with little power and even less flexibility. If the menu didn't have an option for what you wanted to do, you were just out of luck.

Linux has changed all that, and Usermin has helped. Usermin is a graphical tool that allows you to set up and care for all the programs that you need to use in your day-to-day life — kind of like a customization wizard, but with extra flexibility built in. Usermin helps you

- Manage and read your e-mail
- Configure e-mail forwarding
- Manage and use SSH
- Upload and download files across a local network, wide-area network, or the Internet
- Monitor processes on your system
- Schedule jobs to run while you're away
- Digitally sign and encrypt e-mail

You can extend Usermin by plugging in new modules. If you're lucky, someone else may have already written the exact plug-in you need — or, with a little bit of programming skill, you can write your own module. (Open source — gotta love it.)

Installing Usermin

Right now, the RPMs available for Usermin were built for Red Hat 9, so they won't install into Red Hat 10. The Usermin program itself *works* fine, but installing it is going to take just a few more steps than you may be used to. Instead of installing from an RPM, you install from a zipped archive — in geek-speak, a *tarball* (because of the `.tar` in the filename extension). When you install from a tarball, the setup program asks you a few questions including which version of Linux you're using. To install Usermin from a `.tar.gz` file (that is, a compressed tarball), follow these steps:

1. **Insert the companion CD.**
2. **In a terminal window, give yourself superuser privileges with the** `su` **command.**

3. **Mount the CD with the following command:**

```
mount /dev/cdrom /mnt/cdrom
```

4. **Move to the /usr/webmin directory (**`cd /usr/webmin`**) and unpack the tarball with the following command:**

```
tar -zxvf /mnt/cdrom/usermin*gz
```

5. **Type** `cd usermin*` **to move to the new Usermin subdirectory.**
6. **Run the setup program with the following command:**

```
./setup.sh
```

   This starts the Usermin setup program.
7. **You can accept the defaults for the directory-related questions.**
8. **When the setup program asks for your operating system version, choose Red Hat 10 if it's available; otherwise, choose Red Hat 9.**

The basics of using Usermin

Usermin runs in your Web browser. To start Usermin, follow these steps:

1. **Open your favorite Web browser.**

   Mozilla or Konqueror will work fine for the purpose.
2. **Go to** `http://127.0.0.1:20000`**.**

   Pretty simple, huh? Figure 8-2 shows the Usermin Start page.

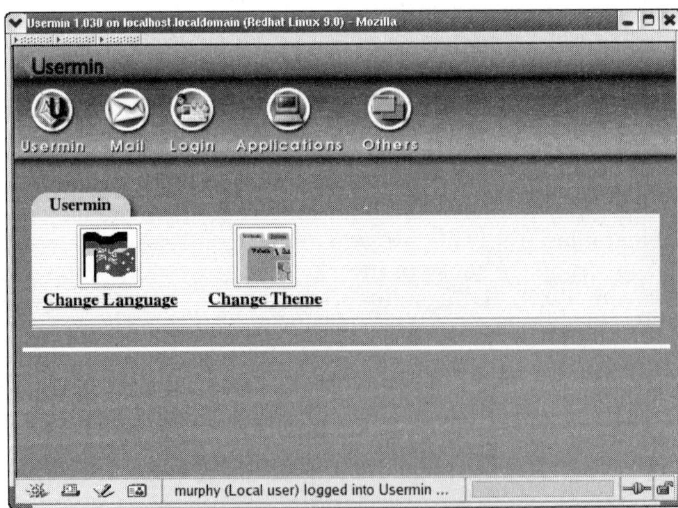

Figure 8-2: The Usermin Start page.

Don't forget — you can keep Usermin handy by adding Usermin to your Mozilla Bookmarks list. On the Mozilla menu, choose Bookmarks⇨Bookmark this Page.

Usermin starts out assuming that you want to converse in English, but you can choose an alternate language from the start page — just click Language and then choose your preference from the list.

You can also change the overall appearance of Usermin from the start page. Click Change Theme, choose a new theme from the drop down list, and click Change.

Across the top of each Usermin page you see a row of icons:

- **Usermin:** This takes you back to the Start page, no matter how lost you might be.
- **Mail:** The mail page lets you configure Usermin to retrieve your e-mail from another server, forward your e-mail to another server, and set up filters (to stop unwanted mail from coming in). You can also read your mail from the mail page.
- **Login:** From the login page, you can log in to the server (using SSH or telnet) and manage login-related things like your password, SSH identity, and startup scripts.
- **Applications:** The applications page gives you a friendly interface for Apache, MySQL and GnuPG Encryption. You can also upload and download files from this page.
- **Others:** The Others page is a hodgepodge of modules that you might find useful in your day-to-day work. You can work with files, schedule commands, set up an HTTP tunnel, or search your documentation (or Google) for information on a given topic.

The upload and download features, while very useful, are also very confusing. If you're sitting in front of your Red Hat Linux computer, connected to the copy of Usermin installed *on* your computer, just ignore the upload and download tools — they won't make any sense. Instead, pretend you're at your office, connected to the Usermin server at your house. Both upload *and* download put files *on the server*. You can't put a file anywhere else with these tools. So what's the difference between upload and download? The *upload* tool copies a file from the computer that you're sitting in front of (the one that's running a Web browser) and places it on the server. The *download* tool pulls a file from a third computer (most likely a computer out there on the Web somewhere) and copies it to the server (that is, pulls it "down" out of the wider realm of cyberspace and stuffs it onto the Webmin server).

Monitoring your system with Usermin

Usermin is a great tool for keeping an eye on your system. You can use the File Manager (on the Others page) to browse through your file systems. If you are running a bit short of disk space (and you're sharing your computer with friends and family), you can impose *disk quotas* — limits on the amount of disk space that any given user can consume. You can also mount and unmount file systems from the Others page.

One of the handiest features in Webmin is the Running Processes page. To see a list of the processes running on your computer, click Login, then Running Processes. You'll only see the processes running under your username.

If you've logged in to Usermin with the administrative username `root`, you'll see most of the system-level processes too (they're owned by the superuser account, `root`).

The first time you open the Running Processes page, the processes are listed in the form of a tree. Every process (except for the init process, process ID 1) has a parent process and the tree view shows the parent/child relationships by grouping all child processes together underneath their parent. You can choose to view running processes in four different arrangements (or *views*). The first view is the one you're looking at now — processes are arranged in a tree and sorted (roughly) by process ID. Click User (near the top of the page) to view running processes sorted by user name. Unless you've modified Usermin (as outlined in the next Tip), the User view is identical to the tree view. If you modified `proc-lib.pl`, the User view displays all processes, grouped by username.

If you want to see *all* processes on your system, find the `proc-lib.pl` file that comes with Usermin (if you chose the default location when you installed Usermin, you can find this file in `/usr/libexec/usermin/proc/proc-lib.pl`) and change the line that reads

```
$user_processes_only = 0;
```

so that it reads

```
$user_processes_only = 0;
```

The Memory view sorts the process list according to the amount of memory used by each process The CPU view displays processes in order of CPU consumption (CPU-hogs are at the top of the list, polite programs that know how to share appear at the bottom of the list).

No matter which view you are using, you can click the Process ID for any process to see detailed information about that process and to control that process. Figure 8-3 shows a sample process.

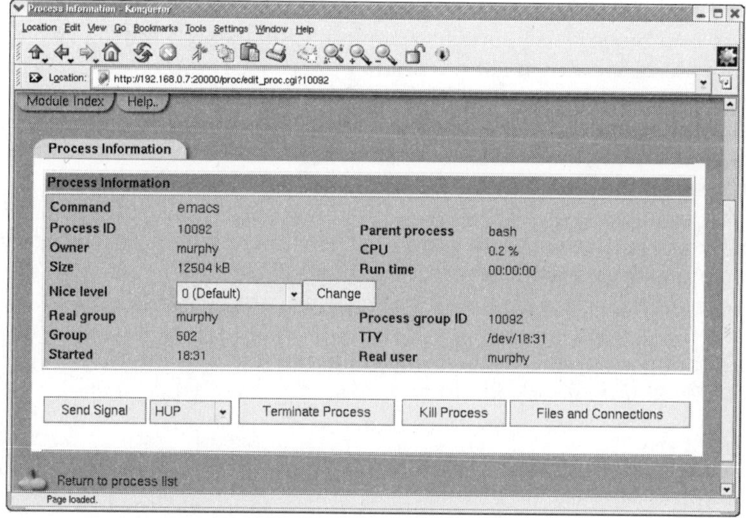

Figure 8-3: Viewing process details.

Notice the buttons across the bottom of the page:

- **Send Signal:** This button does what it says — it sends a *signal* to the process. If that sounds weird, don't worry. The only time you'll ever need to send a signal is when a piece of documentation directs you to, and the documentation will also tell you *which* signal to send.
- **Terminate Process and Kill Process:** The first button terminates the process and the other kills the process. What's the difference between a Terminate and a Kill? Well, when you Terminate a process, you're asking it (politely) to finish its work and go away. When you Kill a process, it's gone right away. Killing a process is much more drastic — the victim may be right in the middle of a file update and you can easily corrupt data files that way. If you need to stop a *runaway process* (that is, a process that doesn't seem to be doing anything other than giving your computer a complete cardio-fitness workout), try to Terminate it first — use Kill *only* as a last resort.
- **Files and Connections:** This is probably the second most useful button in all of Usermin (we show you the number one button in a moment). Click Files and Connections to see a list of files opened by that process and a list of open network connections. Why is this such a great thing? Occasionally you'll find that Linux won't let you do something because another user has a resource that you need.

  For example, you can't unmount the CD drive if a process has opened a file on the drive (and hasn't yet closed it). The Files and Connections button is also handy when you need a file that some tool uses, but you don't know the name of the file. For example, if you need to know where the Mozilla Web browser store history information, fire up a copy of Mozilla, find the process with Webmin, and look at the list of open files.

Okay, if Files and Connections gives you the *second* most useful tool, which tool holds first place? We happen to think that the Search button (which shows up when you're viewing a list of running processes) tops the list. When you click Search, a new page appears that enables you to search for processes according to a number of criteria. You can search processes owned by a specific user, processes using more than, say, 25 percent of the available CPU time, or a process whose name includes a given word.

Cooler yet is that you can search for processes which are using a given file, file system, or network connection. Want to know why you can't unmount a file system? Just search for any processes using that file system. Want to know who's using your network on port number 80? Search for all processes that have that port open. Spend some time playing with the Running Processes tool — you'll be glad you did.

Appendix

About the CD

System Requirements

The companion disc is designed specifically for Red Hat Fedora. If your computer can run Red Hat Fedora, you should be good to go. Your computer should meet the following *minimum* requirements (and exceed them if possible):

- Red Hat Fedora (included in this kit).
- A Pentium-class PC with a 133MHz or faster processor recommended. To run the MAME arcade emulator or MPlayer DVD player, a faster CPU will give you much better results.
- For best performance using the X Window System, we recommend at least 64MB, and preferably 128MB, of main memory. Wine can eat up a lot of memory — memory's cheap, so buy more if you can.
- To install all the software included on the companion disc, you'll need about 500MB (or 1/2GB) of free space on your hard drive. Of course, if you're running short of disk space, install only what you really need.
- If you want to watch DVD movies with MPlayer, you need a DVD drive that's supported by Red Hat Linux.
- MPlayer and RealPlayer require an audio card (one supported specifically by Red Hat Linux.
- Monitor, keyboard, and mouse.

Using the CD with Linux

To install the items from the CD onto your hard drive, follow these steps:

1. **Log in as `root` and then insert the CD into your computer's CD-ROM drive.**
2. **If your computer has Auto-Mount enabled, wait for the CD to mount. Otherwise, mount the CD:**

- *Command-line instructions:* At the command prompt, type **mount /dev/cdrom /mnt/cdrom**. This command mounts the `cdrom` device to the `mnt/cdrom` directory. If your device has a different name, change `cdrom` to that device name (for instance, `cdrom1`).
- *Graphical-interface instructions:* Right-click the CD-ROM icon on the desktop and choose Mount CD-ROM. This mounts your CD-ROM.

3. **Browse the CD and follow the individual installation instructions for the products listed below.**
4. **Remove the CD from your CD-ROM drive:**
   - *Command-line instructions:* At the command prompt, type **umount /mnt/cdrom**.
   - *Graphical-interface instructions:* Right-click the CD-ROM icon on the desktop and choose UMount CD-ROM. This unmounts your CD-ROM.

After you've installed the programs you want, eject the CD and carefully place it back in the plastic jacket of the book for safekeeping.

What You'll Find

Shareware programs are fully functional, free trial versions of copyrighted programs. If you like particular programs, register with their authors for a nominal fee and receive licenses, enhanced versions, and technical support. *Freeware programs* are free, copyrighted games, applications, and utilities. You can copy them to as many PCs as you like — free — but they have no technical support. *GNU software* is governed by its own license, which is included inside the folder of the GNU software. There are no restrictions on distribution of this software. See the GNU license for more details. *Trial, demo, or evaluation versions* are usually limited either by time or functionality (such as being unable to save projects).

MPlayer: This open-source media player from the team at `www.mplayerhq.hu` runs on Linux and other systems. MPlayer is distributed under a number of licenses — the basic player is GPL'ed, but some components use different licenses. You need a DVD player up and running before you can watch DVDs with MPlayer. See `www.mplayerhq.hu` for details.

To run MPlayer, use the Red Hat Package manger to install all the MPlayer package files. Use the following command: `rpm -Uhv /mnt/cdrom/mplayer*.rpm`.

RealPlayer: RealPlayer, from RealNetworks, Inc., is a free version of the Real Networks RealOne audio/video player for Linux. RealPlayer is distributed under a proprietary license but is free for public use. This program is distributed as an RPM (Red Hat Package Manager) package. To install RealPlayer, just type `rpm -Uhv /mnt/cdrom/rpp*`. If you have problems running RealPlayer, try typing `LD_ASSUME_KERNEL=2.2.5 realplay`.

MAME: From the team at `www.mame.net` comes MAME, which stands for *multiple arcade machine emulator* — a program the emulates video-arcade games. MAME is an open-source project, but the game programs themselves are not. See the MAME Web site (`www.mame.net/readme.html` in particular) for licensing information. Details on installing MAME (and a sample game) are in Chapter 4.

Wine: Wine (from the Wine Project at `www.winehq.com`) lets you run Windows software on your Red Hat Linux computer. Wine is distributed under the GNU Lesser General Public License, but programs that you run with Wine (such as Netscape, Microsoft Office, etc.) are covered by their own license agreements.

Be aware that Wine is an evolving program and that not all Windows software will run under Wine. See the WineHQ Web site for a current list. To install Wine, type `rpm -Uhv /mnt/cdrom/wine*.rpm`. That command will also install `winesetuptk` — an open-source configuration tool for Wine.

Webmin: Webmin, from Jamie Cameron and `www.webmin.com`, is distributed under the BSD License (meaning that Webmin is freely distributed and can be used for commercial and noncommercial purposes). Webmin lets you manage your Red Hat Linux computer from within a Web browser. See Chapter 8 for installation instructions (it's a little tricky).

Usermin: Also from Jamie Cameron and `www.webmin.com`, Usermin is distributed under the BSD License. Usermin is similar to Webmin — it lets you perform day-to-day tasks (such as uploading and downloading files, reading e-mail, and so on) from within a Web browser. Detailed installation instructions are in Chapter 8.

Adobe Acrobat Reader: Acrobat Reader, from Adobe Systems, lets you read e-books and other documentation created in Adobe's Portable Document Format (also called *PDF*). You can find PDF documents all over the Web.

Red Hat Linux Fedora Desktop For Dummies PDF: We've included this entire little book (the one you're reading now) on the CD in PDF format. Take the CD with you if you want to read this book on a long trip. The PDF format is nice because you can use the search tool to find whatever you're looking for.

OpenOffice.org For Dummies PDF: And here's another entire book in PDF format! OpenOffice.org is a free suite of tools (similar to Microsoft Office) that you can use to automate your office. OpenOffice.org includes a document processor that can create professional documents, newsletters, brochures, or even complete Web sites. The Calc tool is a powerful yet easy to use spreadsheet. You can also create presentations (fancy, enhanced slide shows) with Impress. OpenOffice.org also includes diagramming tools and database tools.

Coupons: Can't install Red Hat Linux from a DVD? Don't worry — we've included a coupon for the CD installation set of Red Hat Linux on CD. And if you find yourself wanting the actual *OpenOffice.org For Dummies* book, we've included a coupon for that, too.

If You've Got Problems (Of the CD Kind)

We tried our best to test various computers with the minimum system requirements. But your computer may differ, and some of the programs on the companion disc may not install correctly or work as stated.

The most likely problem is that Red Hat Linux doesn't recognize your hardware. If you're having trouble with MPlayer, visit the official MPlayer Web site (`www.mplayerqh.hu`) and make sure that the program supports your specific DVD drive. MPlayer and RealPlayer both require a working audio card. Playing games is more fun with a joystick, but getting a joystick to work with Linux can be challenging. If you find no joy in your joystick, browse through the Web site at `http://atrey.karlin.mff.cuni.cz/~vojtech/joystick`.

If you still have trouble with the CD-ROM, please call the Wiley Product Technical Support phone number: (800) 762-2974. Outside the United States, call 1(317) 572-3994. You can also contact Wiley Product Technical Support through the Internet at `www.wiley.com/techsupport`. Wiley Publishing will provide technical support only for installation and other general quality control items; for technical support on the applications themselves, consult the program's vendor or author.

To place additional orders or to request information about other Wiley products, please call (800) 225-5945.

Red Hat® Linux® Fedora™ For Dummies®

vi commands

Many people find that working in a text-based environment makes everyday systems administration jobs a little easier. You're likely to work from a CLI terminal emulator (see our comments in Chapter 4 about the GNOME Terminal) after you have been working with Linux for a while. The Visual Editor, vi, is almost as old as the Unix operating system and is much older than Linux. The straightforward text editor vi is nothing fancy, like OpenOffice, but is nonetheless quite useful and powerful.

The following list of commands contains the most useful and commonly used commands to control the vi text editor. We have been using vi for more than 20 years, in fact, and have never had to use many other commands than these — proving that you can be lazy and still get work done.

You can start vi by entering the command `vi` from the GNOME Terminal shell prompt:

```
[username@somemachine username]$ vi somefile
```

You enter these commands from the vi editor (see Chapter 4 for more details):

`vi` *filename*	Open *filename* in vi
`I`	Enter Insert mode, inserting before the current position
Shift+`I`	Enter Insert mode, inserting at the beginning of the current line
`a`	Enter Insert mode, inserting after the current position
Shift+`A`	Enter Insert mode, inserting at the end of the current line
Esc	Return from Insert mode to Command mode
`x`	Delete a character while in Command mode
`cw`	Delete the word to the left of the cursor and put the editor in Input mode
`:w`	Write out the file
`:q`	Quit with no additional writes to the disk
`:wq`	Write back the file, and then quit
Shift+`ZZ`	Write back the file, and then quit
`:q!`	Quit the file with impending changes unwritten
/string	Search forward through the file for a string
?string	Search backward through the file for a string
`n`	Find the next string (either forward or backward)
`u`	Undo the last command

For Dummies: Bestselling Book Series for Beginners

Red Hat® Linux® Fedora™ For Dummies®

Systems administration commands

The following list shows several commonly used Linux commands that help you to manage disks, shut down your computer, and gather information about your computer system. You enter these commands from a GNOME Terminal shell prompt. Consult Chapter 4 for more information about how to enter commands.

`mount [options] device file_system`	Mount a file system.
`umount [option] file_system`	Unmount a file system.
`fsck [options] file_system`	Check the structure and integrity of a specified file system.
`mkfs [options] file_system`	Put a directory structure on a low-level formatted disk.
`shutdown`	Shut down the system now rather than wait for a message to be sent. (Ctrl+Del does the same thing).
`vmstat [options]`	Look at the virtual memory performance.
`procinfo`	Gather information about processes.

File permissions

The following examples show different file permission combinations. Consult Appendixes C and D for more information about files and file permissions.

`-rwxrwxrwx`	Creates read, write, and execute permissions for the user, the group, and the rest of the world (mode 777)
`drwxr-xr--`	Creates a directory that is completely open to its owner and that can be read and searched by the group and read (but not searched) by the world (mode 754)
`crw-r--r--`	Creates a character-special file that the owner can read or write to but that the group and the world can only read (mode 644)
`brw-------`	Creates a block-special file that only the owner can read and write to (mode 600)

Item 4232-X.
For more information about Wiley Publishing, call 1-800-762-2974.

Red Hat® Linux® Fedora™ FOR DUMMIES®

by Jon 'maddog' Hall and Paul G. Sery

Wiley Publishing, Inc.

Red Hat® Linux® Fedora™ For Dummies®

Published by
Wiley Publishing, Inc.
111 River Street
Hoboken, NJ 07030-5774
www.wiley.com

Published by Wiley Publishing, Inc., Indianapolis, Indiana

Published simultaneously in Canada

For general information on our other products and services or to obtain technical support, please contact our Customer Care Department within the U.S. at 800-762-2974, outside the U.S. at 317-572-3993, or fax 317-572-4002.

Wiley also publishes its books in a variety of electronic formats. Some content that appears in print may not be available in electronic books.

Library of Congress Control Number: 2003112921

ISBN: 0-7645-4232-X

Manufactured in the United States of America

10 9 8 7 6 5 4 3 2

1B/TR/QR/QU/IN

About the Authors

Jon 'maddog' Hall is the executive director of Linux International, a vendor organization dedicated to promoting the use of the Linux operating system. He has been in the computer industry for more than a quarter of a century (somehow, that sounds more impressive than just "25 years"), the past 18 years of which have been spent using, programming, and admiring the Unix operating system. Jon works for Compaq Computer Corporation, where he is helping to shape Compaq's strategy with respect to Linux. Previously, Jon was the department head of computer science at Hartford State Technical College, where his students lovingly (he hopes) gave him the nickname 'maddog' as he tried to teach them operating system design, compiler theory, and how to live an honorable life.

While working for Digital Equipment Corporation in May of 1994, 'maddog' met Linus Torvalds, and was intelligent enough (his critics say 'maddog' was just lucky) to recognize the potential of the Linux operating system. Linux changed his life, mostly by providing him with 22-hour workdays. Since 'maddog' has started working with Linux, however, he has also started meeting more girls (in particular, his two godchildren). You can usually find Jon speaking at various Linux conferences and events ('maddog' just barks), and he has also been known to travel long distances to speak to local Linux user groups.

Paul G. Sery is a computer systems engineer employed by Sandia National Laboratories in Albuquerque, New Mexico. He is a member of the Computer Support Unit, Special Projects, which specializes in managing and troubleshooting UNIX and Linux systems.

When he is not beating his head against systems administration problems, Paul and his wife, Lidia, enjoy riding their tandem bicycle through the Rio Grande valley. They also enjoy traveling throughout Mexico. Paul is the author of *Linux Network Toolkit* and the co-author of several other books. He has a bachelor's degree in electrical engineering from the University of New Mexico.

Dedication

Jon 'maddog' Hall: To Mom & Pop (TM), whose aversion to things electronic is well known, and who can still call their son Jon rather than maddog.

Paul G. Sery: To my wife, Lidia Maura Vazquez de Sery.

Author's Acknowledgments

I want to thank my wife, Lidia, for her patience, support, and good advice, all of which have made writing this book possible. Without her, I would still be the pocket-protector-wearing, busted-eye-glass-fixed-with-tape-looking, "Star Trek"-watching, wrinkled-shirt-suffering, spaghetti-in-the-pot-over-the-sink eating, Saturday-night-hacking sorry sorta guy. Well, I never was into "Star Trek," and I *am* pecking at this keyboard on Saturday night, but my beautiful wife sure has made me a better man.

I would also like to thank Anne Hamilton and Laura Lewin, who gave me the chance to write in general and this book in particular. Both showed great confidence and patience in me. I am very grateful and wish them success in their ventures.

And, of course, I want to thank the staff at Wiley Publishing, who provided considerable and essential help, too. Terri Varveris and Rebecca Whitney provided constant and essential assistance.

I want to acknowledge a total lack of assistance in writing this book from my dog, the infamous Oso Maloso; eater of many things that should have ended his long career early, including but not limited to ant poison, Advil, many pounds of Tootsie Rolls one Halloween, several bags of chicken bones at one party, beer, and other assorted items; escaper of many fences and gates; and friend of the late, great Paunchy (whose name you see throughout this book) and other local dogs.

How useful was Oso? Well, one night while working on this book I got a phone call. Leaving my apple pie behind next to the keyboard, I went downstairs to take the call and passed him on his way up. I should have known something was up because he had a cell phone with him and no one answered when I picked up to take the call. I went up the stairs while he went down. The apple pie was gone. Oso 1, human 0.

— *Paul G. Sery*

Publisher's Acknowledgments

We're proud of this book; please send us your comments through our online registration form located at www.dummies.com/register/.

Some of the people who helped bring this book to market include the following:

Acquisitions, Editorial, and Media Development

Project Editor: Rebecca Whitney

Acquisitions Editor: Terri Varveris

Technical Editors: Korry and Susan Douglas

Editorial Manager: Carol Sheehan

Permissions Editor: Laura Moss

Media Development Specialist: Angela Denny

Media Development Manager: Laura VanWinkle

Media Development Supervisor: Richard Graves

Editorial Assistant: Amanda M. Foxworth

Cartoons: Rich Tennant (www.the5thwave.com)

Production

Project Coordinator: Erin Smith

Layout and Graphics: Carrie Foster, Joyce Haughey, Kristin McMullan, Mary Gillot Virgin, Shae Lynn Wilson

Proofreaders: Laura Albert, Carl William Pierce, Charles Spencer, Ethel M. Winslow

Indexer: TECHBOOKS Production Services

Publishing and Editorial for Technology Dummies

Richard Swadley, Vice President and Executive Group Publisher

Andy Cummings, Vice President and Publisher

Mary C. Corder, Editorial Director

Publishing for Consumer Dummies

Diane Graves Steele, Vice President and Publisher

Joyce Pepple, Acquisitions Director

Composition Services

Gerry Fahey, Vice President of Production Services

Debbie Stailey, Director of Composition Services

Contents at a Glance

Table of Contents

Part IV: Revenge of the Nerds 197

Introduction

Red Hat Linux Fedora For Dummies is designed to help you install and use Red Hat Linux. This book shows you how to do fun and interesting — to say nothing of useful — tasks with Red Hat Linux. This book is also designed to be an effective doorstop or coffee cup coaster. Whatever you use it for, we hope that you have fun.

About This Book

This book is designed to be a helping-hands tutorial. It provides a place to turn for help and solace in those moments when, after two hours of trying to get your network connection working, your dog bumps into the cable and it magically starts working.

Note: Red Hat Inc. has merged its Red Hat Linux distribution with the Open Source Fedora Core Project to create the new Fedora Core distribution. Red Hat sponsors and maintains editorial control over the project, while the public provides technical development and support. Although the book refers to the product as Red Hat Linux, it is the same product.

We tried our hardest to fill up this book with the things you need to know about, such as how to

- Install Red Hat Linux
- Get connected to the Internet by using broadband DSL and cable modems or old-fashioned dial-up modems
- Get connected to your Local Area Network (LAN)
- Build a simple but effective firewall
- Build Internet and LAN services, such as Web pages and print servers
- Use Red Hat Linux to play CDs and listen to Internet radio stations
- Use the GNOME desktop environment
- Take advantage of useful and usable applications, such as the OpenOffice desktop productivity suite, Evolution desktop organizer and e-mail client, and streaming multimedia MPlayer.

- Work with the OpenOffice desktop productivity suite to satisfy your word processing, spreadsheet, and presentation needs
- Increase your computer and network security
- Know where to go for help
- Manage your Red Hat Linux workstation

You see troubleshooting tips throughout this book, and Chapter 18 is devoted to the subject. It's not that Red Hat Linux is all that much trouble, but we want you to be prepared in case you run into bad luck.

The instructions in this book are designed to work with the version of Red Hat Linux you find on the companion DVD; we also describe how to download several software packages not found on the DVD-ROMs. Feel free to use other versions of Red Hat Linux or even other Linux distributions, but be aware that our instructions may not work exactly or even at all. Good luck!

Foolish Assumptions

You know what they say about people who make assumptions, but this book would never have been written if we didn't make a few. This book *is* for you if you

- **Want to build a Red Hat Linux workstation:** You want to use the Linux operating system to build your personal workstation. Surprise! The DVD-ROM in the back of this book contains the Red Hat Linux distribution.
- **Have a computer:** It's just a technicality, but you need a computer because this book describes how to install Red Hat Linux on a computer.
- **Have no duct tape:** You want to put the Red Hat Linux operating system and the computer together, and using duct tape hasn't worked.
- **Don't want to be a guru:** You don't want to become a Red Hat Linux guru — at least not yet.

However, this book is *not* for you if you're looking for

- **An all-encompassing reference-style book:** We simply don't have enough space, or permission from the publisher, to provide a comprehensive range of topics. We concentrate on providing help with getting popular and useful stuff up and running. We devote more space, for example, to getting your DSL or cable modem working than to describing the theory that makes them work.

- **A system administration book:** Again, we don't have enough space to do the subject justice. We provide instructions on how to perform certain essential administrative tasks, like adding users, packages, and network connections. This book selects certain topics to focus on and leaves the rest for other books.

Conventions Used in This Book

At computer conventions, thousands of computer people get together and talk about deep technical issues, such as

- What is the best hardware for running Red Hat Linux?
- Is Coke better than Pepsi?
- Could Superman beat Batman?
- Could Superman, Batman, and Spiderman together beat The Punisher? (No way!)

But these conventions aren't the types we mean. Our conventions are shorthand ways of designating specific information, such as what is and isn't a command or the meaning of certain funny-looking symbols.

Typing code

We show you how to use graphical interfaces to run most of the programs, utilities, and applications we describe in this book. Sometimes, however, running commands from a text-based interface is better or necessary. In Chapter 4, for example, we describe how to start a terminal emulator window in which to run the command. In anticipation of running text-based commands, we describe the conventions we use.

When you see filenames, directories, commands, and parameters in the text, they're formatted `in monospace type`. That helps differentiate those items from the general text.

When you see words in boldface, they indicate something you should type; for example:

> Type **man chown** at the command prompt and press Enter.

That line means to enter the command `man chown` and press the Enter (or Return) key. The command is then executed. (Throughout this book, we say "press the Enter key" whenever we want you to execute a command; the Enter key is synonymous with the Return key.)

Commands not shown in the text, but set off on lines by themselves, look like this:

```
pwd
```

Here's a rundown of the command syntax in Linux:

- Text *not* surrounded by `[ ]` or `{ }` brackets must be typed exactly as shown.
- Text inside brackets `[ ]` is optional.
- Text in *italics* indicates the part of a command that must be replaced with appropriate text. You should not type verbatim the italicized part of a command. If we say "Enter the command **more *somefile***," we mean for you to replace *somefile* with the name of the file you're interested in. For example, you may end up entering the command **more /etc/passwd**, where you substitute `/etc/passwd` for *somefile.*
- Text inside braces `{ }` indicates that you must choose one of the values inside the braces and separated by the `|` sign. For example, you should enter either **echo "one"** or **echo "two"** or **echo "three"** if you see the command **echo "{one|two|three}"**.
- An ellipsis (. . .) means *and so on* or to repeat the preceding command line as needed.

Don't concern yourself much with these conventions for now. In most chapters in this book, you don't need to know these particulars. When you do need to know something about a particular syntax, come back to this introduction for a refresher course.

Keystrokes and such

Keystrokes are shown with a plus sign between the keys. For example, Ctrl+Alt+Delete means that you should press the Ctrl key, Alt key, and Delete key all at the same time. (No, we don't make you press any more than three keys at the same time.)

Most applications and utilities we describe in this book use a graphical user interface (GUI), such as GNOME, which allows you to control your computer by pointing and clicking with your mouse. Occasionally, however, we give nongraphical instructions that require you to press keys on your keyboard. In those situations, we often simplify the instructions by saying "click OK." That instruction generally means that you press the Tab key, which moves the cursor to the OK button, and then press the Enter key. That two-step process is equivalent to clicking an OK button in a GUI.

How This Book Is Organized

Like all proper *For Dummies* books, this book is organized into independent parts. You can read the parts in any order. Heck, try reading them backward for a real challenge. This book is not meant to be read from front cover to back; rather, it's meant to be a reference book that helps you find what you're looking for when you're looking for it. Between the Contents at a Glance page, the table of contents, and the index, you should have no problem finding what you need.

If you do read the chapters in this book in order, you encounter the useful and interesting things first and the more technical items last. For example, after installing Red Hat Linux in Part I, you may want to proceed immediately to Part II to see how to connect Linux to the Internet or your local network. From there, you can use your new workstation to surf the Internet and use e-mail.

The following sections describe each part.

Part I: Installing Red Hat Linux

In Part I, you find out what Linux is and how to prepare your computer to install Red Hat Linux. We then walk you through the installation and show you the basics of working with Red Hat Linux.

Part II: Got Net?

In Part II, you find out about connecting to the Internet and local networks. You see how to jump on the Internet with your everyday modem or high-speed (broadband) DSL or cable modem. We also show you how to connect to an existing network. If that local network has a high-speed Internet connection, you can use it as your portal to the wonderful world of surfing. The Internet can be dangerous, so we include instructions for creating your own firewall.

Part III: Linux, Huh! What Is It Good For? Absolutely Everything!

Part III guides you through the glorious particulars of *doing* something with Red Hat Linux. You're introduced to the GNOME desktop window environment. You're taken through its paces by finding out how to move, resize, hide, and close windows and how to use the file manager and much more. Two chapters are devoted to using the Red Hat Linux multimedia capabilities, such as listening to CDs and MP3s, in addition to how to rip and record them. The world's radio stations are now available to you with streaming media technology. We introduce you to the Mozilla browser so that you can surf the Net and use the Evolution organizer to read your e-mail, do calendaring, and other tasks. We also describe in detail the full-featured OpenOffice desktop productivity suite. You can use OpenOffice with your Red Hat Linux machine to do all your writing and other work-related functions. You can even write a book with it! Finally, you see how to get organized with Red Hat Linux.

Part IV: Revenge of the Nerds

In Part IV, we guide you through the use of your Red Hat Linux computer's network capabilities. It's Nerd City, but it's also fun and useful. We start by showing you how to build a simple network. After your network is up and running, we describe how to build network services, such as the Apache Web server, Samba, and printer servers. The last two chapters are devoted to exploring the art of network computer security and troubleshooting network problems. Insert your pocket protector, strap the old HP calculator to your hip, retape your glasses, and get ready for Saturday night!

Part V: The Part of Tens

A *For Dummies* book just isn't complete without The Part of Tens, where you can find ten all-important resources and answers to the ten most bothersome questions people have after installing Red Hat Linux. (The folks at Red Hat Software provided these questions.) We introduce the ten most important security concerns too.

Part VI: Appendixes

Ah, the appendixes. Appendix A outlines the Red Hat Linux systems administration utilities. Appendix B describes how to find out about the details of your computer's individual pieces of hardware; this information is sometimes helpful when you're installing Red Hat Linux. Appendixes C and D introduce you to using and managing the Linux file system. Appendix E shows how to use the Red Hat Package manager (RPM). Appendix F completes this book by describing what you can find on the companion DVD-ROM.

What You're Not to Read

Heck, you don't have to read any of this book if you don't want to, but why did you buy it? (Not that we're complaining.) Part I has background information. If you don't want it, don't read it. Also, the text in sidebars is optional, although often helpful. If you're on the fast track to using Linux, you can skip the sidebars and the text next to the Technical Stuff icon, as described in the following section. But we suggest instead that you slow down a bit and enjoy the experience.

Icons in This Book

This section describes the icons you see in this book. Icons amplify the discussion by injecting interesting or important information.

Nifty little shortcuts and timesavers are under this icon. Red Hat Linux is a powerful operating system, and you can save unbelievable amounts of time and energy by using its tools and programs. We hope that our tips show you how.

Don't let this happen to you! We hope that our experiences with Red Hat Linux can help you avoid the mistakes we have made.

This information helps you to recall information presented elsewhere in the book.

This information is particularly nerdy and technical. You can skip it, but you may find it interesting if you're of a geekier bent.

Where to Go from Here

You're about to join the legions of people who have been using and developing Linux. We have been using Unix for more than 20 years, Linux for more than 10 years, and Red Hat Linux for 10 years. We have found Red Hat Linux to be a flexible, powerful operating system, capable of solving most problems even without a large set of commercial software. The future of the Linux — and Red Hat Linux, in particular — operating system is bright. The time and energy you expend in becoming familiar with it will be worthwhile. *Carpe Linuxum.*

Part I

Installing Red Hat Linux

"It's called 'Linux Poker.' Everyone gets to see everyone else's cards, everything's wild, you can play off your opponents' hands, and everyone wins except Bill Gates, whose face appears on the Jokers."

In this part . . .

You're about to embark on a journey through the Red Hat Linux installation program. Perhaps you know nothing about setting up an operating system on your computer. That's okay. The Red Hat Linux installation system is easygoing by nature and straightforward to use. Plus, we help guide you through the installation process.

In Chapter 1, you begin to discover what Red Hat Linux is all about and what it can do for you. Chapter 2 helps you to get ready to install Red Hat Linux and repartition your hard drive, if necessary. The real fun begins in Chapter 3, when you install your own penguin. (Linus Torvalds, the inventor of Linux, loves penguins; and they have been adopted as the Linux mascot.) Chapter 4 gives you a brief, but important, introduction to working with Red Hat Linux.

Chapter 1

And in the Opposite Corner . . . a Penguin?

In This Chapter

- Napping through Linux History 101
- Finding out what Red Hat Linux can do
- Using Red Hat Linux as a workstation
- Using Red Hat Linux network functions

We see a penguin in your future. He's an unassuming fellow who's taking on a rather big competitor — that other operating system — in the battle for the hearts, minds, and desktops of computer users. Red Hat Linux, with its splashy brand name and recognizable logo, is undeniably one of the driving forces behind the Linux revolution — and is by far the most popular Linux brand.

This chapter introduces you to the latest and greatest Red Hat release, Red Hat Linux 10. This book covers all the bases — a good number of them, at least — about how to use Red Hat Linux as a desktop productivity tool, Internet portal, multimedia workstation, and basic network server. You can do lots of things with Red Hat Linux, and this chapter gives you an overview of the possibilities in addition to a brief look at the history of Linux.

History of the World — Er, Linux — Part II

In the beginning of computerdom (said in a booming, thunderous voice), the world was filled with hulking mainframes. These slothful beasts lumbered through large corporations; required a special species of ultranerds to keep them happy; and ate up huge chunks of space, power, and money. Then came the IBM PC and Microsoft, and the world changed. Power to the people — sort of.

In 1991, a student at the University of Helsinki named Linus Torvalds became dissatisfied with the standard PC operating system. Torvalds thought that the Unix operating system might be better suited than MS-DOS or Windows to help him accomplish his work. Unix was invented in the 1970s and, although powerful, was expensive, so he began writing his own version of Unix. Now, writing your own operating system is a simple task — *not!* After formulating the basic parts, Torvalds recruited a team of talented programmers through the Internet, and together they created a new operating system, or *kernel,* now named Linux.

One of the most important decisions Torvalds made in the early days of Linux was to freely distribute the Linux kernel code for anyone to do with as they wanted. These free Linux distributions were and still are available in several forms, mainly online.

The only restriction Linus imposed on the free distribution of his creation was that no version of the software can be made proprietary. (*Proprietary* software is owned and developed by private companies in places that often rival Area 51 in security. *Open source* code is for "the people" — anyone can use and develop it without fear of violating copyrights.) You can modify the heck out of it and also distribute it for fun or profit. What you can't do is stop anyone else from using, modifying, and distributing the software you have modified.

Think of open source software as a chain. You can use the existing chain and add another link to the chain. However, you can't stop anyone from using the chain or adding to it.

The lack of proprietary restrictions on Linux has led to drastic improvements in its technology. Open source software, and Linux in particular, is transparent to all users and developers. That transparency allows people throughout the world to rapidly improve Linux and its associated subsystems. In contrast, proprietary operating systems are like a black box where no one except a small group of insiders knows what goes on inside. Only that select group can make modifications, and that limits innovation and improvements.

Go back to our history lesson. In early spring 1994, the first real version of Linux (Version 1.0) was made available for public use. Even then it was an impressive operating system that ran smartly on computers with less than 2MB of RAM and a simple 386 microprocessor. Linux 1.0 also included free features for which other operating systems charged hundreds of dollars. Nowadays, tens of millions of users enjoy Linux at home and work.

By the way, if you're wondering about the whole penguin thing, the answer is disappointingly simple. Linus loves penguins. The Linux world naturally started using it as its symbol. The friendly and familiar penguin — whose name is Tux, by the way — now symbolizes All Things Linux.

Knowing What You Can Do with Red Hat Linux

Linux is freely available software. The source code for Linux, which is the heart and soul of the operating system, is also publicly available. The Free Software Foundation (FSF) contributes much of the utilitarian software that makes using Linux much easier — FSF is the brainchild of the great Richard Stallman.

Fedora Core 1 combines all those pieces plus some additional applications and then goes another step and adds a few of its own to create an *integrated product.* Red Hat, Inc., combines the basic Linux operating system with software (some made by other companies and some made by Red Hat) to produce a package with a value that's greater than the sum of its parts. That combination is known as a *distribution,* or *flavor,* of Linux.

So that you can get up and running as quickly as possible, we have bundled the Fedora Core distribution on the DVD in the back of this book. It contains all the major parts of the full Red Hat distribution except the source code and some MS-DOS utilities (for example, the Windows File Allocation Table, or FAT, repartitioning program First nondestructive Interactive Partitions Splitting [FIPS] isn't included).

If your computer can't use DVD-ROMs, you can get the full Red Hat Linux distribution on CD-ROMs by sending in the coupon in the back of this book.

Red Hat Linux was initially used almost solely to provide network services. However, Red Hat started working hard to make Linux suitable for your everyday use. The result is that Red Hat Linux is now used in both server and desktop environments. It's used by individuals, businesses, and governments to cut costs, improve performance, and just plain get work done.

You can use Red Hat Linux as a desktop workstation, a network server, an Internet gateway, a firewall, the basis of an embedded system (such as a smart VCR or a robot), or even as a multiprocessor supercomputer. And, thanks to the many, many people who continually make refinements and innovations, Red Hat Linux continues to become more flexible and capable with each release.

This list shows some cool Red Hat Linux features you can use:

- **Desktop productivity tools:** Red Hat has successfully worked overtime over the past few years to make Linux work on your desktop. Red Hat bundles software, such as the OpenOffice suite of productivity tools, so that you can get your everyday work done. The OpenOffice suite includes a full-function word processor plus spreadsheet, presentation, graphical drawing, and Web page creation tools. Its word processor can read and write all Windows Office formats plus many others, such as WordPerfect. When you install Red Hat Linux, OpenOffice is installed and icons are placed on the menu bar to make accessing it easy.
- **Multimedia stuff:** Red Hat Linux packs numerous multimedia tools for you to use. You can play, record, and rip audio tracks from CDs and DVDs. You can listen to streamed media sources, such as radio stations, over the Internet. Linux also lets you transfer photos and other items from your own cameras and MP3 players, for example.
- **Network services:** Red Hat Linux works as a network-based server too. Linux found its initial popularity performing jobs like Web serving and file and printer sharing and hasn't missed a beat. We show you how to create several network services.

Boosting your personal workstation

We cannot emphasize enough how well Red Hat Linux works as a personal workstation. With Red Hat Linux, you can easily create your own, inexpensive, flexible, and powerful personal workstation. Linux provides the platform for most of the applications you need to get your work done. Many applications come bundled with Red Hat Linux, from desktop productivity suites, to web browsers and multimedia systems, for example.

The following list describes just a few major categories of free software available for Linux, along with some examples of popular programs:

- **Office suites:** OpenOffice provides a complete desktop productivity suite that includes an advanced word processor, a spreadsheet, and a presentation editor, for example. The OpenOffice word processor can read and write Microsoft Word files, HTML editors, spreadsheet editors, and graphics editors.

OpenOffice provides its own file format but also reads and writes Microsoft Office 97, Office 2000, and Office XP files. It also can use other formats, such as Rich Text Format. Check out the site, at `www.openoffice.org`.

- **Multimedia players:** Red Hat packages and installs the open source XMMS player. You can use XMMS to play downloaded Ogg/Vorbis files or continuous Ogg/Vorbis streams. You can download the excellent open source MPlayer audio and video player. MPlayer lets you watch DVDs and listen to MediaPlayer streams. You can, alternatively, download a free version of the proprietary RealPlayer, from RealNetworks, to listen to RealAudio streams. The Internet is going nuts with multimedia, and these multimedia players let you get in on the action.
- **Running Microsoft Windows applications and environments:** You can use Linux to run Windows programs. The WINE (Wine Is Not an Emulator) system facilitates running Windows programs directly under Linux. The commercial VMware workstation product creates a virtual computer within your Linux PC. The virtual machine looks, acts, smells, and performs just like a real computer, but is really just a program running under the Linux operating system. You can install Linux or Windows or both on the virtual machine. Both WINE and VMware create a bridge between Linux and Windows to give you the best of both worlds.
- **Web browsers and e-mail clients:** The open source browser, Mozilla, is included with Red Hat Linux 10. The nongraphical, text-based `lynx` and `links` browsers are included too and come in handy if you're using an older, slower modem because they don't require as much speed as Mozilla does. You can use Mozilla or the new Ximian Evolution personal organizer, calendar, and e-mail client.

Linux is for nerds too

The Linux operating system has been *ported* (or converted) from the 32-bit Intel architecture to a number of other architectures, including Alpha, MIPS, PowerPC, and SPARC. This conversion gives users a choice of hardware manufacturers and keeps the Linux kernel flexible for new processors. Linux handles *symmetric multiprocessing* (it can take on more than one CPU or mathematical and logical programming unit per system box). In addition, projects are in the works to provide sophisticated processing capabilities, such as

Real-time programming: Controlling machinery or test equipment.

High availability: Running a server that needs to work all the time.

Parallel processing: Amplifying the problem-solving power of a computer by using multiple processors to work in parallel. Parallel processing systems come in various flavors, such as Symmetric Multi Processing (SMP), extreme Linux systems, and Beowulf clusters. Research organizations and even individuals can create machines with supercomputer capabilities at a fraction of the price of supercomputers. In certain cases, extreme Linux systems have been made from obsolete PCs, costing the organizations that make them nothing in material costs.

Using Linux network tools and services

Linux computers can provide many powerful and flexible network services. Your Red Hat Linux Publisher's Edition DVD comes packed with the tools to provide these services:

- **Apache web server:** Of all the web servers on the Internet, the majority are run by the open source Apache web server. You can start a simple web server by simply installing the bundled Apache software from this book's companion DVD-ROM.
- **OpenSSH:** The open source version of Secure Shell enables you to communicate securely across the Internet. Secure Shell is much safer than Telnet because Secure Shell encrypts your communication when you log in (even when you log in to other computers), making much slimmer the chance that others can discover your passwords and other sensitive information. OpenSSH also provides other authentication and security features and enables you to securely copy files from machine to machine. With OpenSSH, you can prevent people from listening to your communication.
- **Internet accessing utilities:** Red Hat Linux provides several configuration utilities that help you connect to the Internet. The utilities help you to configure DSL, cable modems, and plain old telephone modems to connect to the Internet. They also help you to connect to Local Area Networks (LAN) using Ethernet adapters.
- **Firewalls:** A *firewall* is a system that controls access to your private network from any outside network (in this case, the Internet) and to control access from your private network to the outside world. To keep the bad guys out, Red Hat Linux provides protection by giving you the tools to build your own firewall. Red Hat Linux is flexible in this regard, and many software packages are available, including the popular and simple-to-use `netfilter/iptables` filtering software, which is included on the companion DVD-ROM. Building a firewall is covered in Chapter 8.

This list is just a sample of the network-y things you can do with Red Hat Linux. We describe many of them in this book, but it takes much more exploration to find them all!

Chapter 2

Getting Ready for Red Hat Linux

In This Chapter

- Preparing to install Red Hat Linux
- Determining whether your Windows partition is FAT or NTFS
- Defragmenting your hard drive
- Resizing Windows 9*x*/Me FAT partitions
- Resizing Windows NT, Windows 2000, and Windows XP NTFS partitions

All major personal computer (PC) manufacturers now install Microsoft Windows on their machines by default. However, you can still purchase computers without an operating system via mail-order or from local, nonbrand stores.

What does that mean? Basically, you can skip this chapter if you have a computer with no preinstalled operating system. You can also skip this chapter if you have a Windows computer and are willing to reformat your hard disk, permanently erasing its contents. You can also skip this chapter if your Windows computer includes a secondary partition on which you can install Linux.

A *partition* is a portion of a disk drive used to organize files and directories. For example, the famous Windows C: drive is installed on its own partition. A partition can use all or part of a disk. Most systems use one large partition that hogs up an entire hard drive.

Otherwise, you have to make accommodations so that Red Hat Linux can live alongside your existing Windows partition. Because Linux is an easygoing fellow who gets along well with others, you can install it on the same hard drive with Windows. This type of configuration is a called a *dual boot system:* You choose which operating system to use when you power up, or *boot,* your computer.

This chapter shows you how to prepare your hard drive so that Linux and Windows can live in harmony. It will be a love-fest.

Preparing Your Hard Drive for Red Hat Linux

Before you install Red Hat Linux alongside Windows, you need to get your hard drive ready. This list provides an overview of the disk preparation process:

1. **Put on a red fedora.**
2. **Back up your computer.**

   The processes we describe in this chapter should not affect your existing Windows installation. However, you can never be too safe when dealing with your precious files, so you should back them up. A description of how to back up a Windows computer is beyond the scope of this book. We suggest that you look into using a product like Norton Ghost 2003. That system both backs up and repartitions your computer. A side benefit of Ghost is that you can use it to repartition your hard drive. Numerous other commercial and freeware (not to be confused with open source) backup systems are available.

3. **Determine how your Windows computer's hard drive is formatted.**

   Microsoft Windows uses two types of disk formats: FAT (File Access Table) and NTFS (NT File System). FAT is older and less advanced than NTFS. However, free tools are available for resizing FAT-based disks to make room for Linux. You have to purchase commercial software to repartition NTFS systems.

4. **Defragment your disk.**

   All resizing programs require you to defragment your disk before proceeding. Over time, the bits and bytes that comprise your files tend to get scattered around your hard drive. Resizing may not work or may even cause problems if your computer has too much fragmentation.

5. **Repartition your computer's hard drive to make room to install Red Hat Linux if you want to install it alongside Windows (or another operating system).**

   You can use either destructive or nondestructive resizing to make room for Linux. *Destructive* resizing wipes everything off your hard drive and starts fresh. *Nondestructive* resizing uses Windows utilities to dynamically shrink the existing partition and then uses the freed space to make a new Linux partition.

The open source FIPS (First nondestructive Interactive Partition Splitting) program is supplied with the full Red Hat Linux distribution to repartition FAT disks. You need to use commercial utilities, like PartitionMagic or Norton Ghost, to repartition NTFS disks; both these programs also work on FAT systems.

"Am I Fat or Just NTFS?"

The process of determining your partition type is straightforward. These instructions describe how to use the tools provided by Windows (Windows 9*x*, Windows Me, Windows NT, Windows 2000, and Windows XP) to show the partition type.

Follow these instructions on all Windows systems:

1. **Start your computer.**
2. **Open the My Computer icon.**
3. **Right-click the C:\ drive icon.**
4. **Click the Properties button. You should see information displayed about the partition, as shown in Figure 2-1.**

Figure 2-1 shows the information about drive C:\ (the partition). The upper-middle part of the figure shows, in this case, that the partition uses the FAT.

The following section describes how to defragment both FAT and NTFS partitions.

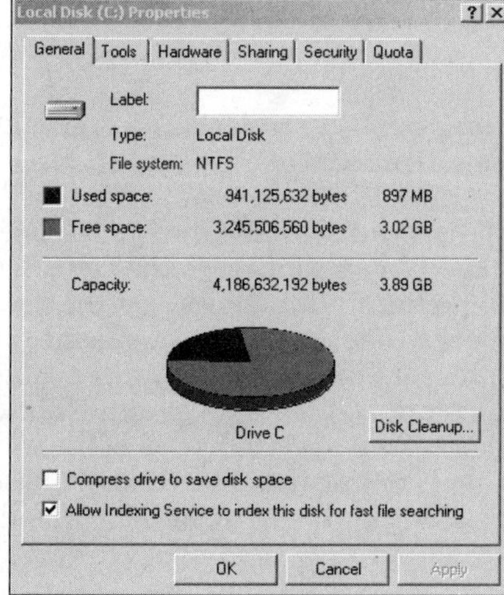

Figure 2-1: The Properties window showing an NTFS partition.

Defragmenting Your Hard Drive

Defragmenting consolidates all files on your hard drive into contiguous portions. This task is necessary because Windows is a slob as operating systems go, scattering data all over the hard drive rather than in any sort of logical order.

These steps show how to defragment your Windows partition:

1. **Close all programs and windows on your computer, leaving just the desktop and icon bar.**
2. **Double-click the My Computer icon on the desktop.**
3. **Select the C: drive by clicking it and then choose File⇨Properties⇨Tools.**
4. **Click the Defragment Now button.**

   The defragmentation program looks at the drive to determine whether it needs defragmentation.

   You may get a message telling you that you don't need to defragment because your hard drive is not very fragmented; don't believe it. Under ordinary circumstances, this statement may be true. But resizing isn't an ordinary occurrence; defragmenting your hard drive is necessary because you're going to move the end of the partition file system and make the partition smaller, erasing any data outside that barrier.

5. **Click Start.**

The defragmentation window appears and the process begins. Defragmenting can take a long time, depending on the size of your hard drive and the number of errors to be corrected.

By clicking the Show Details button, you can scroll up and down the large window to watch the defragmentation process in action, as shown in Figure 2-2.

The colored blocks represent programs and data, and the white space represents free space on your hard drive that FIPS can allocate to the Linux file system. The movement of the blocks around the screen shows that the data is being moved forward on the drive. Expect to see white space appear toward the bottom of the window, which represents the end of your drive. At the end of the defragmentation process, no colored blocks appear at the bottom of the window, and all the blocks are compressed toward the top of the window. After what may seem like quite a long time, defragmentation ends. All useful blocks of information are now at the beginning of the drive, making it ready for the resizing program.

These instructions describe how to defragment your Windows NT, Windows 2000, or Windows XP (NTFS) computer:

1. **Close all programs and windows on your computer.**
2. **Click Start⇨Programs⇨Accessories⇨System Tools⇨Disk Defragmenter.**
3. **Select the partition to defragment. Most computers use a single partition labeled C:\ (the ubiquitous "C drive"). Click the Defragment button and the process starts.**

   Figure 2-3 shows the defragmentation process for an NTFS partition.

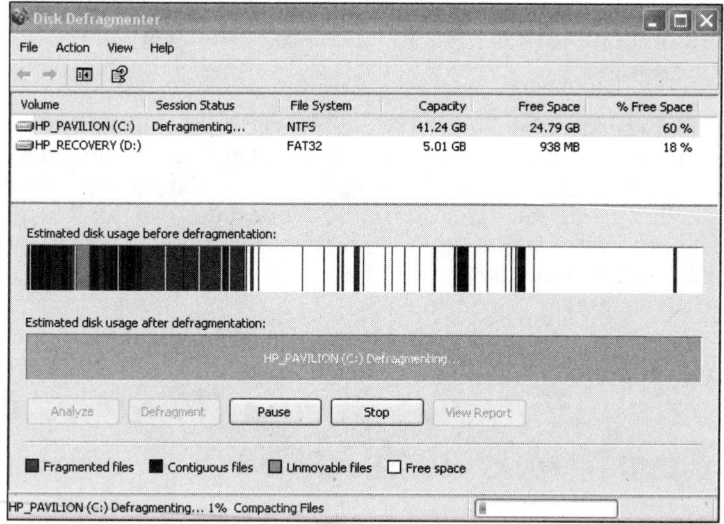

Figure 2-2: Defragmenting a FAT partition.

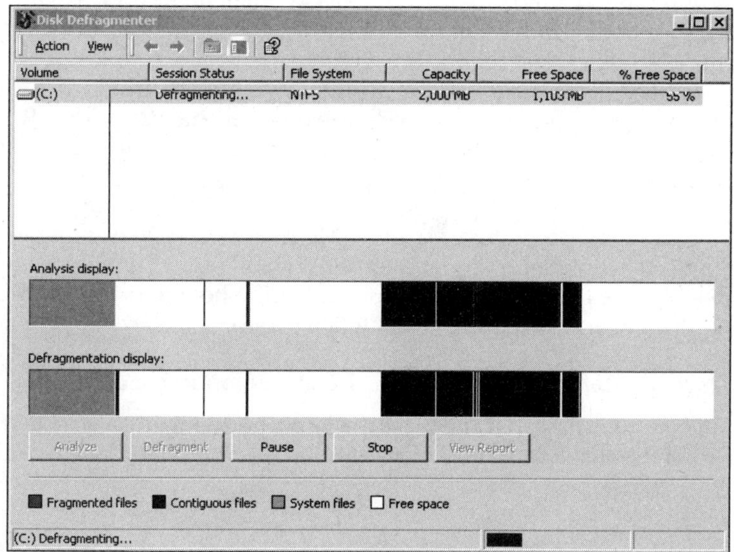

Figure 2-3: Defragmenting an NTFS partition.

Move Over, Windows — Here Comes Linux

You need to make room for Linux. This section describes how to repartition your Windows computer to make the necessary room. You can use the Open Source FIPS program to repartition FAT partitions. FIPS doesn't work on NTFS partitions, so you need to purchase a commercial tool, such as PartitionMagic. The next section is dedicated to using FIPS on FAT. The subsequent section describes using the commercial PartitionMagic program on NTFS partitions.

We strongly suggest backing up your entire computer before proceeding. If that's impractical or impossible, you should back up all important files. You can generally reinstall your operating system and applications from your systems discs, but you can't do that for your data. You don't want to lose any data or programs that you worked hard to create. Refer to your system's owner's manual to find out how to back up your system and how to restore the data if necessary.

Resizing Windows 9x and Windows Me FAT partitions with FIPS

FIPS resizes your FAT-based Windows partitions. Newer versions of Windows (some versions of Windows 95, Windows 98, and Windows Me) use a 32-bit file allocation table (called FAT32) and drive management tools that provide for single-drive configurations larger than 2GB. Older versions of Windows 95 use a 16-bit FAT (called FAT16, oddly enough); to use more space over and above 2GB, the hard drive has to be partitioned into logical drives of 2GB or less. Newer computers have hard drives much larger than the old 2GB limit. If the drive is repartitioned, the large drive-management system is disabled, and DOS and Windows partitions are again limited to 2GB.

You need to use the ancient MS-DOS (Microsoft Disk Operating System) operating system — yes, one way or another, all of Windows-dom owes its existence to MS-DOS. The following instructions describe how to create an MS-DOS boot floppy disk, which you use to run FIPS:

1. **Insert a floppy disk and click the My Computer icon.**

   Please be aware that these instructions permanently erase all information from the disk.

2. **Right-click the 3-½ Floppy (A:) icon and choose the Format option.**

   The Format A:\ window appears.

3. **Click the Make a Bootable Disk option and then the Start button.**

   A confirmation window — labeled Format A:\ again — opens.

4. **Click the OK button and your floppy is formatted.**

The Publisher's Edition Red Hat Linux DVD-ROM, bundled with this book, unfortunately doesn't include the FIPS utility. However, you can download FIPS to the floppy disk you just created:

1. **Open your browser and go to** `www.redhat.com/download/mirrors.html`.

2. **Select any Red Hat mirror.**

   Mirrors are just that — mirror images of downloadable software. Many organizations help out the open source movement by providing their resources, such as Web pages that allow you to download software, to spread the burden of distributing software. Red Hat Linux, a popular download site, greatly benefits from mirrors.

3. **When your browser displays the mirror you selected, go to the subdirectory** `redhat/8. 1/en/os/i386/dosutils/fips20` **if you're using Windows 98 or Windows Me or the newer version of Windows 95 (or Windows NT, Windows 2000, or Windows XP systems that happen to use FAT file systems).**

   Alternatively, go to `redhat/10/en/os/i386/dosutils/fips15c` **if you're using an older version of Windows 95.**

   For instance, go to the University of Oregon Red Hat mirror, at `ftp://limestone.uoregon.edu/redhat/8.0/en/os/i386/dosutils`.

4. **Download fips.exe, restorrb.exe, errors.txt, and, optionally, readme.1st and fips.faq to your floppy disk.**

5. **Boot your computer from the floppy disk.**

   The computer restarts in MS-DOS mode.

6. **Type** cd a: **at the DOS prompt and press Enter.**

7. **Type** fips **at the prompt and press Enter.**

   Some messages appear and flash by, but you can ignore them all except the last one, which asks you to press any key.

8. **When you see the** `Press any key` **message, do so.**

   You see all existing partitions on the hard drive.

9. **When you see the `Press any key` message, do so again.**

   You're getting good at this! A description of the drive and a series of messages flash by. Then FIPS finds the free space in the first partition.

10. **When you're asked whether you want to make a backup copy of sectors, press y for yes.**

    The screen asks whether a floppy disk is in drive A.

11. **Place a formatted floppy disk in drive A and press y.**

    A message similar to `Writing file a:\rootboot.000` appears, followed by other messages and then the message `Use cursor key to choose the cylinder, enter to continue.`

    Three columns appear on the screen: Old Partition, Cylinder, and New Partition. The Old Partition number is the number of megabytes in the main partition of your hard drive. The New Partition number is the number of megabytes in the new partition that you're making for the Red Hat Linux operating system.

12. **Press the left- and right-arrow keys to change the numbers in the Old Partition and New Partition fields to create the space you need for both the Windows operating system and Linux.**

    See Chapter 3 for installation requirements.

13. **When you have the correct amount of hard drive space in each field, press the Enter key.**

    The partition table is displayed again, showing you the new partition that has been created for the Linux operating system. This new partition is probably Partition 2; your C: drive is probably Partition 1.

    You also see a message at the bottom of the screen asking whether you want to continue or make changes.

14. **If you're satisfied with the size of your partitions, press c to continue (if you *aren't* satisfied, press r, which takes you back to Step 12).**

    Many more messages about your hard drive flash by. A message then appears, stating that the system is ready to write the new partition scheme to disk and asking whether you want to proceed.

15. **Press y to make FIPS write the new partition information to the hard drive.**

    The partitioning process begins.

    REMEMBER

    If you press **n**, FIPS exits without changing anything on your hard drive, leaving your hard drive exactly the way it was after you defragmented it.

16. **To test whether the nondestructive partitioning worked properly, remove the boot floppy disk and reboot your system by pressing Ctrl+Alt+Delete.**

17. **Allow Windows to start and then run ScanDisk by clicking the Start button and choosing Programs⇨Accessories⇨System Tools⇨ScanDisk.**

    ScanDisk indicates whether you have all the files and folders you started with and whether anything was lost. Even if everything is found to be okay, consider keeping any backup files around for a while to be on the safe side.

Now you're ready to install Red Hat Linux 10, which we explain how to do in Chapter 3. The Red Hat Linux installation process can use the newly created space to create its own partitions. Chapter 3 describes how to use the new space without stepping on the existing Windows partition.

Resizing Windows NT, 2000, and XP NTFS partitions with a little PartitionMagic

Resizing NTFS requires the use of commercial tools, such as Norton Ghost (`www.norton.com`) or PartitionMagic (`www.powerquest.com`). PartitionMagic works by shrinking the Microsoft Windows partition, leaving free space for a new partition. Ghost 2003, however, doesn't dynamically modify your existing NTFS file system. Instead, it backs up your existing Windows partition (takes a "snapshot"), and then creates one or more new partitions over the original. Finally, it writes the original Windows image to the new partition. Ghost requires a storage device on which to save the snapshot image. If your Windows installation is relatively small (less than 2GB), you may be able to use a Jaz drive, Zip drive, or even a writable CD-ROM as a storage device. However, you have to use a second hard drive, tape backup, or other backup mechanism for larger installations.

We describe in this section how to use PartitionMagic. Norton Ghost is an excellent tool, but is beyond the scope of this book because we can't assume that you have the backup resources to use it. (You need backup media large enough to store your entire Windows installation.) PartitionMagic doesn't give you the warm fuzzies of getting a backup along with your resizing, but it still works well. We have used it a number of times with good results.

These steps describe how to install PartitionMagic:

1. **Get out your credit card, go to your friendly nearby computer store, and buy PartitionMagic 8 or higher; or, alternatively, go to your friendly Internet store.**

This statement is uncomfortable to make in a book devoted to the free, open source Linux operating system. However, the name of the game is getting the job done, and in this case we have no noncommercial alternative. So, until an open source NTFS resizing utility breaks out into the light, go ahead and make the purchase.

Three NTFS variations are available. Older Windows 9*x* systems used one type, Windows NT used another, and the third version is used by current Windows versions. You must use PartitionMagic 8, the current version, because it can recognize and handle all three NTFS versions.

2. **Start the PartitionMagic installation by inserting the disc into your CD-ROM drive.**
3. **Click the PartitionMagic button when the installation window opens.**
4. **Click the Install option when the subsequent screen opens.**
5. **An installation wizard starts. Answer the questions depending on how your computer is configured.**

   In general, you should be able to use the default options.
6. **Create a rescue disk. The installation wizard guides you through the process.**

After you install PartitionMagic, you can use it to repartition your drive. The following instructions show how to select an existing partition, shrink it, and then create a second one from the new space:

1. **Start PartitionMagic, and you see a screen like the one shown in Figure 2-4.**
2. **Click the partition you want to reallocate.**
3. **Click the Create a new partition option in the upper-left corner of the screen.**

   The Create New Partition window opens. This wizard guides you through the process of shrinking the existing partition and creating a second one from the new space.
4. **Click the Next button.**

   The Where to Create window opens. You need to tell PartitionMagic which partition to repartition. In this example, we assume that you have the typical single-partition Windows computer (the ubiquitous C: drive), as shown in Figure 2-5.

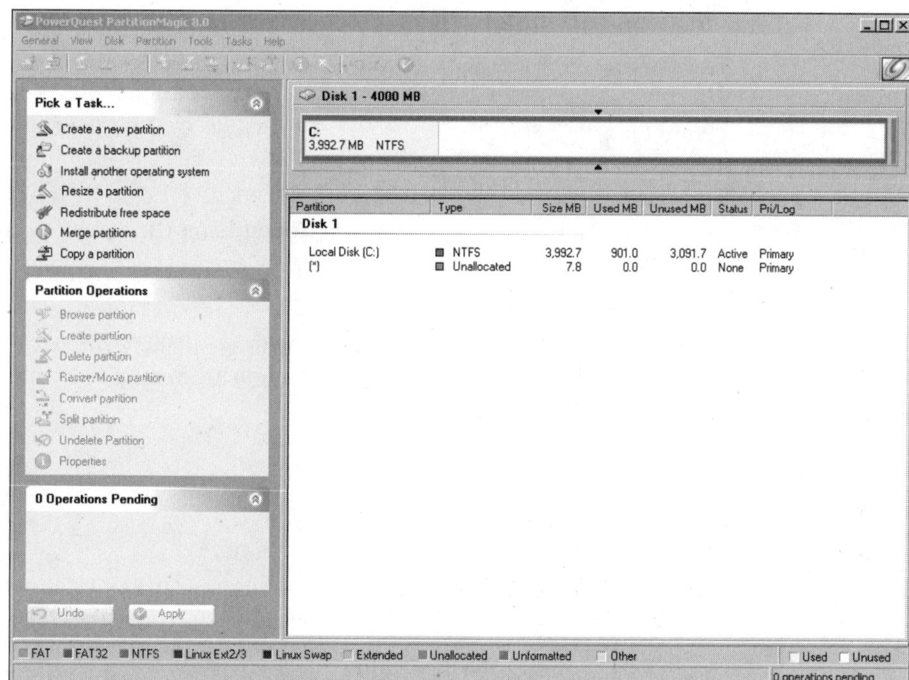

Figure 2-4: The initial PartitionMagic screen.

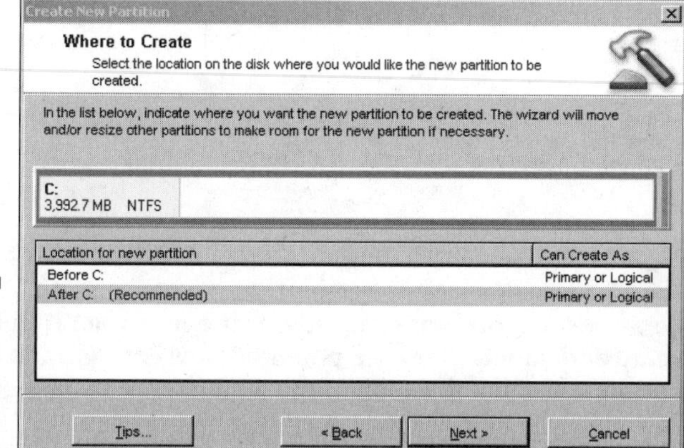

Figure 2-5: The Where to Create window.

5. **Click the Next button.**

   The Partition Properties window allows you to select the options for your new partition. Figure 2-6 shows the settings we have entered for our new partition. This example is 2GB, has a `linux` label, is a logical partition, and uses the `ext3` file system.

   This list shows the Partition Magic options:

   - **Size:** The size of the partition depends on the size of your disk.
   - **Label:** The label is optional and arbitrary. Use any description you want.
   - **Create As:** You have two options: Logical and Primary. PC drives can have as many as four primary partitions and any number of logical ones.

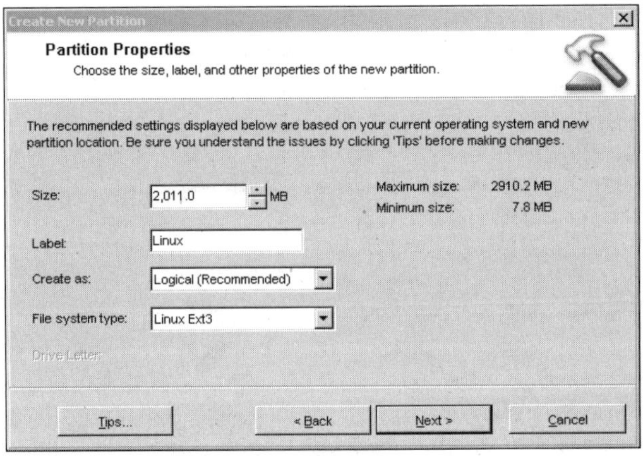

Figure 2-6: The Partition Properties window.

6. **Click the Next button and the Confirm Choices window opens, as shown in Figure 2-7.**

7. **PartitionMagic wants you to be sure about the new partitions you're about to create and summarizes the potential new configuration. Inspect the information and click the Finish button if you're satisfied with the selection.**

   If you don't want to repartition with the current choices, click the Back button to return to the preceding window, where you make new choices.

   After you click the Finish button, the new partition-to-be is displayed in the main window. However, your disk isn't repartitioned until you click the Apply button in the lower-left corner of the PartitionMagic window.

8. **Click the Apply button and a final confirmation window opens.**
9. **Click the OK button in the confirmation window and your disk is repartitioned.**

   The new partitions aren't put into place until you reboot your computer.
10. **Reboot your computer.**

    PartitionMagic applies the changes to make the new partition while your computer boots.

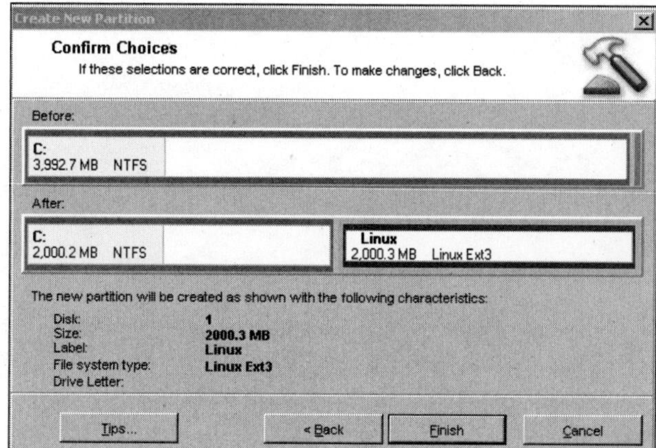

Figure 2-7: The Confirm Choices dialog box.

Chapter 3

Ready, Set, Install!

In This Chapter

- Deciding which Red Hat Linux installation type to use
- Starting the Red Hat Linux installation process
- Automatically selecting Linux partitions
- Configuring your network
- Configuring your system options
- Going beyond the point of no return
- Configuring your graphics system
- Finishing the installation

Installing Red Hat Linux 10 isn't rocket science — it's more like astrophysics. No, no — just kidding. Don't run — just relax, sit down, grab your favorite drink, and contemplate the fun you will have installing Red Hat Linux. After you're done, you will have a powerful computer that's capable of performing most, if not all, of your daily computing chores — all for the cost of this book! That's pretty amazing when you think about it: For a few dollars, you get the same amount of operating power that cost megabucks just a few years ago.

This chapter walks you through the process of installing Red Hat Linux. The process involves inserting the companion Red Hat Linux DVD-ROM disc, powering on your computer, and answering some questions.

This book comes with a companion DVD-ROM disc that contains the entire Red Hat Linux distribution. The single DVD-ROM replaces several CD-ROMs and reduces the need to continually swap CD-ROMs during the installation process; it also makes installing the software easier by eliminating the need to find the particular CD-ROM that contains the needed package. If your computer can't handle DVD-ROMs, however, you can obtain the Red Hat Linux distribution on CD-ROMs by mailing in the coupon in the back of this book.

The Red Hat Linux installation process has a point of no return. That time comes toward the end of the configuration process, after which the disks are partitioned and the software is written to your hard drive (see the later section "Installation Stage 5: The Point of No Return"). If you stop at or before that point, you save whatever operating system (or systems) exists on your computer.

For installation purists only

You can run the Red Hat Linux installation system from either a graphical or text-based interface. If the installation process successfully detects your graphics hardware, the graphical method is selected automatically, and that's what we discuss in this chapter. In addition to the ease of using a mouse to point and click, the graphical method groups similar configuration choices. For example, the keyboard and mouse selections are presented within one window, not two, as in the text-based installation.

You may have to use the text-based installation, for these reasons:

- Your mother told you never to point and click.
- The Red Hat Linux installation system can't use your graphics adapter. You figure out this situation when the graphical installation window doesn't appear, but a text-based window does appear; with the text-based system, you use the keyboard to enter information and the cursor (arrow) keys to move from step to step. It doesn't happen often any more because the folks at Red Hat have done their homework and refined the installation process. However, manufacturers occasionally introduce new graphics systems that the installation system can't use.

You can select the text-based installation method by typing **text** at the `boot:` prompt.

Choosing an Installation Type

Red Hat provides several installation types to choose from. Although we think that you can probably get away with having less space on your system, we decided to give you the minimum disk space requirements Red Hat suggests for each installation option:

- **Server:** Creates an operating system environment for computers that provide services such as hosting Web pages. This installation requires 850MB of free space if you want only minimal bells and whistles, at least 1.4GB of free space if you want to install all the bells and whistles but not the graphical X Window System, and at least 2.1GB to install all the bells and all the whistles and throw in the Acme Bell and Whistle Factory (which includes both GNOME and KDE).
- **Custom:** Installs the minimum base of software and requires you to select additional services, utilities, and applications. A second option installs everything on the companion discs. The former requires at least 475 MB, and the latter, 5.0GB.
- **Upgrade:** Updates the Red Hat Linux software that's already installed on a computer but leaves all existing settings, users, and data alone. You can optionally choose to install additional packages.

- **Personal Desktop:** Installs the software necessary to use your computer as a workstation. Applications such as OpenOffice, Mozilla, and Evolution plus the GNOME graphical environment give you all the tools you need to enjoy the Internet and get your work done. This installation type requires at least 1.7GB of free space.
- **Workstation:** Adds software development tools to the Personal Desktop installation type. You need at least 2.1GB to use this option.

The primary difference between the Workstation and Personal Desktop installation types is that Workstation installs software development tools and Personal Desktop doesn't. We use the Workstation installation option in this book not because we don't discuss software programming but, rather, because the tools often come in handy when installing applications. We encourage you to use the Workstation installation type for your Red Hat Linux installations.

Both the Workstation and Personal Desktop installation types automate otherwise horrifically complicated decisions that no sane person would want to haggle with, such as how to partition your hard drive and select software. The installation includes the GNOME graphical user interface (GUI) and all the tools that an average computer user (that's you) needs to survive. If you want software that the installation doesn't provide, you can always add packages later.

Installation Stage 1: Starting the Journey

Before you install Red Hat Linux, you need to insert the companion DVD-ROM into the DVD/CD-ROM drive and boot or reboot your computer. The instructions in this section describe how to start installing Red Hat Linux on your computer.

This section gets you started with the Red Hat Linux installation process. Use these initial steps to start the installation and perform some basic configuration:

1. **Insert the DVD-ROM that came with this book and boot (or reboot) your computer. Note that if your computer can't boot from a DVD-ROM (or CD-ROM), you have to create a boot floppy and boot from it (refer to Chapter 2 for instructions for creating a boot floppy).**

   After your computer thinks for a while, the first installation screen appears, displaying a welcome message, some options, and the `boot:` prompt.

2. **Press Enter.**

   A series of messages scrolls by, indicating the hardware that the Red Hat Linux kernel detects on your computer. Most of the time, particularly with newer systems, Red Hat Linux detects all the basic hardware.

3. **When Red Hat Linux has detected your hardware, the Red Hat installation process starts and the Welcome message is displayed onscreen. Click the Next button to proceed to the next step.**

You can view information about Red Hat Linux by clicking the Release Notes button, in the lower-left corner of the screen. Additional information about where to find more information is displayed on the sidebar on the left side of the window.

After the Welcome message screen disappears, the Language Selection window appears.

4. **Select a language and click Next.**

Choose the language you speak or, if you're feeling adventurous, one that you don't (not recommended).

The Keyboard Configuration window appears.

5. **Select your keyboard configuration and then click Next.**

The Mouse Configuration window appears.

6. **Select your mouse (squeak!) and click Next.**

Red Hat generally automatically detects your mouse. However, in case Red Hat fails to find your mouse, you can select your mouse manually from the slew of mice you see. If you have a PS/2 mouse, all you have to do is select the manufacturer and number of buttons. If you have the older style of mouse that connects via a serial port, you have to select the manufacturer, number of buttons, and the serial port to which it's connected; you have only four serial ports to select from, and in many cases it's either `ttyS0` or `ttyS1`.

If you have a 2-button mouse (either serial or PS/2), you can choose to have it emulate three buttons by selecting the Emulate 3 Buttons option. You emulate the third (middle) button by pressing both mouse buttons at one time.

7. **Click Next.**

The Red Hat installation system tries to detect and identify your monitor. In most cases, Red Hat can make the identification and doesn't need any input from you, so you can skip to Step 11.

8. **If the installation system cannot automatically identify your monitor, the Monitor Configuration window appears.**

The Red Hat installation process detects your video driver hardware and automatically selects the best resolution. You can manually configure the video card after the installation process finishes. See Chapter 4 for configuration instructions.

We use the word *monitor* generically to refer to both the traditional Cathode Ray Tube (CRT) and the modern Liquid Crystal Display (LCD) devices. CRT monitors use heavy glass tubes, of course, and LCDs use lighter, thin-plastic panels.

If your monitor isn't detected, the screen defaults to the Unprobed Monitor option. You can manually select your monitor by choosing from the list of manufacturers and their models. If you can't find your model, your best bet is to select one of the generic monitors. For example, select the Generic Laptop Display Panel 1024x768 if you have an LCD display. Alternatively, you can simply select the default Unprobed Monitor type; the worst that can happen is that you either have to reconfigure the monitor later or live with slightly less than optimal performance.

9. **Click the Next button.**

   If you selected the unprobed monitor, the Monitor Unspecified dialog box opens. Click the Choose Monitor Type button and control returns to the Monitor Configuration window, as described in Step 8. Otherwise, you don't see the dialog box and should proceed to Step 10.

10. **Click the Proceed button and continue to Step 11.**

Older CRT monitors (not LCD displays) can't handle resolution rates and scan frequencies higher than what they were designed for. A monitor designed for a 640 x 480 resolution (and a low scan frequency), for example, can't display a 2,048 x 1,024 resolution (and a high scan frequency). If you try to make the monitor display a higher frequency than it's capable of displaying, the monitor may burst into flames. (We didn't believe this either until we saw a monitor smoking. Hey, at least you get a new monitor out of it. Welcome to the 21st century.)

Modern CRT monitors (not LCD displays), called *multiscanning monitors,* can automatically match themselves to a series of scan frequencies and resolutions. Some of these monitors are even smart enough to turn themselves off rather than burst into flames if the frequencies become too high. Finding the documentation and matching your vertical and horizontal frequencies properly is the best way to go (particularly with older monitors). If you don't have this information, try a lower resolution first, just to get X Window System running. (LCDs cannot catch on fire in this way.)

11. **The Installation Type window appears. If you have already installed Linux on your computer, however, you're asked whether you want to upgrade or make a fresh installation. Upgrade, if you want; your current software is updated to newer versions. This book is oriented toward installing Red Hat Linux for the first time.**

See the following section to select your Red Hat Linux installation type, and then continue to partition your disk.

Checking your discs

Red Hat provides a validation mechanism for checking its DVD-ROM or CD-ROMs. Red Hat inserts numeric keys into its discs to help verify that they aren't corrupted. If you enter **linux mediacheck** at the `boot:` prompt, the installation process starts up and displays a dialog box. Follow these steps to verify that your DVD-ROM (or CD-ROMs) are in working order.

1. **Select the OK option by pressing the Enter key if you want to verify that your DVD (or CD) is okay.**

   If you have already verified your media, perhaps you have already checked them during an earlier installation — you can select the Skip option to return to the Red Hat installation process without checking the media.

   The Media Check window opens.

2. **Select the Test option and the test starts.**

   The media check system displays a progress meter and then shows the result in the Media Check Result window when it's finished. The possible results are PASS and FAIL.

3. **If you're testing a DVD and the test succeeds, the installation process will start and you should skip step 4. Otherwise, when testing CD-ROMs, click the OK button (the only option) in the Media Check Result window.**

   The CD-ROM is ejected after the check is finished.

4. **Insert the second or third CD-ROM and click the Continue button in the Media Check dialog box. Repeat this step for each CD-ROM. You are finished after checking the third CD-ROM.**

Obviously, if the DVD-ROM (or any of the CD-ROMs) fails the test, you shouldn't use it. You should buy another copy of this book. No, no — just kidding. Contact the Wiley Media Development department, at `MediaDev@wiley.com`, to find out how to get a replacement DVD-ROM (or CD-ROM).

Installation Stage 2: Slicing and Dicing the Pie

You must decide where on your hard disk to install Red Hat Linux, a process called disk partitioning. *Disk partitioning* divides a disk into multiple sections, or slices. Red Hat Linux is then installed on the partitions. You typically use three to seven partitions.

Red Hat provides automatic and manual methods for creating disk partitions. We use the Red Hat automatic method because it's easy to use. The automatic method erases any existing Red Hat Linux partitions, but leaves alone any existing Windows partitions. If you don't have any existing Red Hat partitions or unused space on your disk, you have to make some free space. Refer to Chapter 2 for instructions on shrinking Windows partitions to make space for Linux.

Linux disk partitions are analogous to Windows disk partitions. The well-known C: drive is placed on a disk partition. The Linux equivalent is the root (/) partition. The two operating systems use different terminology, and the analogy isn't perfect, although the concept is the same.

Follow these steps to continue the installation:

1. **Select the Workstation option in the Installation Type window and then click the Next button.**

   The Disk Partitioning Setup window appears. The Red Hat Linux installation system must partition your hard drive in order to install its software. Partitions divide a hard drive into one or more parts. The divisions are used to organize the software and data (user files, for example) that comprise the operating system.

   Red Hat provides two partitioning methods: automatic and manual. The manual method uses the Red Hat Disk Druid utility. Using the Disk Druid requires you to make several decisions to select your disk partitions, so we use the automatic method, which is simpler to use. The automatic method is easier to use, and we recommend it unless you're feeling lucky (or want to experiment or have the experience of manually partitioning your hard drive).

2. **Select the Automatically Partition option and click the Next button.**

   If you're using a new disk that has never been partitioned or your existing disk's partition table has become corrupted in some way, a Warning dialog box appears.

3. **Click the Yes button and a new partition table is created. (Selecting No stops the installation process and reboots your computer.)**

   The Automatic Partitioning window appears. You have three options:

   - **Remove all Linux partitions on this system:** This option leaves any Windows partitions (FAT, VFAT, and NTFS) unmodified while erasing any existing Linux partitions. Use this option if you're reinstalling Red Hat Linux (in either a dual boot or solo configuration).

   - **Remove all partitions on this system:** This option is the most dangerous one because it erases everything on your hard disk. Use this option only if you're absolutely sure that you don't have, or don't want to save, anything on your disk. Your new Red Hat Linux installation is the only operating system on the hard disk if you use this option.

   - **Keep all partitions and use existing free space:** Use this option if you used the nondestructive repartitioning (using FIPS, Norton Ghost, or PartitionMagic, for example) described in Chapter 2 to shrink your Windows partition.

You can use commercial products, like Norton Ghost 2002, to shrink NTFS partitions. Shrinking a Windows partition frees up disk space that you can use to install Red Hat Linux. Using this option creates a dual boot configuration if Windows already exists on your computer.

Never select the Remove All Partitions on This System option unless you want to erase everything on your disk! Use extreme caution because this action destroys all installed operating systems (Windows and Red Hat Linux) and data. You may use this option, for example, if your computer came with Windows preinstalled and you want to convert it to a Red Hat Linux-only workstation.

Select the option labeled Keep All Partitions and Use Existing Free Space if you want to install Red Hat Linux on extra, unused space on your hard drive (for example, if you have shrunk an existing Windows FAT or NTFS partition, as described in Chapter 2).

4. **Select the automatic partitioning option most appropriate for you.**

   If you repartitioned your Windows disk in Chapter 2 to make room for Linux, click the button labeled Keep All Partitions and Use Existing Free Space. The Red Hat Linux installation system uses the extra space on the disk to install.

   Optionally, click the Remove All Linux partitions on This System button if you're installing Linux over an old Linux installation.

   Optionally, if you want to erase any existing operating system and start fresh with Red Hat Linux, click the Remove All Partitions on This System button along with all programs and data on the disk.

5. **(Optional) Select the option labeled Review (and Modify If Needed) the Partitions Created, at the bottom of the screen.**

   Selecting this option lets you review your partitions.

   The Warning dialog box opens, informing you about which, if any, partitions will be erased.

6. **Click the Yes button to continue with the installation. Click the No button to return to the Automatic Partitioning window in Step 3.**

7. **If you selected in Step 5 the option labeled Review (and Modify If Needed) the Partitions Created, the Partitioning dialog box appears, as shown in Figure 3-1.**

   If you didn't select the Review option, proceed to Step 10.

8. **Review the partitions and modify them, if necessary.**

   The Partitioning window shows you how the Red Hat installation process plans to divide the available space on your hard drive into three partitions. (The available space is determined by the option you selected in Step 2.) The partitions created are `root (/)`, boot (`/boot`), and `swap`. (`swap` is used internally by Red Hat Linux and, unlike the other partitions, isn't accessible by you.)

At this point, you can click the New, Edit, and Delete buttons if you want to modify the default disk partitions. You should modify the default partitions only if you're an experienced Unix or Linux user and understand the concept of using multiple partitions. We recommend that unless you feel really lucky or are very experienced, you let Red Hat do the work here.

9. **Click the Next button.**
10. **The Boot Loader Configuration window appears, as shown in Figure 3-2. The defaults should work just fine for you, so click Next.**

    The boot loader helps start your operating system when you start your computer; if you create a dual boot computer, the boot loader allows you to select one operating system or another. The standard Red Hat Linux boot loader is GRUB, a powerful system that can do more than just load an operating system. However, the GRUB default options should be all you need (and a description of its advanced features are beyond the scope of this book).

If your computer has an NIC (network interface card), Red Hat detects it and the Network Configuration window appears, as shown in Figure 3-3. You should proceed to Step 1 in the next section and configure your network. However, if you don't have an Ethernet NIC or are using a wireless device that Red Hat doesn't detect, the installation process skips the network configuration and continues at Step 7 in the following section.

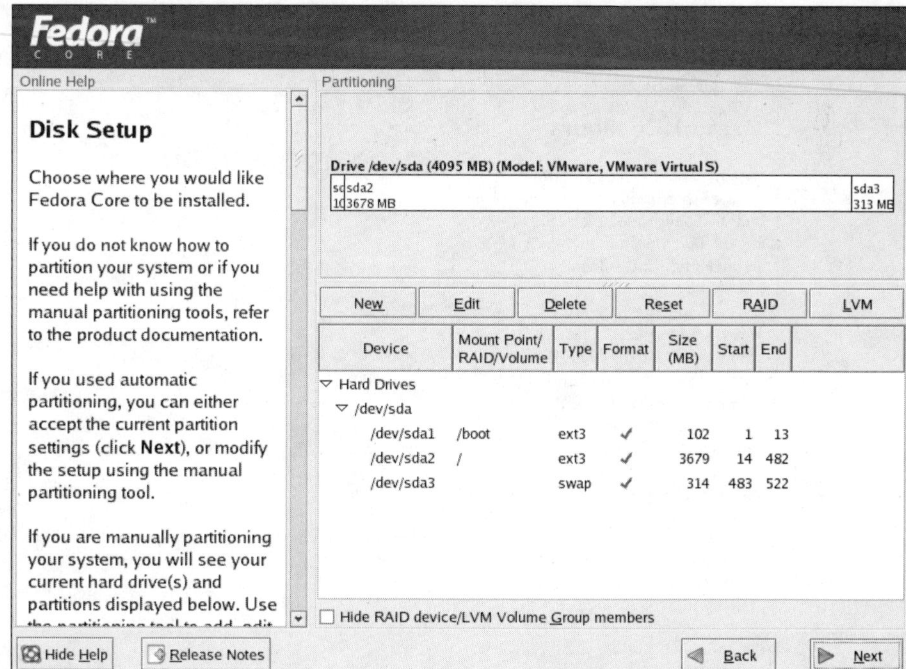

Figure 3-1: The Disk Setup window displays the partitions to be created.

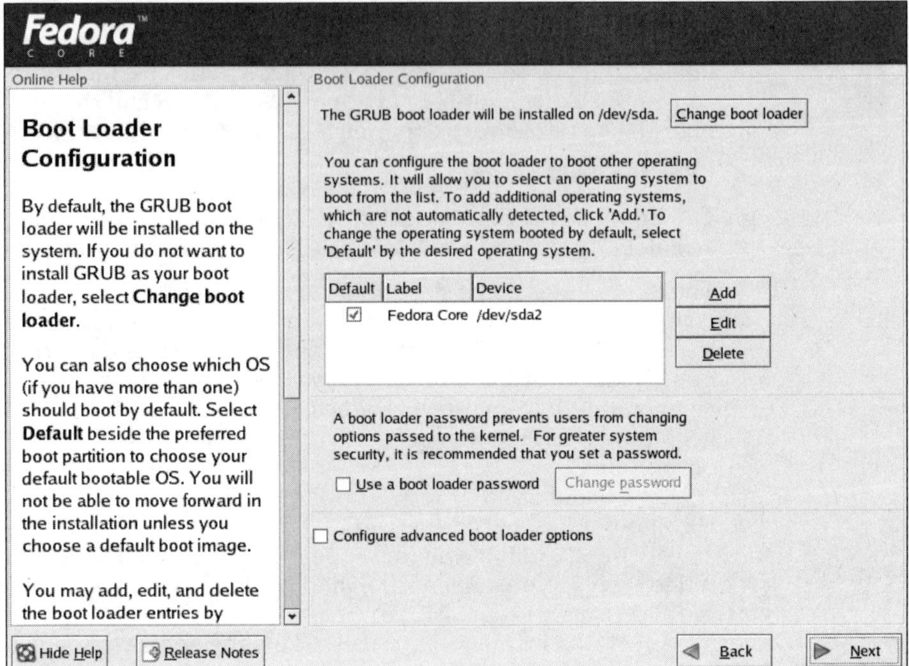

Figure 3-2: The Boot Loader Configuration window.

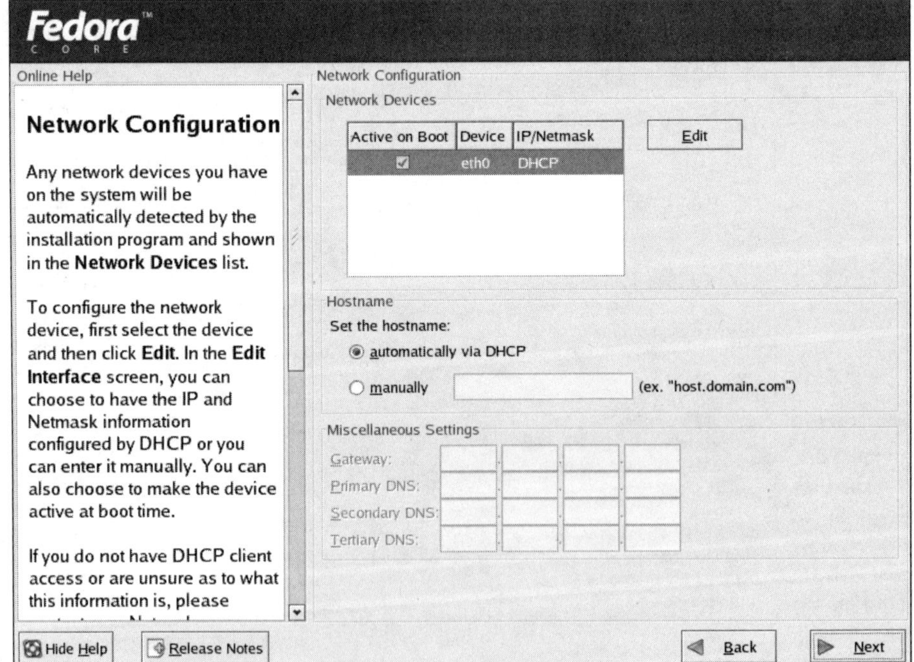

Figure 3-3: The Network Configuration window.

Confidential for Windows users

If you're installing Red Hat Linux in a dual boot configuration with Windows NT, Windows 2000, or Windows XP, your NT boot record is temporarily overwritten, which means that you can't boot Windows NT. Don't panic: Your NT partition isn't erased — it has just been rendered unbootable. (An NT *boot record* is what enables a Windows NT system to start automatically when you start your computer.)

You can install Red Hat Linux without overwriting the NT boot partition if you click the Change Boot Loader button and select the Do Not Install a Boot Loader radio button. When you click the Next button, the Advanced Boot Loader Configuration window opens. Select the First Sector of Boot Partition option and then click the Next button. Your Windows boot configuration continues to operate as before.

In the following section, we show you how to configure your network for Red Hat Linux use. If you don't have a network or just don't want to haggle with it right now, you may want to read the following section anyway because it makes your life easier if your decide to create a network sometime in the future. If you're still not interested, click Next and skip to the section after that, "Installation Stage 4: Configuring Your System."

Installation Stage 3: Configuring Your Network

If you're ready to configure your network and your computer has an Ethernet or Wi-Fi (a wireless network interface using the 802-11b standard) adapter, enter the appropriate information, as described in the following steps. If you have a network adapter but don't have a network to connect to, you should still enter a host name in Step 4. Entering a host name makes life easier down the line if and when you eventually connect to a network.

Sometimes, the installation process doesn't detect a network device and skips the steps described in this section. If that happens, continue with the installation as described in the following section, "Installation Stage 4: Configuring your System." You can configure your network after you finish installing Red Hat Linux. See Chapter 7 for network configuration instructions.

If you pick up from the end of the preceding section, the Network Configuration window appears. Follow these steps to configure your system for a network:

1. **If you're connecting to a network that uses the Dynamic Host Configuration Protocol (DHCP), you don't have to do anything more to configure your network connection. Click the Next button and skip to Step 8.**

You may need to consult with your LAN's administrator to find out whether the LAN (Local Area Network) uses DHCP. If you constructed your own LAN and don't know whether you're running DHCP, you're not. Go to Chapter 15 to find out how to install and configure a DHCP server.

2. **Click the Edit button and the Edit interface subwindow opens.**
3. **Click the Configure using DHCP button and enter your IP address and netmask..**

   The following list briefly explains IP addresses and netmasks:

   - **IP address:** This address is the numeric network address of your Red Hat Linux computer and is the address by which your computer is known on your local network and — in many cases — the Internet. If you haven't registered your private network's address space with InterNIC (the organization in charge of distributing IP addresses), you can use the public address space that goes from `192.168.1.1` to `192.168.254.254`.

     If you're connecting to an existing LAN, consult its administrator to get an IP address that isn't already being used. You have to keep track of unused IP addresses if you're running your own LAN.

   - **Netmask:** Private networks based on the Internet Protocol (IP) are divided into subnetworks. The netmask determines how the network is divided. For IP addresses, such as the example in the preceding bullet (`192.168.1.1`), the most common netmask is `255.255.255.0`.

4. **Click the button labeled Manually under the Set the Hostname section of the window. Type your computer's host name, including the network (domain) name in the text box.**

   For example, if you want to name your computer `cancun` and your network name is `paunchy.net`, you type **cancun.paunchy.net**.

If you don't give your computer a name and domain name during the network configuration process, it's referred to as `localhost.localdomain`. Otherwise, the Welcome screen refers to whatever name you gave it. For example, in the preceding example, you would see `Welcome to cancun.paunchy.net`.

5. **Enter your gateway and primary DNS (and, optionally, the secondary and tertiary DNS) IP addresses in the appropriate text boxes in the Miscellaneous section, at the bottom of the screen.**

   This list describes what these parameters do:

   - **Gateway:** The *gateway* is the numeric IP address of the computer that connects your private network to the Internet (or another private network). Red Hat Linux uses the address `192.168.1.254` by default. You can accept this address, but leaving it blank is a better option, unless that address is really your gateway. Chapters 5, 6, and 7 describe how to configure your Linux computer to connect to the Internet via a telephone, broadband (DSL or cable), and existing LAN connections, respectively. If you do that, setting a default route now can interfere with your connection.

- **Primary DNS:** The Internet Protocol uses the Domain Name Service (DNS) system to convert names such as `www.redhat.com` into numeric IPs. A computer that acts as a DNS server is a *name server.* We suggest leaving this box blank, however, unless you're on a private network with a name server or will be connected to the Internet (your ISP supplies a DNS). When you designate a nonexistent name server, many networking programs work very slowly as they wait in vain for the absent server.
- **Secondary and tertiary DNS:** The secondary and tertiary DNS back up the primary DNS server. If your computer can't find the primary DNS server, it may find the secondary. If not, it should find the tertiary. Best of luck!

6. **If you're connecting to the Internet directly using a modem (regular dial-up, DSL, or cable), leave the Gateway address blank. Otherwise, if your computer is connected to a LAN with Internet access, enter the Internet gateway's address in the Gateway text box.**

   If you're connecting to someone else's LAN — if you're building a Red Hat Linux computer at work, for example — you should obtain this address from your system administrator. If you're connecting to your own LAN at home, consult yourself because you're probably the administrator.

7. **When you complete the Network Configuration form, click the Next button to continue.**

   The Firewall Configuration window opens.

   The firewall is turned on by default. You can turn it off if you want, but we recommend leaving it turned on.

8. **Click the Next button.**

Red Hat creates for your computer a firewall designed for use by a workstation. The firewall is adequate and provides a reasonable amount of protection. However, we show you how to construct a better — safer and simpler — firewall in Chapter 8.

The next section shows you how to finish the configuration of your Red Hat Linux workstation.

Installation Stage 4: Configuring Your Options

This section describes the basic configuration steps for your Red Hat Linux computer. We describe how to set your time zone and the root user password. You also choose to install extra software in addition to the default packages. The following steps describe how to perform these basic tasks. Note that if you

Introducing password etiquette

Your password must be at least six characters long, but you should use at least eight characters: The more characters you use, the harder the password is to break. If you're concerned about security, we recommend that you use a combination of uppercase and lowercase letters, symbols, and numbers to make your password as difficult as possible to compromise. In addition, don't choose anything you can find in a dictionary or names or items that are easy to associate with you. In other words, your name, your name spelled backward, your birthday, your dog's name, or any word in any language are all poor choices. Beer, for example, is a poor selection for Jon's password, even though it has both uppercase and lowercase letters, because Jon and beer are usually seen in close proximity with each other.

A good way to come up with a good password is to select a phrase and destroy it. For example, make "I am not a number" into something like `imN0tun#`. Even though the result doesn't spell out the phrase in any real way, it gives you all the cues to remember the essentially random characters ("I am" = `im`, "not" = `N0t`, "a" = `un`, and number = `#`). Other common substitutions are 3 for *e,* 4 for *a,* 9 for *g,* 1 for *l,* 8 for *b,* and 5 for *s.* In this way, you can create passwords like `s0uthb4y` (southbay) and `14mn0t4g33k` (iamnotageek).

Also, be sure to write down your password where it won't get lost and can't be easily found or stolen. For example, save your work passwords at home or store them in a locked desk or safe. Do not write your password on a sticky note and attach it to your computer monitor!

have been following along in this chapter and completed Step 7 in the preceding section, the Additional Language Support window opens and gives you extra linguistic options.

Follow these steps:

1. **With the Additional Language Support window open, make your selection (although almost anyone in the United States doesn't have to make a selection) and click the Next button.**

   The Time Zone Selection window appears.

2. **To select your time zone, click the dot representing a city closest to where you live.**

   You can use the map to point and click your way to your time zone bliss. When you click one of the thousand points of light, the represented city and its time zone appear in the subwindow below the map. You can also click the slider bar at the bottom of the screen to locate the name of your city or time zone. After you find it, click the text to select your time zone.

3. **Click Next.**

   The Set Root Password window appears.

4. **Type your root password in both the Root Password and Confirm text boxes.**

   The password is for the root user, also known as the *superuser,* who has access to the entire system and can do almost anything — good and bad.

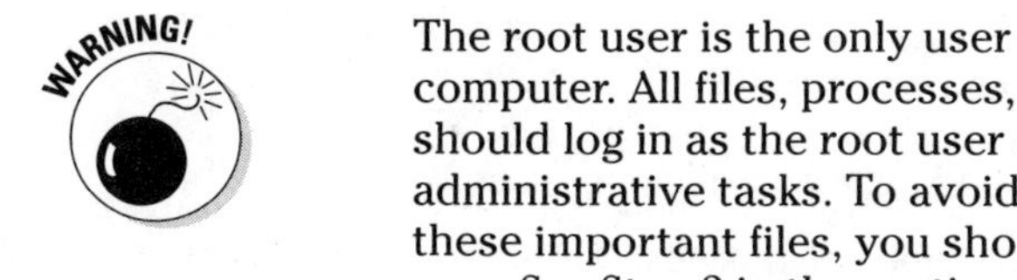

   The root user is the only user who can access all resources on your computer. All files, processes, and devices are controlled by root. You should log in as the root user only to perform system maintenance or administrative tasks. To avoid making unwanted changes or deletions to these important files, you should normally log in as a regular (non-root) user. See Step 2 in the section "Post Installation: Using the Setup Agent," later in this chapter, to find out how to add a user.

   You have to type the password two times to make sure that you typed it correctly. The password appears onscreen as asterisks as you type it. "Holy breach of security, Batman!" You wouldn't want someone to be able to look over your shoulder and get your password, would you?

5. **Click Next.**

   The Workstation Defaults window opens and displays a summary of the important software to be installed. (A summary for whichever installation type you're using is displayed if you're not using the Workstation type.) You're given the choice of selecting either the Accept the Current Package List (the default) option or the Customize the Set of Packages to Be Installed option.

   In this book, we use the default packages from the Workstation installation environment.

   If you select the Customize the Set of Packages to be Installed option, the Package Group Selection window opens. You can select additional packages to be installed individually or by group. For example, if you want to install the KDE environment, simply click the button next to the KDE Desktop Environment menu and all the necessary packages are then selected. Select individual packages by clicking the Select Individual Packages option. After you make you selection, click the Next button and proceed to Step 6.

6. **Click the Next button.**

   The About to Install window appears. A loud voice reverberates that this is The Point Of No Return. Well, not exactly. No loud voice says anything, but it is the point of no return. If you click the Next button, your disk is reformatted in whatever way you selected in the preceding section and Red Hat Linux is then installed. The following section describes how that process goes.

GNOME is the default Red Hat graphical environment for Red Hat and is what we use throughout this book. However, many people prefer the KDE environment. The choice is yours; you can use either environment or both, if you want. (If you install both GNOME and KDE on your computer, you can select one or the other as your desktop environment when you log in.) To install

Customizing the software to install

If you select the Customize the Set of Packages to Be Installed option and click the Next button in Step 5, the Package Group Selection window appears.

Red Hat organizes individual software packages into package groups. (Packages are described in Appendix D.) For example, individual packages used by the GNOME graphical system are grouped into the GNOME package group. The Red Hat installation process selects certain package groups for each of its installation types.

Both the Workstation and Personal Desktop types use the same package groups except that the Workstation type adds the software development package group. The Server installation type uses a different set of package groups.

You generally don't need to modify the default Red Hat package groups when using the Workstation or Personal Desktop installation types. You can certainly do so if you want, but the default creates a computer that serves most of your needs.

KDE, select the Customize the Set of Packages to Be Installed option, as described in Step 5. Click the check box next to the KDE package group and then click the Next button.

Installation Stage 5: The Point of No Return

The instructions described in this chapter, if you have been following along, have not yet resulted in making any permanent changes to your computer. Your selections haven't been written in stone, so to speak. No partitions have been erased. No Red Hat Linux packages have been written to your hard drive either. You can stop the installation process and go back to your good old computer by clicking the Back button.

Make your decision whether to proceed. Take a deep breath and follow these instructions to install Red Hat Linux on your computer:

1. **Click the Next button and the installation process begins. If you're using this book's DVDs, proceed to Step 3 when the installation process finishes.**

   If you're using the CD-ROM discs, the Install Media dialog box opens. (You're a informed which discs you will need.) Go to step 2; you can click the Reboot button if you want to abort the installation process.

2. **Insert the next CD-ROM when prompted and click the Continue button.**

   Your disk partitions are created and formatted, and then the Red Hat Linux distribution is written to it.

Yikes! The Installing Packages window (see Figure 3-4) tells you which package is being installed in addition to how many have been installed, how many remain to be installed, and the estimated time remaining.

The process takes several minutes if you have the latest, greatest high-speed computer and DVD/CD-ROM drive. Otherwise, plan to spend 20 to 40 minutes — or longer — for older equipment.

3. **After installing Red Hat Linux on your computer, the installer asks whether you want to create a boot disk.**

   This option helps you create a floppy disk that you can use to boot your computer just in case something happens to the boot partition on your disk. Microsoft products, for example, have a bad habit of overwriting the master boot record (MBR) — and therefore your Red Hat Linux booting system — when they're installed or even updated. Hard drive boot failures can also happen for any number of reasons — aliens and gremlins are well known for wreaking havoc. The boot disk is a great tool for foiling these dastardly mischief-makers.

   This boot disk is different from the one you use to start the Red Hat Linux installation. You can use the boot floppy to start your Red Hat Linux computer in case the Red Hat Linux boot information stored on your hard drive ever becomes corrupted.

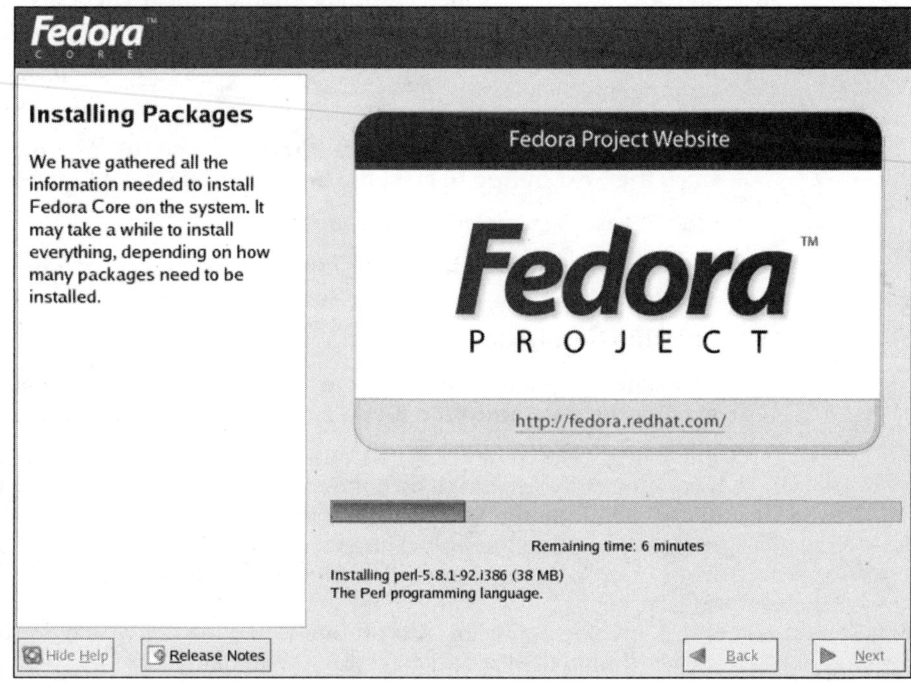

Figure 3-4: The Installing Packages window.

4. **(Optional) Insert a blank disk into your main floppy drive, select the Create Boot Floppy option, and click Next to create a boot disk.**

   The Congratulations window opens. It provides you with information about where to find Red Hat Linux information.

5. **Remove the DVD-ROM (or CD-ROM or floppy disk) from the computer and click the Reboot button.**

Your computer reboots. Consult the following section to finish the installation.

Post Installation: Using the Setup Agent

After your computer reboots, the Red Hat Setup Agent starts. The Setup Agent simplifies the installation process by pushing some configuration work to the post-installation phase. Your new Red Hat Linux computer works just fine whether or not you run the Setup Agent. The Setup Agent helps you to fine-tune your computer. The fine-tuning doesn't need to occur during the installation, which makes that entire process a bit easier.

The Setup Agent automatically runs when your computer reboots after installing Red Hat Linux. The Setup Agent helps you add user accounts, set your computer's date-time, configure your sound system, and optionally install additional packages. The following instructions describe how to use the Setup Agent:

1. **When the Red Hat Setup System starts, you see the Welcome screen. Click the Next button to start the post-installation configuration process.**

   The License Agreement window opens.

2. **Read the license requirements, click the Yes, I Agree to the License Agreement button.**

3. **Click the Next button.**

4. **The Date and Time Configuration window appears, and you can change the date and time if you need to.**

   You can also let your computer automatically and continuously update your clock. If you plan to be connected to the Internet, either through a LAN (Local Area Network) or a broadband modem (DSL or cable), select the Enable Network Time Protocol (NTP) option. You can choose from a drop-down menu full of time NTP servers. The default choices `clock.redhat.com` and `clock2.redhat.com` work well, but you can enter any one you want. Alternatively, you may have access to an NTP server not on the list and can enter it manually.

We recommend that you use the NTP option, if your computer is connected continuously to the Internet on a LAN or a DSL or cable modem. PC clocks tend to drift from seconds to minutes per day. It's better to be up-to-date than not.

5. **Click the Next button.**

   The User Account window opens. Only the root user was created during the installation process, but you have the chance here to create one or more user accounts.

6. **Enter an account name, the name of the account owner, and its password. Click the Next button to continue.**
7. **Red Hat does a good job of detecting hardware, such as sound cards, and should detect yours, if you have one. Click the Play Test Sound button.**

   A dialog box opens, asking whether you heard the music.

8. **Click Yes if you did and No if you didn't.**
9. **An Error dialog box opens if you clicked No. Click the OK button to continue.**

   Consult the section in Chapter 11 about setting up your sound system for help if the sound test fails. Click the Forward button to continue.

10. **Click the Next button.**

    The Finish Setup window opens.

11. **Click the Next button and the Setup Agent closes and your login window opens.**

You can run Setup Agent whenever you want. The Setup Agent is a script named `firstboot`. You can run the Setup Agent by running the `firstboot` script with the `reconfig` option. Just run the following commands as root from a GNOME Terminal window:

```
rm /etc/sysconfig/firstboot
/usr/sbin/firstboot
```

That's it! You have built yourself a Red Hat Linux computer. After your computer reboots itself, you can then use it as your personal workstation.

Chapter 4

Getting Red Hat Linux

In This Chapter

- Checking out the Red Hat Linux file system
- Booting Red Hat Linux
- Comprehending logins and the root user
- Using text-based commands
- Configuring the graphical display
- Adding users with a graphical tool
- Adding users without a graphical tool
- Stopping Red Hat Linux

After you have installed Red Hat Linux is a good time to spend a few minutes perusing some basics. This chapter covers enough of the Linux fundamentals to get you started, including topics such as starting and stopping Red Hat Linux and understanding the difference between graphical and nongraphical applications.

We start by introducing the system Linux uses to store information on a disk. Linux, like Windows, uses files and directories to store and organize information and applications. The following section describes the Linux file system.

Introducing the Linux File System Tree

Linux sees all its parts, except its network, as files. Linux accesses files, directories, and devices as *file addresses*. Linux refers to drives and drive partitions by using a system of letters and numbers; for example, `/dev/hda` may be the name of the first IDE hard drive, and `/dev/sdb` may be the name of the second SCSI hard drive.

You can compare the Linux file system to a tree, as shown in Figure 4-1, which shows three *subdirectories* of root (more than a dozen subdirectories are in the root directory); a *subdirectory* is a directory within a directory. The top of the upside-down tree, represented by a / (slash), is the *root directory.* A series of limbs, branches, and leaves extends below the root: Limbs are mount points, the branches that extend from the limbs are directories, and the leaves on those branches are your files.

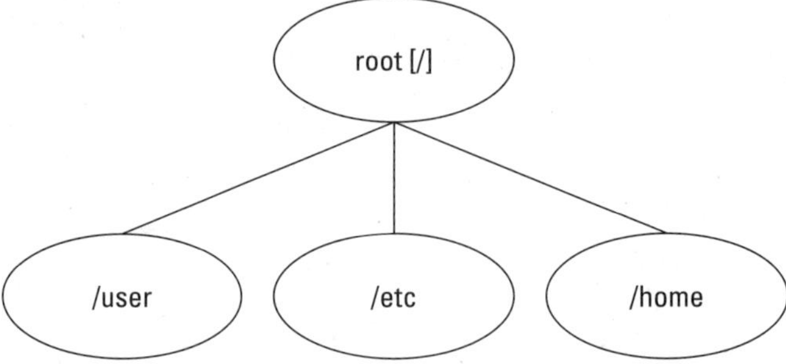

Figure 4-1: The Linux file system resembles an upside-down tree.

Each *mount point* is a drive partition or remote file system (such as your DVD or CD-ROM drive) that is *mounted,* or made visible to, a directory of the limb above it. Whenever a disk partition or remote file system is mounted on the directory branch, it turns that branch into another limb, allowing even more branches to be positioned and attached below the mount point.

Red Hat Linux needs at least a root partition in your directory structure and a swap space partition. The root partition is used to store all your personal and system files and directories; Linux uses *swap space,* the Hamburger Helper of the computer world, to extend your memory beyond the limit of your random access memory (RAM). If you have 512MB of RAM and 512MB of swap space, for example, you can run programs that use 1GB of memory.

This configuration isn't much different from the Windows and MS-DOS file systems. Windows uses the concept of a hierarchical directory tree. However, the syntax is somewhat different. The top-level directory in Red Hat Linux, root, is designated with a forward slash (/). Every subsequent subdirectory name follows that initial slash. For example, the home directory is a subdirectory of root and is shown as `/home`. In the Windows world, the root directory is designated with an initial backslash (\). The famous `C:` is synonymous with `C:\`. The theme for both operating systems is carried forward when dividing subdirectories: Linux uses forward slashes, and Windows uses backslashes. Your home directory is then shown as `/home/me` in Linux and as `\user directories\me` in Windows.

Another primary difference between Linux and Windows file systems is that Linux requires you to explicitly mount file systems. Windows does so automatically. Explicitly mounting the file system isn't as onerous as it sounds. Red Hat Linux installs utilities that automatically sense and mount file systems when necessary. For example, the default Red Hat Linux configuration mounts a DVD or CD-ROM automatically whenever you insert it in the drive.

The Workstation installation type we describe in Chapter 3 automatically sets up your root and swap partitions in addition to an additional boot partition used for storing the Red Hat Linux kernel and other files used for booting your computer. (The Personal Desktop installation type uses the same partitioning scheme as the Workstation installation type.)

The next section describes how to start and stop Linux.

Giving Red Hat Linux the Boot

To *boot* a computer means simply to start it (and to *reboot* means to restart it). Follow these steps to boot your Red Hat Linux system for the first time:

1. **Make sure that your computer is turned off.**
2. **Turn on the power to the monitor and then turn on the computer's main power switch.**

   After a short time, the Red Hat boot menu appears on your screen. If you have only Red Hat Linux installed on your computer, you are given only one choice of operating systems to boot: Linux.

   The default operating system is the one at the top of the list. If you have installed Red Hat Linux along with another operating system, you can change the one that boots by default.

   Linux runs in three different states: 1, 3, and 5 (referred to as *run levels*). Each run level is used to perform different functions. At Level 1 (also called *single-user mode*), Linux operates with a minimum of processes so that you can make configuration changes and debug problems. Level 3 is essentially the same as Level 5 except that Level 3 doesn't run the X server — it's nongraphical. You typically run servers that don't need to run graphical applications, such as word processors, at Level 3. Level 5 is the default for personal workstations. You can use GRUB (Grand Unified Bootloader) to select a different Linux run level. When GRUB appears, press **e** for edit. Three lines appear. Press the down-arrow key to select the line that begins with *Kernel.* Press the **e** key again, append a space, and then press either **1**, **3**, or **5.** Press the Enter key and then press the **b** key. Your computer boots into either single-user mode (1), nongraphical mode (3), or graphical mode (5).

3. **Press the up- and down-arrow keys to highlight the word *Linux* (if it's not highlighted already) and press Enter.**

   If you don't press anything, the default operating system (Linux sets itself as the default when you install it) starts automatically after a five-second delay.

   If you're running more than one operating system (for example, Red Hat Linux and Windows), you can select any of the listed operating systems to boot; we assume here that you choose Linux.

   After you press Enter, Red Hat Linux boots. During this process, lots of information is displayed on your screen. Red Hat Linux gleans this information as it probes your computer in order to determine what hardware (disk drives and printers, for example) is present.

Because Red Hat Linux is a multiuser system, one or more users can use it at the same time; for example, you can be logged in at the computer console (the attached keyboard and monitor) while someone else is logged in via a network connection). Therefore, you and every other user need a user account in order to use the computer. Each account requires an individual account name and password to protect your information and keep your tasks separate from other people's tasks.

Logging In

When you use Red Hat Linux, you must log in as a particular user with a distinct login name. Why? Because Red Hat Linux is a multiuser system and therefore uses different accounts to keep people from looking at other people's secret files, erasing necessary files from the system, and otherwise (intentionally or unintentionally) doing bad things.

The use of unique identities helps to keep the actions of one person from affecting the actions of another because many people may be using the same computer system at the same time (for example, over a network). A benefit of this strategy is that Red Hat Linux systems are essentially invulnerable to viruses simply because each user's files and directories can't be used to corrupt the system as a whole. (Not that we're keeping score or anything, but viruses can destroy or just make life miserable for Windows 9*x* systems because they don't have this capability.)

As Red Hat Linux boots, you see all sorts of messages scrolling by on the screen. After the scrolling stops, the login screen appears.

If you chose (during installation) not to have X start automatically whenever you boot your system, you see the `login:` prompt.

If you make a mistake while typing the password or your login, the system asks you to retype it.

We strongly recommend that you do most of your experimentation with Red Hat Linux as a nonprivileged user and log in as the root user only when necessary. By operating as root, you run the risk of corrupting your system, having to reinstall again, or losing data because you can delete or change anything and everything. When you are logged in as a regular user, you can accidentally erase your own files and data, but you can't erase someone else's files or system files.

Fortunately, Red Hat Linux provides many graphical administration utilities you can start as a nonprivileged user. Each Red Hat administrative utility prompts you to enter the root password as it starts and then performs its specific function, but only that function, with root privileges. You're prevented, therefore, from doing unintended damage to other systems. (See Appendix C for information about how file permissions work and how you can modify them.)

The Command-Line Interface (CLI) versus the Graphical User Interface (GUI)

Red Hat Linux installs the X Window System by default. You can perform most administrative tasks with the GUI-based tools (GUI stands for *g*raphical *u*ser *i*nterface) that Red Hat provides. Most of the how-to instructions in this book use the X-based applications and utilities. We do that because they're generally easier to use and because this book wasn't written for systems administrators.

Occasionally, a utility or program doesn't run graphically; at other times, using nongraphical methods and systems is just more interesting or convenient. Believe it or not, some geekier Linux users *prefer* to use a text-based, command-line interface (CLI). If you're not familiar with doing some basic administrative tasks with a CLI, we don't recommend using one just to prove that you can. Being less of a geek is okay. We still like and respect you. On the other hand, it makes good sense to know some basics, just in case a need arises for you to have to wing it with the text-based interface.

Command-line interfaces are generally run from a *shell,* which acts as a text-based interface between the Red Hat Linux operating system and you. The `bash` shell, which Red Hat Linux uses by default, displays a prompt like `[lidia@cancun lidia]$`. You enter commands at the shell prompt. That's where the term command-line interface (or CLI) comes from.

You can start a shell from within the GNOME interface by starting a GNOME Terminal (also known generically as a terminal emulator). Click the GNOME Menu and then choose System Tools➪Terminal (you can also right-click anywhere on the GNOME Desktop and choose New Terminal) to start a terminal session, as shown in Figure 4-2. (You can find out more about the GNOME interface in Chapter 9.)

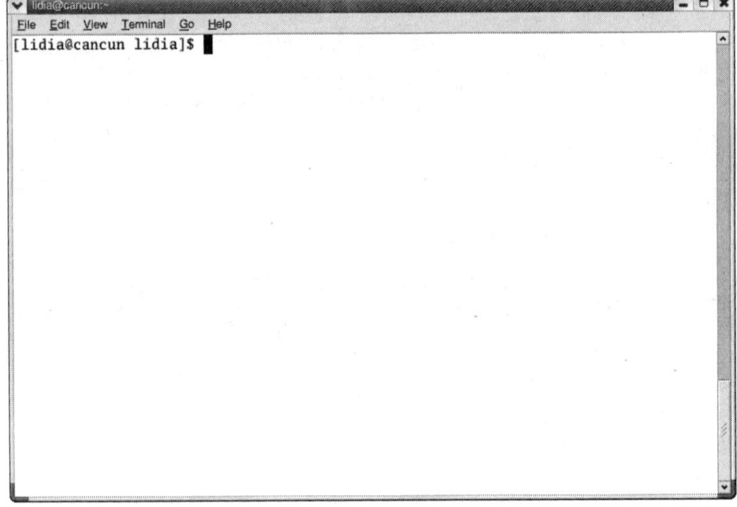

Figure 4-2: A GNOME Terminal session.

You can run individual programs without starting an interactive shell by using the GNOME Run Program menu. Click the GNOME Menu button — the red hat in the lower-left corner of the screen — and choose Run Program. The Run Program window opens; type the name of any program in the text box. The program then runs — if it's graphically oriented. You don't see the output if the program is designed to interact with the terminal screen (the technical term is *standard output*). Entering **xclock**, for example, displays a graphical clock on your screen.

The GNOME Menu button looks like a red hat and is on the toolbar in the lower-left corner of your desktop. The button works in a manner similar to the Windows Start button.

The GNOME Terminal is similar to the MS-DOS window in Windows. Opening an MS-DOS window provides a CLI in which to enter DOS commands. The underlying technology of a Windows CLI is different from that of a Linux CLI. However, its capabilities are more or less the same.

Configuring Your Graphical Display

The Red Hat installation process is good at automatically configuring itself to use your video hardware and display — Linux uses the X Window System (X, for short) to display graphics. However, occasionally the X configuration process fails, or you may want to reconfigure it. Red Hat gives you access to the same configuration tool it uses during the installation process.

The Red Hat X configuration utility is the `redhat-config-sxfree86` program. We refer to it as simply the *Display Configurator.* Generally, the Display Configurator automatically detects your display (monitor) and graphics card. After they have been detected, you can set your display's resolution and color depth.

Configuring with the Display Configurator

You can start the Display Configurator even if you're not running X Window (if you're running in nongraphical mode; nongraphical mode is run level 3):

1. **Log in as root.**

   You're automatically placed in a CLI.

2. **Enter this command at the Bash prompt:**

   ```
   redhat-config-xfree86
   ```

   The Display Configurator window opens. The utility runs within a graphical interface.

You can, of course, start the Display Configurator if your computer is running X. You may want to reconfigure your system, for example. Follow these instructions to start the utility:

1. **Click the GNOME Menu.**
2. **Choose System Settings⇨Display.**
3. **Enter the root password, if you're prompted.**

   The Display Configurator opens. Use the following set of steps to configure your graphical (X Window) interface.

The X Window System (X, for short) was invented at the Massachusetts Institute of Technology (MIT). MIT designed X to display graphical applications across a wide range of machines. It was originally built to run on Unix platforms, but has been adapted to Linux, Windows, and other platforms.

Old monitors that aren't multiscanning can be damaged if you try to use them at a higher resolution than VGA, which is 640 x 480 and 60Hz (a multiscanning monitor can switch to the same signal frequency that a video card is generating). Most newer monitors have built-in protection mechanisms to keep them from burning up in what is known as *overdriving,* but older monitors don't have this type of protection. Older monitors can literally catch on fire. If you hear weird noises from your monitor or smell burning components, turn off your computer immediately!

Configuring manually

You can manually change your display settings if the Display Configurator doesn't automatically detect them. These steps describe how to access and use the advanced Display Configurator features:

1. **Start the Display Configurator and click the Advanced tab.**

   Figure 4-3 shows that you can configure the monitor, the video card, and multiple-head computers (to use more than one monitor at a time). A description of multiple-head systems is beyond the scope of this book.

Advanced Settings
Monitor | Video card | Multi Head
Please select the model of your monitor.
Generic CRT Display
Generic LCD Display
ADI
AOC
AST
AT&T
Aamazing
Acer
Action Systems, Inc.
Horizontal Sync Range: 31.5-48.5
Vertical Refresh Rate: 40.0-70.0
Reset to default
Cancel
OK

Figure 4-3: The monitor Advanced Settings dialog box.

The Advanced Settings window shows the monitors available to you by default.

2. **Try to locate and select your particular monitor.**

   You have dozens and dozens of monitors to choose from, so you have at least as good a chance of finding yours as winning the PowerBall. If not, your best bet is to rummage around in the Generic section.

   Generic monitors include several laptop configurations and old-fashioned heavy ones. If you don't know what type fits your monitor, take a guess and try one. Keep trying different generic monitors if your first choice doesn't work.

   Click the OK button and return to the advanced settings window.

3. **Click the Video Card Configure button. Control is sent to the Video Card Settings window, as shown in Figure 4-4. Select your video card from the long list of choices.**

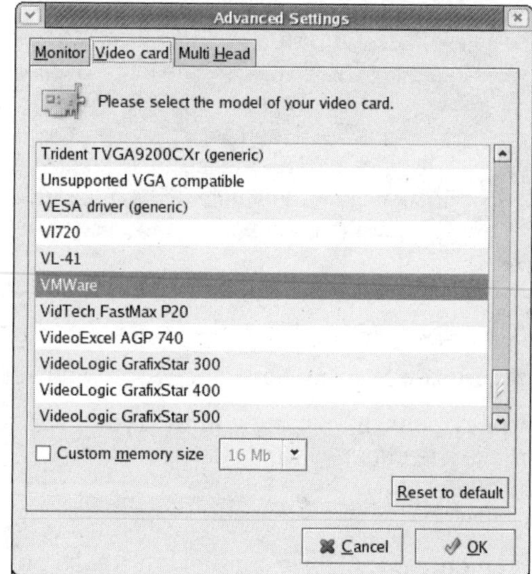

Figure 4-4: The video card Advanced Settings dialog box.

   You can tell the Display Configurator to probe and locate your video card for you by clicking the Probe Videocard button. Your card is most likely detected and highlighted for you.

   The lowest (8-bit) option allows only 256 colors on the window at one time. The 16-bit option allows for 65,535 colors, and 24-bit allows for more than 16 million colors (also known as *true color*).

4. **Click the OK button to return to the Advanced Display Settings window.**

Delving deep into color depth

Color depth, the number of colors your system can have active on the window at any one time, is loosely a function of both the amount of video memory contained by your system and the window resolution.

If your system has a small amount of memory (such as 1MB), your screen can have a resolution of 1024 x 768 pixels (dots) with 256 colors (8 bits) on the screen at one time. If your system has 2MB, you can have 64K colors (16 bits) on the screen at the same time at the same resolution. If you have an older video board with a small amount of video memory but some additional video memory sockets, you may be able to upgrade the amount of video memory on the video card.

If you have only 1MB and want to see 64K colors on the screen at one time, you can reduce your resolution from 1,024 x 768 to 800 x 600 pixels. If you want true color (24 bits), you can set your resolution to 640 x 480 pixels. The picture you're viewing takes up more of the screen, but color depth versus resolution is a trade-off you can make by choosing the right options.

When you want to display an image and the color depth isn't correct, nothing drastic happens. The picture may look lackluster or not quite normal. X has an interesting capability to have virtual color maps, which allow the active window to utilize all the colors of the bits of color depth, even if other windows are using different colors. When this option is turned on (as it is with the Red Hat distribution on this book's companion DVD-ROM), the various windows turn odd colors as your mouse moves from window to window, but the window that your mouse activates is shown in the best color available. With newer video cards and larger video memories, which allow for true color at high resolutions in every window, this option is less useful.

5. **Click the OK button and the Display Settings window closes.**

   An Information window opens, informing you that you need to log out and log back in to make the changes take effect.

   Log out and log back in to make the changes take effect.

You can also restart X in emergencies (for example, if it freaks out) by pressing Ctrl+Alt+Backspace. Your current X session is stopped and eventually restarted. You can then log back in.

Creating User Accounts with the Red Hat User Manager

If you have cause to add new users (if you have a home network, for example) or you forgot to create a nonroot user during installation, this section shows you how. Red Hat offers several systems administration tools for your convenience. The Red Hat User Manager is an excellent administration tool that can make your life easier.

The following instructions assume that you're using the GNOME window system, which is the Red Hat default. But the User Manager works the same under the KDE window system as with GNOME. KDE comes bundled with Red Hat Linux and can be selected rather than GNOME during the installation process. (We discuss GNOME in Chapter 9.)

You can use the Red Hat User Manager to modify an existing user account. Click the user name and then the Properties button, and a window similar to the Create New User window opens. You can then modify any aspect of the account.

Use the User Manager to create a new account by following these steps:

1. **Open the User Manager by clicking the GNOME Menu button and then choosing System Settings⇨Users & Groups.**

   If you're not logged in as the root user, you're prompted to enter the root password.

   The Red Hat User Manager window appears.

2. **Click the Add User button in the upper-left corner of the screen.**

   The Create New User window appears, as shown in Figure 4-5.

Figure 4-5: The Create New User dialog box.

3. **Enter your username, real-life name (full name), and password twice (to confirm that it's correct); accept the Login Shell default of** `/bin/bash`.

   The Red Hat User Manager also creates a home directory by default.

Most of these items are self explanatory, but here's some additional information:

- Your user name (also known as a *login name*) is the name you use to log in to your computer. Make your login name easy to remember and use all lowercase letters. Cute names may not seem appropriate later. Avoid choosing a name that is too long because you may have to type it several times a day. You may also end up using your login name as your e-mail address and have to give it over the telephone, so a login name such as `phool` results in missent messages, leaving you feeling phoolish.
- You can enter your full name, if you want. That information is saved in the `/etc/passwd` file, which anyone with an account on your system can read. This information is generally useful to system administrators because it allows them to connect a person with each account. It's probably superfluous if you're configuring your personal system.
- The new password should be different from the one you use for root.

  As you type the password, little asterisks, rather than the actual password, appear onscreen in case someone is looking over your shoulder as you type. (Red Hat Linux is showing its paranoid side here.) In text mode, you don't get any feedback (asterisks or other characters).
- Among your many choices for a default shell, `/bin/bash` is a good choice (`bash` is a popular shell that is the default for Red Hat Linux).

4. **Click OK.**

   Your account is created.

Red Hat Linux uses the Pluggable Authentication Module (PAM) that prevents you from entering trivial or otherwise dangerous passwords; don't use that as assurance, however, that your new password is a good one. A good password can't be found in any dictionary because password crackers have programs that automatically try all dictionary words to crack your password. Avoid birthdays and anniversaries — or anything someone could associate with you. For ideas about good passwords, check out Chapter 3. Just don't forget it, and *don't* write it on a sticky note and put it on your monitor!

You can also use the Red Hat User Manager to delete an existing user account. Click the user name and then the Delete button, and the account is immediately removed. Be careful because you're not asked to confirm the account deletion. However, because the account home directory is left intact (not deleted) you can go back and re-create the account if necessary.

Creating an Account without X

If X isn't working or you want to work from a terminal emulator, you can still add user accounts. To do so, follow these steps:

1. **Open a GNOME Terminal window by clicking the GNOME Menu button and choosing System Tools➪Terminal.**
2. **Log in as root by entering this command:**

   ```
   su -
   ```

3. **Enter the root password when prompted.**
4. **Type** useradd *name* **at the command prompt, where *name* is the login name for the new login account.**
5. **Type** passwd *name* **at the command prompt and press Enter.**

   This step changes the password of the new account, which had a default password assigned to it by the `useradd` command in Step 1. What good is a password if you use the default one?

6. **Type your password again.**

   Red Hat Linux asks you to retype your new password to ensure that the password you typed is the one you thought you typed. If you don't retype the password exactly as you did the first time (which is easy to do because it doesn't appear onscreen), you have to repeat the process.

   Red Hat Linux updates the password for the new login.

Ending Your First Session

Logging off the system and restarting the login process is simplicity itself. To do so, click the GNOME Menu button and choose Log Out. The Are You Sure You Want to Log Out? window appears, and you're asked to confirm that you want to log out. If you do (do you really?), click the OK button and you're outta there. Click No if you change your mind and want to play around with your new operating system a little while longer.

You can also choose to reboot or halt your computer from this window by clicking either the Shutdown or Reboot button and then clicking OK to confirm your decision. Depending on which you choose, your system stops completely or reboots. You can also press the Ctrl+Alt+Backspace keys to shut down your current session. This method is less graceful but still effective, especially in case some renegade process freezes your X session.

Part II
Got Net?

"When we started the company, we weren't going to call it 'Red Hat'. But eventually we decided it sounded better than 'Beard of Bees Linux'."

In this part . . .

After you have created your Red Hat Linux workstation, it's time to get to work. The chapters in this part show three different ways to connect to the Internet: the traditional, slow dial-up (analog) modem; a fast broadband DSL or cable modem; or an existing Local Area Network (LAN) that's connected to the Internet.

Chapter 5 concentrates on telephone-based modems. Modems are much like old, reliable pick-up trucks: They may not be the fastest way of getting somewhere, but they still get you there. In fact, modems provide the simplest, most economical and effective Internet connection available.

Chapter 6 introduces broadband Internet connections. Telephone, cable, and other types of companies now provide broadband service to many communities. For not altogether unreasonable prices, you can get high-speed, always-on service.

Many people have access to existing computer Local Area Networks (called LANs) at work, school, and home. Chapter 7 shows how to connect your computer to a LAN, and, if your LAN has an Internet connection, you can find out how to configure your workstation to use it.

Your computer becomes vulnerable after you connect to the Internet. This statement is especially true if you use a service, such as DSL, that is constantly connected. The difference is similar to living on a quiet street versus a busy one. You're more vulnerable on the busy street. That's why we show you in Chapter 8 how to build a firewall.

Chapter 5

Dial-Up Modems Still Get the Job Done

In This Chapter

- Finding an Internet Service Provider (ISP)
- Configuring your Internet connection
- Configuring your modem
- Connecting to your ISP

Surfing the Internet is lots of fun and sometimes a useful activity. Come on, admit it: You know you want to tie up your phone line for hours in order to annoy your family or roommates, browse sites with ridiculous addresses such as `www.theonion.com`, and chat chummily with people you would never dream of speaking to in person. The catch is that before you join the fray of the new online universe, you have to have access to the Internet.

This chapter describes how to use a modem to connect to an Internet Service Provider (or ISP) and create your bridge to the Internet. After you're hooked up to the Internet, you too can go to a party and drop this casual phrase: "I found this while surfing the Net this afternoon — on my Red Hat Linux system." People then know that you're really cool. And, if you've never been the life of the party, this statement certainly makes you more popular.

This chapter assumes that you're connecting to the Internet using a standard dial-up modem. We describe how to configure your Red Hat Linux computer to use faster connection technologies, referred to as *broadband connections,* in Chapter 6.

Many people have access to Internet-connected networks at work and school. (Or, maybe your 5-year-old has constructed an Internet-connected home network.) Chapter 7 describes how to connect your Red Hat Linux computer to an existing private network and gain access to the Internet through its connection. You can then surf at light speed until the cows come home.

Desperately Seeking an ISP

To get connected using a dial-up modem, you have to successfully hook up a modem to your computer and then find a good Internet Service Provider (ISP) to dial up to. Odds are that you have an internal modem that came installed with your computer. If you don't, you may want to consider upgrading. Check out *Upgrading & Fixing PCs For Dummies,* 6th Edition, by Andy Rathbone (Wiley Publishing, Inc.).

The best way to find a good ISP is by word of mouth. Getting personal recommendations is a good way to find out both the good and bad points of an ISP that you can't find from reading advertisements. Before you sign on with an ISP, make sure that the company supports Linux.

If you don't have any friends and your acquaintances don't speak to you, try finding a local Linux user group (LUG) to ask. You can look up LUGs at the Red Hat community Web page at `www.redhat.com/apps/community`.

Table 5-1 shows a sample of ISPs that support Linux.

Table 5-1 ISPs That Support Linux

ISP	*Toll-Free Phone Number (U.S. Only)*	*Web Address*
Access4Free	866-MyFreei/ 770-349-3430	`www.access4free.com`
AT&T WorldNet	800-967-5363	`www.att.net`
CompuServe	800-336-6823	`www.compuserve.com`
Earthlink	800-EARTHLINK	`www.earthlink.net`
Prism Access	888-930-1030	`www.prism.net`
SprintLink	800-473-7983	`www.sprint.net`
CompuGlobalMega HyperNet Network	867-555-5309	`www.compuglobalmegahyper.net`

Whichever one you want to use, make sure to ask your potential new ISP whether it offers a dial-up PPP service. PPP (which stands for *p*oint-to-*p*oint *p*rotocol) is what Linux uses to connect to the Internet. If the person you talk to gives you the verbal equivalent of a blank stare, you may have troubles. If you encounter some kind of a hitch, be forewarned. The ISP's tech staff probably can't walk you through the procedures. You're on your own.

If you're buying a modem

Dial-up modems are an old technology, but still the most common method for making personal or small-business Internet connections. This statement may not be true much longer because the number of users with broadband connections is rising fast, and most large businesses also use broadband services.

An *internal modem* plugs into a PCI or ISA slot on your computer's motherboard and receives power from the computer. An *external modem* comes in its own enclosure, requires its own power supply (those clunky, boxy plugs), and connects to the computer via a serial (RS232) connection. Both types of modems use your phone jack to connect to the Internet.

Internal modems are generally less expensive than external ones, but external modems have several advantages. You can easily turn them on and off, you can connect them to a computer without opening the computer case, and if your telephone line is struck by lightning, the charge passing through the modem doesn't damage your computer. On the other hand, internal modems need only a telephone line cable, whereas external modems require a telephone line, a serial connection, and power-supply cables.

A third type of serial line modem is a *PCMCIA card* (sometimes called a PC card). These cards are used most often with laptop computers. Most modern laptops come with internal modems already installed.

Now is a good time to verify that your own telephone service is billed at a flat rate and not metered; you should make sure that the dial-up number you use isn't a long-distance call either. If you have metered service or end up making a long-distance toll call, you run up huge phone bills while you're spending hours chatting about lone gunmen and reading about interdimensional space travelers.

After you choose your Internet Service Provider and arrange payment, the ISP provides certain pieces of information, including

- Telephone access numbers
- A username (usually the one you want)
- A password (usually the one you supply)
- An e-mail address typically, your username added to the ISP's domain name
- A primary *Domain Name Server (DNS)* number, which is a large number separated by periods into four groups of digits
- A secondary Domain Name Server (DNS) number, which is another large number separated by periods into four groups of digits
- An SMTP (mail) server name

- An NNTP (news) server name
- A POP3 or IMAP server name, used to download e-mail from the ISP's server to your machine

Access4Free provides a nice combination of free and subscription Internet service. After you register, you get your first 10 hours of service per month free. You're charged on an hourly basis up to $9.95 over 10 hours. You can also subscribe for unlimited dial-up access for $9.95 per month; subscribing gives you telephone support (866-693-7334) that costs $5 per call otherwise. (That's not bad either!) Access4Free also provides local dial-up and PPP access in many U.S. cities.

When you're shopping for a new modem, avoid WinModems like dot.com stock because these modems are designed for only Windows computers. They're cheaper than regular modems because they're lazy (or smart, depending on how you look at it) and depend on the Windows operating system to do much of their work for them. Linux drivers are only now beginning to appear for these types of modems. See the preceding sidebar, "If you're buying a modem," for more information about purchasing a modem for your Red Hat Linux computer.

Configuring Your Internet Connection

You need to configure your modem so that Red Hat Linux can use it to connect to your ISP. The Red Hat Dialup Configuration utility does a good job of detecting, and then configuring, your modem. It also sets up a dial-up account to connect your computer to your ISP and thus to the Internet.

Get started by following these steps:

1. **Click the GNOME Menu button and choose System Tools⇨Internet Configuration Wizard.**

   The GNOME Menu button is the icon that looks like a red fedora in the lower-left corner of your screen.

   If you're not logged in as root, you're prompted to enter the root password in the Input dialog box. Enter the root password.

2. **The Select Device Type window opens. You use this window to configure any type of communications device, such as a modem or network interface. Click the Modem connection option from the menu and then click the Forward button.**

   The Searching for Modems dialog box appears while the Dialup Configuration Tool scans your computer for modems; the window disappears quickly if it detects your modem. If no modem is found, a Warning window pops up informing you that no modem was found. Click the OK button.

3. **If no modem is detected, the Select Modem window appears, as shown in Figure 5-1. (The information displayed may differ on your computer.) Otherwise, if the modem is detected, skip to Step 5.**

   If the Internet Configuration Wizard doesn't find a modem, it guesses that a modem is attached to your first serial port: `/dev/ttyS0`.

   You can modify the modem settings, if you want, in the Select Modem window. (See the following sections "Locating Your Modem with Linux" and "Locating Your Modem with Windows" for instructions on how to get information about your modem.)

4. **Click Forward again.**

   The Select Provider window appears.

5. **Enter your phone number, the name of your Internet Service Provider (ISP), and your login name and password in the appropriate boxes in the Select Provider window.**

   You should also enter your ISP's prefix and area or country code, if necessary, in the appropriate text boxes.

6. **Click Forward when you're finished filling in the info.**

   The IP Settings dialog box opens, as shown in Figure 5-2, and allows you to further configure your dial-up connection.

   The default options are Automatically Obtain IP Address Settings and Automatically Obtain DNS Information from Provider.

   Using the default options permits your ISP to automatically assign an IP address and DNS server address to your computer every time you connect. You should nearly always be able to use these settings.

7. **Click the Forward button.**

   The Create Dialup Connection window appears, showing a summary of the information you just entered.

8. **Click Apply.**

   The Network Configuration window opens. You see your new modem and any other network device, such as an Ethernet interface, in the window.

9. **Choose the File⇨Save menu option to save your modem configuration.**

10. **Click the Activate button to connect to your ISP.**

    The Network Configuration tool dials up your ISP, authenticates with your ISP, and provides your computer with an Internet connection. Your IP address, default route, and DNS provider are automatically set by the

ISP (using the PPP protocol). Those numbers take precedence over any existing parameters, such as an Ethernet interface, as long as the dial-up connection is active. When you deactivate the connection, your existing (if any) IP address and default route are reset. Your previous DNS provider is reset only if you're using DHCP on your private network; otherwise, the dial-up DNS provider remains in effect. See the section in Chapter 7 about configuring DNS and an Ethernet or wireless interface.

You now have configured your modem to connect to the Internet. The following two sections help you if you have problems using the Internet Connection Wizard to configure your modem.

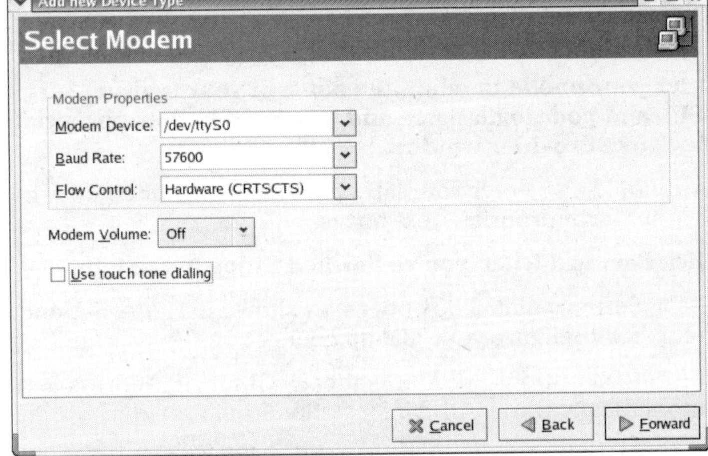

Figure 5-1: The Select Modem dialog box.

Figure 5-2: Configuring your dial-up IP settings.

Locating Your Modem with Linux

Linux uses device files to communicate with peripherals. Device files occupy the `/dev` directory and are somewhat equivalent to Windows drivers: You need them so that your hardware works.

Your modem can connect to one of four serial ports available on your PC. A *serial port* is the mechanism your computer uses to communicate with a device, such as a modem. An external modem is generally connected to port `/dev/ttyS0` or `/dev/ttyS1`, although configuring it as `/dev/ttyS2` or `/dev/ttyS3` is possible. If you have an internal modem, it can be any one of the `tty` devices.

During the boot process, Red Hat Linux provides the `kudzu` utility, which automatically tries to locate new devices on your system. The `kudzu` utility is good at detecting equipment like modems (both internal and external). When `kudzu` detects a new device, it prompts you to configure the device, and you should let it do so.

If the Linux hardware detection system `kudzu` cannot find your modem during the boot process, you have to do so manually. One manual method is the process of elimination; it's crude, but effective. The following two numbered lists describe how to find your modem. The first method, for an external modem, involves sending a string of characters to the modem and watching for the light-emitting diodes (LEDs) to light up. The second method is for internal modems, which don't have LEDs, so you have to use the hideous screeching sound of your modem to track it down.

To use `kudzu` to find an external modem, follow these steps:

1. **Open a terminal emulator window by the clicking GNOME Menu button and choosing System Tools⇨Terminal.**
2. **Run this command from a command prompt in the terminal:**

   ```
   echo "anything" > /dev/ttyS0
   ```

   Honestly, it doesn't matter what you put between the quotation marks in the preceding commands. It just has to be some text — *any* text.

   If your modem is connected to the target serial port, you see the send-receive LEDs (sometimes marked as RX/TX) light up in a short burst.
3. **In the unlikely situation that your modem isn't found, try sending the string to `/dev/ttyS1`, `/dev/ttyS2` and, finally, to `/dev/ttyS3` by altering the number at the end of the command in Step 1 to match the port you're targeting.**

Life is a bit harder if you have an internal modem because you don't have a visual response. You can, however, listen to the modem's speaker to find out what's going on. Follow these steps:

1. **Open a terminal emulator window by clicking the GNOME Menu button and choosing System Tools⇨Terminal.**
2. **Enter this command at a command prompt:**

   ```
   echo "atdt5555309" > /dev/ttyS0
   ```

   If you hear the modem pick up and dial, you have won the game of hide-and-seek and know which device the modem is connected to. You can then skip to Step 4.
3. **If you don't hear anything, make sure that you have the speaker turned on by entering the following command and then retry Step 1:**

   ```
   echo "atv" > /dev/ttyS0
   ```

   If you hear the modem pick up and dial, skip to Step 4.
4. **If you still can't hear anything, try using the other serial ports by trying again, substituting** `ttyS1`**,** `ttyS2`**, and** `ttyS3` **in the command.**
5. **After your modem is found, send this command to the modem to kill the connection:**

   ```
   echo "atz" > /dev/ttyS0
   ```

Locating Your Modem with Windows

If you're running a Windows 9*x*, Windows Me, Windows NT, or Windows 2000 computer, you can see which port your modem is connected to by following these steps:

1. **Send e-mail to Bill Gates and ask him for your configuration.**

   If he's tied up in court or is otherwise too busy to respond, see Step 2.
2. **Choose Start⇨Settings⇨Control Panel.**

   The Control Panel window appears.
3. **Double-click the Modem icon or the Phone and Modem Control icon in Windows NT or the Phone and Modem Options icon in Windows 2000 systems.**
4. **When the Phone and Modems Options window opens, click the Modem tab. Select your modem from the list that appears.**

5. **Click Properties.**

   The Modems Properties dialog box appears.

6. **Select the Diagnostics tab.**

   You see your modem listed with a COM line number beside it. That's the Windows designation for your modem's serial communications line. If the number 1 appears, it means that Windows knows it as COM1; if the number is a 2, it's on COM2; and so on. These number designations translate directly to the matching number of `ttyS0`, `ttyS1`, `ttyS2`, and `ttyS3` in Red Hat Linux.

If you're running Windows XP, follow these steps to see which port your modem is connected to instead:

1. **Click the Start button and then click the Control Panel icon.**

   The Control Panel appears.

2. **Double-click the System icon.**

   The System Properties window appears.

3. **Select the Hardware tab and click the Device Manager button.**

   The Device Manager appears.

4. **Click the little plus sign next to the Modems menu item.**

   Your modem should be listed under the Modems menu item.

Firing Up Your Internet Connection

Red Hat Linux provides the Red Hat PPP dialer utility to help you establish a PPP connection. You establish this connection by using the PPP configuration you set up with the Dialup Configuration Tool (which we describe earlier in this chapter, in the section "Configuring Your Internet Connection").

To connect to the Internet with the Red Hat PPP dialer, follow these steps:

1. **Log in to Linux as any user.**

2. **Click the GNOME Menu button and choose System Tools⇨Network Device Control.**

   The Network Device Control window appears, displaying all the network interfaces you have.

3. **Click the name of your modem (for example, Myconnection) and then click Activate.**

If you have an Ethernet network adapter, it shows up as `eth0` or `eth1`. You generally can ignore the Ethernet device because it probably doesn't interfere with your modem. However, if a network device appears to cause interference with your modem, you should deactivate it in the same way as you deactivate a modem. Step 4 describes how to deactivate a device.

The Network Device Control utility dials and connects to your ISP.

4. **When you're finished using the Internet, click the Deactivate button in the Network Device Control window.**

Your connection comes to an end.

The firewall Red Hat installs is quite good. However, we describe an even more secure firewall in Chapter 8.

Chapter 6

Broadband Rocks!

In This Chapter

- DSL and cable Internet connections
- Using cable connections
- Using DSL connections

You're probably familiar with the ubiquitous dial-up Internet connection: You log on to the Internet, hear that screeching modem sound and — presto! whammo! — you're online. If you're lucky, the entire dial-up process takes less than a minute, but it can take longer. And then there's the fact that Web pages take so-o-o lo-o-ong to build onscreen.

You have a better way to get online, called broadband. *Broadband* is a generic term for high-speed cable and digital subscriber line (DSL) connections. Cable connections are provided by cable television companies, and DSL by telephone companies. Both are much faster than dial-up connections, and both have their advantages and disadvantages.

The *broad* in broadband means that wires and cables that connect a modem to the Internet have a wide *bandwidth;* they can handle more data at faster speeds and with greater reliability. Plain old telephone service (POTS) was created for transferring analog voice data. Needless to say, POTS just doesn't do as well as broadband media when it comes to the Internet.

The two most popular broadband connections you can use to access the Internet are cable modems (which use your existing cable television lines to transfer data) and DSL (which use fancy-schmancy digital phone lines). Broadband connections work from roughly 500 kilobits per second (Kbps) to several million bits per second (Mbps). That's enough to transfer graphics-rich Web pages in a few seconds; it's also enough to listen to several audio streams or to watch a low-resolution video stream.

If you're ready to make the switch to a DSL or cable Internet connection, believe us when we tell you that you will never want to go back to a dial-up modem. This chapter describes how to obtain and configure a broadband connection.

We recommend avoiding ISDN, satellite, and mental-telepathy Internet connections. The old ISDN technology is rapidly being replaced by DSL. ISDN is also difficult to configure and isn't much faster than a dial-up modem connection. Satellite Internet connections are just now being introduced and suffer from problems, such as transmission delays *(latency)*, that wreak havoc with your communications. Some people say that mental telepathy works great, but we don't think that Intel makes a chip yet. Satellite systems may improve quickly, but until that happens, we recommend using a plain old dial-up modem or, if you can, a DSL or cable modem connection.

Introducing DSL and Cable Connections: The Proof Is in the Wiring

Although the telephone network system is now modern in many ways, its underpinnings haven't fundamentally changed since the early 20th century. The telephone network consists of pairs of copper wire that connect homes and businesses with a telephone company's central offices (CO). The phone company use switches in its COs to connect you to your destination when you make a call. The switches are designed to limit the range of frequencies — called *bandwidth* — that a phone call can use. The bandwidth is roughly 3,000 cycles per second (Hz), enough to recognize a voice but not much more. Those limits prevent today's analog modems from pushing more than approximately 56,000 bits per second, or 56 Kbps, through the telephone network. (That 56 Kbps speed varies, mostly downward, depending on the condition of the copper wires you're connected to.)

What does all this mean to you? Improve your modem and the wiring, and you get faster Internet access. Two of the most commonly used broadband alternatives are

- **Cable television (CATV):** Although CATV companies don't provide service to as many residences and businesses as the telephone companies do, their fiber and coaxial cable networks can carry much more bandwidth than telephone wires can. CATV networks don't have the 3- to 4-mile limits that DSL has. Typically, you can get Internet cable through your CATV company if the company offers it and if the company serves your neighborhood.

- **Digital subscriber lines (DSL):** Designed to skip the restrictions of the traditional telephone system by making an end run around the voice switches, DSL rewires your existing telephone setup. Your local telephone company can connect your computer to new equipment that provides more than ten times the speed a dial-up modem can.

  The main limitation of DSL is that traditional copper wire can carry a high-speed connection for only a few miles. Your telephone company can tell you whether it can provide you with service.

The Cable Modem Option

Cable companies have invested lots of capital (much more than telephone companies) to upgrade their networks in order to gain Internet market share. Their effort has paid off for you consumers, and many places in the United States now have access to high-speed Internet connections.

However, you have to consider some downsides:

- Unfortunately, not all cable companies have caught up with 21st century technology. Many companies may provide you with TV service, but not with Internet service.
- Many people don't live in an area served by cable TV. Internet cable is also not a good medium to provide services such as Web page hosting.
- Most cable companies require you to connect to their ISP. Many people like to use a different ISP because it provides better service. Using your own ISP also makes it easier to set up your computer (or network) to provide services going out to the Internet. Cable companies can't prevent you from using a different local ISP, but they don't charge you less — so you end up paying for two services, one of which you're not using.
- Few cable companies support Linux. You may get a connection, but you're on your own if you need to troubleshoot problems, even problems that have nothing to do with Red Hat Linux but affect your machine.

If you decide that cable access is the right choice for your Internet access needs, here's an overview of the process for connecting your Red Hat Linux computer to the Internet via a cable modem:

1. **Do some research and subscribe to an ICP service.**

   Locate an Internet cable provider (ICP) — usually, your existing cable TV company — and subscribe to its ICP service.

2. **Make a hardware commitment.**

   Obtain an Internet cable modem through your ICP. Many ICPs provide cable modems as part of their service. Otherwise, you can purchase the modem from the ICP or a consumer electronics store.

3. **Get registered.**

   Register the cable modem with your ICP. You do have to register your modem with your ICP. During the registration process, your computer is assigned a network address to connect to the ICP. Network addresses are called Internet Protocol (IP) addresses.

   You register your modem by giving your ICP the modem's Media Access Control (MAC) address. The ICP generates an IP address by using the MAC address as its reference. You don't need to do anything to your cable modem. The registration process is all done by your ICP, and your modem automatically is assigned an IP address. You're ready to use your Internet cable modem to connect to the Internet. Woo-hoo! Blazing speed is yours now!

4. **Set up the cable modem.**

   Cable modems have two connectors: a 75-ohm coaxial port and a twisted-pair (RJ-45) connector. (The coaxial connector is the same type that's used for cable TV. The RJ-45 connector looks like a large telephone plug.)

   - Connect a coaxial cable from the cable modem's coaxial port to the cable jack on your wall, just like you would a TV set.
   - Connect a network cable from the RJ-45 modem port to your Red Hat Linux computer. Normal network cables (referred to as Category 5 cables) don't work if they're connected directly from the modem to your computer. You need to use a *crossover* cable if you want to directly connect a computer to a cable modem. You can use normal Category 5 cables if you connect the cable modem and your computer to an Ethernet hub or switch.

5. **Set up your Internet protocols.**

   Configure your computer to use DHCP on the network interface that connects to the modem. Restart your computer's network interface, and you should be good to go.

The following sections take you through the process of finding a cable provider and setting up your access.

Finding an Internet cable provider

Finding an Internet cable provider (ICP) is as simple as calling your cable television company. Not all cable TV systems carry Internet traffic, but many do.

Locating a cable television company that provides broadband Internet connections is unfortunately quite easy. It's unfortunate because little competition exists within the cable industry. Federal law effectively restricts competition within municipalities and creates the environment for monopoly-like companies. The result, of course, is that prices remain higher than necessary. Oh, well, at least many cable companies are offering Internet connections.

Your ICP is your default Internet Service Provider (ISP). Most cable companies give you one or more e-mail addresses. However, cable companies don't generally provide login accounts, like other ISPs do.

Login accounts are used for launching applications and storing information. They aren't essential, but they're useful. However, nothing stops you from maintaining a regular ISP and using its login account. You then have a high-speed Internet connection you can use to log in to any account you have.

We don't run you through the process of signing up for cable Internet service; we think that the process is simple enough. A good portion of the sign-up process involves waiting on hold and listening to Muzak. One suggestion, though: Make sure that you have pertinent information about your system and that the cable company knows you're using Red Hat Linux 10.

Dealing with the hardware

One great thing about Internet cable is that you can buy the cable modems from your local electronics store or an Internet distributor. DSL equipment is less readily available. Cable modems are generally priced the same whether you purchase through your provider, the Internet, or a bricks-and-mortar store. (Cable companies sometimes run promotions where they return by rebate most, if not all, of the price of the modem.) But the convenience of running to a local store is great, especially if your cable modem breaks on a Saturday night and you just *have* to download the latest game patch.

Before you purchase a cable modem, make sure that you

- Ask whether you have to buy your modem through the cable provider. If not, you can shop around for the best price.
- Make sure that the modem you buy is compatible with your service provider. The cable industry is converging on using the Data Over Cable Service Interface Specification (DOCSIS) as its Internet hookup standard. DOCSIS modems are quite easy to configure, so keep your fingers crossed that your service provider uses them.

  If your provider doesn't use DOCSIS, you likely have to purchase your modem through your provider.

How cable modems work

Modern cable modems do more than just transmit network packets. They transmit data packets by modulating and demodulating electrical signals over the cable TV wires — thus, the name modem (*mo*dulate/*dem*odulate). Cable modems now use the industry standard Data Over Cable Service Interface Specification (DOCSIS) protocol to deliver electrical signals across the cable network. The electrical signal carries the actual bits and bytes that comprise the network packets. A good analogy is an AM-FM radio system. The DOCSIS–based electrical signals carry data packets just like radio waves transmit speech or music.

The instructions we provide later in this chapter are designed for DOCSIS modems.

Setting up your cable modem is usually a straightforward process. Modern DOCSIS cable modems act as network bridges. A *network bridge* simply rebroadcasts network packets in both directions — incoming and outgoing. One side of the bridge connects to the cable TV company. The other side connects to your computer through your Ethernet NIC through a Category 5 crossover cable; you can also connect through a network switch or hub (LAN). If your modem is the bridge type — we believe that the cable industry in the United States mostly uses that system — it doesn't require any configuration.

Setting up Internet protocols

You don't have to configure your cable modem for it to work. What you *do* need to do, however, is tell your Red Hat Linux computer how to connect to the modem. Cable modems typically connect to your computer via an Ethernet network interface. Therefore, you need to connect the cable modem to your computer using an Ethernet-based network.

You need to configure your Red Hat Linux computer's Ethernet adapter using the Dynamic Host Configuration Protocol (DHCP); you need an Ethernet adapter, of course, installed on your computer. Your cable modem sets the IP address of your Ethernet NIC by using DHCP. These instructions show how to do that:

1. **Log in to your computer.**
2. **Click the GNOME Menu button (the button in the lower-left corner of your screen that looks like a red fedora) and choose System Settings⇨Network.**

The Network menu pops up, prompting you to enter the root password if you're not logged in as the root user.

3. **Enter the root password if prompted, click OK, and create an Ethernet connection by clicking the New button.**

   The Select Device Type window opens.

4. **Select the Ethernet connection option and click the Forward button.**

   The Select Ethernet Device window opens, showing the Ethernet device (or devices) that the Network utility found.

5. **Click the Forward button.**

   The Configure Network Settings window opens, as shown in Figure 6-1. By default, the Automatically Obtain IP Address settings with DHCP option is selected; the Automatically Obtain DNS Information from Provider button is activated too. These are the settings you need to use with DOCIS cable modems. However, you can select a name for your computer.

6. **Pick a name for your computer and enter it in the Hostname (Optional) text box.**

   This step is optional, so you can skip it and go to Step 7, if you want.

7. **Click the Forward button.**

   The Create Ethernet Device window opens, showing a summary of your Ethernet interface's configuration.

8. **Click the Apply button and control returns to the original Network Configuration window.**

   The Network Configuration window shows your new Ethernet device. However, you still need to save your changes before exiting the configuration system.

9. **Choose File⇨Save and click the OK button.**

   Before you click OK, an Information window pops up, telling you that your changes have been saved and that you need to restart your network or computer to make them take effect.

   Control returns to the Network Configuration window.

10. **Click the Activate button and your new Ethernet NIC turns on.**

11. **Choose File⇨Quit to close the Network Configuration window.**

    You have created and saved the configuration necessary to use your cable modem. You have also activated that connection. You can start using your broadband Internet connection. Open Mozilla, for example, and start browsing at lightning speed.

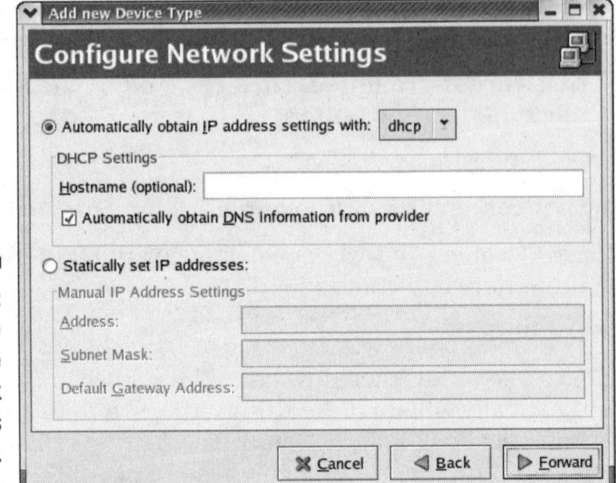

Figure 6-1: The Configure Network Settings window.

We strongly advise against leaving your Internet connection permanently active until you protect yourself with a firewall. Turn off your Internet connection — turn off the modem, for example. If you're not using the default firewall that comes with Red Hat Linux, of if you're looking for a more secure firewall, go to Chapter 8. After the firewall is working, you can restart your Internet connection and be reasonably safe from hackers.

The DSL Option

The world is wired — wired for telephones, that is. DSL modems take advantage of this old, but common, technology to provide a high-speed Internet connection to consumers. The DSL option uses special equipment to pump much more data through the POTS lines than a traditional analog modem does.

The telephone system is referred to as plain old telephone service (POTS) in the telecommunication industry.

DSL provides high-speed Internet connections by electronically converting your computer's digital information into a form that can be transmitted from your home or business to the telephone company. When your data finds its way to the telephone company, it's converted into another form and sent to your ISP.

DSL uses frequencies in the millions of cycles per second — the megahertz (MHz) range — compared to traditional analog modems, which work with signals in the thousands of cycles per second (KHz). You get much higher connection speeds when you use higher frequencies. The problem is, however, that the telephone system wasn't designed to work with higher frequencies.

Fortunately, the brainiacs of the world have figured out how to get high-speed DSL connections from old, slow POTS wiring. They have designed new digital signal processing chips to overcome the POTS architecture. The result is that if you live close enough — roughly three to four miles — to your DSL provider's equipment, you can use DSL to get connected to the Net.

Facing DSL configuration woes head-on

This section describes the basic DSL modem-configuration issues. We take the time to give you an overview because you can easily get confused if you concentrate on just the details. Please check out the following list and get familiar with it. Getting your DSL modem working is easier after you do so.

Most consumer DSL providers now use the asymmetrical DSL (ADSL) type of connection. The following list describes the process for getting an ADSL connection working. (Please note that we use the generic acronym DSL interchangeably with ADSL. Most consumer DSL connections are really ADSL, and that's the type of connection we describe in this chapter.) Follow these steps to set up DSL service:

1. **Find a DSL provider.**

   You need to find out whether you live or work close enough to the DSL provider's equipment to get a connection. DSL providers check your address and tell you whether they can take your business.

2. **Connect your DSL modem to your telephone jack and your computer.**

   Your DSL modem acts as the intermediary between your computer and your DSL service provider. You must connect one side to the phone jack and the other to your computer's Ethernet NIC.

3. **Configure your Red Hat Linux computer to communicate with the DSL modem.**

   Your Red Hat Linux computer connects to the DSL modem via an Ethernet NIC. You must configure your Ethernet NIC to work with the modem.

4. **Set up the DSL modem user and administrative passwords.**

   DSL modems provide a reasonable level of security. You should take advantage of this security by assigning your own password to the modem. That action prevents hackers from breaking into your modem and causing problems.

5. **Set up your ISP PPP account name and password.**

   You must authenticate your DSL modem to your ISP. DSL connections get logged on to your ISP just like traditional analog modems do. You configure your DSL modem with your ISP username and password.

6. **Configure the DSL modem's internal (private) network interface.**

   Your DSL modem must be able to communicate with a Red Hat Linux computer over an Ethernet connection. You must configure the DSL modem so that it uses the same network parameters as your computer.

7. **Configure the modem's network address translation (NAT) settings.**

   The Internet was designed to send — or *route* — information as quickly as possible to its destination. Internet Protocol (IP) addresses are used to designate where the information is coming from and where it's going. IP addresses can be routable or nonroutable. Nonroutable addresses can be reused; you can use the same nonroutable addresses that your neighbor uses without interfering with one another.

   NAT is used to convert nonroutable IP addresses into routable ones, which is useful when you're connecting your private network to the Internet by translating your internal IP addresses into one of your ISP's routable IP addresses. You need to configure your DSL modem to convert your computer's private (for example, `192.168.1.1`) and nonroutable address into an address assigned to your DSL connection by your ISP.

8. **Save the settings to nonvolatile memory and reboot.**

   You need to save your DSL modem's settings after you have them working. You don't want to enter the configuration every time you turn on your modem.

Finding a DSL provider

You must obtain both DSL and ISP services to make your broadband connection. Some companies — notably, the regional Bell telephone companies — can provide both services. However, in our case, we preferred our ISP to the ISP that was aligned with the DSL provider. We were fortunate enough to retain our existing ISP when we purchased our DSL service.

The DSL provider market is fluid. Analyze the DSL service providers in your area carefully before choosing one, and remember that longevity is as important as a low price. Regional Bells are more likely to provide long-term service than many of their competitors.

One advantage of DSL service is that you often don't have to sign a service contract; you can reasonably switch providers if you're not satisfied with the service.

Usually, you have to select an ISP after you choose a DSL provider. DSL providers either provide their own ISP or allow you to select from several independent ones (the DSL provider makes the arrangements and works directly with the third-party ISP).

The many faces of DSL

DSL comes in a variety of flavors. Most consumers end up using ADSL because it offers inexpensive Internet connections at reasonably high speeds. ADSL serves an individual computer user's Internet needs very well; it even provides a small business with adequate service. ADSL is, not surprisingly, the most available of all DSL flavors.

The other types are more suited for business use. Most locales probably have access to only two or three of these services. This list describes the DSL variations:

- **ADSL (Asymmetrical DSL):** The ADSL download *(downstream)* speed isn't the same as its upload *(upstream)* speed. (That's why it's asymmetrical.) The maximum ADSL speed is 8 Mbps, but it's usually limited to less because of the POTS infrastructure limitations.
- **G.Lite:** Also known as Universal DSL or splitterless ADSL, G.Lite is a low-speed version of ADSL that doesn't require filtering out the POTS signal. It provides as much as 1.5 Mbps downstream and 512 Kbps upstream.
- **HDSL (high bit-rate DSL):** HDSL is a symmetrical protocol with equal upstream and downstream speeds. You can use HDSL as a substitute for T1 connections because it provides the same data rates of 1.544 Mbps.
- **HDSL2 (high bit-rate DSL 2):** HDSL2 provides the same specifications as HDSL but works over a single twisted-pair connection.
- **IDSL (ISDN Digital Subscriber Loop):** IDSL, the successor to the current ISDN technology, uses the same line encoding (2B1Q) as ISDN and SDSL. IDSL is used mostly to provide DSL service in areas where the more popular forms, such as ADSL and SDSL, aren't available. IDSL is capable of providing upstream and downstream rates of 144 Kbps.
- **SDSL (Single-line DSL):** SDSL is commonly called *Symmetric DSL* because SDSL upstream and downstream speeds are the same.
- **VDSL (Very high bit rate DSL):** VDSL provides as much as 50 Mbps over distances up to 1,500 meters on short loops. VDSL is particularly useful for campus environments — universities and business parks. VDSL is now being introduced in market trials to deliver video services over existing phone lines. You can also configure VDSL in symmetric mode.
- **xDSL:** xDSL is a generic term for all the DSL flavors.

Connecting your Cisco modem to your Red Hat Linux computer

Writing explicit configuration examples is always difficult and liable to leave some readers disappointed. But the DSL world is still young, and we're not convinced that any standards have emerged. Therefore, we think that it's better to provide the following instructions rather than none. (Chances are that many of you use the same DSL modems, and we hope that our instructions match your equipment.)

This section shows you how to use one of the more common DSL modems. Qwest, which is a "baby Bell" and one of the larger DSL providers, uses this equipment. Our Cisco 675 or 678 DSL modem-router is the Qwest-recommended equipment. Cisco is one the largest network equipment suppliers in the world, and many people use its DSL modems.

Even if you're using different equipment, our instructions should still be useful in outlining the general process of configuring a DSL connection. The process goes like this:

1. Connect your Red Hat Linux computer to the modem so you can configure it.
2. Start Mozilla and open the modem's IP address. DSL modems typically use public addresses by default, such as `192.168.1.1`.
3. Set the modem's passwords.
4. Tell the modem how to connect to your DSL provider.
5. Set up the modem's firewall and NAT configuration, if it's available.
6. Save the configuration.

The details of how to accomplish each step vary between manufacturers, but the idea is still the same. Consult your modem's user guide for detailed configuration information.

Chapter 7

Connect Locally, Communicate Globally: Connecting to a LAN

In This Chapter

- Networking with an Ethernet or wireless NIC
- Using the Red Hat Network Utility
- Starting and stopping your local network connection

This chapter shows how to connect your Red Hat Linux computer to an existing Local Area Network (LAN), also referred to as a *private network.* It's different from connecting directly to the Internet with a dial-up modem or broadband connection, as we describe in Chapters 5 and 6; those chapters show how to connect a single, stand-alone Red Hat Linux computer directly to the Internet. In this case, you connect your Red Hat Linux computer to a LAN.

You may be building your Red Hat Linux computer to use at home, work, or school. It doesn't matter what the venue is — you can use the information in this chapter to connect your computer to any existing LAN. Note that your computer has access to the Internet if that LAN is connected to it.

Don't get discouraged if you don't have access to a LAN. You can make your own! Chapter 15 describes how to put one together.

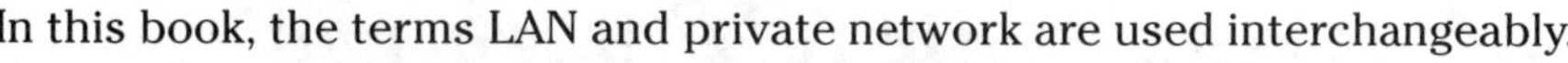

In this book, the terms LAN and private network are used interchangeably.

If you configured your Ethernet card to connect to your LAN during the installation process we describe in Chapter 3, that's great! You can skip this chapter or just browse through it for fun. Otherwise, you can use this chapter to connect your computer to a LAN.

Although forming a private network isn't exactly rocket science, a detailed description of how to network two or more computers is beyond the scope of this book because so many network configurations are possible. Many good books are available that explain how to do that, and the best place to start is at the Wiley Web site: `www.wiley.com`.

Introducing Local Area Networks

The invention of Linux revolutionized computer networking. Creating a LAN before Linux existed was complicated and expensive. LANs were the nearly exclusive domain of big corporations, universities, and other monstrous organizations.

But the TCP/IP networking protocols were built into Linux from the beginning. In the mid-1990s, if you could afford a couple of PCs, a cheap piece of coaxial cable, and a few 10 Mbps (megabits per second) or faster Ethernet adapters, a LAN was born. Ethernet adapters, also commonly known as *network interface cards* (NICs), cost about $150 at the time. Prices, fortunately, have crashed since then, falling to earth like Ziggy Stardust: A 100 Mbps NIC now costs as little as $15, and you can buy an 11 Mbps wireless NIC for less than $100.

To get your Red Hat computer on a network, you have to configure only a handful of networking subsystems. Here are the tasks that need to be performed in order for your networking to work:

- Load your wireless or Ethernet NIC kernel module. Red Hat Linux generally detects your hardware and loads the correct kernel modules.
- Configure your network interface card (NIC).
- Configure your domain name service (DNS), which converts Internet names into Internet Protocol (IP) addresses.

Wireless networking suffers from some security vulnerabilities. Consult the "Wireless network warning" sidebar, later in this chapter.

Performing these steps is pretty heavy lifting. The load is eased considerably by using the graphical Network Configuration Utility system administration tool provided by Red Hat. Have fun!

Configuring Your NIC with the Red Hat Network Utility

To use your Red Hat Linux computer with an existing Local Area Network (LAN), you need a wireless or Ethernet NIC installed on your computer and a network hub, or switch, to which to connect the NIC. After you set up the hardware, you need to configure your Red Hat Linux network settings.

If your LAN also has an Internet connection, you can set up that connection too. Although a high-speed Internet connection is best, in terms of the network configuration the type of connection doesn't matter.

IEEE and wireless networks

The dominant wireless standard is based on the IEEE 802-11b (and the older 802-11a and the about-to-be-released 802-11g) standard; 802-11b is also referred to as *Wi-Fi* (which is short for the wireless industry's trade term *wi*reless *fi*delity). If you hear people talking about a Wi-Fi NIC, they're just talking about wireless NICs.

IEEE (pronounced "eye-triple-e"), or Institute of Electrical and Electronic Engineers, is a worldwide professional society of nerds. (Is it necessary to use words like nerds or geeks to convey some technical meaning?) The IEEE, the "triclops" of wireless networking, concerns itself with issues such as which frequency wireless networking devices should use. Fortunately, this group has devised this wonderful standard that now enables everyone who's interested to communicate without stringing wires between machines.

Preparing to configure your wireless NIC

Before you can configure your wireless NIC, you need to figure out two things:

- Which type of wireless NIC you have (or need)
- How your wireless NIC should connect to your network

Two main types of wireless electronics (or *chip sets*) are now in use: Wavelan, built by Lucent Technologies, and Prism2, designed by Intersil. Both types are supported by Red Hat. The following list shows the manufacturers of each type. You can use the list to help figure out what kind of chip set your device uses:

- **Wavelan:** Orinoco, Apple Airport Enterasys RoamAbout 802, Elsa AirLancer 11, and Melco/Buffalo 802.11b.
- **Prism2:** D-Link DWL-650, LinkSys, Netgear, WPC11, and Compaq WL110. Other, less popular models include Addtron AWP-100, Bromax Freeport, GemTek WL-211, Intalk/Nokia, SMC 2632W, YDI, Z-COM X1300, and Zoom Telephonics ZoomAir 4100.

You need to figure out how your wireless NIC (or network adapter) should connect to your network. Wireless NICs can connect to a LAN in two ways:

- **Adapter-to-adapter:** This type, referred to as an *ad hoc* connection, is useful if you have two or more computers that you want to talk and form their own, exclusive private network.

- **Adapter-to-wireless hub:** This type, called *infrastructure,* provides a single entrance (an access point) into a LAN. An *access point* allows one or more computers to be connected to a network. However, unlike an ad hoc network, the individual computers can connect to any access point that allows them to.

The wireless-configuration instructions we provide work with either the infrastructure or ad hoc connection methods. Your wireless NIC can connect to either the access point or other computers (Linux and Windows) as long as you correctly configure your Network ID (ESSID) and encryption key.

Choosing between ad hoc and infrastructure

Using ad-hoc mode provides three advantages:

- **Lower costs:** You don't have to purchase an access point; an access point starts at around $50. Computers using wireless NICs running in ad-hoc mode communicate directly with each other, eliminating the need for a common access point.
- **Simpler configuration for Linux users:** Older access point devices could be configured using only Windows-based software — the simple network management protocol (SNMP), to be exact. You had to physically connect a Windows computer to the access point via a wired Ethernet network and then use the software supplied with the device. That was difficult if you didn't have any Windows-based computers. Newer access points tend to use HTML-based configuration systems, so you can use Mozilla to configure these newer devices.
- **No need to configure any access point:** You need to configure only the wireless NIC in each computer on your network. You can use the Red Hat Network Configuration Utility to configure a wireless NIC, which simplifies the process. Each NIC must have the same Network ID and encryption key.

Ad hoc networks can also provide a bit more security because they connect to other networks — and the Internet — through a network router. Access points work as network bridges. Routers examine IP addresses and then decide where to direct network traffic from one network to another. Bridges automatically pass on all traffic. Ad hoc networks can be configured to more tightly — but not completely — control network traffic than access-point-based networks. You can configure ad hoc networks with a firewall more easily than a network using an access point. (Many of the current crop of access points now provide NAT and firewall support, however; using NAT effectively creates a firewall.)

Wireless network warning

Wi-Fi, the standard for wireless technology, uses an encryption system named *wireless equivalent privacy (WEP)* to provide security. WEP encrypts communication between wireless devices to prevent someone with the right equipment from listening to and using your wireless network. But WEP is flawed and can be broken using tools available on the Internet (that's a big surprise). If a hacker breaks in to your Wi-Fi network, he can read your communications. But your problems don't end there. Hackers can use your wireless network to connect to both your private network and the Internet; you give the bad guys a free lunch and a launch pad to the Internet.

On the other hand, wireless networking is so useful that many people make accommodations for the risk. The logic? If you assume that your wireless network has already been hacked, you don't have to worry about *when* it might be hacked in the future.

You should use OpenSSH, Secure Sockets Layer (SSL), and virtual private networks (VPN) — all bundled with Red Hat Linux — to conduct all your internal and external communication. Keep in mind that using SSH, SSL, and VPN protects your information, but doesn't prevent someone from connecting to your network. The next generation of Wi-Fi, 802.11g, is supposed to fix the WEP weakness. Until the WEP problems are solved, be aware of the risks.

Configuring your Ethernet or wireless NIC

To get your Red Hat Linux computer working on a LAN, you must first configure its network interface card, or NIC. The *NIC* is the device that electronically connects your computer to your LAN. To work with the other computers on your network, your Ethernet or wireless adapter must be given a network address and a few other pieces of information.

We have divided the configuration instructions between Ethernet and wireless (or Wi-Fi) NICs. The instructions start by explaining how to start the Red Hat Network Configuration Utility. We then devote a subsection apiece to describing the particulars of configuring Ethernet and wireless devices. After we cover the device specifics, we discuss general configuration issues. The overall configuration process is outlined in these steps:

1. Start the Network Configuration Utility.
2. Configure your Ethernet or wireless device.
3. Configure your computer's host name.
4. Configure your computer's domain name service.
5. Restart your network.

Starting the Network Configuration Utility

Follow these steps to start the Network Configuration Utility:

1. **Click the GNOME Main Menu button and choose System Settings⇨Network.**

   Alternatively, you can click the GNOME Menu button and choose System Tools⇨Network Device Control. When the Network Device Control window opens, select the Ethernet or wireless device and click the Configure button. The Network Configuration Utility starts.

2. **Enter the root password if you're prompted to do so.**

   Figure 7-1 shows the initial configuration window. A NIC may or may not be displayed in the window. The NIC is displayed only if you configured your networking during the Red Hat installation.

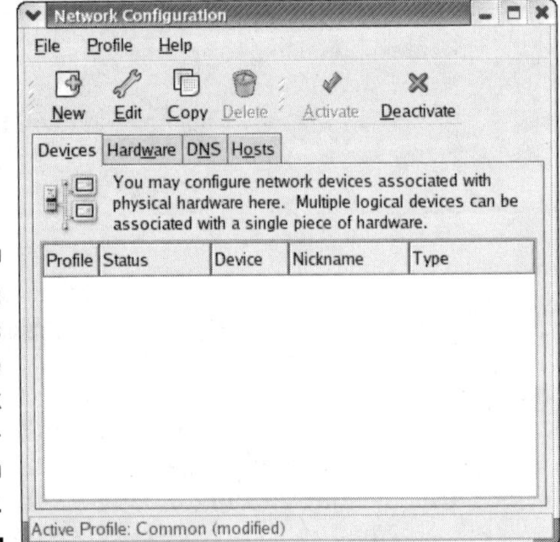

Figure 7-1: The Devices tab in the Network Configuration window.

3. **Click the New button if no NIC is displayed on the Devices tab or if you want to configure an additional one.**

   Otherwise, skip to Step 3 in the following section when you're working with an Ethernet device; skip to Step 1 in the section "Configuring a wireless NIC," later in this chapter, if you're working with a Wi-Fi NIC.

   The Select Device Type window appears.

4. **Select the appropriate type from the list of devices and then click the Forward button.**

   For example, select Ethernet if you're using that type of interface. If you're using a Wi-Fi (also referred to as wireless or IEEE 802.11b) device, select Wireless Connection.

What you do next depends on whether you're configuring an Ethernet or a wireless NIC. The following two sections are devoted to Ethernet and wireless NICs, respectively.

Configuring an Ethernet NIC

If you're using an Ethernet NIC, follow the steps in this section to configure its parameters (if you're using a wireless NIC, go to the following section):

1. **Follow the steps in the section "Starting the Network Configuration Utility," earlier in this chapter.**

   When you choose Ethernet from the drop-down list in Step 4 on the preceding list, the Select Ethernet Device window appears.

2. **Select the appropriate Ethernet device and click the Forward button.**

   The Network Configuration utility detects all Ethernet devices attached to your computer. Most PCs have only one Ethernet device, so you don't have to make a decision about which one to select.

   The Configure Network Settings window opens as shown later in this section, in Figure 7-2.

3. **Configure your TCP/IP address settings.**

   The Red Hat Network Configuration Utility selects DHCP (Dynamic Host Configuration Protocol) as the default method for determining your machine's IP address. (DHCP dynamically assigns an IP address and other parameters to your Ethernet NIC, and you're finished configuring your NIC.) If you're connecting to a network that provides DHCP service, type your computer name in the Hostname (optional) field (for example, **Cancun**), click the Forward button, and go to Step 9.

   If your network doesn't use DHCP, you need to manually configure your IP address. Proceed to Step 4.

4. **Click the Statically Set IP Addresses radio button.**

   You should ask your friendly local system administrator (unless you're the administrator, in which case you may want to avoid talking to yourself) which system your network uses.

   Life is a bit more complicated if you have both a wireless and an Ethernet NIC on your computer. You can run both devices at one time, but the configuration is more difficult. You can solve the problem by clicking the Automatically Obtain IP Address Settings With radio button so that the dot disappears. This simple mouse click prevents the Ethernet NIC from starting automatically.

5. **Assign an IP address to your computer by typing it in the Address text box.**

IP addresses are analogous to street addresses: They provide a number that uniquely distinguishes your machine from all others. Private IP addresses don't require any registration with the powers that be — the InterNIC organization that distributes IP addresses. Public IP addresses aren't routed on the Internet and can be used on LANs for your own use.

If you're on a network with registered IP addresses, be sure to get an IP address from your system administrator. Otherwise, go ahead and use a private IP address. (Use any Class C address between `192.168.1.1` and `192.168.254.254`; for example, `192.168.1.20` or `192.168.32.5`.) Private IP addresses in this range are designated for use by private networks. By design, private IP addresses don't get *routed* (sent from one machine to another) through the Internet, and anyone can use them. Private IP addresses would wreak havoc on the Internet if they were routed.

6. **Type** 255.255.255.0 **or the netmask for your IP address in the Subnet Mask text box.**

The Internet Protocol (IP) defines only three network address classes: A, B, and C. Only Class C addresses are assigned by InterNIC. Use the `255.255.255.0` netmask for Class C networks, `255.255.0.0` for Class B, and `255.0.0.0` for Class A.

Class C netmasks are used almost universally now, and we use only Class C addresses here. If you're not using a Class C address, you're probably experienced in the ways of TCP/IP and know which netmask to use. Godspeed. Otherwise, don't fool with Mother Nature: Use a Class C address.

7. **In the Default Gateway Address text box, type the IP address of the Internet gateway for your LAN.**

The Internet gateway is the device (router or computer) that connects your network to your ISP and the Internet. Obtain the address from your system administrator if you're at work and have one. If you're a home user, a typical convention is to assign the highest address — 254 — of a Class C subnetwork as the gateway. For example, type **192.168.1.254**.

Your TCP/IP Settings should look similar to the dialog box shown in Figure 7-2.

8. **Click the Forward button.**

The Create Ethernet Device dialog box opens, indicating that you have finished the configuration process. The dialog box shows a summary of the information you entered in the preceding steps.

9. **Review the summary and click the Apply button.**

You return to the Network Configuration window that now displays the newly configured Ethernet NIC.

Figure 7-2: Entering your static (non-DHCP) IP address settings.

10. **Save the new configuration by choosing File➪Save.**

    A dialog box opens, informing you that your changes have been saved. Click the OK button to continue.

11. **Start the NIC by clicking the Activate button.**

    This step completes your Ethernet NIC configuration.

Your Ethernet NIC is now active. But you still need to configure your domain name service (DNS) if you aren't using DHCP. Proceed to the section "Configuring DNS service," a little later in this chapter.

Kernel modules are the Linux equivalent to Microsoft Windows device drivers. Usually, Red Hat Linux can detect your Ethernet adapter and automatically load the correct module. However, if Red Hat Linux can't find your Ethernet adapter, you probably can't find the correct one on the supplied list. You can still go ahead and try; there's no harm in that.

Configuring a wireless NIC

This section describes how to configure the parameters for a wireless NIC, also called a Wi-Fi NIC. (Skip this section if you don't have a wireless NIC.)

The following steps describe how to configure your wireless device:

1. **Follow the steps in the section "Starting the Network Configuration Utility," earlier in this chapter.**

   When you choose Wireless from the drop-down list in Step 4 on the earlier list, the Select Wireless Device window appears.

2. **Select the appropriate wireless device.**
3. **Click the Forward button.**

   The Configure Wireless Connection window opens, as shown in Figure 7-3.

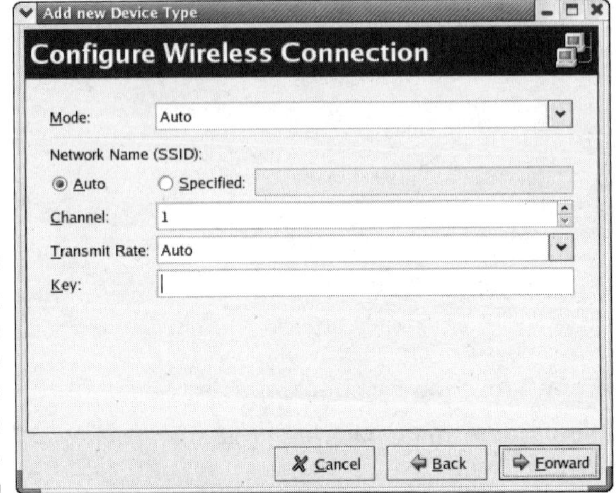

Figure 7-3: The Configure Wireless Connection dialog box.

4. **Select either Managed or Ad-Hoc from the Mode drop-down list.**

   You use Managed mode when you're using an access point. Use ad-hoc mode if you configured a wireless network without an access point.

5. **Type** ANY **in the ESSID (Network ID) text box if you use an access point. Type the specific ESSID name for an ad hoc network.**

   All machines connected to an ad hoc wireless network must share the same ESSID. For example, you may choose the string `mynetwork` as your ESSID. In that case, you must enter **mynetwork** as the ESSID for all machines connected to your ad hoc network.

6. **Enter the encryption key in the Key text box and then click the Forward button.**

   You should obtain the encryption key from your network administrator. If you have set up your own wireless home network, you can generate the key yourself. An *encryption key,* similar to a password, protects your wireless network from casual eavesdropping. Enter in the text box a key that's 13 characters or fewer — for example, **this_is_a_password**; using all 13 characters maximizes the encryption key's effectiveness.

Encryption keys are 40- or 128-bit binary numbers. They can be represented as text strings, as described in Step 6, or as a string of hexadecimal — hex — numbers. Hex numbers are commonly used in computer science to represent binary numbers. For your purposes, it's sufficient to know that a hex number is represented by 16 characters: 0 through 9 and A through F. For example, hex 0 is represented as decimal 0; hex 3, as decimal 3; and hex 9, as decimal 9. But decimal 10 is hex A, and the decimal 16 hexadecimal value is F. The hexadecimal value of this sample key:

```
-- this_is_a_password --
```

is

```
746869735F69735F615F6B6579
```

You can enter the hex value in the Key field by prepending the string *0x* to the key. In the example, you enter this line:

0x746869735F69735F615F6B6579

After you enter your encryption key and click the Forward button, the Configure Network Settings window opens. The processes of assigning a host name, IP address, netmask, and gateway to your computer are the same as for an Ethernet interface. Consult Steps 3 through 9 in the preceding section for instructions on how to configure your wireless NIC TCP/IP parameters.

Your wireless NIC configuration is complete. You still need to configure your domain name service (DNS) if you aren't using DHCP. Proceed to the following section if that's the case.

Configuring DNS service

You need to configure your computer to use from one to three DNS servers. You can use your LAN's DNS servers, if they're available. You can also use external DNS servers whether or not any exist on your LAN. To configure your Red Hat Linux computer to use DNS, follow these steps:

1. **Click the DNS tab in the Network Configuration dialog box, which is where you leave off in the preceding list of steps.**
2. **Type the host name of your computer in the Hostname text box.**

   The host name is any name (for example, Cancun) that you want to use.

   If you're connecting to a network controlled by someone else (for example, at work), check with the system administrator before selecting a host name.

3. **Type the IP address of your DNS server in the Primary DNS text box.**

   If your LAN provides a DNS server, you can use it as your primary name server (DNS).

4. **If you have one, type the IP address of your secondary name server in the Secondary DNS text box.**

   Most ISPs provide a backup DNS server address. If your LAN has its own DNS server, you can specify your ISP server as your secondary DNS server, if you want.

5. **Type the domain name of your network in the DNS Search Path text box.**

   Figure 7-4 shows a sample DNS configuration screen.

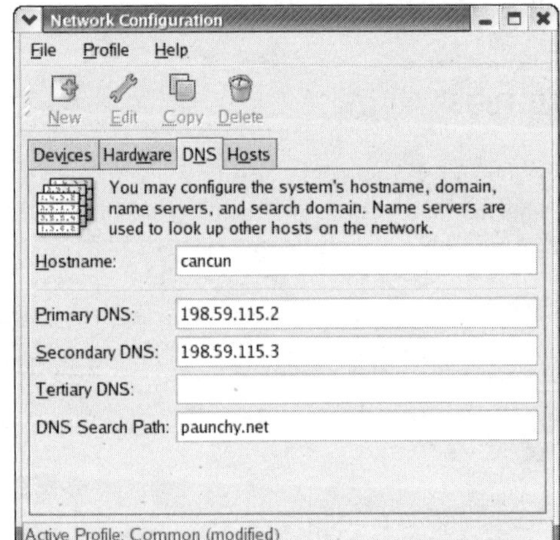

Figure 7-4: A sample DNS configuration.

   A *domain name* is a 2-part name separated by a period. For example, `paunchy.net` is a domain name, which is the domain name of the sample LAN used in this book. You should replace the `paunchy.net` domain name, of course, with the name of your LAN.

6. **Choose File⇨Quit.**

   The Network Configuration Utility closes. Your settings are saved and are activated the next time you reboot your computer. Proceed to the following section to activate your settings immediately.

Manually Starting and Stopping Your Network

Sometimes, the Network Configuration Utility configures your network stuff but cannot activate it. Why does that happen? Who knows? It may be because the Network Configuration Utility is still relatively young and should become better with age. In the meantime, you can start your networking systems another way, by following these steps:

1. **Click the GNOME Menu button, choose System Settings⇨Server Settings⇨Services, and then enter your root password, if you're prompted.**

   The Service Configuration Utility appears. Scroll down until you find the Network option.

2. **Select the Network option and then click the Restart button.**

   The Information window opens and confirms that your network has been restarted. Your new network settings take effect.

3. **If you're using a wireless NIC that doesn't communicate, you may have to restart your PCMCIA system. Here's how:**

   a. Locate and click the PCMCIA service in the Service Configuration Utility.

   b. Click the Restart button.

   c. Repeat Step 3 to restart your network.

All networking is stopped and then started again.

Alternatively, you can log in as root in a terminal emulator and run this command: `/etc/init.d/network restart`. (Or to stop your network, run `/etc/init.d/network stop`.)

Chapter 8

Only You Can Prevent Network Break-Ins

In This Chapter

- Introducing firewalls
- Using the Iptables firewall system
- Designing and viewing your filtering rules
- Automatically starting your firewall

After connecting to the Internet, you run the very real risk that bad guys will try to break into or otherwise harm your computer. The bad guys wear black hats, just like in the movies (as opposed to red hats, which are a bit odd but still good). You may also have heard them called hackers, crackers, the Joker, and whatever. Whatever their names and whatever their intentions, the Internet is getting more dangerous every day, so ya gotta protect yourself.

A *firewall* is a device that enables you to use the Internet while minimizing the possibility that the Internet will use you. Firewalls basically allow your network communications to go out but minimize the possibility of anyone making unwanted connections to your computer or private network.

This chapter describes, not surprisingly, how to build a firewall to help protect your Red Hat Linux computer from the bad guys. First, in case you doubt that you truly need a firewall, we explain why firewalls are important. Then we introduce you to Iptables, the Linux firewall system, and describe how to set up your firewall-filtering rules. After you set up your firewall filters, you need to know how to run the firewall automatically. You do that by setting up a script — something else we explain in this chapter. And, of course, what good would your firewall be if it didn't work? So, we show you how to do a simple test to make sure that your firewall is burning brightly.

The firewall described in this chapter is designed to protect a single Red Hat Linux computer that's connected to the Internet. The firewall isn't designed to protect an entire network. Chapter 15 describes how to modify this firewall to protect your private network.

Understanding Why You Need a Firewall in the First Place

You may think that there's safety in numbers. After all, literally millions of people, businesses, and organizations are connected to each other at any given time through networks and the Internet. What do you, an individual with a simple computer and possibly a small network connected to the Internet have to be concerned about? The bad guys are usually interested in big money or big publicity, right?

Well, that's mostly true, and chances are that you may never get hacked. If you subscribe to that world view, you're — in technical jargon — relying on security by obscurity.

Many hackers use tools that automatically scan and attack entire networks. The happy hacker doesn't have to work hard to search large numbers of networks to find and exploit unprotected computers. Don't risk needlessly getting *owned* — when your computer gets broken into and controlled — by a hacker, especially when Linux provides effective tools for protecting yourself.

Using a firewall is one simple but quite effective method for protecting yourself when you connect to the Internet. A firewall allows you to connect to the Internet while blocking unnecessary and unwanted connections from coming in.

Firewalls provide good bang-for-the-buck protection. However, they're not the only security measure you should take. For example, locking your doors certainly helps to protect against burglars but is not 100 percent effective — they can still break through a window. You best bet comes from using layers of security, such as locking your windows, using alarms, and keeping tabs on neighborhood activities. The idea is to have each layer reinforce the others. Chapter 17 describes how to add security layers to your computer.

Building an Effective Firewall

Linux comes bundled with a simple but extremely effective firewall system named Netfilter/Iptables. The Netfilter part refers to the firewall system that's built into the Linux operating system — the kernel, to be exact — and Iptables is the interface that controls it. We refer to the overall system as Iptables because that is the part that you work with.

Designing filtering rules: Permissive and restrictive methods

Firewall-filtering rules are like the bricks (or asbestos, if you prefer) that build your firewall. Basically, filtering rules determine what network communication can go out of and come into your computer.

When designing firewall-filtering rules, you can choose between two philosophies:

- Allow all connections by default and then deny specific access.
- Deny all connections by default and then allow specific access.

Allowing all connections takes the view that you should start by allowing all communication with your computer and then denying connections one by one. (This method is used by the Red Hat firewall, which you create during the installation process.) The danger with this method is that you unintentionally allow dangerous traffic to reach your machine. The alternative method is to start by denying *all* communication and then selectively allowing certain traffic. This more restrictive method is, from a security standpoint, the best way to create a firewall because you know exactly what access you're allowing. However, the restrictive method can also create problems because you may unintentionally prevent needed or wanted network traffic from reaching your computer.

We explain in this chapter how to use the restrictive method, for several reasons:

- **It's the safest method.** The restrictive method is safer because it minimizes all external contact with your Internet-connected computer. For example, it minimizes the information about your firewall that port scanning and other tricks can provide to hackers.
- **It's easier to configure.** Because Iptables provides stateful filtering, you have to configure only two rules to create a safe firewall. However, you have to configure numerous individual rules when using the permissive model. Extra, unnecessary complexity reduces security.

The Iptables system filters IP packets, which are the backbone of the Internet (IP stands for Internet Protocol, in fact). When you're connected to the Internet, all the information (graphics and text) that you send and receive is sent in the form of IP packets. All the information that enters and leaves your computer via the Internet is packaged in the form of IP packets. You can use Iptables to accept or deny IP packets based on their destinations, source addresses, and ports.

The Iptables system is effective because it uses *stateful filtering,* which means that the firewall can keep track of the state of each network connection. It's a technical way of saying that Iptables knows which IP packages are valid and which are not. For example, if you're browsing `www.dummies.com`, Iptables keeps track of all packets that belong to that connection. The Iptables utility can deny packets that are trying to reach your computer but don't belong to your connection, thus preventing any hackers from sneaking packets through your firewall.

Red Hat Linux installs an Iptables-based firewall by default. The installation system configures a medium level of protection during the installation process. You may recall from Chapter 3 that we advise you to use the default firewall configuration. However, the default firewall isn't as secure as we would prefer for connecting to the Internet. Therefore, we describe in this chapter how to construct a more comprehensive and secure firewall.

The concept of ports is an essential part of the Internet Protocol. *Ports* are used to organize the communication between clients and servers. For example, when you click a Web page, your browser communicates with the web server by using a port. That's a gross simplification, of course, but it describes the basic idea. Suffice it to say that ports are used to control the internal workings of the Internet for such tasks as Web browsing.

Setting Up a Firewall

So you know that you need a firewall and want to create one. What's next? The following sections explain how to set up an Iptables-based firewall by using the restrictive model. This section describes how to manually create the firewall-filtering rules. When you're done setting up your rules, see the section "Saving your filtering rules to a script," later in this chapter, so that you don't have to enter these rules every time you turn on your computer.

In this section, you design an Iptables-based firewall that turns off all incoming connections on your modem and still enables you to establish an outgoing connection to the Internet. You then back off the total restriction of incoming communication to allow incoming Secure Shell connection. (Secure Shell provides encrypted communications.)

Don't execute these instructions from a remote connection! You must run these commands from your computer's console. That is, you must be sitting at your computer and not be working on it over a network connection. The reason is that these firewall rules shut off external network connections before restoring them.

These instructions describe how to build your firewall, brick by brick:

1. **Log in to your computer as root and then open a GNOME Terminal window, by right-clicking any empty portion of the desktop and choosing New Terminal from the menu.**
2. **Make sure that you're not already running a firewall, by entering these rules at the command prompt in the terminal window:**

```
iptables --flush
iptables --flush -t nat
```

The `iptables` entries remove any existing filtering or Network Address Translation (NAT) rules. *NAT rules* masquerade your network address as another address, making your computer appear to be used by someone else. NAT is frequently used to make your computer appear to be coming from your ISP so that you don't have to register your computer for an official Internet Protocol (IP) address.

3. **Filter out all network communication to, from, and through your computer by entering these rules:**

```
iptables --policy INPUT   DROP
iptables --policy OUTPUT  DROP
iptables --policy FORWARD DROP
```

These commands set the default policy of your firewall to not allow any network traffic into (the INPUT rule) or out of (the OUTPUT rule) any network interface; nor is any traffic allowed to pass between multiple network interfaces (the FORWARD rule) if you have them. At this point, you have an extremely safe firewall. However, your computer is useless in terms of using it for any network-related tasks. The next step opens the firewall a little bit so that you can access the Internet (or any network you're attached to) in a safe way.

4. **Enter these rules to allow network traffic to pass through the loopback device:**

```
iptables -A OUTPUT -j ACCEPT -o lo
iptables -A INPUT -j ACCEPT -i lo
```

Linux computers use an internal network, called a *loopback interface* (`lo`). The loopback isn't a physical device, but rather is a virtual one. Linux uses `lo` for internal communications. (A great deal goes on behind the scenes on a Linux computer.)

5. **Turn on all outgoing communication from your computer:**

```
iptables -A OUTPUT -m state --state NEW,RELATED,ESTAB-
        LISHED -j ACCEPT
iptables -A INPUT -m state --state RELATED,ESTABLISHED -j
        ACCEPT
```

These rules don't specify any particular network interface. However, because the filter is stateful, these rules effectively work on your Ethernet, wireless, or a dial-up Point-to-Point (PPP) interface.

The first filter rule permits all outgoing communication. The `--state NEW, RELATED, ESTABLISHED` option tells the firewall to allow packets of both new and already established connections to pass. (*Packets* are the basic part of all network communication.) Packets that are related to existing connections but use a different port, such as FTP data transfers, are also permitted.

The second filter rule controls the packets coming back from outgoing connections. When you connect to a Web site, for example, your browser sends out packets and the web server responds to them. You may click a button on the Web site, and a new display pops up. Clicking a button sends a packet out, and the web server sends packets back. You have previously blocked packets from the Internet. This rule creates an exception that allows packets which belong to an existing connection — such as the connection that represents you clicking a button — to return to your computer through the firewall. Note that we don't allow new incoming connections (`--state NEW`) to be established because that would defeat the purpose of this firewall.

6. **(Optional) Use the following rule to allow SSH connections to your Linux computer:**

```
iptables -A INPUT -p tcp -m state --state NEW,ESTABLISHED
         -j ACCEPT --dport 22
```

This rule permits SSH connections on Port 22 to enter into your computer. You can install an OpenSSH server by logging in as root, mounting your companion DVD, and running this command:

```
rpm -ivh /mnt/cdrom/RedHat/RPMS/openssh-server*
```

Start the OpenSSH server by running this command:

```
/etc/init.d/sshd start
```

You can modify this rule to allow other types of incoming connections to your computer. For example, add a new rule using `-dport 80`, and the firewall allows incoming HTTP packets. All you need to do is install the Apache web server (included on this book's companion DVD-ROM and described in Chapter 16), and your workstation morphs into a web server.

You have just created a simple, effective firewall that protects your computer from the werewolves of Netdom. ("They'll rip your heart out, Jim!") Your firewall remains active until you turn the rules off or reboot your computer. The following section shows how to display your new firewall rules.

Displaying Your Firewall Rules

After you configure your firewall, you naturally want to verify that the filtering rules are set up correctly. To display the firewall rules, follow these steps:

1. **Open a GNOME Terminal emulator window, by right-clicking any empty portion of the desktop and selecting the New Terminal menu.**

2. **If you're not already the root user, enter the** su - **command in the GNOME Terminal window.**
3. **Enter the root password and type this command to display the firewall rules:**

```
iptables -L
```

After you complete these steps, you see the firewall-filtering rules displayed in the terminal window as follows (use the verbose *-v* option in the preceding command to display extra information, including the network interfaces — for the sake of brevity, we don't use the option in this example):

```
Chain INPUT (policy DROP)
target   prot opt   source     destination
ACCEPT   all  --    anywhere   anywhere
ACCEPT   all  --    anywhere   anywhere    state
              RELATED,ESTABLISHED
ACCEPT   tcp  --    anywhere   anywhere    tcp dpt:ssh
              stateNEW,ESTABLISHED

Chain FORWARD (policy DROP)
target   prot opt   source     destination

Chain OUTPUT (policy DROP)
target   prot opt source       destination
ACCEPT   all  --    anywhere   anywhere
ACCEPT   all  --    anywhere   anywhere    state
              NEW,RELATED,ESTABLISHED
```

The first *chain,* INPUT, is for incoming packets. You can see that the default policy is to deny all packets. The first rules in the INPUT chain direct `iptables` to allow all internal packets on the logical loopback (`lo`); many programs use the internal (`lo`) network to communicate with each other. The second rule allows the return packets, RELATED and ESTABLISHED, from outgoing connections to come back in. The last rule, which is optional, allows the incoming Secure Shell connections to your computer.

The next chain, FORWARD, denies all packets from being forwarded through your Linux computer. Forwarding is necessary only if you use your computer for routing or other advanced networking functions.

The last chain, OUTPUT, defines which IP packets are allowed out of your computer. Again, the first rule allows unlimited traffic through the loopback (`lo`) interface. The second and last rule allows any and all packets to leave your firewall.

The following section describes how to save the rules you just created and displayed so that they can be started automatically.

Firing Up Your Firewall (And Dousing the Flames)

The preceding section describes how to display your firewall-filtering rules. However, you certainly don't want to manually enter these rules every time you reboot your computer. This section shows you how to automate your firewall. We show you how to make use of the Red Hat utilities that save the rules you just created and start up the firewall whenever you boot your computer.

These instructions assume that you have configured the firewall as described in the preceding section and that the configuration is still in effect.

Saving your filtering rules to a script

You need to save your rule set after you have created your firewall. Red Hat provides a utility for doing just that. The `iptables-save` utility reads your current firewall rules and converts them into script-compatible form. Red Hat also provides a script to start up your firewall whenever you start your computer. The `/etc/init.d/iptables` script is run whenever you start your computer and, thus, your firewall is started too. Follow these steps:

1. **Log in as root, if necessary, and open a GNOME Terminal window (refer to Chapter 4), if necessary.**
2. **Run this command and your firewall rules are saved to a script:**

```
iptables-save > /etc/sysconfig/iptables
```

Turning your firewall off and on

Red Hat uses the `/etc/sysconfig/iptables` script to start `Netfilter/iptables` firewalls. The `/etc/init.d/iptables` script uses the filtering rules stored in the `/etc/sysconfig/iptables` file to implement the filtering rules.

You can start the `Netfilter/iptables` firewall by running this `iptables` script:

```
/etc/init.d/iptables start
```

You must be logged in as root, of course. Note that you can turn off your firewall by replacing `start` with `stop`:

```
/etc/init.d/iptables stop
```

You can also use the graphical Red Hat Service Configuration utility. These instructions show you how to use the utility to start or stop your firewall:

1. **Click the GNOME Menu button and choose System Settings⇨Server Settings⇨Services.**

   If you're not logged in as root, the Input window pops up and you're asked to enter the root password.

2. **Enter the root password you set during the Red Hat installation process.**

   The Service Configuration window appears. This window controls all the Linux *daemons* (processes that provide services).

3. **Scroll down the Service Configuration window until you find the** Iptables **service.**

   The check mark should be set in the check box.

4. **Click the Restart button in the upper-left corner of the window.**

   You could click the Start button, but we advise you to use the Restart function. The Start and Restart buttons give you the same result, but restarting works if the service is already running. Using the Start function doesn't work if the service is already running.

   Click the Stop button to turn off your firewall.

   After the service restarts, you see a confirmation message.

5. **Click OK.**

   Your firewall is restarted, and you can exit from the Service Configuration window.

You can also prevent the Iptables script from being automatically started when you boot the system. Click in the box immediately to the left of the service name to remove the check mark. Click the Save button, and the pointer (`/etc/rc.d/rc5.d/S08iptables`) to the startup script (`/etc/init.d/iptables`) is removed. You can restore the pointer by clicking in the box so that the check mark reappears.

Part III

Linux, Huh! What Is It Good For? Absolutely Everything!

"Think of our relationship as a version of Red Hat Linux – I will not share a directory on the love-branch of your life."

In this part . . .

One thing you can do with your computer is put up your feet and wait for the screen saver to kick in. You can confide to all your friends at the next party you attend that you have a "Red Hat Linux box." (That will make you popular as they clamor to know when your stock options will mature.) Or, you can use your new Red Hat Linux workstation to get things done.

To that end, Chapter 9 introduces the friendly world of the GNOME windows environment. GNOME, a friendly li'l guy who likes to put a friendly face on Linux, can help you set up the "look and feel" of Linux so that you feel comfortable and at home. Chapter 10 goes further and introduces cool things you can do with GNOME applications.

In Chapter 11, the fun starts. Can you say "Par-*tay*"? (Sorry.) Find out how to use the Mozilla browser and how to use multimedia players to listen to audio CDs and Ogg or MP3 files. We show you how to record music from CDs and how to become your own recording studio by recording audio (and data, if you're a nerd) to CD.

Chapter 12 takes the audio thing one step further. It describes how to use the open source multimedia players XMMS and MPlayer to listen to flowing streams — no, not water streams, but, rather, audio and video streams flowing from the Internet. You can listen to radio and audio clips and watch video too. With this knowledge, you never have to leave your couch again.

Lucky Chapter 13 describes how to get work done with OpenOffice. Sorry — reality bites and personal productivity suites (word processors and spreadsheets, for example) are a necessary evil. Gotta make the doughnuts.

Chapter 14 describes how to use WINE and VMware. The WINE system lets you run Windows applications, like Word 2000, directly from your Linux workstation! VMware creates virtual computers that run both Windows and Linux.

Chapter 9
Gnowing GNOME

In This Chapter

- Introducing the X Window System
- Introducing and exploring the GNOME desktop environment
- Exploring the GNOME desktop
- Using GNOME windows
- Making GNOME icons
- Exploring the GNOME Panel
- Adding GNOME Panels
- Exiting from GNOME and X
- Modifying the look of your desktop
- Introducing GNOME applications
- Configuring MIME types

The Red Hat Linux operating system provides two interactive interfaces for you to work from: the text-based command-line interface (CLI), as we describe in Chapter 4, and the graphical X Window System. The command-line interface is similar to the old Microsoft Disk Operating System (MS-DOS) environment, which requires you to feed individual commands to the operating system; you can use the GNOME Terminal (emulator) as your CLI. The X Window System, also known simply as *X,* provides a graphical "point-and-click" environment from which most people prefer to work.

Red Hat Linux provides two desktop environments for you to use: GNOME and KDE, or the K Desktop Environment. Both GNOME and KDE run on top of X, and both environments include a menu system to access utilities, applications, and shortcuts in the form of icons and other numerous other enhancements. Using either of these desktop environments makes using Red Hat Linux as your workstation easy and pleasurable.

GNOME is the default desktop environment for Red Hat Linux. Red Hat also gives you the option of installing KDE, an excellent system that many people prefer. However, because of limited space in this book, we discuss only GNOME.

The excellent Red Hat Linux "minibook" describes KDE in more detail.

In this chapter, you find out a little about X and the basics for working with GNOME. You also get to mess around with the GNOME Panel and desktop (the GNOME Panel is similar to the taskbar in Windows computers). We show you some simple but effective maneuvers to manage your desktop and describe some applications.

Introducing the X Window System

Red Hat gives you the option of using the GNOME and KDE desktop environments. GNOME and KDE, however, run on top of X, and X runs on Linux. *X* is the software that provides the low-level graphical tools that systems like GNOME use. X is the middleware that makes building complex systems like GNOME possible.

The version of X that comes with Red Hat Linux is both sophisticated and simple to use. That wasn't always the case, though; in fact, it took lots of natural — dare we say Darwinian? — selection to arrive at the current arrangement of X, and the result works well.

X is composed of three main parts:

- The X server
- Numerous graphics libraries
- A set of X client graphics applications

The *X server* is a program that talks to the human-interactive hardware on your computer — such as the video card, keyboard, and mouse — and runs interference between this hardware and other graphics software. It uses the graphics libraries to work properly with the graphics hardware.

X clients are graphical programs, such as Mozilla and xclock. X clients display their graphical output through the X server; they also get their keyboard and mouse input through the X server. X clients can be run on the same computer that the X server runs on or across a network to any computer running an X server. For example, by using X, you can run an X client on a computer on the other side of the world and view it on the X server running on your home computer.

Suppose that you're logged in to a computer in Australia and you want to see what time it is there. You could run the `date` command (from a command line) to see the date and time, but that would be boring. Instead, you could run the `xclock` program on the remote machine and see a graphical clock displayed on your local computer. You can then verify that the Aussies use clocks that run clockwise and have 24-hour days.

The X server program, often called simply *X,* isn't part of the operating system, as it is in some other operating systems. Instead, the X server is a *user-level* program — although it's special and complex.

The X Window System provides the foundation for these graphical-based systems:

- **Desktop environment:** GNOME and KDE provide a desktop environment that makes using your computer easy. Desktop environments provide high-level functions like menu systems, icons, and backgrounds. A desktop environment is equivalent to a house where X is the foundation.
- **Graphical applications:** Red Hat installs numerous applications, such as games, system administration utilities, Mozilla, and Ximian Evolution to provide the functionality that helps you use your computer and the Internet. Graphical applications are equivalent to the appliances in a house.

Introducing the GNOME Desktop Environment

GNOME stands for GNU Network Object Model Environment. (GNU itself stands for GNU's Not UNIX, a recursive acronym designed by guys who probably never went to their prom but did change the world.) If you have trouble remembering acronyms, just think of GNOME as great graphics for *nada* money. However you remember it, GNOME is an open source graphical desktop environment. It provides a platform for completing your everyday tasks, such as word processing and Internet browsing, on your Red Hat Linux computer.

Log in to your Red Hat Linux computer and check out the GNOME interface. It should look something like Figure 9-1 and consists of these three major elements:

Figure 9-1: The GNOME desktop.

- **The desktop:** Quite simply, the desktop is what you see on your computer screen. It's the space where you do your work and is equivalent — ta-da! — to the top of a desk. The desktop comes preconfigured with a background and several icons that include links to such places as your home directory and the trash bin. Icons are equivalent to the junk you pile on your desk: Some is useful and some isn't.

  When you double-click the home directory (or right-click and choose Open), a Nautilus window opens and displays the contents of those directories. *Nautilus* is a graphical system for working with not only files and directories but also administration utilities and Web pages. See Chapter 10 for more information about Nautilus.

- **The Panel:** The menu bar that runs across the bottom edge of your GNOME screen is the Panel. You can access every GNOME function and Red Hat or third-party application from the GNOME Panel. It represents the drawers in a desk.

- **Applications:** These elements include user system and GNOME-level applications. User programs include applications such as Mozilla, Evolution, XMMS, and Xine. System applications include the Red Hat Linux system administration utilities, such as network configuration and user management utilities, and GNOME utilities, such as the Help browser. Applications are equivalent to the toys and work to be done on and in your desk.

Exploring the GNOME Desktop

GNOME performs all the basic graphical functions you expect from a desktop environment. You can set the background and create icons, for example. This section shows how to perform some basic GNOME desktop maneuvers and configurations. After you master the basics, you can continue to explore on your own.

The default GNOME desktop — as installed by the Red Hat Linux installation — comes with several elements preinstalled. Let's take a quick trip around the desktop.

Introducing the default desktop icons

In the upper-left corner of the desktop are three icons: your home directory, Start Here, and Trash (refer to Figure 9-1). They perform these tasks:

- **Home directory:** This icon, which looks like a folder, represents your home directory. For example, if you create a user account named `lidia`, a directory named `/home/lidia` is created; the icon is labeled `lidia's Home`. When you log in as `lidia`, the home directory icon is linked to that directory. Double-click the home directory (or right-click and choose Open) and a Nautilus window opens, displaying the contents of the home directory.

  Double-clicking an icon opens the window associated with the icon. For example, double-clicking your home directory opens a Nautilus file manager window linked to your home directory. You can also open an icon by right-clicking it and choosing the Open option.

- **Start Here:** GNOME provides a Preferences window that includes links to the major GNOME and Red Hat configuration utilities and applications. Double-click the Start Here icon and the Start Here window opens. Opening any of the icons — Applications, Preferences, Server Settings, or System Settings, for example — opens another Nautilus window that provides access to utilities and applications:
  - **Applications icon:** Clicking the Applications icon is equivalent to clicking the GNOME Menu. You see a window of icons that mirrors the GNOME Menu. Any item you can reach from the GNOME Menu, you can access from the Applications icon.
  - **Preferences:** Clicking the Desktop Properties icon is equivalent to choosing GNOME Menu⇨Preferences. You get to choose from a number of GNOME configuration options. The GNOME Preferences window is described later in this chapter, in the "Making GNOME Recognize MIME Types" section.

- **System Settings:** Double-clicking the System Settings icon opens the System Settings window, which allows you to start various administrative utilities. You find icons, such as Red Hat Network Configuration, and the Printing utilities here.

- **Trash icon:** GNOME provides a method to dispose of files and directories in the form of the Trash directory. Click any icon, file, or directory and drag it to the Trash icon. Although Jesse James' Monster Garage automated trash minivan doesn't come for your file, it's placed in the Trash directory; the Trash directory is in your home directory.

  Trashed items aren't really deleted until you right-click the Trash icon and choose Empty trash. You can undelete items by opening the Trash (double-clicking the icon) and then clicking the item and dragging it out onto the desktop or an open Preferences window.

Changing themes and backgrounds

GNOME provides the ability to change the look and feel of its elements. The look and feel of an element — typically, a window opened on the desktop — is referred to as its *theme. Themes* determine the size, shape, texture, and color of the buttons, slides, menus, borders, and other pieces of an open window.

You can change your theme more easily and quickly than a politician during an election by choosing GNOME Menu➪Preferences➪Theme; alternatively, you can open the Start Here icon and select Preferences in the window that opens. Double-click the Theme icon when the Preferences window opens.

When the Theme Preferences window opens, the Application tab is activated by default. You can select any theme and all your open windows immediately adopt it. The application theme changes the tint and texture applied to each window. For example, clicking the Metal theme gives your windows a brushed surface appearance.

Click the Window Border tab. Click any of the themes and your window borders change. Window borders consist of the tint and texture of the strip that surrounds each window and the buttons on the strip.

Keep selecting different themes until you find one you like. Click the Close button when you're finished.

You can also select the image that's displayed on your desktop. The image can be a picture, a pattern, or solid colors. Change the desktop to find one you like by right-clicking any blank (uncluttered) section of the desktop.

Choose Change Desktop Background from the menu and the Background Preferences window opens. Select an image by clicking the Picture section or one of its variations. The Please Select an Image window opens. You can select any listed image or search for another image on your disk. Alternatively, you can select a solid color by clicking the No Picture button.

Open the Background Style menu and select either a solid color or colors that change on the vertical or horizontal axis. You can then change the color (solid or gradient) by clicking the Color button. Select your color from the Pick a Color window. Repeat the process for the other color, and you get a screen full of colors.

Right-clicking anywhere on a blank section of the desktop and then choosing Use Default Background resets the background. The default background gets reactivated.

Toiling in your workplace

After using GNOME for a while, you find that as you start more and more applications, you create lots and lots of windows on the screen. You may even lose windows behind other windows. Perhaps you want to strap together several monitors so that you can display all the windows at one time.

Monitors are expensive and bulky, so you're probably stuck using a single monitor. But you don't have to be stuck with one *screen.* GNOME lets you spread your work across multiple virtual monitors.

Imagine that you have a large GNOME desktop spread equally across four monitors. Life would be good if you could open windows on any of the monitors. You would have lots of real estate to spread out on.

However, because you probably don't have four monitors, GNOME simulates four virtual monitors, called *workspaces.* Each workspace is equivalent to a real monitor, and you can spread out your work across it. The only limitation is that you can view only one workspace at a time.

Trading places on your workspace switcher

Switching between workspaces is easy. GNOME provides a utility, the Workspace Switcher, to select any workspace. The Workspace Switcher is on the GNOME Panel.

You use the GNOME Workspace Switcher to access each workspace. The Workspace Switcher is divided into four quadrants. Clicking any of the quadrants places you in the corresponding desktop. Click the lower-right one and you enter that workspace.

You can force a window into any or all workspaces. Click the downward-facing arrow in the upper-left corner of a window. The menu that opens provides all the expected functions that close, minimize, maximize, and resize the window. However, toward the bottom of the menu are options for placing the window in any of the remaining three workspaces; or, you can put the window in all the workspaces. You may want, for example, to put an application like Mozilla in all workspaces in order to use it no matter what you're doing.

Messing Around with Windows

Before you can do anything to a window, you have to get its attention. When you have a window's attention, it has *focus*. Depending on how you have set up GNOME, you can give a window focus with GNOME in several ways:

- Click the window's name on the GNOME Panel.
- Click the window's title bar, at the top of the window.
- Click a part of the window itself, which typically also makes the window the topmost one. This method is the default.
- If you're working in an office with lots of people, you can shout, "Hey, you — wake up!" Although this tactic isn't likely to wake up your window, it sure is fun.

In this book, we stick with the Red Hat and GNOME default of clicking a window to give it focus.

Moving windows

To move a window, click anywhere on the window's title bar and hold down the left mouse button. As long as you continue to hold down that button, the window moves anywhere you move your mouse. Release the button and the window stays there.

Resizing windows

Sometimes, a window is a little too big or a little too small, and you know that life would be much easier if you could just nudge that window into shape. To do just that, position the mouse cursor on any border of the window. Click and drag the window's outline to the size you want. Release the mouse button and the window takes the new size.

Minimizing windows

Now that you have put lots of windows on the screen, how can you get rid of a few or all of them? You can *minimize* (or *iconify*) a window by clicking the bold, underscored button toward the upper-right corner, which removes the window from the desktop and places it in a storage area of the GNOME Panel. If you're in a particularly devilish mood, you can be more drastic and *close* a window. Figure 9-2 shows an open Mozilla window minimized — you can see its icon on the GNOME Panel along the lower, central edge of the screen.

Figure 9-2: Mozilla minimized inside GNOME.

Here are a few ways to get rid of a window, starting with the least drastic and escalating to outright window death:

- Take advantage of any exit buttons or menu options that the window or application in the window gives you. For example, many applications allow you to choose File⇨Exit to close the application.
- Click the X button in the upper-right corner of the window's title bar to close the window.
- Click the upper-left corner of the window (or right-click the title bar) and choose the Close option from the menu that opens.

You can return a minimized window to the desktop by clicking the icon that corresponds to the window on the GNOME Panel.

Maximizing windows

To make a window fill the entire screen, click the Maximize button, in the upper-right corner of the window. Check out the buttons to the right of the title bar in a typical window. The Maximize button is the one in the middle; it looks like a square and is similar in action to the Cascade button in Windows.

The Making of a Desktop Icon

You can create an icon on your desktop for any application on the GNOME Menu. Just click the GNOME Menu button, find the menu item for the application you want an icon for, and then left-click the application's icon and hold down the mouse button. While continuing to hold down the button, drag the mouse cursor to any open area on the GNOME desktop (or the GNOME Panel). Release the mouse button and an icon for that application is placed on the desktop. You can then start the application by double-clicking the icon on the desktop (or just clicking an icon that lives on the GNOME Panel).

With GNOME, you can enhance icons with emblems. *Emblems* provide additional information about what an icon is meant to do. You can assign an Emblem by right-clicking an icon and choosing Properties. The Properties window opens. Click the Emblems tab and select one of the emblems. For example, if you select the Cool emblem, a pair of Wayfarer sunglasses is displayed with the icon on the desktop — cool. You can see the cool icon dude in the margin of this paragraph.

Another cool GNOME icon feature is the ability to stretch an icon's boundaries. Right-click an icon and choose Stretch. A dashed line and four square buttons bracket the icon. Click any of the buttons and you can stretch the icon image as much as you want.

Playing with the GNOME Panel

The GNOME *Panel* is the menu bar along the bottom of the desktop. The GNOME Panel, similar to the taskbar in Windows, provides a location to place common menus and applets for easy starting or viewing. The GNOME Panel also gives you a view of the virtual desktop and enables you to keep track of minimized windows.

By default, Red Hat Linux places icons on the GNOME Panel for accessing the GNOME Menu, Mozilla, Evolution, OpenOffice (Writer, Impress, and Calc), and the GNOME Workspace Switcher. You can start any of these programs or use the switcher by clicking its icon.

The most important element on the GNOME Panel is the GNOME Menu button, on the far left side, which you use to access all the standard GNOME applications and configuration tools. The GNOME Menu button, which looks amazingly similar to a red hat, is in the lower-left corner of the screen. You can choose from any of the menus that are displayed when you click the GNOME Menu button. For example, the System Settings and System Tools menus contain many of the Red Hat utilities you can use to administer your

Red Hat Linux computer. The Sound & Video menu provides access to a CD player, and the Graphics menu provides access to graphical applications. You get the idea.

You can use the Add to Panel submenu to modify the configuration and behavior of the GNOME Panel. For example, if you right-click any unused portion of the GNOME Panel and choose Add to Panel⇨Amusements⇨Geyes, you get a nifty pair-of-eyes applet added to the GNOME Panel. The eyes follow your mouse around the screen — ooh, scary. Geyes demonstrates the tremendous extra dimension of functionality that enters your life when you use Red Hat Linux. (You can remove the eyes by right-clicking its icon and choosing the Remove from Panel option.)

One other interesting function of the GNOME Panel menu is the Add New Launcher function. Click any unused section of the GNOME Panel and choose Add to Panel⇨Launcher. The Create Launcher Applet window opens. By entering the pathname of an application, you can add a new applet to the GNOME Panel that *launches,* or opens, that application.

GNOME provides a file searching utility, named Search Tool. Click the GNOME Menu button and choose Search for Files, and the Search Tool opens. Enter the name of a file you want to find and click the Find button. Click the Advanced tab and you can conduct a more finely tuned file search.

Give it a try. For example, if you frequently use MPlayer to listen to Internet audio streams (described in Chapter 12), you can add an applet for it to your Panel so that you can easily launch MPlayer on a whim. Open the Create Launcher Applet window again and add the name, the generic name, any comments, and the command (`gmplayer`) to launch the program. If you click the No Icon button, you see a few pages of standard icons you can use to distinguish your new applet from others on the GNOME Panel; in this case, we chose a generic apple as our icon mascot. Figure 9-3 shows the finished applet launcher window.

Figure 9-3: The MPlayer icon is born.

After you finish editing the Create Launcher Applet window, click OK. The icon is added to your Panel, as shown in Figure 9-4. You can create a launcher for any application on your Red Hat Linux computer in the same way.

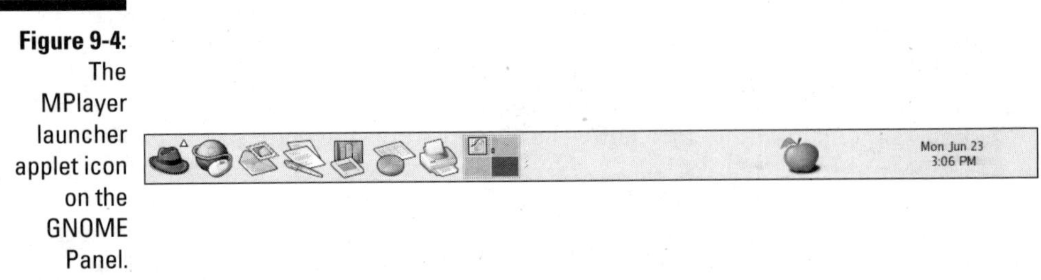

Figure 9-4: The MPlayer launcher applet icon on the GNOME Panel.

Adding and Deleting Panels

You're not limited to the default GNOME Panel. You can create additional panels at will. Click anywhere on an unused portion of the GNOME Panel and choose New Panel. For example, choosing Edge Panel places a blank panel along the top of the screen.

The new panel is blank and doesn't contain any icons, like the default GNOME Panel does. The new panel does have a basic menu you can use to populate it with icons and other menus. Right-click the new panel and the Add to Panel submenu opens. You can use the Add to Panel menu to build up the new panel. For example, choose Accessories⇨Clock and a digital clock is added to the panel, as shown in Figure 9-5. Or, choose Amusements⇨Geyes. Keep adding icons until you're satisfied with the new system.

Figure 9-5: A new panel with a clock and kooky eyes.

You can, of course, remove any panel you create, but you can't remove the default GNOME Panel. The process is simple: Right-click any unused section of the panel and choose Delete This Panel. Click the Delete button in the Delete Panel window that opens, and the panel is depaneled.

Any panel can be made to hide when it's not in use. Right-click any unused section of the panel and choose Properties from the pop-up menu, and the Panel Properties window then opens. Select the Autohide option and click the Close button. The panel disappears off the edge of the screen until you move the mouse cursor back to that edge. The panel then reappears.

Every new panel contains arrows at each end, called Hide buttons; the original default Panel does not. Clicking either of the arrows forces the panel to slide off to one side or the other. The panel is hidden except for those same arrows. Clicking the arrow uncovers the hidden panel.

Leaving GNOME and X

If you want to leave your computer on but don't want to leave it open to anyone just walking along, you can save yourself the time spent logging out of your GNOME desktop by using the screen lock. To do so, click the GNOME Menu button and choose Lock Screen; the screensaver is displayed. To return to productive life and your desktop, press any key or wiggle your mouse and enter your password in the X Screensaver window that opens.

Securing your computer while you step out for a moment

Locking your screen is one of the best security features you can use. To lock your screen, click the GNOME Menu button and choose Lock Screen. Your screen locks up and you must enter your password to get back in. Locking your screen is a good idea when you're going to be away from it for even a minute or two.

Going home for the night

After you have finished for the day and want to go home (or just upstairs), you need to log out. Click the GNOME Menu button and choose Log Out. The Are You Sure You Want to Log Out? window opens. Click Log Out to — you guessed it — log out. You also have the options to shut down or reboot your computer.

GNOME configures a random screensaver by default. You can select a single screensaver by clicking the GNOME Menu button and choosing Preferences⇨Screensaver. The Screensaver Preferences window opens. For example, you can switch from the default random screensaver to the Xjack (we all know that all work and no play makes Jack a dull boy) screensaver. It's not a bad selection for those long winters spent at peaceful resorts with plenty of time to write Linux books!

eXterminating X

When you can't get your applications to respond to you, you can simply stop X, which kills all programs running under it. To do so, press the Ctrl+Alt+Backspace keys all at one time. If you started X manually, you can then log out of the account. If X is started automatically at boot time (as we assume in this book), you see the X login screen and you can log back in.

Making GNOME Recognize MIME Types

You can modify the look and feel of your desktop by using an assortment of GNOME configuration utilities. Double-click the Start Here icon on the desktop. When the window opens, double-click the Preferences icon. (You can access the same functions by clicking the GNOME Menu button and then opening the Preferences menu. A submenu opens, showing the same options as in the Preferences window.)

Figure 9-6 shows the Preferences window, where you can modify GNOME properties. For example, double-click the File Types and programs option and you can associate applications with MIME types.

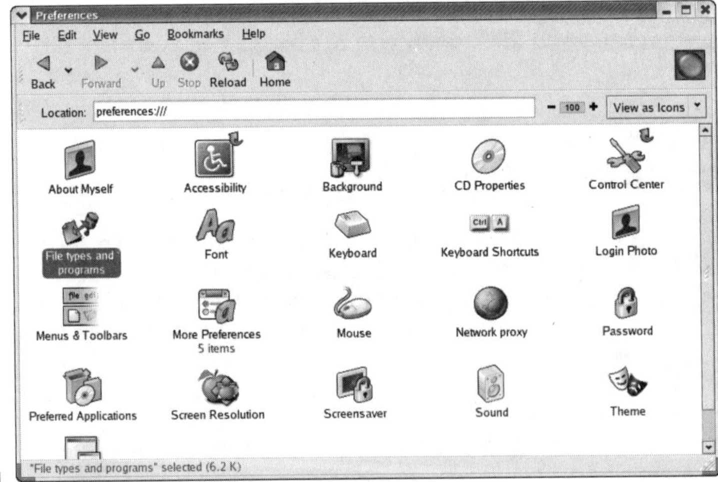

Figure 9-6: The Preferences window.

Double-click the Files Types and programs icon and the File Types and Programs dialog box is displayed. GNOME recognizes MIME types by the information stored by this utility. For example, choose Audio⇨OGG and then Edit. The File Types and Programs window opens (see Figure 9-7).

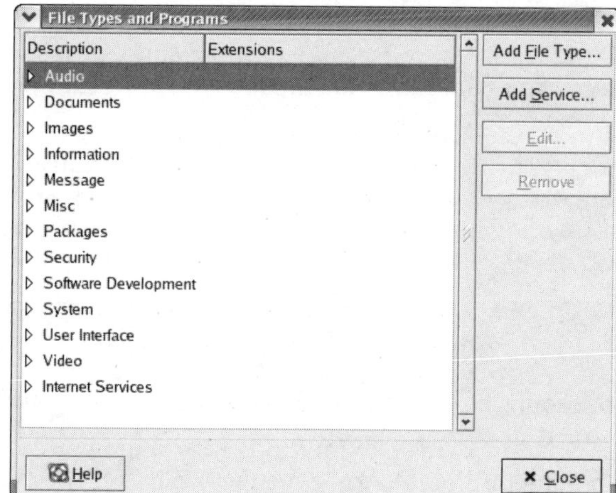

Figure 9-7: The File Types and Programs dialog box.

The Edit File Type window shows that Ogg audio files belong to the MIME type `application/x-ogg`. The window also shows that Ogg audio files use `.ogg` file suffixes. No default action is specified. You can open the Default action pull-down menu and then choose X Multimedia System if you want XMMS to play your Ogg files or enter the name of a program manually in the Program to run subwindow. Whatever program you select is used to play Ogg files whenever you click them in any Nautilus or other file manager window. XMMS is a standard audio player bundled with Red Hat Linux.

The Preferences window also lets you configure items other than screen savers with maniacal rantings. We leave it to you to explore the wonderful world of setting your keyboard bell and other items.

Accessing GNOME Applications

The last GNOME element consists of the applications that come packaged with GNOME. GNOME provides numerous applications intended for work and fun. Red Hat also provides a wide range of applications, some of which are accessible via GNOME. (You can also add your own applications from the open source community and third parties.)

Nautilus provides another way of accessing many applications on your Red Hat Linux computer. Applications that don't have links to GNOME aren't accessible via the GNOME Menu system; you can generally correct that situation by manually adding links with the GNOME Add to Panel option.

This list describes the methods used to access applications:

- **Start Here:** Open the GNOME Start Here window and double-click the Applications icon. You can then start most of the applications Red Hat Linux installed on your computer.
- **Nautilus:** Clicking your Home directory icon opens a Nautilus window. You can then start any executable application stored in your home directory by double-clicking its icon. You can also change to any other directory — that you have access permission to — to run an application.
- **GNOME Menu:** Opening the GNOME Menu provides access to every application GNOME "knows" about (every application that GNOME has been configured to access). Using the GNOME Menu provides access to the same set of programs as the Start Here⇨Applications windows.
- **Old School:** GNOME provides two methods for running programs from a CLI (a command-line interface). You can start a GNOME Terminal emulator window or use the GNOME Run Program function. The former opens a `bash` shell in a Terminal emulator window from which you can launch applications. The latter opens a window in which you can enter the name of a program to execute. The primary difference between the two systems is that you can interact with an application more when using the terminal emulator. The Run Program system allows you to interact with an application only if it creates a GUI.

The following list illustrates the rich application landscape you get with Red Hat and GNOME. The list corresponds to the menu selection you see when you click the GNOME Menu button:

- **Accessories:** Applications that don't belong to any groups on this list are labeled as accessories. Applications such as the GNOME calculator, gedit, and a dictionary are placed in this category; the dictionary is quite useful — enter a word and its definition is displayed.
- **Games:** Because Linux was initially oriented toward running services, you may not see it as being oriented toward game players. But it has lots of games. Open the Games icon and you see many of them. You can waste your life with Linux just as easily as with Windows! Ha!
- **Graphics:** You can view and manipulate images with these graphical utilities; ImageMagick and The Gimp are excellent tools for working with pixels. You can use the Scanning tool to scan images on a scanner. DVI,

Adobe Acrobat Reader, and general-purpose image viewers are included, as is a digital camera tool. You can access some utilities by choosing Graphics from the GNOME Menu. More graphics applications are accessible via the GNOME Menu: Choose Extras⇨Graphics.

- **Help:** Clicking the Help menu opens the GNOME Help browser. It provides information about many GNOME topics.
- **Internet:** The new Red Hat default e-mail client Evolution is in this folder. You also find a graphical chat application, Instant Messenger.
- **Network Servers:** You can view Samba servers on your network. Network Servers provides the same function that Microsoft Network Neighborhood provides.
- **Office:** The open source OpenOffice applications are stored in this folder. OpenOffice provides a word processor, spreadsheet, presentation manager, and drawing tool, all of which you access here. You can also find the OpenOffice repair and printer configuration utilities here. (Icons are automatically placed in the GNOME Panel.)
- **Programming:** Linux provides a good programming environment. Red Hat Linux provides links, via this menu, to several programming utilities, such as Emacs, that many people use for editing source code.
- **Search for Files:** This function helps you search for files and directories on your computer. Selecting this function opens a window where you can enter filenames to search for.
- **Sound and Video:** Fun stuff is stored here. The Red Hat Linux CD player, XMMS, is here, for example. You also find in this folder more mundane items, such as the volume control and volume monitor utilities.
- **Server Settings:** You can access the Services utility, which allows you to start and stop Red Hat Linux services.
- **System Settings:** Red Hat places many of its fabulous configuration utilities here. For example, the Red Hat Network Configuration, X configuration, and Soundcard Detection utilities are here.
- **System Tools:** You can access more of the Red Hat system administration utilities from this folder.

Chapter 10

Gnowing More Applications

In This Chapter

- Nautilus, the GNOME file and integration manager
- The Ximian Evolution e-mail and personal organizer

Many applications help make your Red Hat Linux computer useful. In this chapter, you find out how to use several of the most useful applications that come packaged with Red Hat Linux. The first one is the Nautilus File Manager, an integral part of the GNOME desktop system. The second application is the new e-mail and organizer application named Evolution. We also introduce several other useful applications.

Chapter 11 describes how to use the Mozilla web browser. Chapter 13 introduces the OpenOffice desktop productivity suite, which gives you Microsoft Word–compatible word processing, a spreadsheet program, a PowerPoint–compatible presentation program, and other functions. These programs, combined with Evolution, give you all the functions you need to make your Red Hat Linux computer a fully functioning workstation.

Navigating with the Nautilus File and Internet Integration Manager

Being the boss doesn't make you a bad person. It's just a job. Right? Well, that little GNOME guy is a good worker and doesn't get paid much. Just press a key here, click a button there, and you can boss him around like any worthy pointy-headed Dilbert manager. GNOME even comes with its own file and integration manager that saves work and makes time for those long lunches.

Nautilus is the GNOME file and Internet navigator system. Nautilus follows in the tradition of all good file managers by graphically displaying the files and directories on your computer. You can copy, move, delete, and execute files by pointing and clicking; creating directories and viewing file details are a snap too. Nautilus even goes a step further: You can use it to configure your GNOME desktop. And, that's not all! Nautilus can also navigate the Internet, access multimedia applications, and slice and dice! It's not a bad deal, considering that it works for free.

Waking up Nautilus

Red Hat Linux configures Nautilus to start automatically when you log in. Nautilus appears toward the end of the login process and works as a file manager (see Figure 10-1, which shows the contents of your home directory). If you want to start it manually — after you have closed it, for example — right-click anywhere on the desktop background and choose New Window.

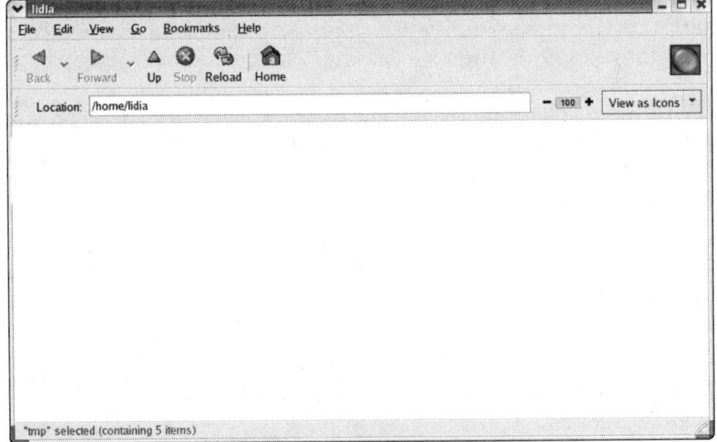

Figure 10-1: The Nautilus File Manager.

The main menu follows familiar menu formats (File and Edit, for example) and does all the things you would expect those menus to do. The toolbar immediately below the main menu enables you to quickly move up one directory (Up) and skip back to previous moves (Back and Forward). It also lets you rescan a directory, go to your home directory, and change the way icons are displayed.

The Reload function is useful if you create a new file — for example, via a terminal emulator. The file doesn't show up in the File Manager until you move to another directory and return, or else reload.

Moving files and directories

Moving a file or directory is as simple as clicking and dragging the item you want to move to the directory you want to move it to. Release the button and you have moved your file or directory.

You can move multiple files by clicking and dragging the mouse cursor over the files you want. The mouse cursor creates a rectangular outline and highlights all files within that box. Next, click anywhere within the highlighted box and drag the mouse cursor to the directory you want. Release the mouse button and the files move to the specified directory.

Copying files and directories

Copying a file or directory is a bit more complicated than moving one. Rather than simply click and drag an icon someplace, you have to right-click the file or directory icon and choose Copy from the menu that opens. Next, enter the directory you want to copy to by double-clicking its icon. When the directory opens, right-click anywhere on the background and choose the Paste option. The file or directory is copied to the new location.

You can copy multiple files and directories in the same manner as you copied individual ones. Trace a box around the files or directories you want to copy by clicking and dragging the mouse cursor. Next, right-click any of the blue highlighted icon names (but not the white space around the icon and names themselves) and choose the Copy option. Double-click the directory to copy to, right-click the background, and choose Paste. Release the mouse button and the files are copied to the specified directory.

Deleting files and directories

Deleting files and directories is much the same process as copying them. You right-click the file or directory icon you want and choose Move to Trash from the menu that opens. The file or directory is moved to the Trash directory.

"Trashed" files and directories aren't immediately deleted. When you use the Move to Trash option to delete a file, for example, the file is moved to the Trash folder. Open the Trash directory by double-clicking its icon and then right-clicking the file or directory to delete. Choose the Delete from Trash option. The Delete from Trash warning window opens and prompts you to confirm the deletion. Click the Delete key and the file is erased.

You can delete multiple files and directories. Again, you trace a box by clicking and dragging the mouse cursor. Right-click the blue highlighted icons or icon names (but not the white space around the icon and name). The files or directories are moved to the Trash directory.

Creating directories

Right-click anywhere in a Nautilus window and choose New Folder to create a new directory. A new folder is displayed with the name Untitled folder. Enter any name for the directory as you please.

Viewing files and directories

Files and directories are displayed onscreen as icons by default. The only information an icon shows is the name and whether an item is a file or directory (directory icons also show the number of files and directories they contain). You can display additional information by clicking View⇨View As List or View⇨View As⇨View As Catalog.

This list describes the differences between views:

- **Icons view:** The default display option; shows the icon and indicates whether an item is a file or directory. Regular file icons take several forms, but text and configuration files look like pieces of paper with a corner folded. Files containing specific types of data have small subicons overlaid on the file icon. For example, PDF files have a PDF subicon. Links, devices, and other objects take other forms. Directories take the form of a partially open manila folder. Icons are evenly placed across the entire File Manager screen. Icons tend to make distinguishing files and directories easier but take up more space onscreen.
- **List view:** Displays the size and time stamp of each file and directory in addition to their names.
- **View as:** Enables you to select icons or lists as your default folder view for all or specific directories. You can also associate MIME types with specific applications.

You can use Nautilus to create on your desktop some shortcut icons that point to files or applications. In Nautilus, just click and drag any file or application to any blank part of the desktop and then release the mouse button. An icon is placed on the desktop. You can then start the application by double-clicking its icon. If the icon points to a data file (a text file, for example) and Nautilus knows how to handle its MIME type, Nautilus launches the appropriate application to open the file. Otherwise, Nautilus prompts you to tell it which application to use to open it.

Nautilus is programmed to recognize numerous Multipurpose Internet Mail Extensions (MIME) types, and they define what type of information a file stores — in other words, MIME keeps its own Rolodex, of sorts. Each MIME type is associated with certain file extensions. For example, when you double-click a `.doc` file, Nautilus recognizes that the `.doc` file suffix corresponds to a Word document MIME type and opens the OpenOffice word processor (as described in Chapter 13), which loads the `.doc` file.

Nautilus provides the ability to bookmark your favorite locations. The Nautilus bookmark function works just like Mozilla's or any other web browser's. Go to any directory and click Bookmarks⇨Add Bookmark. You only have to click Bookmarks and select the particular bookmark to go to that location. You can modify existing bookmarks by choosing Bookmarks⇨Edit Bookmarks.

Running programs

Nautilus is such a hard worker that it happily launches commands for you. Right-click the icon you want to run in order to open a submenu and then choose Open. For example, if you click the xclock icon in the `/usr/bin/X11` directory, xclock appears on your desktop. (Double-clicking the icon also works.)

Managers are generally not very smart. But Nautilus is smarter than the average manager, and it knows what to do when it encounters various file types. If you open a non-executable file, such as a PDF file, File Manager knows which program to use in order to view it.

Come the Ximian Evolution Revolution

The Ximian Evolution system is the new workhorse of the GNOME and Linux world. Evolution provides the next significant step in the evolution of the Linux desktop by combining excellent e-mail and calendar clients with other functions to create a single, integrated package. Evolution provides these capabilities:

- Calendar
- Contact manager
- E-mail client
- Personal Digital Assistant (PDA) manager
- Task master (to-do list)

The following two sections describe how to configure the Evolution e-mail and PDA functions.

Using Evolution for your e-mail

Red Hat uses Evolution as its default e-mail client. Evolution makes it easy for you to configure one or more e-mail accounts. These steps describe how to configure Evolution to send messages to and receive messages from your ISP e-mail account:

1. **Log in to your Red Hat Linux computer as a regular user (not root) and click the Evolution Email icon on the left side of the GNOME panel.**

   The first time you start Evolution, the Setup Assistant (wizard) opens.

2. **Click the Forward button. Then enter your name and e-mail address in the appropriate text boxes in the Identity window and click the Forward button.**

   You can optionally enter your organization and *signature file* (a file where you keep personal or business information to be appended to the end of every message you send).

   Figure 10-2 shows some sample entries in the Identity window.

   The Receiving Mail window opens.

3. **Click the Server Type drop-down menu and choose the option that matches your ISP's e-mail system. Most ISPs use the Internet Message Access Protocol (IMAP) server type.**

   The Receiving Mail window expands so that you can enter more information about your ISP's e-mail system.

4. **Enter the host name of your ISP's e-mail server and your ISP username.**

   Figure 10-3 shows a sample screen in this window.

   Your ISP provides you with the name of its incoming and outgoing e-mail servers when you first subscribe. You need to enter the incoming server name in the Host text box. For example, your ISP incoming server may be `mail.myisp.com` or `imap.myisp.com`.

   Your ISP username may be different from your username on your Linux computer. For example, your ISP username may be based on your first initial and last name — *garagon* — but your home Linux computer username may be just your first name — *gabe*.

5. **Click the Forward button.**

   The second Receiving Email window opens.

   You can change options, such as having Evolution automatically look for incoming messages, by selecting the Automatically check for new mail option.

6. **Make any necessary changes and click the Forward button.**

   The Sending Mail window opens.

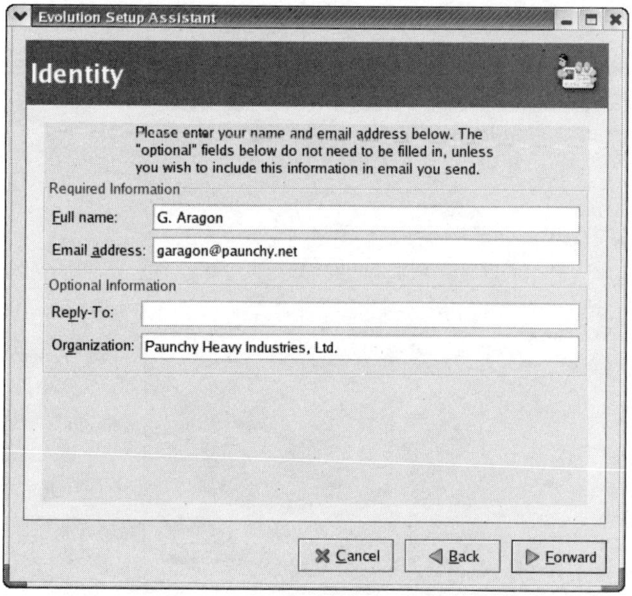

Figure 10-2: The Identity dialog box.

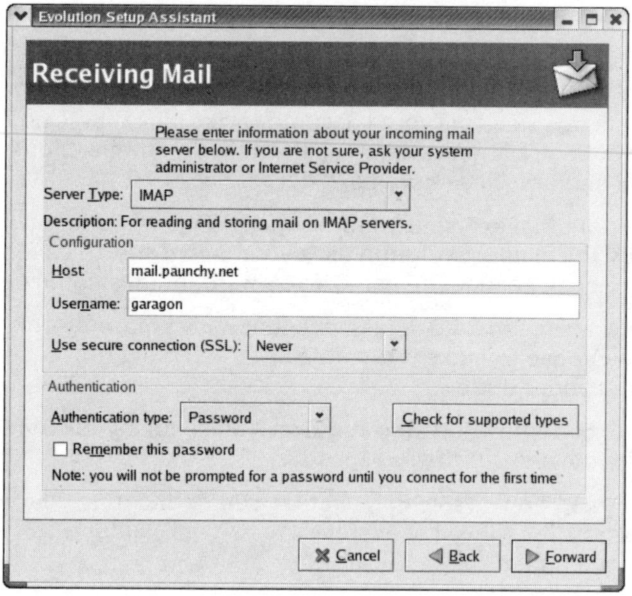

Figure 10-3: The Receiving Mail dialog box.

7. **Enter your ISP's outgoing mail server name and click the Forward button.**

   Figure 10-4 shows a sample screen in this window.

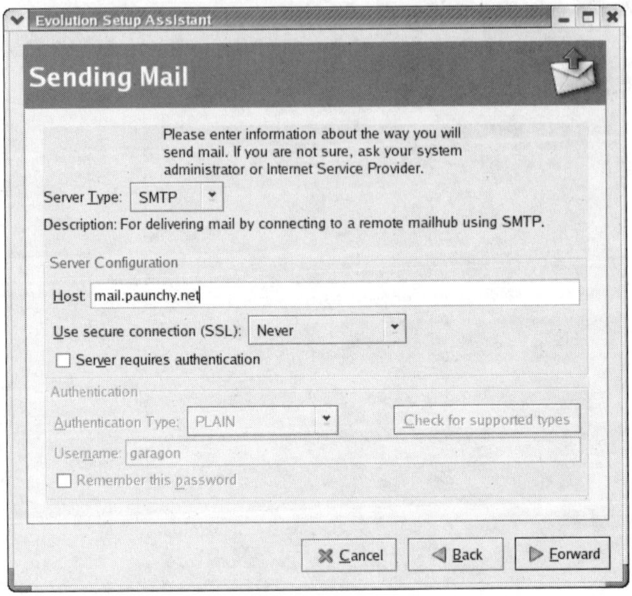

Evolution Setup Assistant

Sending Mail

Please enter information about the way you will send mail. If you are not sure, ask your system administrator or Internet Service Provider.

Server Type: SMTP

Description: For delivering mail by connecting to a remote mailhub using SMTP.

Server Configuration

Host mail.paunchy.net

Use secure connection (SSL): Never

Server requires authentication

Authentication

Authentication Type: PLAIN Check for supported types

Username: garagon

Remember this password

Cancel Back Forward

Figure 10-4: The Sending Mail dialog box.

The default outgoing Evolution e-mail protocol is SMTP. SMTP is used frequently by ISPs, so you may not need to change it. Your ISP should supply you with the protocol it uses.

A few ISPs may use encrypted Secure Service Link (SSL) connections and require authentication. Again, you need to obtain this information from your ISP and use those options, if necessary.

The Account Management window opens. The account you're creating is called by this name. Evolution uses your e-mail address as the default name. You can change the name if you want, but it's not necessary.

Your new account is the default account if it's your only one. Otherwise, you can choose to make it the default by selecting the Make This My Default Account option.

8. **The final configuration step requires you to pick your time zone. Click the closest dot to your location.**

   A bigger map appears, which enables you to fine-tune your location, if necessary. It's the same system you use in Chapter 3 to set your computer's time zone.

9. **Click the Forward button.**

   The Done window pops up.

10. **Click the Apply button and you're finished.**

    Evolution opens and displays a Summary window; a separate dialog box also opens and displays information about Ximian (click the OK button after you finish reading the information in the dialog box). Shortcuts to the Evolution function are on the left side of the window. Click your e-mail account shortcut to see your new e-mail account listed. (You can also access your account by clicking the Summary button, toward the upper-left corner of the window.) Select your account to make it active. You can then send and receive messages. You can also perform any other typical actions on your account, such as sorting, moving, and deleting messages.

You can add new e-mail accounts as desired. You can also go back and modify or delete existing accounts. Click your e-mail account shortcut icon and choose Tools➪Mail Settings. The Mail Settings window opens and you can modify your account, add new ones, and delete old ones. Note that the Evolution Account Assistant opens when you click the Add button.

Using Evolution with your PDA

You can use the Evolution calendar, to-do manager, and contact manager with your PDA. In this section, we concentrate on showing you how to use Evolution to back up your PDA because that's one of more interesting and fun things you can do. You can find out more about using the calendar by reading the online Evolution documentation (click Help or visit `www.gnome.org/gnome-office/evolution.shmtl`) or by simply experimenting with it.

You can use the Evolution pilot-link utility to back up your PDA databases to your computer. Follow these steps:

1. **Plug your Pilot cradle into your computer's serial port.**

   The cable attached to your cradle has a female 9-pin (a *DB9*) plug attached to it. Most, if not all, modern computers have a 9-pin male plug that connects to a serial port socket controlled by the `/dev/ttyS0` Linux device. (In the Windows world, `/dev/ttyS0` is equivalent to COM1, `/dev/ttyS1` is COM2, and so on.)

2. **Click the Evolution icon on the GNOME panel.**

   The Ximian Evolution (revolution?) application opens.

3. **Click the Contacts button and choose Tools➪Pilot settings.**

   The Welcome to GNOME Pilot Wizard window opens.

4. **Click the Forward button and the Cradle Settings window opens, as shown in Figure 10-5.**

   You have to tell Evolution where to find your PDA. Open the Port menu and choose the serial device.

   The device is probably `/dev/ttyS0` or `/dev/ttyS1`. There's no shame in trial and error, so choose each port in order until you find the right one.

Don't worry about selecting the speed. The default value is adequate unless you have a very old computer.

5. **Click the Forward button.**

   The Pilot Identification window opens.

6. **Click the No, I've Never Used Sync Software with This Pilot Before button.**

   Your username is inserted into the User Name text box. (For example, if you're logged in as `paul`, `paul` is your default Pilot ID.)

7. **Click the Forward button to accept the username; otherwise, type the name you want to use for your Pilot ID.**

8. **Press the synchronize button (for example, HotSync for a Palm Pilot) on the PDA cradle.**

   The calendar database is copied to your Red Hat Linux computer.

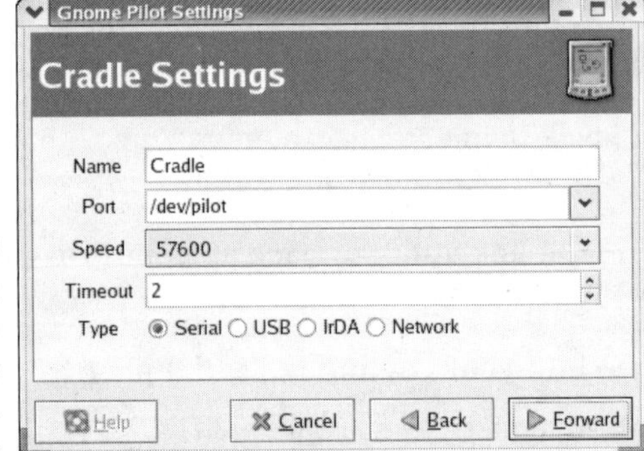

Figure 10-5: The Cradle Settings dialog box.

Evolution can also synchronize your contact list and address book. Pretty cool, eh?

Chapter 11

Surfin' the Net and Groovin' to Tunes

In This Chapter

- A brief history of the Web
- Using Mozilla to surf the Web
- Plugging in plug-ins
- Playing your CDs
- Building your sound system
- Working with CDs

In this chapter, we introduce the open source Mozilla web browser. Mozilla provides all the capabilities of other popular browsers. We show you how to set up Mozilla for your Red Hat Linux computer so that you can surf the Net. You can use your computer as a multimedia device. After working with Mozilla, we describe how to configure your Linux box to listen to music and create CDs.

Our goal in this chapter is to describe how to use the basic Mozilla features. However, we want you to know that Mozilla can do far more than we describe here. For more information about Mozilla, check out the features available on the Help menu, such as the Reference Library or Help contents.

Making the World Wide Web Possible

Once upon a time, a company named Netscape created a browser to surf the Internet. The browser was originally named Navigator, and later, Communicator. Millions of people downloaded it from the Internet for free. Netscape put in the hands of millions of people (including us, your authors) the power to access the exploding number of web servers. Netscape made history and changed the world because it changed the Internet from a medium that served scientists into a tool that anyone can use.

Even though Netscape Communicator is freely distributed to anyone who wants it, it isn't open source software in the same way that Linux is. Quite simply, Netscape Communicator is a moneymaking venture, and Netscape considers the way the software works to be proprietary.

On the other hand, Netscape recognizes the importance of the open source dynamic, which is why it released an open source version of Netscape, named Mozilla. Now, countless numbers of people are developing and enhancing Mozilla, the default browser for Red Hat Linux computers.

The DVD that comes with this book includes Mozilla, the open source brother to Netscape Communicator. Netscape and Mozilla are quite similar, although they have a slightly different look and feel.

Surfin' the Net with Mozilla

If you have ever browsed the Internet (and who hasn't, these days?), the first thing you want to do is to tailor Mozilla to your preferences. You can complete this task without connecting to the Internet. Follow the steps in this section to customize Mozilla to your liking and set up Mozilla to be your e-mail client.

When you connect to the Internet, the first page you see is your home page. You have the option to set your home page to a Web page you want to see rather than look at a page that someone else wants you to see. You may also want to tweak your history settings for whatever reason (but certainly not a paranoid one). These steps explain what you need to do:

1. **Start Mozilla by clicking the blue globe icon on the GNOME Panel.**

   The Welcome to Red Hat Linux screen appears in Mozilla. You can use this page to find out more information about Red Hat and its products.

   Concentrate on configuring Mozilla and skip over all the Red Hat information; lots of good information is there, however, so explore its world at your leisure.

2. **Choose Edit⇨Preferences.**

   On the left side of the Preferences window is a list of categories, which you can think of as a map of where you are in the Preferences window.

3. **Click the arrow plus sign next to the Navigator category to expand it.**

   Here, you determine which Web page appears when you start Mozilla and which Web page loads when you click the Home button on the Navigation toolbar.

4. **In the Home Page area of the Preferences window, fill in the Location field with the URL of the Web page you want to be your home page.**

   You can also surf to the site of your choice, click Preferences, and then click the Use Current Page button.

   For example, type **www.linuxworld.com** and you see interesting information about Linux whenever you start up your browser or click the Home button, in the upper-left corner of the Mozilla window.

Mozilla remembers where you have been and lets you select (and go to) a previous location. How long Mozilla remembers (and then how big the list becomes) depends on how many days of history you choose. The History configuration option determines the number of days that the locations you visit are saved. If you're short on disk space, choose a lower History number, such as one or two days. Otherwise, leave the default setting alone.

If your Linux computer is connected to a network with a proxy firewall, you have to configure Mozilla to work with it. To do so, from the Preferences window choose Advanced⇨Proxies. Click the Manual Proxy configuration radio button and enter the name of your firewall. For example, enter **proxy.mynetwork.com** in the HTTP Proxy text box (if that's the name of your firewall) and enter **80** in the Port text box. You don't have to perform this configuration if you're using the Red Hat default firewall or the packet-filtering firewalls we describe in this book.

Plugging In Plug-Ins

Mozilla performs the tasks you expect from a browser, like displaying graphics along with text. Without help, Mozilla doesn't go the extra mile and display things like animation and JavaScript. When it comes to special functions, Mozilla is a blank slate.

However, with a little help from friends such as you, Mozilla can go that extra mile. That help comes in the form of plug-ins. A *plug-in* is software Mozilla uses when needed to perform extra functions. To make use of plug-ins, all you need to do is — sorry — plug it in.

The plug-in process is straightforward:

1. **Obtain the plug-in and place it in the Mozilla plug-in directory.**
2. **Optionally, configure the Mozilla preferences to use the plug-in.**

We describe how to download and install several popular — and necessary — plug-ins. Let's start with the popular Macromedia Shockwave Flash plug-in. Mozilla can show animation and other cool stuff. Follow these steps:

1. **Start up Mozilla and your Internet connection (if necessary) and then check to see which plug-ins Mozilla already has access to by clicking the Help⇨About Plug-ins menu.**

   Mozilla shows that only the default plug-in, libnullplugin.so, is installed. You need to download and install some useful plug-ins.

   Clicking the Netscape.com link at the top of the Installed Plug-ins page sends you to the Netscape plug-in Web page. That page describes what plug-ins do and which popular ones are available.

2. **Enter the address** www.macromedia.com/downloads **in the text box and press Enter.**

   The Macromedia download page opens.

3. **Click the Get Macromedia Flash Player button in the Download Free Players section (in the middle of the page).**

4. **Click the Download Now button and the Opening install_flash_player_6_linux.tar.gz window opens.**

   You need to save the file that contains the Flash software, so click OK.

   A second window opens, labeled Enter name of file to save to. Mozilla saves by default to the directory you're working from — generally, your home directory.

5. **Click the Save button and the software is saved to your computer. (The Download Manager window shows the progress of the download.)**

6. **Now you need to unpack and install the Flash plug-in. Open a Gnome Terminal window.**

7. **You need to become root (the superuser), so enter this command in the terminal window:**

   ```
   su
   ```

   Enter the root password when prompted.

8. **Enter this command to unpack the Flash Media software:**

   ```
   tar xzf install_flash_player_6_linux.tar.gz
   ```

   The directory `install_flash_player_6_linux` directory is created, in which the Flash plug-in is placed.

9. **Copy the Flash plug-in to the Mozilla plug-in directory:**

   ```
   cp install_flash_player_6_linux/libflashplayer.so
          /usr/lib/mozilla-*/plug-ins
   ```

We specify using the asterisk (*) in this command because you may be using a different version of Mozilla than we are. The asterisk substitutes for the Mozilla version number.

10. **Choose Help⇨About Plug-ins and the window opens, as shown in Figure 11-1.**

    The Mozilla window described in Step 1 opens and displays the new Flash Player plug-in you just installed.

Figure 11-1: The Plug-in window shows the Flash plug-in.

Your Mozilla browser can now display any Web page that uses Flash content.

Installing the Macromedia Flash Player plug-in helps you a great deal. This list shows some more common plug-ins, available for Linux, that you should consider installing:

- **Acrobat (Adobe):** Reads the Adobe Portable Document Format (PDF) files. Many Web sites provide information via PDF files rather than via HTML or other formats. You can download the Adobe Acrobat plug-in from `ftp://ftp.adobe.com/pub/adobe/acrobatreader/unix/4.x`. (Note that you can use the open source xpdf program to view PDF files.)
- **Shockwave (Macromedia):** Provides multimedia, graphics, and game-oriented support. You can download the Shockwave plug-in from `www.macromedia.com/downloads`.

- **RealPlayer (RealAudio):** Allows you to play the RealNetworks audio and video streams. Many Internet radio stations still use the RealNetworks protocols to stream their content. You can download the RealPlayer plug-in from

  ```
  http://proforma.real.com/real/player/unix/unix.html?src=d
        ownloadr,000814rpchoice_c1
  ```

  Install the RPM package and then copy the plug-in to the Mozilla plug-in directory, just like with Macromedia Flash:

  ```
  cp /usr/lib/RealPlayer8/rpnp.so /usr/lib/mozilla-*/plug-
        ins
  ```

  You can also use the RealPlayer8 application to listen directly to RealAudio streams.

- **Java (Sun Microsystems):** A programming language that many Web sites use to provide dynamic content. Although dynamic content comes in many forms, it's basically anything that changes over time. Java is good at providing those interesting and often annoying Web thingies that spin around and do other silly tricks. Download the Java 2 Platform, Standard Edition (J2SE) RPM for Linux from `java.sun.com/j2se/1.4.1/download.html`.

Speaking of tunes, the next section shows how to play music from your CD-ROM.

Groovin' to Tunes with CD Player

Imagine that you're sitting alone, working at your computer. Or, you could be reading a book that's boring you. It's Saturday night too, of course. What a drag. Want some diversion? Perhaps some music? We can't provide music, but we can show you how to use your computer to listen to some tunes.

In the following sections, we show you the tools Red Hat Linux provides to make your workstation into a sound system, including all the necessary applications to play CDs, and tools for connecting your PC to a sound card and speakers. Start by making sure that your computer can play music.

Setting up your sound system

Red Hat Linux should have automatically configured your computer's sound system during the post installation process we describe in Chapter 3. However, you may run into problems — especially on older computers — so Red Hat provides a sound card detection utility.

You can configure and test your sound card at the same time by following these steps:

1. **Log in to your Linux computer, click the GNOME Menu button, and choose System Settings⇨Soundcard Detection.**

   Enter the root password, if prompted.

   The Audio Devices window opens, as shown in Figure 11-2.

2. **Click the Play test sound button.**

   If you hear some mellow music, your computer is ready to rock.

3. **Click OK and you're ready to go.**

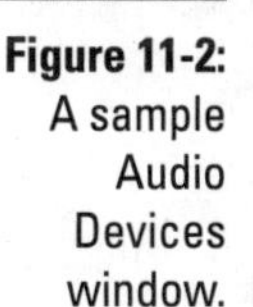

Figure 11-2: A sample Audio Devices window.

If you're plugged in correctly and you repeated the steps, but *still* didn't hear any sound, one of these reasons may explain why:

- Your computer has an old, unrecognizable sound card.
- You don't have a sound card.
- Someone else's stereo is way too loud.

You definitely have to purchase a sound card if you don't have one. Using old sound cards is generally difficult, so we also recommend purchasing a replacement. We can't help you much with the third possibility.

The Red Hat Esound daemon (referred to as *ESD*) is designed to allow multiple applications to use your computer's sound system at the same time. Sometimes, however, an application may not be able to take advantage of this elegant system. For example, when you start XMMS, you may have to turn off the ESD daemon. You can turn off ESD by starting a GNOME Terminal window and entering this command:

```
HUP esd
```

Playing CDs

Everyone wants a little music in their life. But you went ahead and bought a computer rather than a stereo system. D'oh! No problem: It happens that you indeed spent your money wisely because your Red Hat Linux computer functions well as a stereo system. This section describes how to set up your computer to play music CDs.

Red Hat bundles two open source CD players for Linux users: CD Player and XMMS. We describe CD Player in this chapter because it automatically starts when you insert a CD in your computer. (We don't ignore XMMS, however, because we show you in Chapter 12 how to use it to play Internet audio streams.)

Anyway, these steps show how to start playing music:

1. **Log in as any user and pop a CD into the CD drive.**

   The GNOME CD Player application appears.

2. **Listen as your CD starts playing.**

Those are the easiest steps in this book. However, if you exit from CD Player, you have to restart it manually (unless you insert another CD, in which case CD Player starts automatically again). You can start CD Player by clicking the GNOME Menu button and choosing Sound & Video⇨CD Player. Nothing to it!

The CD Player controls should be familiar territory for anyone born in the 20th century. Here's a quick refresher for those cavepeople out there:

- To change the volume, click the vertical slide bar on the right side of the CD Player window. Hold the mouse button while you adjust the volume.
- Click the crossed tools (a screwdriver and wrench) button, toward the middle-left area of the window, to open the Preferences window. You can then select how CD Player reacts when you start and stop it. You can also control the default CD device (the default is `/dev/cdrom`, but you many want to change it to `/dev/cdrom1`, or other devices, depending on your computer hardware). You can also select the theme of the CD Player skin. A simple help system is available too.
- The remaining controls are self explanatory: start, stop, forward, yada-yada.

As you can see, playing CDs is pretty simple. Note that in Chapter 12 we show you how to use simple XMMS and the general-purpose MPlayer players to play Internet music streams and files.

Ripping CDs

Are you paranoid? If not, do you want to be? Well, cdparanoia can help fulfill all your fears. Just kidding. Really, cdparanoia is used for ripping the audio information — music files — from CDs to your hard drive or to other CDs. *Ripping* refers to the process of copying audio from a CD to your computer.

The following steps show how to use the GNOME RIP (Grip) interface to simplify using cdparanoia to copy music from a CD to your hard drive:

1. **Insert your favorite CD in the drive, click the GNOME Menu button, and choose Sound & Video➪More Sound & Video Applications.**

   The Grip window opens, as shown in Figure 11-3.

2. **Click the Rip column (on the right side of screen) of each track you want to use.**

   A check mark appears next to each track you select.

3. **Select the Rip tab at the top of the window (next to the Tracks tab).**

4. **Click the Rip Only button.**

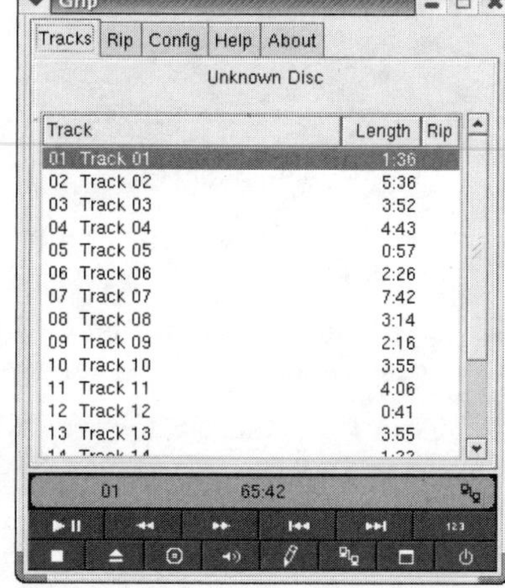

Figure 11-3: The Grip window shows a CD's tracks.

Grip opens the cdparanoia program and feeds it the options you just chose. The music is stored in Ogg, the up-and-coming open source protocol. Grip creates by default the `ogg` directory in your home directory (assuming that you haven't changed the defaults). Grip creates a subdirectory (in `ogg`) named after each

CD you record. Individual tracks are stored in files named after each song; those files live in the directory named after the CD.

After you create the music file, you can listen to it with XMMS or GNOME-CD.

Entering the Ring of Fire: Burning CDs

Back in the 1980s, when vinyl melted away under the invasion of CDs, building the factories to create the CDs cost megabucks; back then, it took a huge effort to make a CD. Now, for roughly the $100 it costs to purchase a CD burner (to *burn* means to record to CD), you can build your own, personal factory. Amazing!

If you don't have a CD burner (or writer), this section doesn't do you a bit of good. Sorry.

A one-time recordable CD is referred to as a *CD-R;* a rewritable CD is a *CD-RW.* CD burners look like regular read-only drives and are connected with either an IDE or SCSI interface.

Using the Nautilus Burn:/// Utility

Nautilus provides an alternative CD-burning utility. Just insert a CD-R or CD-RW into a CDR drive and Nautilus does the rest. These steps describe how to use the system:

1. **Log in as any user and insert a CD-R or CD-RW disc into your CD writer drive.**
2. **Double-click your home directory icon, in the upper-left corner of your desktop.**

   A Nautilus window opens, showing the contents of your home directory.
3. **Click and hold any file or directory and drag it to the burn:/// window.**

   All the files and directories are displayed in the burn:/// window; those files and directories aren't really copied, but instead are linked to the burn:/// window.
4. **Click any and all of the files and directories in order to highlight them.**

   Selecting a file or directory enables it to be written to CD.
5. **Click the Write to CD button and you're off to the races.**

   After a little thought, the Writing CD dialog box opens.

   When the CD write is finished, the disc is ejected by default.
6. **Click the Close button when you're finished.**
7. **Close the CD tray by pushing it back into the drive.**

   A Nautilus window opens, showing the contents of the disc you just finished writing.

Burn, Baby, Burn: Burning CDs

The steps in this section describe how to create, or *burn,* a CD-ROM. You can copy any kind of file to your CD-R or CD-RW:

1. **Log in as any user and insert a CD-R or CD-RW disc into your CD writer drive. (Close the Burn:/// window when it opens.)**

   What can you burn? The world's your oyster, and you can make a CD of anything you want: data, software, or music. A good place to start is by backing up your `/home` directory on CD.

2. **Click the GNOME Menu button and choose System Tools⇨More System Tools⇨CD Writer.**

   The GNOME Toaster window opens, as shown in Figure 11-4; an Information dialog box that you can read and close by clicking the OK button opens too.

3. **Click the Folder icon, near the lower-left side of the window.**

   Gtoaster contains its own file manager.

4. **Find the file or directory you want to record by clicking the directory where it's stored.**

   For example, double-click `/home` and then the `paul/ogg/Pat Metheny` directory.

5. **Click and drag the files or directory (the `rh18fd` directory, in this example) to the Folder subwindow you opened in Step 3.**

   You don't have to use the GNOME Toaster file manager to select the file or files to record. You can open a Nautilus window and drag the file over to the Track subwindow.

6. **Click the CD icon, immediately below the Track button in the lower-left corner of the window.**

   The Record subwindow opens and replaces the Track subwindow. You're presented with several options that control the CD-R/RW drive. The default settings should work for your ISO image. ISO (International Organization for Standards) is in this context a type of file system that can be read by many different types of computer operating systems.

7. **Click the Record button and the CD recording process counts down.**

   You have nine seconds to abort your mission.

8. **You can stop the process by pressing the Stop button.**

   Your home directory is burned to the CD, creating a simple, reliable, and effective backup system. It's easy to use.

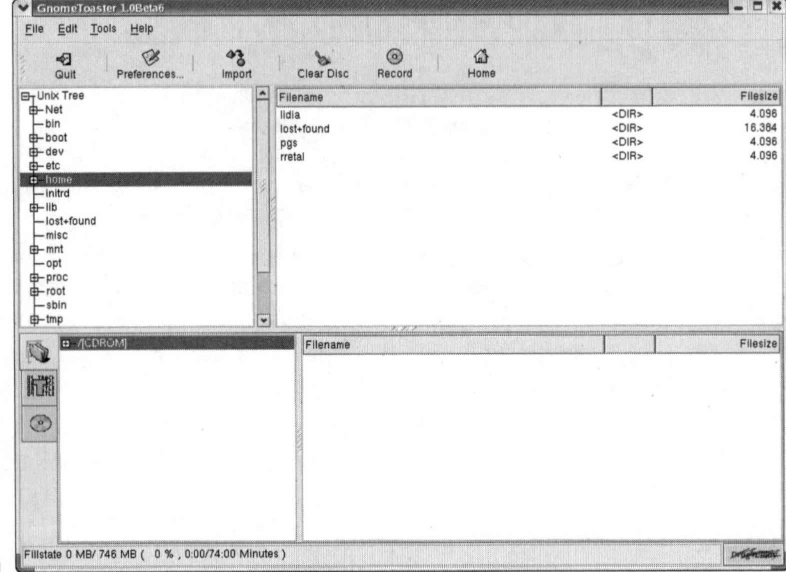

Figure 11-4: The GNOME Toaster window.

Chapter 12

Live from the Net

In This Chapter

- Using XMMS to listen to Internet audio streams
- Listening to live radio and playing DVDs with MPlayer

One of the great innovations of recent times is the use of the Internet to transmit — stream — audio and video programs. Streaming technology provides the ability for anyone to create a radio or TV station unlimited in terms of geography and governmental approval; it also can be done inexpensively. Using streaming technology, computer users can listen to or view those broadcasts from anywhere.

This chapter describes how to use your Red Hat Linux machine as both an audio radio receiver and a DVD video player. We use the open source XMMS and MPlayer applications to listen to the Net.

Using the XMMS Audio Player

The open source XMMS (X MultiMedia System) application is a great tool for listening to audio streams and files. XMMS plays `.wav` files produced by `grip/cdparanoia` by default. It also plays the up-and-coming open source Ogg/Vorbis format (codec).

The Ogg codec doesn't use any proprietary or patented algorithms. Ogg is free for anyone to use, and people and organizations that don't want to depend on proprietary systems are discovering it; Ogg also produces higher-fidelity audio streams than other popular systems, such as MP3. Why depend on another corporation's whims when you don't have to?

You can use XMMS to listen to some of the music you may have saved in Chapter 11. If you used `grip` to save music to your home directory and you want to listen to it, open XMMS and right-click the window. Choose Open⇨File and select any of the WAV files you created.

Ogg is the system used to format audio streams, and *Vorbis* is used to compress formatted audio streams. Unlike most other technological systems, Ogg/Vorbis isn't an acronym but rather is named after science fiction characters. For more information about Ogg/Vorbis and similar open source multimedia systems, go to `www.vorbis.com`.

Now that you have a bit of technological background, you can start using XMMS to listen to Ogg/Vorbis streams:

1. **Log in to your computer and open Mozilla by clicking the blue globe icon in the GNOME Panel. Enter the address** www.vorbis.com/music.psp **in the Mozilla text box.**
2. **Click any of the Track links.**

   For example, click the first one, Lepidoptera.

   The Downloading Epoq-Lepidoptera.ogg dialog box opens.
3. **Click the OK button and then the Save button.**

   The Enter the Name of File to Save to window opens, and Mozilla saves the music file to your home directory.
4. **Start XMMS by clicking the GNOME Menu and choosing Sound & Video⇨Audio Player.**

   An XMMS window opens. Figure 12-1 shows the player.
5. **Right-click the XMMS window, choose Play File, and click the filename you just saved to disk. When you click the OK button, XMMS starts playing the music.**

Figure 12-1: The XMMS window.

The Vorbis Web page provides links to other Ogg-capable sources. For example, click the Music Sites Page link, near the top of the `www.vorbis.com/music.psp` page. You see a page with links to other sources. For example, click the WCPE link to go to a Web page that streams classical music.

Now is a good time to describe how to configure Mozilla to automatically start XMMS whenever you click Ogg/Vorbis sources and streams:

1. **Log in and open Mozilla and then click the Edit⇨Preferences menu.**

   The Preferences window opens.

2. **Choose Navigator⇨Helper Applications.**

   The Helpers Applications subwindow opens in the Preferences window.

   Red Hat has added a MIME (Multipurpose Internet Mail Extensions) entry for Ogg, which is displayed as `application/x-ogg` in the File types subwindow.

3. **Click `application/x-ogg` and then the Edit button.**

   The Edit Type dialog box opens, displaying the information that it knows how to handle the Ogg-formatted media. Figure 12-2 shows the completed Edit Type dialog box.

   This list describes the various fields:

   - **MIME type:** The MIME type associated with the helper application. If you have read Chapter 10, you know that MIME types help your computer decide how to handle different media formats and types. Enter **audio/x-ogg** in this field.
   - **Description:** Any short text describing the MIME type.
   - **Extension:** The file type extension in this field. In this case, Ogg files use the `ogg` extension.
   - **When a file of this type is encountered:** What you want to do with the stream when the MIME type is encountered. You can choose to use the default application, which in this case is XMMS; specify an application to use; or save the information to disk as a file.
   - **Always ask me before handling files of this type:** Forces Mozilla to prompt you before doing anything with the MIME type.

4. **Click the Open it With button and enter** /usr/bin/xmms **in the text box.**
5. **Click the OK button in the Edit Type dialog box to return to the Preferences window.**
6. **Click the OK button in the Preferences window to return to Mozilla.**

Figure 12-2: Using the Edit Type window.

Mozilla now launches XMMS whenever you click a link to an Ogg/Vorbis source. XMMS starts and connects and then plays the stream.

XMMS uses the Enlightened Sound Daemon (esd) process by default to access your computer's speakers. Designed to allow multiple audio players to simultaneously use your computer's speakers, esd sometimes gets confused and you have to restart it. Log in as root, open a GNOME Terminal window, and run the command **killall -HUP esd**. If that doesn't work, you can configure XMMS to use another output system. Right-click the XMMS window and choose Options➪ Preferences. Click the Output Plug-in subwindow and select the OSS Driver 1.2.7 plug-in. Click the Apply button and then the OK button.

Using the Fabulous MPlayer

Whenever a desperate need exists, the Superman — err — the open source movement, comes in to save the day. Until recently, you couldn't use any single Linux application to listen to and view most popular streaming formats. Now, MPlayer has burst on the scene and fills that gap.

MPlayer can play most popular (and many obscure) audio and video streaming formats. Although it's under intense development, it's still technically in the beta development phase. However, MPlayer is quite usable, and we think that you should consider using it. We do!

This list shows some streaming formats MPlayer can play:

- **MPEG-1/Layer 3 (MP3):** MP3 is a popular but proprietary codec used for both storing and streaming audio.
- **Ogg/Vorbis:** This new up-and-coming open source streaming format is unencumbered by any copyrights or patents, like other formats are.
- **Microsoft Media Server (MMS):** You can listen to radio broad casts that use the popular MMS format with MPlayer. Previously, you needed to use the Microsoft client to listen to MMS streams.
- **Digital Versatile Disc (DVD):** You can play DVDs from your computer with MPlayer.
- **RealAudio:** You need to download, compile, and install the RTSP package to use RealAudio.

MPlayer is not now included in the Red Hat Linux distribution. We hope that it will be later, but for now you have to obtain it from its developers. These steps describe how to download, install, and use MPlayer:

1. **Log in, open Mozilla, and go to** `www.mplayerhq.hu/homepage/dload.html`**.**
2. **Click the latest Red Hat RPM version.**

   At the time this book was written, the latest Red Hat RPMS was found in the MPlayer Red Hat 7.*x* RPM packages. The 7.*x* packages work on Red Hat 10 systems.
3. **Download each of these packages:**

   ```
   mplayer
   mplayer-common
   mplayer-gui
   mplayer-skins
   ```

   and this font package:

   ```
   MplayerISO-885901-font
   ```

   At the time this edition of the book was written, the most recent MPlayer RPM package was version 0.92. You may see — and should use — the most recent version available.
4. **Open a GNOME Terminal window and change to root:**

   ```
   su -
   ```

   Enter the root password when prompted.
5. **Install the package:**

   ```
   rpm -ivh --nodeps mplayer*
   ```

One good source for audio streams is `www.shoutcast.com`. Click any of the Tune In! buttons and Mozilla downloads several playlists and launches MPlayer to play the music via the playlists.

Playlists are files that store the locations of one or more audio and video streams. For example, if you click any of the Shoutcast streams (at `www.shoutcast.com`), Mozilla saves the playlist to the */tmp* directory, starts MPlayer, and directs it to play the playlists. The playlist MIME type, x-scpls, was inserted into Mozilla as a helper application when you installed the MPlayer packages.

Alternatively, you can click the Save to disk button and save the playlist to your home directory. You can then manually start MPlayer from a terminal emulator window or the Run Program utility with the command `mplayer -playlist playlist.pls`.

You can use MPlayer to play music files too. Suppose that you use `grip` in Chapter 11 to save some music to a file named `track1.wav`. Enter this command to play that file:

```
mplayer track1.wav
```

Press the Control key and then the C key (Ctrl-c) to end the session.

You can use MPlayer to listen to all sorts of streams. The entire world of Internet radio and — hopefully, soon — video broadcasts is open to you. MPlayer will only become more versatile and useful.

MPlayer plays DVDs too! Use the command `grep -i dvd /var/log/dmesg` to locate the DVD device file. For example, your DVD device file should be something like `/dev/hdd`. Next, create a *soft link file* so that MPlayer knows where to find the DVD drive: `ln -s /dev/hdd /dev/dvd`. Start MPlayer, right-click the MPlayer – Video window and choose Open⇨Play DVD. The DVD plays.

The first MPlayer RealAudio (using the RTSP protocol) plug-in was just recently released from `www.live.com/mplayer`. The plug-in is still too young for easy use, but soon will be. Keep an eye on this system. When the Live.com RTSP plug-in for MPlayer matures, you can listen to an outstanding interview with The Man himself — Linus Torvalds — by opening this URL from gmplayer or MPlayer:

```
rtsp://audio.npr.org/fa/20010604.fa.rm
```

In this clip, Terri Gross, from National Public Radio, conducts an interview during the summer of 2001 on her program, "Fresh Air." Linus discusses the development of Linux, his life in Silicon Valley, and other matters. You can also use the commercial RealPlayer8 to listen to this or any RealAudio stream. The section in Chapter 11 about plugging in plug-ins describes where to obtain the RealPlayer8 RPM package.

Audio by proxy: Getting XMMS to work through your firewall

Firewalls are necessary to fight the evil guys who lurk on the Internet, but they can put a kink in your listening pleasure. A *firewall* is used to prevent unauthorized access from the outside — in most cases, the Internet — from reaching your computer or network.

The firewall we show you how to build in Chapter 8 and the default Red Hat firewall don't affect either of the players described in this chapter. However, many LANs are connected through *proxy* firewalls, which intercept packets sent to the Internet and rewrite them according to certain rules; our firewalls are filter packets based on their source and destination addresses and ports.

If your Red Hat Linux workstation sits on a network with a packet-filtering firewall, such as the one you may have installed in Chapter 8, you don't need to modify XMMS. The key is that the filtering firewall allows all outgoing TCP and UDP connections (or ports). However, if your network uses a proxy-based firewall, you may have to modify XMMS. (gmplayer doesn't have any mechanism specifically designed to work with proxies.)

To configure XMMS to work with proxy firewalls, follow these steps:

1. **Start XMMS, right-click the XMMS window, and choose Options⇨Preferences.**
2. **Click the Ogg Vorbis plug-in in the Input Plug-ins subwindow and click Configure.**

   The Ogg Vorbis Configuration window opens. You need to enter the address of your proxy server. You may need to contact your friendly neighborhood systems administrator to get that information.
3. **Click the Use Proxy button and enter the proxy server address in the Host subwindow.**
4. **Click the Use Authentication radio button and enter your username and password in their respective subwindows if your proxy server requires them.**

Launching gmplayer from the GNOME Panel

Until now, you have been manually launching MPlayer. Now it's time to put gmplayer in its place on the GNOME Panel. You can create an applet launcher (an icon to click) for gmplayer on the GNOME Panel.

The *Panel* is the gray bar that rests along the bottom of your screen.

Follow these steps to create a launcher applet for gmplayer:

1. **Right-click any blank section of the GNOME Panel and choose Add to Panel⇨Launcher menus.**

2. **Type a name for the gmplayer launcher icon and press the Tab key to display the Generic Name text box. Enter any name you want.**

   An entry such as `Radio Player` or `Streaming Audio/Video player` describes what the launcher is meant to do.

3. **Press the Tab key again and enter a descriptive comment in the Comment text box.**

   The comment is displayed whenever you place the cursor over the MPlayer icon.

4. **Press the Tab key one more time and type** /usr/bin/gmplayer **in the Command text box.**

5. **Click the Icon button at the bottom of the Launcher window to pick an icon for the launcher.**

   The Browse icons window opens and displays the generic GNOME icon images. You can select any image you want by clicking the image and then clicking the OK button. You return to the Create Launcher window.

   Selecting an icon image in this step means that you can skip Steps 7 through 9, which help you find custom icon images. Skip to Step 9.

6. **Click the Browse button to select a custom image.**

   The Browse window opens.

7. **Select any generic icon you like and click the OK button.**

   The gmplayer icon is displayed in the Launcher window, ready and waiting to launch the program.

8. **Click the Close button and the gmplayer icon is placed on the GNOME Panel.**

9. **Click the OK button in the Launcher window and click the new gmplayer launcher you just created on the GNOME Panel.**

   The new icon is inserted into the GNOME Panel and the gmplayer window opens.

You can also reach gmplayer from the GNOME menu. After you install the MPlayer packages, log out and then log in again. Click the GNOME Menu button and choose Sound & Video➪More Sound & Video Applications➪gmplayer.

You can easily copy the gmplayer icon (or any icon) from the GNOME Panel to your desktop. Click and hold the gmplayer icon in the GNOME Panel and drag it to your desktop. Release the mouse button and the icon is copied to your desktop background. You can then right-click the desktop icon and choose Properties from the menu that pops up. The gmplayer Properties window opens and enables you to modify the icon's look and feel.

Chapter 13

Going to the Office

In This Chapter

- Introducing OpenOffice
- Using OpenOffice Writer
- Printing from OpenOffice

Red Hat Linux is a great product that comes with a large base of services and applications. It has always been an outstanding platform for providing services and technical applications. But you didn't find Red Hat, until recently, on many of the world's workday computers; in other words, it lacked a presence on the "desktop."

The Red Hat problem was its lack of a full-blown office suite to work with word processing documents, spreadsheets, and similar documents. Fortunately, desktop productivity suites — such as OpenOffice and its sister application, StarOffice — have taken Linux out of the back office and into the front.

Opening Your Office

The OpenOffice desktop productivity suite does nearly everything Microsoft Office does, but for less money. How much less? Well, 100 percent less because it's 100 percent free. Sun Microsystems, Inc., sells the version named StarOffice and also provides an open source version named — you guessed it — OpenOffice. OpenOffice is licensed under the GPL/LGPL and SIISL licenses. What do all those letters mean? They mean f-r-e-e, and they also mean that Linux can integrate office productivity features from OpenOffice because Linux and OpenOffice share the GPL license. You can find more information about the licenses at `www.openoffice.org/project/www/license.html`.

OpenOffice is not only free (did we mention that it's free?), but it's also powerful, providing you with these functions:

- **Word processor:** A full-function what-you-see-is-what-you-get (WYSIWYG) word processor named Writer. OpenOffice Writer comes with many functions you would expect — formatting, cutting and pasting, graphics, spell checking, and more, as shown in Figure 13-1. It uses its own format and can also read from and write to Rich Text Format (RTF); plus, it handles Microsoft Word 6.0, Word 95, and Word 97, Word 2000, and Word XP files.
- **Spreadsheet:** A full-function spreadsheet program, named Calc, used by Wall Street brokers to calculate their option strike prices and similar items. If you're familiar with spreadsheet software, Calc should be straightforward to use. Figure 13-2 shows the initial Calc window.
- **Presentation:** A graphics program named Impress with all the bells and whistles for creating presentations. You can also import and export PowerPoint documents with Impress. Figure 13-3 shows the Impress window.
- **Drawing:** The OpenOffice Draw program gives you graphics tools for creating anything from a novice drawing to a masterpiece, as shown in Figure 13-4. Draw provides your creative side with a tool for creating graphics.
- **Miscellaneous:** OpenOffice provides other functions, such as an HTML editor, a math editor for supernerds, and label and business card creation tools. You can also create word processing templates.

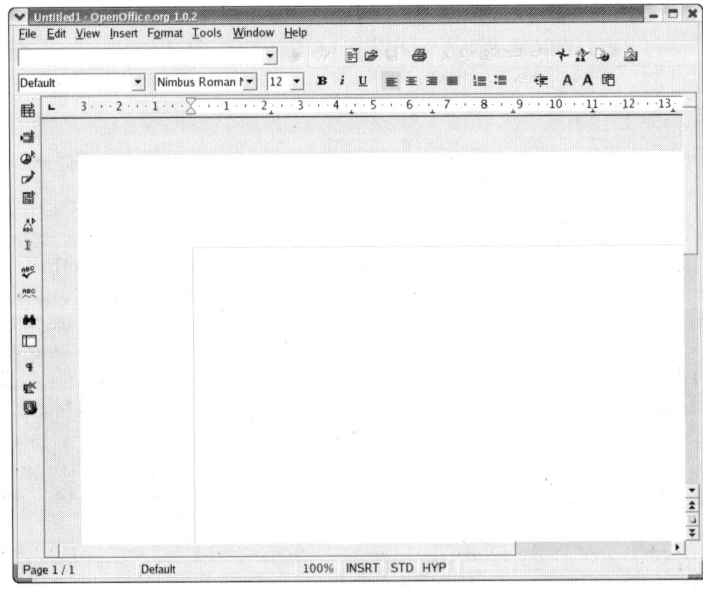

Figure 13-1: The OpenOffice word processor window.

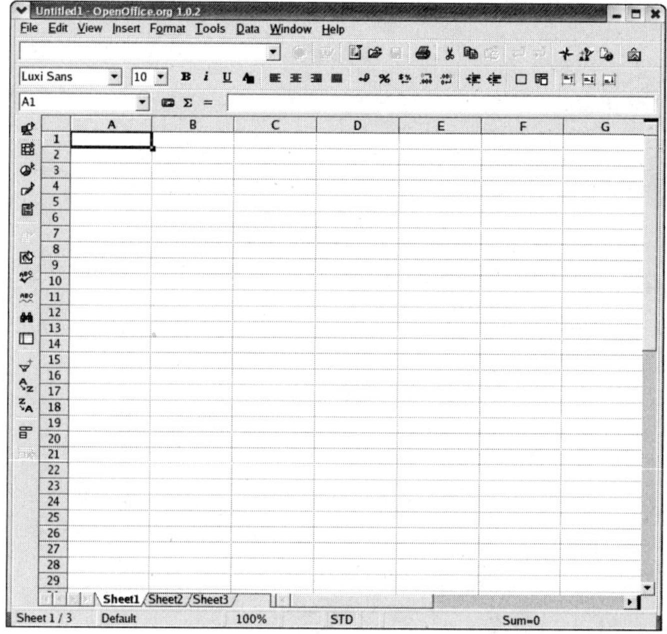

Figure 13-2: The OpenOffice spreadsheet window.

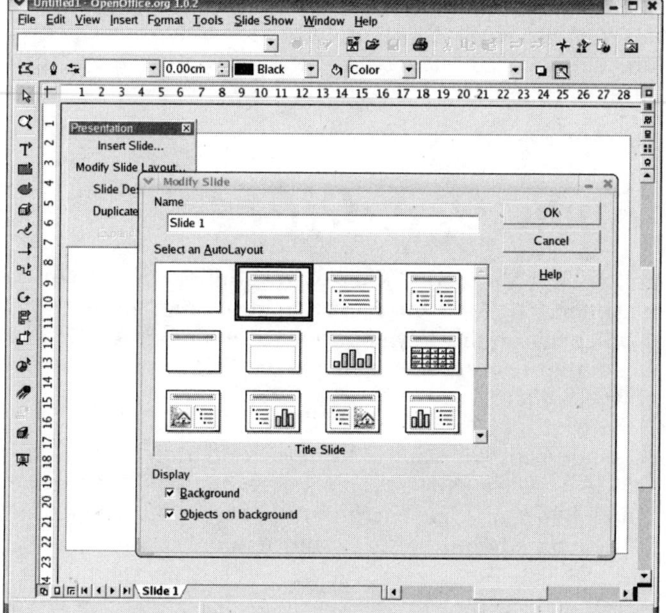

Figure 13-3: The OpenOffice Impress window.

Figure 13-4: The OpenOffice graphics program, Draw.

Okay, so OpenOffice has lots of great features. How good are they? Can they get the job done? Well, we wrote this edition of the book using OpenOffice, and we wrote the preceding edition using StarOffice. That's not a bad testimonial to the capabilities of OpenOffice.

Getting to Know OpenOffice

If you're familiar with Microsoft Office, you should be able to find your way around OpenOffice. The look and feel are a little different, but the idea is the same. OpenOffice is also morally superior to Office because it's free *and* a part of open source. This section briefly describes some of the most common functions of OpenOffice.

The next few sections provide only a basic introduction to the things you can do with OpenOffice. No, we're not lazy; it's just that it would take too much space to describe it all in detail. Please experiment with your own test documents and consult the online help system for more information.

Firing up and using OpenOffice

Red Hat Linux provides OpenOffice and installs it by default. OpenOffice is easy to access. Click the GNOME Menu button and then choose Office⇨OpenOffice

Writer. You can choose some of, but not all, the other OpenOffice functions from this menu too. (However, you can start the spreadsheet program, Calc, only from an OpenOffice window. From any window — Writer or Impress, for example — choose File⇨New⇨Spreadsheet to open Calc.) After thinking about life for a few seconds, the OpenOffice window appears.

The first time you start OpenOffice, it asks whether you want to use the workstation or personal model. The former installs the OpenOffice programs in a central location accessible to all users; the latter option installs a copy of OpenOffice in your home directory. We use the workstation configuration in this section, but you can select the personal model.

When you use OpenOffice for the first time, you're also asked a few questions about importing an address book. We cancel the operation because we prefer to use the Ximian Evolution address book.

You can access all OpenOffice functions by clicking the File button, in the upper-left corner of the window, and then the option you want.

The following list introduces the functions. You're probably familiar with the layout and operation of the menu if you have used Microsoft Office:

- **File:** As you may expect, you can open, close, save, and otherwise manipulate OpenOffice documents by using the File menu. Writer files have the `.sxw` extension. Other file formats, such as Microsoft Word and HTML, must be imported and exported.
- **New:** You can create a new document for any OpenOffice function. When you choose File⇨New, you're given the option to create a new text document, spreadsheet, presentation, or other function.
- **Edit:** This menu provides all the functions you need to modify documents. Functions such as cut, copy, paste, and delete are all provided. The functions that are active at any time depend on whether you're editing a document, spreadsheet, or presentation. For example, the cut, copy, and paste options aren't active if you're not editing a document (like just when you first start up OpenOffice and have not opened any files).

  You can also track changes, just as you can in Microsoft Word. Choose Edit⇨Changes and you can track changes on a character-by-character basis. You can display the changes or keep them hidden from view. When you're satisfied with your edits, you can make the changes permanent and save only the finished document to disk. It's pretty cool.

  OpenOffice also provides the Find and Replace function from the Edit menu. The Find and Replace feature enables you to find text strings and either replace them with another string or delete them. You can search forward or backward through a document. You can replace one instance or all instances.

- **Spell check:** OpenOffice provides a spell checker, of course. You can tell the spell checker to check an entire document by choosing Tools⇨Spell Check⇨Check. You're prompted to act on each possible spelling error the checker detects.

  Alternatively, you can set the spell checker to operate continuously. Choose Tools⇨Spellcheck⇨AutoSpellCheck to toggle on the real-time spell checker; when it's activated, a check mark appears next to the menu option. The Continuous option tells OpenOffice Writer to check each word you enter and underlines possible misspellings with a squiggly red line. The red line disappears when you successfully correct the mistake.

- **View:** This menu displays or hides the various menu bars. You can display a document's formatting characters and also increase or decrease the size (zoom in or out) of the text displayed on the screen. The zoom function enables you to make smaller fonts more readable without changing the document.

- **Insert:** This menu enables you to insert special characters, objects, files, and macros into your documents. Special characters include various symbols (accents and umlauts, for example) that aren't part of the everyday character set (unless you happen to use words like *café* frequently). Objects include graphics, symbols, and figures. (You can create your own figures with Draw.) You can also insert macros and hyperlinks into your documents.

  You can insert tables into documents with any number of rows and columns. OpenOffice can automatically adjust the row height, or you can do it manually. Choose Insert⇨Table and play around with this feature.

- **Tools:** From this menu, you can access the spell checker, thesaurus, various OpenOffice configuration settings, and other functions. Tools such as the spell checker are self explanatory.

- **Window:** This menu enables you to control the look of your desktop. In addition to enabling you to modify and move windows, the menu provides other manipulation capabilities.

- **Help:** OpenOffice provides pretty good online help services. Many are context sensitive. If you're editing a text document, click the Help menu to get access to information related to the Writer module.

  For example, choose Help⇨Help Agent and the Help Agent window appears. The Help Agent provides assistance in several areas of interest to new users, including

  - **Introduction to Writer:** Provides an introduction to the word processor
  - **Basic tips text documents:** Tells you all you ever wanted to know (and then some) about reading, writing, and printing text documents

- **Advanced tips:** Extends the preceding basic text document tip to more advanced subjects
- **Menus:** Describes how all the OpenOffice menus work together
- **Toolbars:** Describes the toolbars that provide information and shortcuts
- **Shortcuts:** Describes which key combinations can be used to perform various word processing functions
- **New stuff:** Describes what's new since the last OpenOffice version
- **Support:** Displays brief information about getting support from Sun Microsystems

Printing with OpenOffice

Printing from OpenOffice is a simple process after you have configured Red Hat Linux to use a printer. OpenOffice uses the default Linux printer, so all you have to do is configure it. This section first describes how to configure a Red Hat Linux printer and then shows you how to set up OpenOffice to use that printer.

Configuring a printer attached to your Red Hat Linux computer is a simple process. All you have to do is run the `printconf-gui` printer configuration utility and enter the information about your printer. These steps describe how to do it:

1. **Log in to your Red Hat Linux computer as root.**
2. **Attach a printer to your Linux computer's parallel (printer) port.**

   The parallel port is a 25-pin female connector on the back of your computer case. New computers usually label the parallel port with some kind of printer icon (although sometimes it's hard to imagine how they came up with the symbol). If yours isn't marked, there's no harm in finding the appropriate port through trial and error.
3. **Start the printer configuration tool by clicking the GNOME Menu button and choosing System Settings⇨Printing.**

   Enter the root password if prompted. The Printer configuration window opens.
4. **To add a printer, click the New button. When the introductory Add a New Print Queue window opens, click the Forward button.**

   The Add a new print queue dialog box opens.

5. **Enter a descriptive queue name (for example,** Epson777**) and, optionally, a description of the queue. (You can, of course, use the default name —** `printer` **— but we prefer to use descriptive names.)**

6. **Click the Forward button to open the Queue Type dialog box.**

   Assuming that your printer is directly connected to your computer, you see the device name `/dev/lp0` in the Queue Type dialog box.

7. **Select the** `/dev/lp0` **device and click the Forward button.**

   The Printer model dialog box opens. You can choose from various manufacturers or generic models.

8. **Click the Generic (Click to Select Manufacturer) button.**

   Select your printer's manufacturer from the drop-down menu.

9. **Use the vertical slide bar to locate and select your particular model and then click the Forward button.**

   When you finish, the Add a new print queue dialog box opens.

10. **Click the Finish button.**

    A Question window opens. You're asked whether you want to print a test page. Click the OK button and a test page is printed.

    An Information window opens and you're prompted to check whether the test page printed successfully.

11. **Click the OK button to return to the Printer Configuration window.**

    You can create an additional print queue or modify existing ones.

The GNOME Print Manager window opens and shows an icon for the new print queue you just created. Double-click the new icon and a status window opens that shows current and past print jobs.

Now that you have a printer connected to your Red Hat Linux computer, you can print from OpenOffice without any further configuration. OpenOffice uses the Red Hat Linux printer configuration by default. Open a file you want to print. From the OpenOffice desktop, choose File⇨Print. You can choose to print the entire document, individual pages, or a range of pages.

Chapter 14

Days of Wine and Applications

In This Chapter

- Introducing and using Wine
- Using CodeWeavers CrossOver Office
- Using VMware to run virtual Windows and Linux computers

As you know if you have been reading other chapters of this book, Linux provides for many, if not most, of your desktop needs. The applications described in the preceding chapters satisfy most of your daily work requirements. All the essential applications, such as OpenOffice and Evolution, are at your disposal.

Sometimes, however, you need to perform some function that isn't provided for in the Linux world. For example, most games are written for the Microsoft world and aren't available for Linux. At times, such as when you're editing documents with complex macros, you must use Microsoft Word. That's when Wine and VMware come to the rescue.

Still, there's always room for improvement, and the open source world works hard to provide new and useful applications.

Introducing Wine

Wine doesn't come from the Sonoma Valley or even from the south of France. You can't get tipsy or spend much money on it either. Wine isn't a beverage, but rather a software system that allows you to run Windows applications on a Linux computer. Wine helps to fill the Linux application gap.

Modern Windows applications, at their core, are written to run on Intel, or Intel-compatible (AMD, for example) Pentium processors. (Some Windows applications are run on Apple Macs; for purposes of this discussion, however, we're talking about only Intel-based PCs.) However, you can't just load a program like Microsoft Word on your Linux computer and expect it to work.

The Microsoft Windows operating system provides a platform for running Microsoft applications, such as Word. That platform is a little like an electrical plug that provides the power to run various appliances; the appliances are analogous to applications. What the Windows plug provides is a library of commonly used low-level functions that are referred to as an Application Program Interface (API). Those functions perform tasks common to every application, such as opening a file or talking over a network. Using a common library prevents every single application from having to reinvent the wheel. Instead, the applications just plug into the common "outlet" and concentrate on performing their particular function.

The problem is that the Windows platform, or "plug," has square holes and Linux has round ones. You can't plug Word directly into the Linux operating system, for example. That's where Wine comes in and provides the adapter so that you can plug the round peg into the square hole.

Wine stands for Wine Is Not an Emulator. This typical acronym is the type that Linux and Unix programmers love. The Wine acronym means not only that some people just need to get out more, but also that it doesn't simulate (emulate) the entire Windows environment. Rather, it duplicates the interface between the application and the operating system. Using the electrical plug analogy, Wine doesn't emulate the entire electrical grid (as in Windows) but, rather, simply provides the adapter.

Downloading Wine

Unfortunately, because Red Hat doesn't include Wine in its distribution, you have to download it from the Internet. These steps describe how to do so:

1. **Log in to your Red Hat Linux computer as any user.**

   You can log in as the superuser (root) if you want, but that's not necessary. By not logging in as the superuser, you don't run the risk of unintentionally damaging your computer (for example, deleting all your files).

2. **Open your Mozilla browser by clicking the blue globe on the GNOME Menu.**

   Using Mozilla is described in Chapter 11.

3. **Enter the address** www.winehq.com **in the text box at the top of the browser and press Enter.**

   You go to the Wine project's home page.

4. **Under the Download heading on the center-left side of the Web page, click the Binaries link.**

   Your browser displays the Wine Binary Downloads page. This page contains links to various noncommercial and commercial repositories.

(We describe the commercial Wine versions later in this chapter.) This section describes how to obtain and use the noncommercial version of Wine.

5. **Click the SourceForge.net link under the From heading.**

   The SourceForge site contains Wine packages for various Linux distributions, including Red Hat's. (SourceForge is a well-known and popular repository for many Linux systems and isn't limited to carrying just Wine.)

6. **Select the latest Red Hat RPM.**

   RPM, or Red Hat Package Manager, is used to install and manage software. See Appendix E for information about using RPMs.

   The latest version at the time this book was written was `wine-20031016-1rh9winehq.i686.rpm`.. The package was compiled for Red Hat Linux 9, but works with Red Hat Linux 10. (Don't download packages dated earlier than 20030618. Packages dated earlier than June 18, 2003, generally work. However, they require modification to work with Microsoft Office and Word.)

   Select the i386 version if you're not sure about which class of Intel (or Intel-compatible) processor your computer uses. Even if your computer uses an i686 class processor, using an i386 version of Wine works — just not as efficiently as an i686.

   The SourceForge.net Download Server page opens and provides you with several geographical locations to download from.

7. **Click the link under the Download heading that's closest to you.**

   A dialog box opens with the Save this file to disk button selected.

8. **Click the Save button and the dialog box labeled Enter Name of File to Save To opens.**

   The default location is your current working directory. Click the Save button and the download process begins. A progress window opens, showing a progress bar and a time-to-completion estimate.

Installing Wine

You have to install Wine after you download it. These steps describe the installation process:

1. **To install the Wine package, open your Nautilus file manager by double-clicking the Home icon in the upper-left corner of your desktop.**

   The Home icon is labeled as X's Home, where X is the username you're logged in as. For example, if you're logged in as the user Gabe, it reads Gabe's Home.

2. **Right-click the Wine RPM package file and choose Open With⇨Install Packages.**

   A Query window opens and prompts you to enter the root password if you're not logged in as root.

3. **Enter the root password, if you're prompted.**

   The package manager checks the current state of your computer and opens the Completed System Preparation window.

   You can optionally click the Show Details button to see a summary of the Wine package you're about to install.

4. **Click the Continue button and the Wine package is installed.**

   When the window disappears, your package is installed.

Alternatively, you can "manually" install the package by opening a terminal window, changing to root (`su -`) and entering the command `rpm -ivh wine*`. See Appendix E for more information about the manual installation process.

Running Notepad and Wine File

The Wine package you just installed, if you have read the preceding section, contains several simple Windows applications. The applications are *emulated* versions of the applications. The Wine contributors have done the work to duplicate the functionality in addition to the look and feel in order to provide some immediate gratification.

We take advantage of the situation by demonstrating a couple of programs. These steps describe how to run the Notepad and file manager programs:

1. **Log in as a regular user (not root).**
2. **Click the GNOME Menu, and open the Run Program menu.**
3. **Click the Run in terminal radio button.**
4. **Enter this command in the text window:**

```
wine notepad.exe
```

Running the Wine program — for example, `wine notepad.exe` — for the first time creates a `.wine` directory in your home directory. The `.wine` directory contains all the configuration information that the Wine system needs in order to run. The configuration information is contained in the `config` file. Several additional files — all with the `.reg` suffix — mimic the Windows Registry. The Windows operating system uses the Registry to organize its configuration parameters; Linux on the other hand, uses separate files, such as those in the /etc, /etc/sysconfig, and /usr/local/etc directories, to hold its configuration information.

5. **Click the Run key and the Notepad window opens, as shown in Figure 14-1.**

   You can use Notepad to create, modify, and save text files.

   Wine provides a Windows-like file manager too.

6. **Repeat Steps 2–5, and substitute** winefile **in place of** `wine notepad.exe`**:**

   The Wine File (file manager) opens, showing the contents of your current working directory.

Playing games

Now that you may have had enough of text editing, you can investigate Wine's true power. Wine is good at running programs that are not yet available in Linux form. Start by downloading a Windows-based shareware game.

Shareware is software that the developer lets you test for free; sometimes, the software is usable for a limited trial period. If you like it, you can — and should — send the programmer a small fee.

Figure 14-1: The Wine Notepad utility.

Wine utilities

Wine provides several useful utilities that help you to configure and test it. This sidebar describes some of them.

wineboot: Simulates the rebooting of a Windows computer. Rebooting is necessary when you're installing numerous Windows applications (for example, Microsoft Word), and this utility provides that function.

winedbg: Debugs Wine applications. This utility shows what's going on under the surface, so to speak. You need to use this utility only if you're developing a Wine application.

winecfg: Helps set many Wine configuration options.

clock: Duplicates the simple Windows clock.

regedit: Duplicates the Registry editor.

progman: Functions as a program manager.

You can try running one of the Wine utilities. For example, test the winefile utility, which acts as a file manager.

Dull, old guys like us still like dull, old games like PacMan (wow! — even our misspent youth was dull), so we show you how to download a PacMan-like arcade game. These steps describe where to download and how to install the software (figuring out the heuristics of PacMan is up to you):

1. **Log in as a regular user and open your Mozilla Web browser by clicking the blue globe (with a mouse wrapped around it) on the GNOME Panel.**
2. **Enter the address** www.tucows.com **in the text box at the top of the browser and press Enter.**
3. **Under the Computer Games heading, near the center of the Web page, click the Windows link.**

   Your browser displays a page with many classes of games.
4. **Under the Arcade heading, click the PacMan link.**
5. **Click the WinPac2 link in the next window.**

   The WinPac 2 1.03b page opens.
6. **Click the Win98 option and the Downloading WinPac2_103b.exe dialog box opens.**

   The Choose a Region window opens.

   The Win95 program runs, but frequently has problems.
7. **Click the appropriate geographical pull-down menu, select your state or country, and click the Go button.**

   The Choose a Mirror window opens.

8. **Click the mirror closest to you.**
9. **Click the OK button when the Opening WinPac2_103b.exe dialog box opens.**
10. **Click the Save button in the Enter Name of File to Save To dialog box.**

    The WinPac2 installation program is saved to your home directory.

The following steps describe how to install and run the game. Most Windows application installations should be similar to this one; you start the installation program and then see a graphical user interface (GUI):

1. **Click the GNOME Menu and open the Run Program menu.**

   The Run Program window opens.
2. **Click the Run in Terminal button and enter this command in the text window:**

   ```
   wine WinPac2_103b.exe
   ```
3. **Click the Run key and the WinPac2 Setup: License Agreement window opens.**

   Read the license.
4. **Click the I Agree button.**

   The WinPac 2 Setup: Installation Options window opens and shows the typical installation options.
5. **Click the Quick Launch Icon and Desktop Icon options.**

   Installing the icons makes starting the game more convenient for you.
6. **Click the Next button and the WinPac 2 Setup Installation Directory window opens, showing the location where the game files will be installed.**

   The C: token is an alias for the `.wine/c` directory in your home directory. If your home directory is `/home/gabe`, for example, C: corresponds to `/home/gabe/.wine/c`.
7. **Click the Install button and the WinPac2 Setup Installing Files window opens. When it's finished, it becomes WinPac2 Setup: Completed.**
8. **Click the Close button and you're finished with the installation.**

The Wine Web page provides a database of tested applications. Go to `http://appdb.winehq.com/` to browse the applications known to run under Wine. The main Wine Web page provides more information about applications, at `www.winehq.com/?page=supported_applications`. The applications are divided into Gold and Silver lists. Gold-rated programs run the best; Silver programs run, but not flawlessly.

You have several ways to start a Wine-based application:

- **Manually, by using a terminal emulator:** Open a terminal emulator window in the usual way and enter this command:

```
wine "C:Program Files/WinPac  2/WinPac2.exe"
```

- **By using the GNOME Run utility:** Open the GNOME Run utility and enter this command:

```
wine "C:Program Files/WinPac 2/WinPac2.exe"
```

- **By creating and clicking a GNOME icon:** This method is described in the following set of steps.

We show you how to create a GNOME icon to make using the new game easy. These steps describe the process:

1. **Right-click anywhere on the GNOME Panel and choose Add to Panel⇨Launcher.**

   The Create Launcher window opens.

2. **Enter** WinPac2 **in the Name text box and enter this command in the Command text box:**

```
wine "C:Program Files/WinPac 2/WinPac2.exe"
```

3. **Click the Icon button and select an image from the Browse icons windows that opens.**

   For example, select the Apple icon.

4. **Click the OK button and the icon is created on the Panel.**
5. **Click the new WinPac2 icon and the game starts, as shown in Figure 14-2.**

Running Microsoft Word (now, that's useful)

You can also run primary applications with Wine. You may prefer Microsoft Word over OpenOffice, for example. Well, you're in luck because Wine provides that capability.

In this section, we show you how to install Microsoft Word 2000 on our Red Hat Linux computer. You have to own a Word 2000 license, of course, but you don't need a Windows 2000 operating system license. Wine provides all the library hooks and sundry items to run an application like Word 2000.

Wine is continually modified and updated to remain as compatible as possible with Microsoft. Wine occasionally has trouble, however, running such complex applications as Office and Word. The problems were solved before we published, but please be aware it's possible that you might have problems with future releases of Wine. If you encounter this type of problem, please consult our help page at `www.dummies.com/go/rhlfedorafd` for possible fixes. You can also use commercial Wine variants, such as CrossOver Office, to run Office or Word.

Figure 14-2: The WinPac2 game introduction window.

Go find your Word 2000 (or Word 97, Word XP, or whatever) disc and get ready to rumble. These steps show how to install and use that word processor:

1. **Log in to your computer as a nonroot user and insert the Microsoft Word 2000 CD into the CD-ROM drive.**

   These steps should work reasonably well with a Microsoft Office 2000 CD.

2. **Click the GNOME Menu and choose System Tools⇨Terminal.**

   The Run Program window opens.

3. **Enter the following commands in the text window:**

   ```
   rm/usr/lib/wine/wine/msi.dll.so
           wine/mnt/cdrom/setup.exe
   ```

   You may have to substitute `cdrom1` for `cdrom` if you have two drives.

Depending on the state of Wine you installed, you may see a Microsoft Word 2000 Setup window informing you that it can't find a font. Missing fonts generally don't affect the functionality of the application.

4. **Click the OK button whenever a missing font warning appears.**

   The installation process displays lots of information as it proceeds. You can ignore the lines as they pass by. They don't affect the installation process.

   The Microsoft Word 2000: Welcome window opens.

5. **Enter in the five text boxes the product key from your Microsoft Word 2000 disc (or from the physical package in which Microsoft enclosed the disc).**

   Remember that Wine provides only the *platform* on which to run valid Windows applications. It doesn't provide the applications.

6. **The next window you see gives you the option of installing a standard Word configuration or, optionally, customizing the installation.**

   For simplicity, we suggest that you click the Install Now button. (We leave it to you to navigate through the various additional configuration steps if you choose the Customize option.)

   The installation continues until you're prompted to reboot your computer. You're not running a Windows computer, of course, so click the No button. The installation process seems to end.

7. **Wine provides a Windows reboot simulation utility. Repeat Steps 2 and 3 and enter this command:**

   ```
   wineboot
   ```

   The installation process starts up again and finishes. You have installed Microsoft Word 2000 on your Linux computer!

8. **You can start the word processor by repeating Steps 3–5 and entering this command in the text window:**

   ```
   wine "C:Program Files/Microsoft
           Office/Office/winword.exe"
   ```

Backslashes (\) are escape characters in the Linux world; in the Windows world, backslashes separate directory names. That is, they prevent Linux (the bash shell) from interpreting the following character literally. Without the backslash, Linux (bash) interprets the directory name `Program Files` as two separate entities, Program and Files, because the bash shell figures that the space character is a separator and not part of a directory name or filename. Therefore, the combination of a backslash and a space — `Program\ Files` — allows Linux to process the directory name correctly: `Program Files`. The preceding command (refer to Step 8) is interpreted by Linux as `wine C: Program Files/Microsoft Office/Office/winword.exe`.

Introducing CodeWeavers CrossOver Office

The outstanding Wine system lets you tap the deep resources of the Windows world. Wine is developed under the open source system, where volunteers provide countless hours of service to the computing world. The open source community, however, doesn't limit the use of its software to only noncommercial use. Software developed under the General Public License (GPL) permits commercial use as long as no restrictions are placed on the original GPL software.

The commercial use of open source software can provide an extra punch in certain circumstances. Open source for profit? Indeed. Companies such as CodeWeavers (`www.codeweavers.com`) and TransGaming (`www.transgaming.com`) deliver just such a punch. Both companies have added features to the basic Wine software to make the installation process simpler. CodeWeavers concentrates on making Wine easier to use on the general desktop; the company makes installing and using Microsoft Office, Internet Explorer, and various plug-ins easy. The TransGaming product WineX, on the other hand, provides a gaming-oriented system.

This book is oriented toward using Linux as a useful day-to-day workstation. Our work is tilted toward using word processors and similar programs. We leave it to you to experiment with WineX. Suffice it to say that our game-oriented colleagues find WineX useful.

CodeWeavers produces two products: CrossOver Office and CrossOver Plugin. Office provides value as an installation utility that helps with installing Windows applications. The Plugin product provides internally developed software that helps in using plug-ins. CrossOver Office uses mostly unmodified Wine software, but provides a slick installation system. CrossOver Plugin uses its own custom libraries to make Windows plug-ins, such as QuickTime, work with your Linux browser. CrossOver Office costs $54.95 and Plugin costs $24.95. You can purchase both for $69.95. (Those prices are for when you download the product from the Internet. The CD version costs $64.95, $34.95, and $79.95, respectively.)

Downloading the trial version of CrossOver Plugin

CodeWeavers graciously provides a 30-day evaluation license for CrossOver Plugin and CrossOver Office. You can therefore test the full version of its products. These steps describe how to download the trial version of CrossOver Plugin:

1. **Log in to your Red Hat Linux computer as the superuser.**

2. **Open Mozilla and go to** www.codeweavers.com/products/download_trial.php.
3. **Click the CrossOver Plugin button at the top of the page.**
4. **Fill out the registration form and click the Request Evaluation button.**

   The Download Trial Version of CrossOver page opens, informing you that instructions for installing CrossOver are being e-mailed to you.
5. **When the information is e-mailed to you, open the this page in Mozilla:** http://crossover.codeweavers.com/download/plugin-trial.

   The CrossOver Secure Download window opens.
6. **Enter the access key (your e-mail address) and serial number that was just e-mailed to you in the Access Key and Serial Number text boxes.**
7. **Click the Download button.**

   The Downloading install-crossover-plugin-1.2.1-demo.sh dialog box opens.
8. **Click the OK button.**

   The Enter Name of File to Save To dialog box opens.
9. **Click the Save button and the software is saved to your current directory.**

Installing CrossOver Plugin

After you have downloaded the CrossOver Plugin installation system, your next step is to install CrossOver Plugin. These steps describe how to use the installation system to install and configure the software:

1. **Log in as the (root) superuser.**
2. **Open a GNOME Terminal window.**
3. **Enter the following commands:**

   ```
   chmod +x install-crossover-plugin-1.2.1-demo.sh
   ./install-crossover-plugin-demo-2.0.2.sh
   ```

   The License Agreement dialog box opens.
4. **Read the license and click the I Agree button.**

   The CrossOver Plugin Setup window shows the location where the Plugin software will be installed. The default directory is /opt/cxplugin (which is created for you).
5. **Click the Begin Install button, and the CrossOver Plugin software is installed for you.**

   When the installation finishes (it can take several minutes), the CrossOver Plugin Setup window displays the message Installation complete.

6. **Click the Configure Now button.**

   The Plugin Setup window opens.

7. **Click the Install button.**

   The Install Software window opens, showing a selection of plug-ins you can install.

8. **Click the Next button.**

   The Browser Selection window opens, showing plug-ins to be installed for both Netscape and Mozilla.

9. **Click the Next button.**

   The HTTP Proxy Configuration window opens and allows you to configure the plug-ins to work with a Web proxy server. *Proxy servers* filter the locations you can browse. Enter the information about your proxy, if you have one.

10. **Click the Finish button.**

    The CrossOver Plugin Setup window opens, as shown in Figure 14-3.

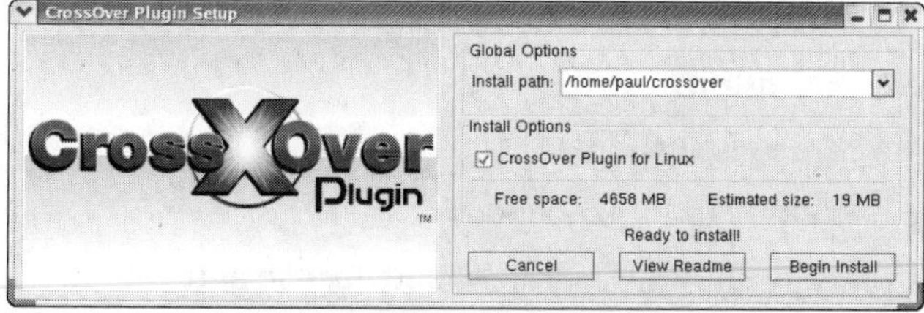

Figure 14-3: The CrossOver Plugin Setup window.

Using CrossOver Plugin

The next phase of the configuration process allows you to choose from numerous popular Windows plug-ins. When you select a plug-in to install, it's automatically downloaded from the Internet for you. No muss, no fuss.

These steps describe how to select and automatically download a Windows plug-in:

1. **Click the Install button and the next CrossOver Plugin Setup window opens.**

   Figure 14-4 shows the Install Software window.

2. **Click the QuickTime 6 plug-in.**

3. **Click the Next button**

   The Express Install (Recommended) button is selected by default.

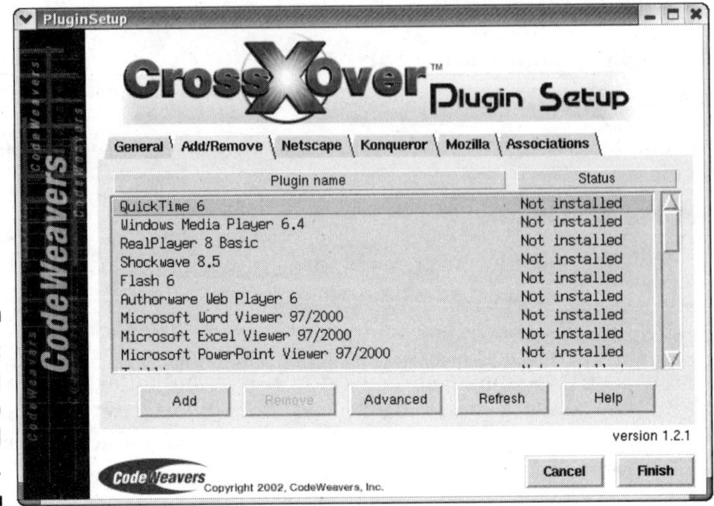

Figure 14-4: Selecting plug-ins to download and install.

4. **Click the Next button and the QuickTime 6 plug-in is downloaded from the Internet.**

   The QuickTime 6 Setup window opens, as shown in Figure 14-5.

5. **Click the Next button.**

   A welcome screen is displayed.

6. **Click the Next button to proceed.**

   The next window shows the QuickTime license agreement.

7. **Read the license (preferably with a room full of lawyers) and click the Agree button.**

   The next window shows the installation location in which the QuickTime plug-in will be installed. The default is the simulated Windows directory, which is really the `.wine/c/program files` directory in your home directory.

8. **Click the Next button.**

   The Choose Installation Type dialog box opens.

9. **You can select various levels of sophistication. The minimal level (the default) should suffice, so just click the Next button.**

10. **When the Select Program Folder opens, click the Next button to select the default folder name:** `QuickTime`**.**

    Take a deep breath because you're almost home. The next window is the Enter Registration window.

11. **Enter your name and organization, if you have one. (You don't have to enter a registration number.) Click the Next button.**

12. **The last step is to enter any proxy information. If you have a proxy (for example, if your company's network uses one), obtain the information about it and enter it.**
13. **Click the Continue button.**

    The installation system thinks for a while and then displays a progress dialog box as it downloads the QuickTime plug-in from the Internet.

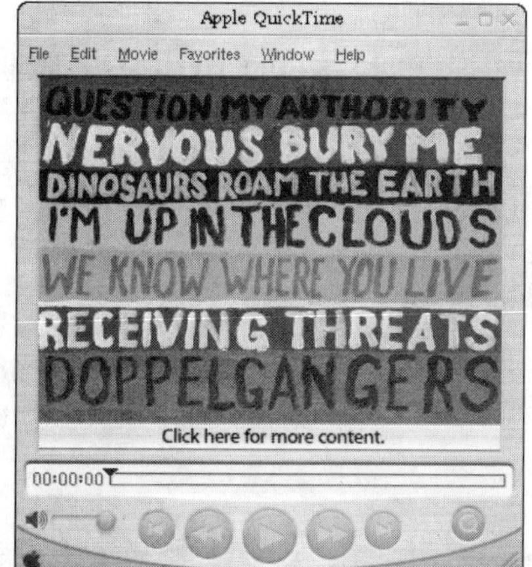

Figure 14-5: The QuickTime 6 Setup dialog box.

Configuring QuickTime

The final QuickTime configuration process begins when the QuickTime Settings/Introduction window opens. These steps describe how to complete the QuickTime configuration:

1. **Click the Next button and the Connection Speed dialog box opens.**

   The Connection Speed dialog box wants to know what kind of Internet connection you use.
2. **Select the speed and type of your connection from the pull-down menu and click the Next button.**

   The Browser Plug-in window opens and wants to know which, if any, MIME settings you want to change.
3. **The default settings should be all right, so click the Next button.**

   In the File Type Associations window that opens next, you can select which types of files QuickTime should work with. The default option is QuickTime, to work with Mac files (PICT and AIFF, for example).
4. **Make any changes that are appropriate for you and click the Finish button.**

The last dialog box asks whether you want to read the README file and or start QuickTime.

5. **Click the Yes, I Want to Launch QuickTime Player button and click the Close button.**

   The Installation Report window opens, showing information about all your plug-ins.

6. **Click the OK button and control returns to the CrossOver Plugin Setup window.**

   The CrossOver installation system installs links to the QuickTime player application in addition to the plug-ins. CrossOver also installs menus on the GNOME Main Menu.

7. **Click the GNOME Menu button and choose Programs⇨QuickTime⇨ QuickTime Player.**

   The QuickTime Player opens, as you can see in Figure 14-6.

CrossOver also installs its own utilities. Click the GNOME Menu and open the CrossOver menu. You see several utilities. Click the Plugin Setup option and the Plugin Setup window opens.

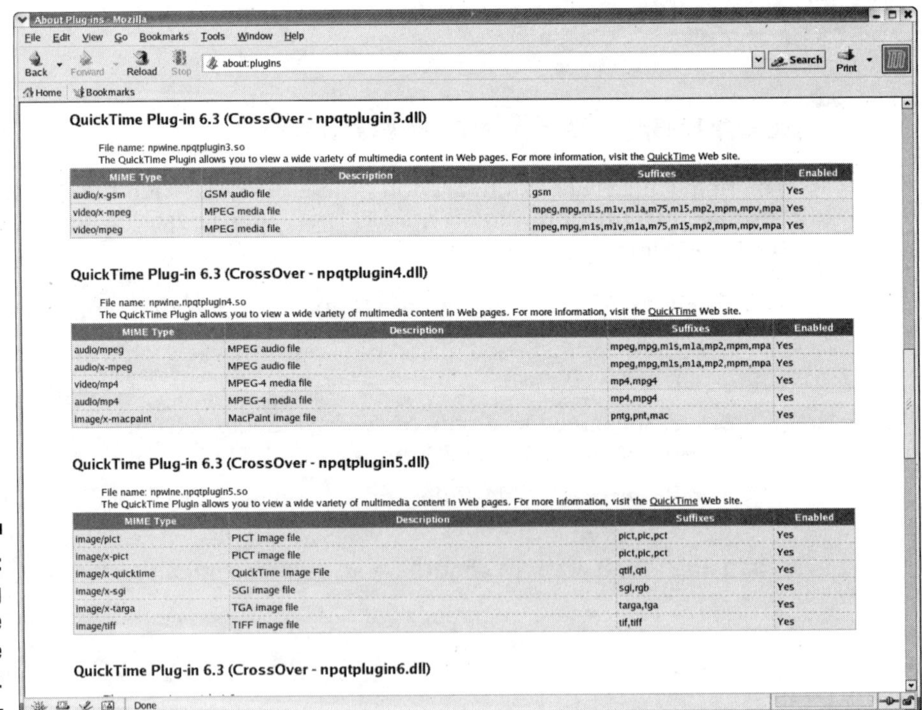

Figure 14-6: Playing with the QuickTime Player.

The QuickTime plug-in and its supporting software are installed in the `.mozilla/plugins` directory in your home directory. You can verify that the plug-in was installed by opening Mozilla and choosing Help⇨About Plugins. Mozilla displays all installed plug-ins.

VMware: A Virtual Reality Machine

Sometimes, you need to use an application that just doesn't run under Linux — even with the help of Wine. For example, one of us has to use a trouble-ticket system to fix customers' problems. The problem is that the trouble-ticket application doesn't run under Linux, with or without Wine. That author must then install both Windows and Linux on his computer (a *dual-boot* system) or else maintain a separate one for the sole purpose of running the single application.

Nothing is wrong with using a dual-boot computer, of course. But it's sort of a waste of time if all you need to do is run one or two applications. Dual-boot computers also have to be rebooted when you need to use the other operating system. An alternative to dual booting is VMware, a commercial product from VMware, Inc. This program creates a virtual computer within a physical computer. The virtual computer runs as an application, just like OpenOffice or Mozilla.

VMware looks and works just like a real PC. The virtual VMware PC can run an operating system, such as Linux or Windows, just like any real computer can. The operating system running on the virtual machine behaves just like the real operating system. Any applications it hosts, therefore, look and work just like the real applications!

VMware is also good for writing Linux books. Writing techy books like this one requires you to use early beta versions of new releases during the initial draft phase. The old method required installing the beta on your computer and using it for both testing and writing; alternatively, you can use two computers side-by-side. Both methods are clunky and cause numerous headaches when the beta does some funky thing. VMware solves the problem by allowing you to run the current production version of Red Hat Linux on your host computer and install the beta on the virtual computer. You can test the beta to your heart's content while writing at the same time in OpenOffice — all on the same virtual computer. Updating from one beta version to another is a snap too.

You can download the VMware Workstation product for free. It requires a license that costs approximately $300 for commercial use and $100 for educational use. It's money well spent.

VMware networking

The VMware virtual computers can use your host computer's network connection. VMware provides two methods for accessing a private LAN and one method for accessing the host computer's local file system:

Bridged network: "Bridges" the virtual machine to the host machine's private network through the host's network interface card (NIC). The virtual machine appears to be an independent network device to the LAN. The virtual computer has its own virtual NIC with a real IP address. The bridged configuration provides the most flexible network configuration possible to the virtual machine. However, the virtual machine must be configured and maintained like any other device.

Network Address Translation (NAT) network: A process that makes one networked computer appear as another computer. NAT translates the source network address (and port) to that of another address (and port). This method is widely used by private networks to funnel all their hosts through a single gateway to the Internet.

VMware uses NAT to make the virtual machine appear to be the host machine on the host machine's LAN. NAT is easy to configure because you have to configure only the virtual machine's network configuration to use the dynamic host configuration protocol (DHCP). You have to select only DHCP, therefore, and nothing else. (We describe NAT in Chapter 16.)

Host-only network: Configures the virtual machine to use the host machine's file system. VMware sets up Samba on the host machine, and then the virtual machine can mount the host's file system. (*Samba* is a Linux/Unix system that speaks the same protocol, or language, as the Microsoft file sharing system. Samba allows Linux computers to access file systems on Windows computers and vice versa.)

VMware also offers a 30-day evaluation license for no charge. The temporary license, which isn't limited in any way other than the time limit, is ideal for testing this powerful tool. The steps in the following section describe how to download the product and its temporary license to find out about its power.

Downloading VMware

VMware, Inc., allows you to easily download and use its software. These steps describe the process — virtual computing for everyone!

1. **Log in to your Red Hat Linux computer, open the Mozilla browser, and enter** www.vmware.com/download **in the text box.**
2. **Under Desktop Products, click the Download button.**

   The VMware Workstation 4 window opens. You need to obtain a temporary license to use the software.
3. **Click the Evaluation Serial Number link.**

   The Try VMware Workstation 4 window opens.

4. **Click the Register button and the registration form opens.**

   Fill out the form, making sure to fill all boxes marked with a red asterisk.

5. **Click the Continue button and your browser goes to the Download page.**
6. **Click the Download Binaries for Linux Systems link.**
7. **Read the VMware End User License Agreement and click the Yes button.**

   You see the Download VMware Workstation 4 (for Linux Systems) link. You can download from several sites across the globe.

8. **Click on the RPM version from the site closest to you.**

   The Enter Name of File to Save To dialog box opens.

9. **Click the Save button.**

   The VMware-workstation RPM file is saved to your home directory.

   You're not limited to saving this file or any other to your home directory. You can select any location in which you have write permission. For example, you may want to save to the `/tmp` directory.

10. **Click the Evaluation Serial Number button.**
11. **Click the Register button and enter your name, e-mail address, and other information in the form that's displayed.**

    Make sure that you specify Linux in the Product Host Platform section. After you complete the form, the evaluation license key is e-mailed to the address you provide.

After you download the software and evaluation license, read the following section to install the software.

Installing VMware

After the VMware software is downloaded, you only need to install it. The software, provided in Red Hat Package Manager (RPM) format, is self-installing; you can read more about working with RPMs in Appendix D. These steps describe how to unpack the RPM package and install the license:

1. **Open the Nautilus file manager by double-clicking the Home icon, in the upper-left corner of the desktop.**
2. **Right-click the VMware-workstation RPM package file and choose Open With⇨Install Packages.**

   A Query window opens and prompts you to enter the root password if you're not logged in as root.

3. **Enter the root password, if you're prompted.**

   The package manager checks the state of your computer and opens the Completed System Preparation window.

4. **Click the Continue button and the VMware-workstation package is installed.**

   When the window disappears, VMware Workstation is installed.

Installing Linux kernel headers

VMware makes use of Linux kernel modules, which are similar to Windows device drivers, to interact with the host Linux computer. VMware ships kernel modules that automatically work with some versions of Red Hat Linux. However, we can't be certain that those modules match your Linux kernel — the one that ships with this book. Therefore, the following steps help you build your own VMware kernel modules.

Building VMware modules requires the presence of Linux kernel headers, which may not be installed on your computer. You need to install the headers by installing the Linux kernel source RPM package. Follow these steps:

1. **Insert the companion DVD into the DVD-ROM/CD-ROM drive.**
2. **Click the GNOME Menu button and choose System Tools⇨Terminal.**
3. **If you're not logged in as root, run the following command:**

   ```
   su -
   ```

4. **Enter the root password when you're prompted.**
5. **Enter the following command to install the Linux kernel headers:**

   ```
   rpm -Uvh /mnt/cdrom/RedHat/RPMS/kernel-headers*
   ```

The kernel source package is installed and you're ready to configure VMware.

Configuring VMware Workstation

This section guides you through the process of building (if necessary), installing the correct kernel modules for, and configuring any or all of the virtual networking connections. After completing this section you have a running virtual PC capable of running both Linux and Windows workstations.

Starting the VMware configuration process

This section describes how to get the started configuring your VMware virtual PC. The following steps describe how to use the VMware configuration script.

1. **Log in as the superuser (root).**
2. **Click the GNOME Menu button and choose System Tools➪Terminal.**
3. **After the terminal emulator window opens, enter the command** vmware-config.pl **in the terminal emulator window.**

   The `vmware-config.pl` script displays the VMware license agreement.
4. **Press Enter to start displaying the entire agreement, and keep pressing the spacebar to display each new page.**
5. **Assuming that you're a lawyer and know what you have just read and accept it, type** yes **and press Enter when you're prompted.**

   The configuration script tries to locate an existing module for your version of Linux. If the script finds the correct module, skip over to the "Configuring VMware networking" section. Otherwise, read the following section.

Building VMware kernel modules

In case the VMware Workstation package you installed doesn't have the correct kernel module, you have to create one. The following steps describe how to create your own VMware kernel module.

If the kernel modules shipped with VMware doesn't match your kernel, you see the following text:

```
None of VMware Workstation's pre-built vmmon modules is
suitable for your running kernel. Do you want this
program to try to build the vmmon module for your
system (you need to have a C compiler installed on your
system)? [yes]
```

1. **Press Enter to accept the default Yes answer.**

   You then see text describing your C compiler (a *compiler* is software that translates human-readable computer code into a form that computers can understand).
2. **Accept the GNU C compiler gcc by typing** yes **and pressing Enter.**

   The `vmware-config.pl` script shows you where it found your kernel header files:

   ```
   What is the location of the directory of C header files
           that match your running
   kernel? [/lib/modules/2.4.20-8/build/include]
   ```

   The exact module version number and location vary, depending on the version of kernel headers package you installed. The value, however, should be correct.

3. **Press Enter.**

   The configuration script proceeds continues to create the kernel modules it needs. After it finishes, it prompts you to configure VMware networking.

   You're prompted to configure VMware networking.

Configuring VMware networking

This set of steps describes how to configure VMware networking:

1. **We assume that you want to use virtual networking, so press Enter. The script automatically configures both bridged and NAT networking.**

   Bridged networking doesn't work if the host computer uses a wireless NIC. NAT works on wireless NICs, however. This limitation should be fixed eventually.

2. **Answer Yes to allow the script to probe for unused subnetworks.**

3. **You need have to accept the DHCP license, so type** yes **and press Enter.**

   The DHCP license is stored in `/usr/share/doc/vmware/DHCP-COPYRIGHT`. The license makes for good reading.

4. **Optionally, type** yes **and press Enter to use host-only networking.**

   Host-only networking consists of a virtual network interface that communicates with only the VMware host computer (the one you're configuring now). Host-only networking is used primarily to share the host's file system with the virtual computer.

5. **Type** yes **and press Enter when prompted to probe for an unused subnetwork (for the host-only networking).**

   We're assuming that you will, or may want to, share files from your host computer (Linux) to your virtual computer (Linux or Windows). You can answer No here if you don't want to share — but then your mom may get mad.

6. **Answer No when prompted to configure another (second) host-only network.**

7. **Answer Yes to allow the system to automatically access the host file system.**

   The installation script wants you to accept the Samba license. (Samba is used, in this case, to share Linux files with virtual Windows and Linux computers.

8. **Press Enter to accept the license.**

   The Samba license is stored in the `/usr/share/doc/vmware/SAMBA-LICENSE` file — *more* interesting reading).

The installation script starts the VMware *daemons* (programs that run continuously in the background to provide system-wide services) and asks whether you want to share files with the virtual machine.

9. **Press Enter.**

10. **Enter the username and password of an account on the host machine.**

    For example, you should enter the username and password of your Linux account. When the script prompts you for your SMB password, use your Linux password.

11. **You're prompted to enter additional usernames and passwords. Enter** yes **if you want to do so. Otherwise, press Enter to accept the default No answer, and the configuration process ends.**

The VMware server is now configured on your host machine. The `vmware-config.pl` script starts up the virtual machine processes when it finishes. You can rerun `vmware-config.pl` whenever you want to reconfigure VMware.

Installing an operating system on a virtual computer

VMware is great at providing a platform on which to run other operating systems under Linux. You can install either Windows or Linux on your virtual PC. After you install and configure VMware, you can run and use your virtual PC.

This section describes how to install Linux on your new VMware Workstation. We use Linux because we can't include Windows on the companion DVD or expect you to go out and purchase that expensive puppy. (We asked Microsoft whether we could bundle its operating system, but we never heard back about it. Not until recently did we realize that it uses a different license from Linux. Just kidding!) Because we can, and already do, bundle Red Hat Linux, we can easily show you how to install it. However, if you have a legal copy of Windows, go ahead and install it.

Creating a VMware icon on the GNOME Panel

You start the installation process by first creating a GNOME applet that you click to start VMware. This action makes starting VMware a breeze. Follow these steps:

1. **Right-click the Gnome Panel and choose Panel⇨Add to Panel⇨Launcher.**

2. **Enter, on the Name submenu, the name you want to call your icon; for example,** VMware.

3. **Enter any information you want in the Comment field and then type** /usr/bin/vmware **in the Command field.**
4. **Click the Icon button and a selection of numerous generic icons appears. Select any one that tickles your fancy.**
5. **Click the OK button. The new launcher appears on the GNOME Panel.**

Starting your virtual machine

Now, you use the new icon to start your VMware virtual machine. The following steps describe how to start the machine:

1. **Click the VMware icon and the VMware Workstation appears.**
2. **You need to enter your evaluation license serial number, so choose Help⇨Enter Serial Number.**

   Enter the temporary serial number that was e-mailed to you. Also, enter your name and, optionally, your company name.
3. **Click the OK button and then click New Virtual Machine.**

   The New Virtual Machine Wizard opens. The default setting should work for you, so you don't have to make any changes.
4. **Click the Next button, open the Guest Operating System pull-down menu, and choose Linux.**

   You can safely accept the default settings in the next set of steps.
5. **Select Use Network Address Translation (NAT) when you see the Network settings window and then click the Finish button.**

Congratulations! You have started your first virtual computer.

Installing Red Hat Linux on your virtual machine

You have your virtual machine running, so what can you do with it? You can install Linux and Windows and on it. The next step in the process installs Red Hat Linux on that virtual computer:

1. **Insert the companion Red Hat Linux DVD.**

   Alternatively, insert a Windows CD in the drive, if you have one. Proceed through this set of steps and substitute the Windows installation process where appropriate.
2. **Click the Power On button.**

   The VMware workstation starts up. You see the BIOS menu, just like you do on a real machine. The virtual computer should detect your Red Hat Linux CD and start the installation process, just like in Chapter 3.

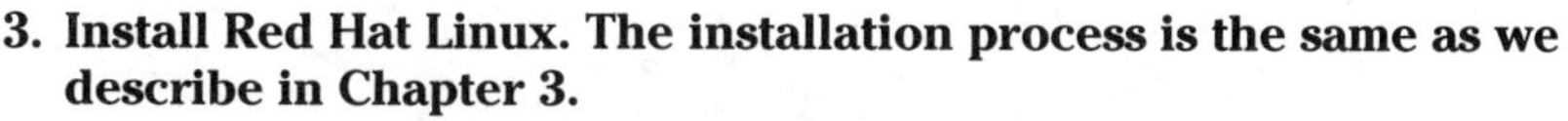

3. **Install Red Hat Linux. The installation process is the same as we describe in Chapter 3.**

VMware uses simple Linux files on the host machine to simulate the virtual computer's disk partitions. (You have the option to use a separate partition for the virtual computer, but the most common method is to use the host file.) Installing an operating system (OS) on a VMware virtual computer places the operating system's virtual disk on a file. Therefore, you don't have to worry about harming your host computer whenever you're installing a virtual OS. Any problems you encounter during the installation or use of the virtual OS are limited to the host computer files. The files used for the virtual OS are labeled with the `.vmdk` suffix.

4. **When you're prompted for the network configuration, select DHCP.**

   Using DHCP shortens the network configuration process because you don't have to select a static IP address, netmask, and other parameters.

5. **When you finish installing the operating system, click Reset.**

   Your virtual PC reboots and you have a fully functional virtual computer running Red Hat Linux. Cool.

Experiment with your newfound tool. Virtual machines provide you with a new killer application that can be used to do almost anything you want it to do. You have an exciting, fun, and powerful device.

VMware creates not only virtual computers, but also virtual networks. Each virtual computer you configure to use bridged networking connects to a virtual switch. If you create two virtual machines on a single host, therefore, each machine can communicate with the other — and the host itself — as though they were connected to an Ethernet hub. This capability allows you to create experimental and production virtual networks. For example, you can use a single powerful PC to create several virtual servers rather than purchase and maintain individual ones. Cool.

Plex86 is the open source world's answer to VMware. The Plex86 system provides a virtual computing platform similar to VMware in function. Plex86 works, but at the time this book was written was still in alpha development — it cannot run production systems. We encourage you to experiment with the system, which you can find at `http://plex86.sourceforge.net`.

Part IV
Revenge of the Nerds

"Drive carefully, remember your lunch, and always make a backup of your directory tree before modifying your hard disk partition file."

In this part . . .

In the great tradition of slackers and procrastinators, we have put off the real work as long as possible. In this part, you find out about how to make a server out of your Red Hat Linux computer. These chapters don't turn you into a Linux guru capable of commanding six-figure consulting fees, but they introduce you to the technical side of Linux.

We start by describing in Chapter 15 how to build a simple Local Area Network (LAN). Building a LAN isn't as difficult as it first sounds. You need to connect your computers, configure them to recognize each other, and then create an Internet gateway or firewall.

Chapter 16 shows how to use your Red Hat Linux computer as a network server on your newly created network; you can also provide services to the Internet.

We get serious in Chapter 17 and describe how to quickly but effectively secure your servers and network. This chapter is really an introduction to security methods and systems.

If (okay, *when*) you need to troubleshoot Red Hat Linux, check out Chapter 18. It provides some detailed help in fixing computer problems, with a special focus on networking. When you're done with this part, you'll be wearing pocket protectors with the best of us!

Chapter 19 returns from the serious world of computer security to have some fun. The chapter describes how to run a streaming audio service. Yes, you can run your own Internet radio station.

Chapter 15

Building Your Own, Private Network

In This Chapter

- Designing your private network
- Building an Internet gateway
- Building a firewall to protect your private network

A *private network* is a group of two or more computers linked so that they can communicate with each other; also referred to as a *Local Area Network* (LAN). The computers are generally in close proximity within a room or building. Unlike the Internet, which is designed to allow the world's computers to communicate with each other, LANs are designed to keep the communication local and private. (You can always connect your LAN to the Internet, of course, but we talk about that topic elsewhere in this book.)

Building a private network isn't as difficult as it may sound. First, you have to decide on a general network layout. Second, you have to physically connect the computers with cables and wireless devices. Third, you have to configure each computer's network settings. Design, connect, configure — one, two, three — it's as simple as that.

This chapter shows how to build a simple LAN. If you want to know how to add a Linux computer to an existing network, check out Chapter 7. To find out about adding a firewall to your LAN, check out Chapter 8.

In this chapter, we show you how to wire computers together; you should depend on the Linux networking instructions from Chapter 7 to get your computers connected on your network. The steps in Chapter 7 are also designed to work with the new LAN you're building here.

In this chapter, we describe how to connect computers to form a LAN. However, you can connect many other devices to a network. Devices such as broadband Internet modems (cable and DSL), routers, switches and hubs, network-capable printers, and even some personal digital assistants (PDAs) all can be connected to a network. In the future, we fully expect to be able to connect nearly every electronic device to a LAN. We discuss only computers here because we're focusing on Red Hat Linux computers. However, remember that you're not limited to just networking computers.

Designing and Building Your Private Network

Private networks take on many shapes and sizes. As you may expect, the design of a LAN for a large- or medium-size organization is different than for a small office or home. Individuals and small organizations generally don't require complex networks unless they perform complex work. For the purposes of this book, we assume that you want and need a simple network. We describe how to design a basic LAN that is both powerful and reliable. This network can be used for many small- or medium-size businesses and most households.

This chapter shows you how to design a flat network. *Flat* refers to the fact that all the computers connected to the network communicate over a single *subnetwork* (or *subnet,* for short). Subnets can be combined within a single LAN, but that makes the network more complex to design, build, and maintain.

The network we describe here is also designed to use a Red Hat Linux Internet gateway. The *Internet gateway* is a computer that acts as a portal, connecting the private network to the Internet. The networked computers in the private network — also referred to as *hosts* or *clients* — are connected through one of two methods:

- **Wired connections:** Hosts are connected to the LAN through a device called an *Ethernet hub* or *Ethernet switch* (hub or switch, for short). Switches are superior to hubs in performance and are becoming the standard. For your LAN, we suggest that you connect all computers (hosts), including the Internet gateway, by using an Ethernet switch. Figure 15-1 shows an example of our private network, where the interconnecting fabric is the Ethernet switch. (In recent years, Ethernet switches have become inexpensive and common, and Ethernet hubs have been disappearing.)
- **Wireless connections:** Wireless devices make it possible to build a network without interconnecting cables. Wireless networks can take two forms:

  Using an access point: Using a device called an *access point,* you can connect wireless hosts to a LAN. This design has the hosts connect to the access point via radio frequency (RF) signals. The access point also connects to a wired network, and the wireless hosts communicate to the wired network through that connection.

The RF signals used by wireless networks are the same ones you tune in to on your radio or communicate with on your cell phone or open your garage door with. The only differences between the RF signals coming from an AM radio station and a wireless network device are its frequency and strength. The Federal Communications Commission (FCC) permits anybody to use the 5 GHz (billions of cycles per second) frequency portion of the spectrum for any purpose as long as the signal strength is low.

Access points have become the most popular system for creating wireless LANs. You can find access point devices in consumer electronics stores for much less than $100.

Using ad-hoc mode: The alternative wireless-connection method, called *ad-hoc mode*, doesn't require a separate access point, other than a wireless device for each host. Wireless hosts communicate directly with each other by using ad-hoc mode. (You can read more about ad-hoc mode in the section "Wiring your network with wires," later in this chapter.)

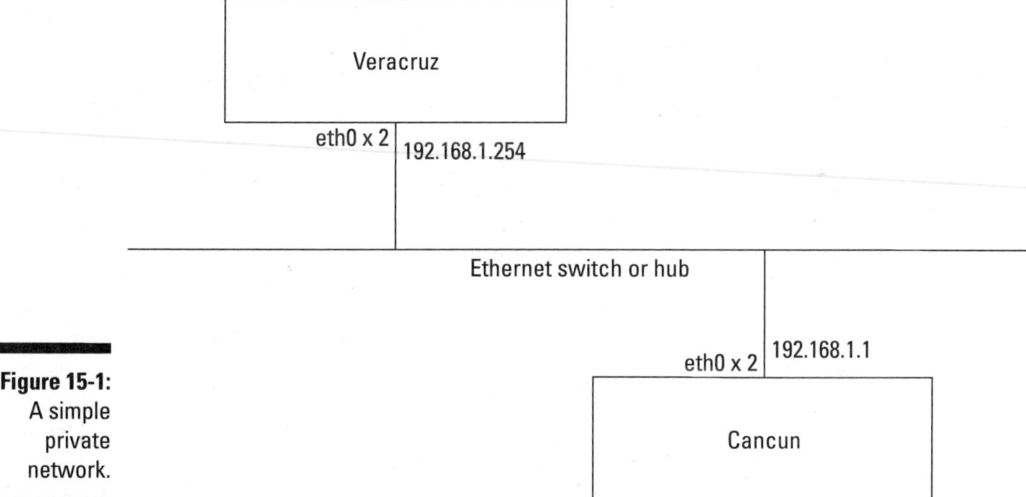

Figure 15-1: A simple private network.

The ABCs of switches and hubs

Switches are slightly more expensive than hubs because they do a little more work. Suppose that your network consists of three machines — A, B, and C — all connected to a switch. When machine A wants to communicate with machine B, the switch transmits the network traffic from A directly to B.

Machine C is totally out of the loop. By making sure that C doesn't know what A and B are saying, the switch keeps network communication private. Hubs, on the other hand, broadcast the network traffic from one machine to all machines connected to the hub. When A sends information to B, the hub broadcasts that information to both B and C.

The following section describes how to build a wired network; the section after that shows a wireless one. You can mix wired and wireless networks, but, for simplicity, we describe how to build a pure wired or wireless network.

Wiring your network with, uh, wires

Way back in prehistoric times (circa 1996), you had to be technically savvy to wire your own network. Wiring consisted of coaxial cables like those used for cable TV connections. Coaxial cables are bulky and require you to use special tools to attach the connectors to the cable ends.

Life is easy now. Wiring your network requires that you obtain *Cat 5* cables, similar in appearance to telephone cables. Cat 5 cables are manufactured with telephone-like connectors that are a snap (pardon the pun) to use. No muss, no fuss.

You can buy Cat 5 cables at any electronics store. They come in many colors and sizes. Cat 5 cables aren't cheap, but they aren't terribly expensive, either. They're reliable and much easier to work with than coaxial cables.

You have to use a network switch or hub in conjunction with Cat 5 cables. Switches and hubs are the glue that holds your network together. Both switches and hubs connect individual computers so that they can communicate with each other.

Most — if not all —networking equipment is now based on the Ethernet protocol. Ethernet is inexpensive and readily available. You can purchase it from any consumer electronics store, mail-order catalog, or online computer seller. You don't need to know any of the technical aspects of Ethernet because it requires no configuration. You need to know only that an Ethernet connector looks similar to a telephone jack. However, Ethernet and telephone jacks aren't compatible.

One byproduct of a switch's design is that it effectively makes your network faster. Network traffic flows only between the machines that are talking to each other. The computers that aren't talking to each other don't use the switch's bandwidth. For example, when machine A is sending information to B, machine C doesn't see any of the traffic.

For your network, start by connecting your machines to a central switch. (You can use a hub, if you want.)

Although you can connect as many computers as your switch or hub can handle, to keep the job as simple as possible, these steps describe how to wire two computers, Cancun and Veracruz. These steps assume that you have a switch or hub, and at least two Cat 5 cables:

1. **On the first computer, plug one end of a Cat 5 cable into the Ethernet network interface connector (NIC) on the back of the machine.**
2. **Plug the other end of the cable into the switch.**

   A green light should appear near the connector you used on the switch. The green light indicates that you have *link status,* indicating that an Ethernet connection has been established: You have an active connection between the computer and the switch.

   If you don't get a link status, make sure that both connectors on the cable have been properly inserted. Pull each connector out and firmly press it back in (called *reseating*).

   If this suggestion doesn't fix the problem, make sure that the cable is working correctly. Check the cable for cracks and cuts, for example. Check the cable's connectors for loose wires. Substitute another cable, if possible; using a cable that you know works can help you determine whether the suspect cable is at fault.

   If neither of these options works, you may have either a broken switch, cable, Ethernet NIC, or any combination. You may have to replace either or all of the devices to determine the real problem. Perhaps you can borrow a known good cable and NIC from a working network and use them to eliminate the problem.
3. **Repeat Steps 1 and 2 for each additional computer.**

After you have successfully connected all your computers to the switch, you can proceed to the section "Building an Internet Gateway," later in this chapter. That section describes how to build an Internet gateway on a Linux computer. The Internet gateway connects your entire private network to the Internet.

Wiring without wires

Life has gotten easier in the past few years (circa 2000). Wireless networking is the best technological advance for home or small-business network users in the past five years, and it's now affordable for consumers.

Going wireless means

- **Not having to string cables around your house or office:** You don't have to spend money and time pulling wires through walls, ducts, attics, and cellars, for example. (The authors have enjoyed all these activities.) You also save the cost of the cables themselves.
- **Geographical freedom:** You have the freedom to use your computers anywhere, regardless of where your server or Internet gateway or printers are located. Ah, life is easier when you can sit outside on a nice day and clack away at the keyboard.
- **Looking good:** You look high-tech even if you're not. You can impress your friends and family.

The process of constructing a wireless network is straightforward. You have to decide how to connect your wireless devices to your private network. You can do that in two ways:

- **Use a wireless access point:** A *wireless access point* (WAP) is a device through which wireless devices communicate. An access point provides a single point of contact through which all other devices communicate.

  An access point uses two network connections. One is an Ethernet port that connects to your private LAN through a Cat 5 Ethernet cable, and the other point connects to your wireless devices. The access point serves as a common connection point to your LAN.

  The other connection point is the access point's wireless receiver. The wireless "port" communicates with all other wireless devices on your network.
- **Use point-to-point (ad-hoc) communication:** Contrary to popular opinion, you can create a wireless network without an access point. Wireless NICs are designed to communicate directly with each other as well as through an access point. You configure each NIC to know a common network name and a common encryption key, and the NICs form their own ad hoc network by communicating directly with each other. We show you how, later in this section.

  Point-to-point communication is referred to as ad-hoc mode. The term *ad hoc* means that you put something together with what you have in whatever way you can. Using wireless ad-hoc mode means that each wireless device can communicate with the other wireless devices. (Setting up a network with wireless NICs is less expensive than using WAPs.)

You can purchase an access point to construct your wireless LAN. That's simple and quick, if a little expensive. If you choose that route, we leave it up to you to follow the access point's instructions for connecting other computers to it. You can follow the steps in Chapter 7 for configuring your Red Hat Linux wireless NIC to an access point.

We describe how to save a few bucks and use a Linux computer to build an ad hoc network. Building an ad hoc network requires you to put a Wi-Fi NIC on a Linux gateway. You then configure every computer, on your private network, to use the same network name and encryption key. The computers can then communicate directly with each other through the Linux gateway to the Internet.

Follow these steps to create a wireless LAN:

1. **Install both a Wi-Fi and Ethernet NIC on the Internet gateway computer.**

   Each of your private network's computers can talk to the Internet gateway through the wireless NIC. The Ethernet connects the gateway to the Internet through either a DSL or cable modem; you can substitute a telephone modem for the Ethernet NIC, if necessary.

   The next section in this chapter describes how to build an Internet gateway.

2. **Install a Wi-Fi NIC on each of your Linux and Windows computers.**

3. **Configure each Wi-Fi NIC to use the same network name and encryption key.**

   Refer to Chapter 7 to find out how to configure a Wi-Fi NIC; use the network IP addresses, netmasks, and other items described there.

4. **Configure your Internet gateway to forward your private network traffic to the Internet.**

5. **Configure a firewall on your Internet gateway.**

   Refer to the section "Protecting your LAN with a firewall," later in this chapter.

One advantage of using infrastructure mode is that a wireless device can move from access point to access point without reconfiguration. Access points provide mobility and flexibility, which can be a good thing if you happen to work on a large, dispersed environment. For example, if your company is spread across several locations, you want to be able to use your computer anywhere. However, if you don't correctly configure your access point correctly — for example, not using an encryption key — then flexibility becomes a security liability. Make sure that you correctly configure all your wireless devices.

Building an Internet Gateway

Okay, you have built your LAN. Woo-hoo! That wasn't too hard. The next question is "What can you do with it?" One answer is that every computer on your private network can communicate with all the others and share information and services. (We describe in Chapter 16 how to share some useful network-based services. You find out how to share files and printers, dole out IP addresses to your LAN devices, configure a Domain Name Server (DNS), and — ta-da! — build a Web server.)

One essential network function is to be connected to the Internet. Chapters 5 and 6 show you how to connect a single, stand-alone Linux computer to the Internet. We expand that process a step further and show you how to turn the Internet connection into one that can be used by the entire private network. Any computer connected to your LAN subsequently has Internet access. Sharing is good, and your mom should be pleased.

The remainder of this chapter deals with building an Internet gateway. We assume that you have a working Internet connection, as we describe in Chapters 5 and 6. This connection is the conduit from your LAN to the Internet. You only have to configure a Linux computer to redirect Internet-bound traffic from your LAN to the Internet *(routing)* and modify the firewall we describe in Chapter 8 to work with the gateway.

Understanding IP forwarding and network address translation (NAT)

An Internet gateway requires a Linux computer that has two network connections. You need one Ethernet or wireless NIC to connect to your LAN. The other network connection is used to make the Internet connection; this connection may be a traditional telephone-based modem, a DSL modem, or a cable modem. You use an Ethernet NIC to make the second connection.

Suppose that you open Mozilla on the sample Red Hat Linux computer Cancun (with the IP address `192.168.1.1`) and enter the URL `www.redhat.com`. Network packets bound about your LAN and then fly out to the Internet (and back again), and Mozilla ends up displaying the Red Hat Web page.

Lots of things have to happen to make all these things happen. Here's a simplified version of how it all works:

1. Mozilla asks Linux to look up the address — via the Domain Name Service (DNS) — which translates `www.redhat.com` to the numeric IP address `66.187.232.56`.
2. Linux compares the IP address to its internal routing table. The operating system directs network traffic to the default route if the address doesn't match its local networks. (In other words, if the IP address belongs to a machine on the private network, Linux directs its communication to the Ethernet device connected to the LAN. However, if the IP address is external to the LAN, Linux forwards the packets to the appropriate router.)

In this case, 66.187.232.56 doesn't exist on the LAN, so all traffic for the browsing session is directed to the default route.

3. On your private network, the default route of each host is directed toward the sample Internet gateway, the Red Hat Linux computer Veracruz. All the network packets that Cancun produces that are destined for the Internet, for example, are sent to Veracruz.
4. The Internet gateway Veracruz receives the outbound packets from Cancun on its internal connection and forwards them to its external connection. Packets going through its external connection are directed to the Internet.
5. Veracruz (192.168.1.254) also converts the source address of packets from Cancun (192.168.1.1) to the source address of its external connection. For example, if Veracruz has a DSL Internet connection with the address 192.168.32.254, the source address of Cancun packets is changed to 192.168.32.254. (This supposedly external Internet address has been changed to protect the innocent.)
6. The packets go to their intended destination. The www.redhat.com server responds to the query and sends back the requested information.
7. Veracruz receives the return packets, converts their destination address back to that of Cancun, and forwards them to the private network.
8. Cancun receives the packets, and the browser displays the information.

Forwarding network traffic through your gateway

This section describes how to configure a Linux computer to work as an Internet gateway. The process requires you to configure the Linux kernel to forward packets from one network interface to another — between the LAN port and the Internet port. Because Red Hat Linux turns off forwarding by default, the steps in this section describe how to turn on forwarding (you also need a Linux computer with two network connections in order to construct a gateway):

- One network connection should be either an Ethernet or wireless NIC that connects the gateway to the LAN. We refer to it as the *internal network connection.*
- The other connection is either the telephone-based modem or an Ethernet NIC connected to a DSL or cable modem. We refer to it as the *external network connection.*

Figure 15-2 shows Veracruz modified to work as an Internet gateway.

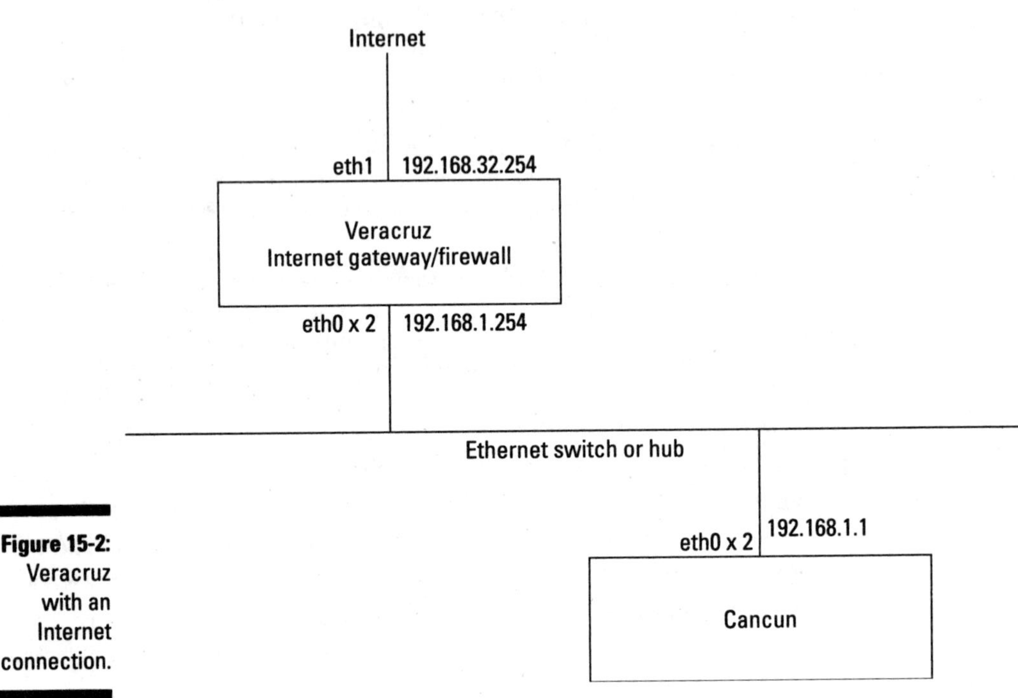

Figure 15-2: Veracruz with an Internet connection.

Turn off your external network connection for now. You turn on IP forwarding to enable the transmitting of network traffic between the Internet and your private network, which can be a security hazard. Disconnecting your Internet connection removes the insecurity: Unplug your modem's (DSL, cable, or telephone) external (Internet) cable.

These steps describe how to configure a Linux computer as the Internet gateway for a LAN:

1. **Add the appropriate internal and external network connections to your intended Internet gateway.**

   For example, the internal network connection is `eth0`, and the external network connection is `eth1`.

2. **Log in to your Internet gateway (in the example, Veracruz) as root.**

3. **Click the GNOME Menu button, choose Accessories➪Text Editor, and click the Open button.**

   The Open File window opens.

4. **Enter** /etc/sysctl.conf **in the Selection text box and click the OK button.**

   The gedit program displays the contents of `sysctl.conf`, as shown in Figure 15-3.

5. **Locate this line (which should be close to the top of the file):**

   ```
   net.ipv4.ip_forward = 0
   ```

6. **Change the 0 to a 1:**

   ```
   net.ipv4.ip_forward = 1
   ```

7. **Click the Save button and then choose File⇨Quit to close gedit.**

   You can view the change by clicking the Nautilus Refresh button. You have to restart Linux networking for the change to take effect.

8. **Open the Service Configuration utility by clicking the GNOME Menu button and choosing System Settings⇨Server Settings⇨Services.**
9. **Enter the root password, if you're prompted.**
10. **Locate and click the Network service.**
11. **Click the Restart button to turn on IP forwarding.**

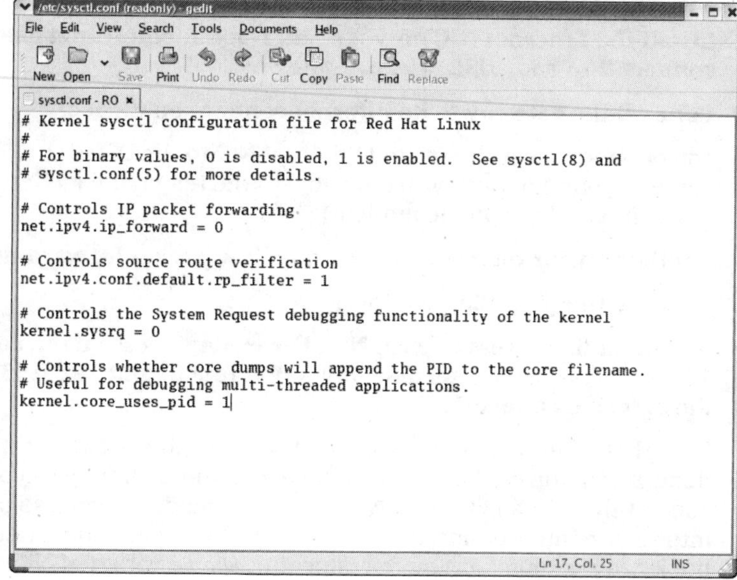

Figure 15-3: The gedit editor opens the `sysctl.conf` file.

Connecting your Internet gateway

After you configure your Internet gateway to forward network traffic from your private network to your Internet connection (see the preceding section), you need to make that connection. In this section, we describe how to use the Internet connections introduced in Chapters 5 and 6. You build on those instructions to connect your entire network to the Internet through these connections.

From a functional viewpoint, the type of Internet connection you use — telephone, DSL, or cable — doesn't matter because all these Internet connections send and receive the same network traffic. (Practically speaking, of course, the higher throughput and lower latency of broadband make it more desirable than old telephone modems.) For this reason, you can treat as interchangeable the Internet connections you may have read about in Chapters 5 and 6.

The forwarding we describe in the preceding section takes care of routing the packets to and from the Internet via your Internet gateway. Follow these steps to configure the Internet gateway:

1. **Install the Ethernet or Wi-Fi NIC on your Red Hat Linux Internet gateway to connect it to your private network.**
2. **Install the Ethernet NIC on your Red Hat Linux Internet gateway to connect it to your DSL or cable gateway.**
3. **Connect the gateway to its Internet connection device.**

   You either connect the second Ethernet NIC to the DSL or cable modem or connect your computer's serial cable to the telephone modem (or simply to the internal telephone modem).
4. **Configure your Internet gateway to allow packet forwarding.**

   (Refer to the preceding section.)
5. **Assign an IP address to each NIC. For example, assign the address** `192.168.1.254` **to your internal connection (**`eth0`**) and** `192.168.32.254` **to the external connection (**`eth1`**).**

   Note that when you're using a telephone or cable modem, this action is done automatically for you — modems connect directly to your gateway and not through an Ethernet NIC; some DSL modems can also plug directly into your computer and don't require an Ethernet connection. For this book, we assume that you're connecting via an Ethernet NIC.

Telephone modems use the Point-to-Point Protocol (PPP), whereas cable and some DSL modems use DHCP, which assigns an IP address to their respective interfaces.

6. **Assign a default route that points to the Internet connection device.**

   The PPP and DHCP protocols do this step automatically.

Follow these steps to configure computers or network devices on your private network to connect to the Internet through the gateway:

1. **Configure your computer with its network parameters.**

   In other words, assign an IP address and netmask (and optionally, but highly recommended, a host and network name) to each computer when using an Ethernet-based LAN. On a wireless network, you have to assign the IP address, netmask, common network name, and encryption key.

   For example, Chapter 7 describes how to set up the sample computer Cancun. You assign it the host name `cancun`; the network name `paunchy.net`; the IP address `192.168.1.1`; and the netmask `255.255.255.0`.

   If you use a Wi-Fi NIC on Cancun, you can assign the network name (ESSID) `myfi` and the encryption key `iamnotanumber`.

2. **Configure the default route on each device to point to the Internet gateway.**

3. **Rinse and repeat. (Repeat these steps for each computer on your private network.)**

After you have configured your Internet gateway and each additional computer on your private network, you should test whether they can communicate with the Internet. Consult Chapter 18 for pointers on troubleshooting network problems if you encounter difficulties. After you're satisfied that you have your LAN happily connected to the Internet, turn that puppy off. You still need to set up your firewall (as we describe in the following section) because you don't want to stay connected without one.

Protecting your LAN with a firewall

After you have configured your gateway for IP forwarding, you need to protect your network from the bad guys of the Internet. This section describes how to turn your gateway into a firewall. You use the same process and many of the same rules we describe in Chapter 8; however, this firewall is designed to protect your entire network, whereas the one in Chapter 8 is oriented toward protecting a single machine.

The firewall you're building helps to protect both your computer and network. The firewall also provides the network address translation (NAT) function, which allows the computers on your private network to access the Internet. NAT, you may recall, converts the nonroutable source IP addresses (`192.168.1.1`, for example) into the routable source IP address of your Internet connection.

Network address translation is also referred to as IP masquerading, or simply masquerading.

The basic configuration of the firewall we describe in Chapter 8 works in the new configuration. The firewall performs these functions:

- **Block all incoming, outgoing, and forwarded packets:** Start by blocking all network traffic by default. This firewall completely protects your private network but also makes it useless! Start with this policy to ensure that the firewall blocks all except the connections you explicitly allow.
- **Allow all loopback traffic:** You must allow all network traffic on the Internet gateway's internal loopback (lo) interface. The loopback interface is used by the Linux operating system for its own, internal communication. Many internal processes communicate over this virtual network.
- **Allow all internal NIC traffic:** Allowing computers on the private network to communicate with the gateway provides convenience. For example, you may want to administer the gateway via SSH. Take a lenient approach and allow any internal machine to communicate with the gateway; this strategy makes constructing the firewall easier. You may decide to limit internal access if your security needs demand it.
- **Allow all outgoing traffic from the firewall:** Allow all outgoing connections from within the firewall. The firewall needs to perform its own internal processes, such as making DNS queries.
- **Allow forwarding:** A gateway needs to pass traffic from one interface to another. You change the forwarding policy to permit communication from the private network to pass through the firewall to the Internet. The downside is that traffic from the Internet can pass through the firewall to the private network — not a good idea. You fix that problem by adding NAT. It effectively prevents external access through the firewall.

  You may want to set up specific forwarding rules to provide more protection to your private network. We believe that using NAT to effectively block externally originated connections is adequate for your needs.

- **Use NAT for outgoing connections:** Create a NAT rule to make all connections originating on the private network appear to be coming from the Internet gateway. All private network machines have their source addresses and port numbers changed to that of the gateway.

  The network address translation isn't necessary if your Internet connection device (telephone, DSL, or cable modem) performs NAT. However, by providing a NAT filtering rule, you ensure that your Internet gateway works with any connection device — whether or not it performs NAT. NAT also prevents external access to your private network.

- **Allow incoming SSH connections:** Secure Shell (SSH) is a protocol for encrypting network connections. SSH provides a reasonably secure system for connecting to your private network from the Internet. We configure the firewall to allow SSH connections into our firewall.

The firewall on the Internet gateway is similar to the firewall we describe in Chapter 8, except that you add IP forwarding and NAT. IP forwarding allows packets from the private network to pass through the firewall and on to the Internet. In this case, NAT makes all Internet-bound traffic appear to be coming from the firewall or gateway and prevents incoming packets from being forwarded into your private network.

Chapter 16

Creating Basic Linux Network Services

In This Chapter

- Preparing a network server
- Building a Linux web server
- Building a Linux file server with Samba
- Building a Linux print server
- Building a DNS server

Linux was built from scratch with networking in mind. Therefore, networking is fully integrated into Linux and is not merely an afterthought. Linux also comes bundled with software that provides file sharing, printer sharing, and other functions. Thus, Linux gained initial popularity by inexpensively and reliably providing network services. (Linux moved to the desktop only when applications such as word processing were written for it.)

In earlier chapters, we show you how to use a Red Hat Linux computer with an existing network. We also show you how to build a private network using Red Hat Linux computers as both clients and the Internet gateway, or firewall. In this chapter, we describe how to configure a Linux box to provide some popular services to the private network.

Preparing a Network Server

All examples shown in this chapter can be run from any Red Hat Linux computer, such as the one you construct in Chapter 3. Linux doesn't care what your intentions were when you built your computer. Linux calmly does what it is told and works gracefully as either a workstation or a server.

Linux works equally well whether it's running a word processor or a web server; the difference between them is just the software that's used and how it's configured. For example, you start the Open Office program when using your computer as a word processor, or you use the Apache program for Web services. In fact, you can run both programs at one time and do word processing while running a web server. (The basic web server uses fewer resources than OpenOffice, for example.)

Regarding performance, maintenance, and security, workstations and servers should be run on dedicated machines, if possible. Workstations require a wider range of software than do servers. Your workstation is a jack-of-all-trades by nature. Servers work better when they're configured to do just a small — preferably one or two — jobs.

When you get to the point where your business and livelihood depend on providing network services, you want to build and dedicate machines for this purpose. However, until that time comes, you can use the simple workstation we describe in Chapter 3, which is what we assume you're doing for this book.

You can configure the Red Hat Linux computer from Chapter 3 to provide services to a private network, like the one we describe in Chapters 7 and 16. This chapter describes how to make the Apache web server visible to the Internet. Services such as Samba and printing, however, definitely should be kept private and not be shown to the Internet.

We also assume in this chapter that you're connecting to the Internet through a private network as described in Chapters 7 and 15. (Chapter 15 tells you how to use a Red Hat Linux computer as an Internet gateway and firewall.) This chapter assumes that you want to use this same computer to provide services to your private network. This assumption is reasonable for small-office and home-office (SOHO) networks because the demands put on a modern PC by a small network aren't excessive. Using a single computer for multiple purposes greatly simplifies the work you must do and is an efficient way to use your resources.

Using a single Linux computer to act as an Internet gateway and provide network services is a cost-effective way of using your limited resources. However, this type of configuration is more difficult to secure. Each function you place on a single machine increases the potential number of vulnerabilities. Think of adding functions like adding doors and windows to a house: A house with a single door and no windows is more secure than a house with 5 doors and 15 windows. However, who wants to live in a dark house? Security, like everything else in life, is a matter of compromise. Consult Part II and Chapters 17 and 21 in this book for discussions on how you can increase security.

Building an Apache Web Server

The Web is the Internet, and the Internet is the Web. Well, that's not completely true because the Internet provides the foundation for widely used functions, such as e-mail. However, the Internet became immensely popular because of the World Wide Web (WWW).

The Web isn't as mysterious as it may seem at first. It's essentially all the world's web servers that are connected to the Internet. The Internet serves the same function as the world's telephone system: It interconnects everyone. You can think of web servers as the telephones that allow people to contact each other, businesses, and other organizations. Just as you can start a business or organization and let people contact you via your phone, you can also allow people to contact you via your web server. This section describes how to construct a simple web server.

Describing how to set up anything more than a simple web server is beyond the scope of this book. Needless to say, you can configure Apache to provide a whole world of Web services. If you want to utilize the powers of Apache, consult such books as the excellent *Apache Server 2 Bible,* by Mohammed J. Kabir, published by Wiley Publishing, Inc.

Installing and starting the web server

Linux provides the ideal platform for providing Web services. The Apache web server system is bundled with Red Hat Linux. Apache is easy to set up and use.

Because you're entering the world of creating and administering Linux services, you switch your orientation from performing work in GUIs to the command-line interface (CLI). Linux system administrators should become comfortable with using the CLI because many functions are best performed with the command line. You enter commands in the GNOME Terminal (terminal emulator) window in this chapter rather than use graphical utilities.

Follow these steps to install and configure a basic web server:

1. **Log in as root and mount the companion DVD-ROM.**

   Now you need to install the Apache RPM packages.

2. **You manually install the packages by first starting a GNOME Terminal window by clicking the GNOME Menu and choosing System Tools➪Terminal. Enter these commands:**

   ```
   rpm -ivh /mnt/cdrom/RedHat/RPMS/apr*
   rpm -ivh /mnt/cdrom/RedHat/RPMS/httpd*
   ```

The Apache RPM package puts all configuration files in place, so all you have to do is start the appropriate daemon.

3. **Enter this command from the GNOME Terminal window:**

```
/etc/init.d/httpd start
```

Linux uses the term *daemon* when referring to a process that runs continually in order to provide a service. The Apache daemon is named `httpd`, short for HyperText Transport Protocol Daemon. *HyperText Transport Protocol (HTTP)* is the system used to coordinate the transfer of Web pages between the server and the client (for example, the Mozilla browser). HTTP is the common language that both sides speak.

4. **Start your Mozilla Web browser and enter** localhost **in the URL window. Your new web server is displayed, as shown in Figure 16-1.**

5. **If you want your web server to start automatically every time you boot your computer, enter this command in the terminal emulator window:**

```
chkconfig --level 35 httpd on
```

The *level 35* option configures the web server to start in either non-graphics mode (system level 3) or graphical (system level 5) modes.

Running the chkconfig utility creates *soft links,* which are roughly analogous to a pointer. In this case, the soft link `S85httpd` is run automatically whenever you boot your computer.

Your web server should now be visible on your private network. (If your computer isn't connected to a LAN — for example, if it's a stand-alone machine with a telephone, cable, or DSL Internet connection — you can still use your web server from the machine itself.) However, keeping your web server all to yourself isn't much fun. The following section describes how to allow access to your web server from the Internet.

The Open Office suite has an HTML editor you can use to create Web pages. It's simple to use and can produce great-looking documents. Open any Open Office program (Writer or Spreadsheet, for example) and choose File➪New➪HTML Document. The HTML editor window opens, and you can create Web pages.

Accessing your web server through your firewall

This section describes how to open your firewall to allow access to your web server. Exactly how you allow access depends on whether you're connecting to the Internet directly from your Linux computer or through a LAN. The steps in this section describe how to modify your firewall and a DSL Internet connection to allow the Internet to view your Web page.

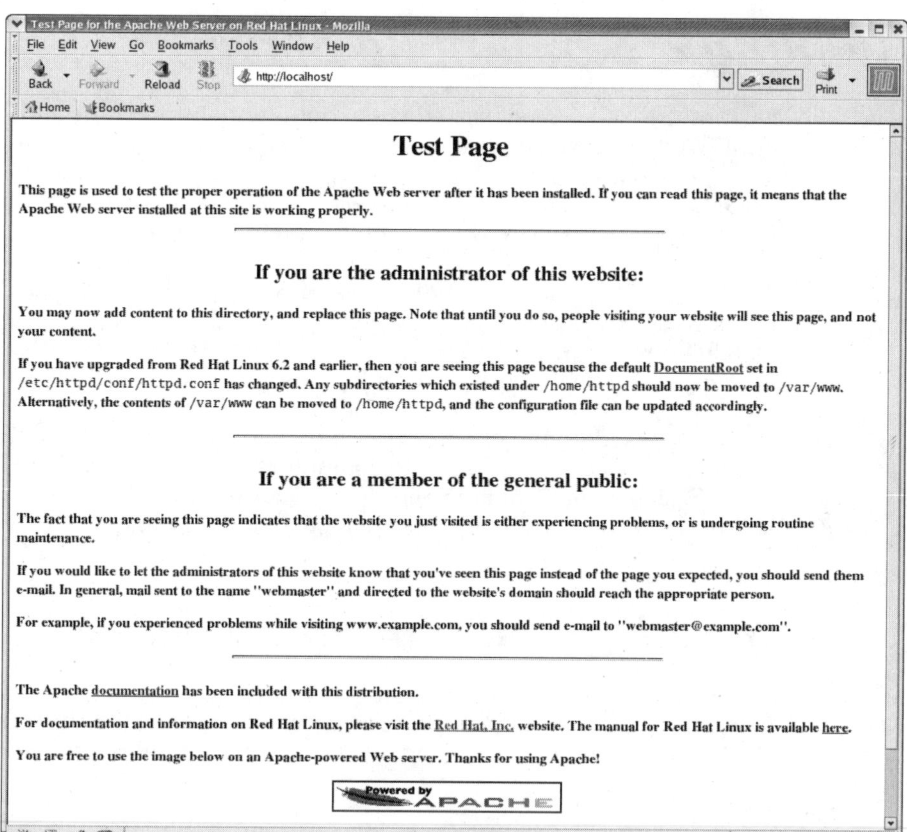

Figure 16-1: Your first web server!

You must modify the network address translation (NAT) configuration if you're using a DSL modem like the one we describe in Chapter 6. Connect to the DSL modem as described in Chapter 6 and run these commands:

```
set nat entry add 10.0.0.1 80 192.168.32.254 80
write
```

You have to modify your Internet gateway or firewall too. You have to allow external web browsers to connect to port 80 on your Apache server. Create the firewall rule by entering this command:

```
iptables -A INPUT -p tcp -m state --state NEW,ESTABLISHED -j
         -dport 80
```

Amazons of the world, watch out! Okay, it takes just a bit more than the default Apache Web page to upset the big boys, but you have the basics in place. All you have to do is figure out what to sell. How about a great Linux book?

Building a Samba File Server

Early in the game, Linux gained much popularity by acting as a file server for both Windows and Linux computers. It did that by dancing the Samba. Samba is more than just a dance routine — it's a suite of programs that speaks the same file-sharing language (the *protocol*) as Microsoft Windows. Using Samba produces a way to share the Linux file system on a network.

This section describes how to install and configure Samba on your Red Hat Linux computer. Samba comes bundled with Red Hat Linux, of course, so installation is a breeze. Samba is also configured to automatically share the ubiquitous `/home` directory, so configuration is also easy.

Samba is based on the client-server model in which a computer (server) provides services to one or more computers (clients). Samba uses the term *share* (which comes from the Microsoft Windows world) to refer to any object it exports to a network. An object can be a directory or a printer.

Installing and starting Samba

Samba consists of several programs, configuration files, and documentation files. The complete Samba package consists of four RPM files that come bundled on the DVD-ROM accompanying this book. This list describes the purpose of each RPM file:

- **samba-client:** This package contains the utility and other supporting software to connect a Linux computer to a Samba server. You can use the interactive utility `smbclient` to connect to a Samba share. The default Red Hat Linux installation installs this package by default.
- **samba:** The Samba server software is included in this package. All the programs for sharing files, directories, and printers are included here; the two essential daemons are `smbd` and `nmbd`; the essential configuration file is `smb.conf`. The utilities for controlling the daemons are also included.
- **samba-swat:** You can manually configure the Samba configuration file, `smb.conf`, if you're an expert. However, Samba provides a Web-based system that is much easier to use and produces clean and readable configuration files.
- **samba-common:** All the software required by the other three packages is included in this file. This package is also installed by default.

Samba was originally designed and coded by Andrew Tridgell, of Australia. Samba instantly became popular worldwide and became too much for a few people to handle. Thus, the Samba project was started in order to take care of the phenomenon. You can find more information about Samba at `www.samba.org`.

Follow these steps to dance the — er, install, configure, and use — Samba:

1. **Log in as root and insert this book's companion DVD-ROM.**
2. **Open a terminal emulator window and enter this command:**

   ```
   rpm -ivh /mnt/cdrom/RedHat/RPMS/samba-client*
   ```

   The Samba server consists of two daemons: `smbd` and `nmbd`. You must start both daemons before anyone can access your Samba server.
3. **Enter this command to start the daemons:**

   ```
   /etc/init.d/smb start
   ```

   You can stop the daemons by substituting the *stop* option for the *start* option. You can restart the Samba server by using the *restart* option:

   ```
   /etc/init.d/smb restart
   ```
4. **Automate the startup of the Samba daemons by creating these soft links with the chkconfig utility:**

   The following command tells Linux to automatically start Samba for Level 3 (nongraphical) and Level 5 (running the graphical X server); Samba is started whether your Linux computer starts in graphical or nongraphical mode:

   ```
   chkconfig --level 35 smb on
   ```

   Samba is configured by default to use its own password file. You must create the password file by using the `mksmbpasswd.sh` script.
5. **Use the smbpasswd program to create the Samba user account and password.**

   The `-a` option tells the script to add the user account to the `smbpasswd` file:

   ```
   smbpasswd -a paul
   ```

   You're prompted to enter a password twice.

6. **Here's the acid test: Run this command to look at your home directory (in this example, it's Paul's home directory):**

   ```
   smbclient //localhost/paul -U paul
   ```

7. **Enter the password you entered in Step 6, and you gain access to Paul's home directory, which should look similar to this:**

   ```
   added interface ip=192.168.1.1 bcast=192.168.1.255
           nmask=255.255.255.0
   Password:
   Domain=[MYGROUP] OS=[Unix] Server=[Samba 3.0]
   smb: \>
   ```

8. **Enter** help **at the** `smb: \>` **prompt and you see all the commands at your disposal.**

   For example, enter **dir** and you see all the files in your home directory.

9. **You can mount Samba file systems on a Linux computer. Enter this command to mount your home directory (**`/home/paul`**) on the same computer you're logged in to:**

   ```
   mount -t smbfs -o username=paul //localhost/paul /mnt
   ```

   This example doesn't require that you have a network to work on and mounts your home directory on the `/mnt` mount point. You can mount a Samba share from another Linux computer by specifying the remote machine name. For example, if you're logged on to the computer Cancun and the Samba server runs on Veracruz, enter this line:

   ```
   mount -t smbfs -o username=paul //veracruz/paul /mnt
   ```

Your home directory is now mounted on the `/mnt` directory. That's great! Now you can use your Linux computer to provide files and directories to the rest of your network.

Configuring Samba with SWAT

Call in the SWAT team! (Sorry, that couldn't be helped.) SWAT, which stands for Samba Web Administration Tool, is used to graphically configure Samba. SWAT helps you to configure all aspects of a Samba server and also to start, stop, and look at Samba's status.

You must configure the `inetd.d` daemon to start up SWAT. These steps show you how to get `xinetd.d` to run SWAT:

1. **Log in to your Samba server as root and open a terminal emulator window (refer to Chapter 4).**

2. **Insert the companion DVD-ROM and install the SWAT package by entering this command:**

   ```
   rpm -ivh /mnt/cdrom/RedHat/RPMS/samba-swat*
   ```

3. **Edit the** `/etc/xinetd.d/swat` **file and change the last line from** `disable=yes` **to** disable=no.

4. **Restart** `xinetd.d`:

   ```
   /etc/init.d/xinetd restart
   ```

5. **Start Mozilla on your Samba server and enter this address in the URL window:**

   ```
   localhost:901
   ```

   SWAT starts up and prompts you for a username and password. SWAT is configured, via the `/etc/xinetd.d/swat` file, to use the root user and password.

6. **Enter** root **at the User Name prompt and the root user's password at the Password prompt.**

   Mozilla shows the SWAT configuration system, as shown in Figure 16-2.

   You can now use SWAT to configure any aspect of Samba. These steps describe how to use Samba to export your DVD-ROM/CD-ROM drive:

   Samba comes configured to export users' home directories and printers on the server where it resides, so the basics are already covered. One good Samba share to provide to users on your LAN is your DVD-ROM/CD-ROM drive.

7. **Click the Shares button.**

   The Shares window opens.

8. **Enter** cdrom **in the text box next to the Create Share button and then click the Create Share button; the word *cdrom* is arbitrary but descriptive.**

   The configuration window for the new `cdrom` share opens.

9. **Enter** /mnt/cdrom **in the Path text box, as shown in Figure 16-3.**

   Optionally, you can enter a comment to describe what you're exporting.

10. **Click the Commit Changes button and the new share is saved to the** `/etc/samba/smb.conf` **file.**

The changes also take effect immediately because a new `smbd` daemon is spawned every time a share request is made to the Samba server. You can now mount the new Samba share from any machine on the LAN, including the server.

11. **Create a new directory on which to mount the Samba share (the name is arbitrary):**

```
mkdir /samba
```

12. **Restart the Samba daemon.**

```
/etc/init.d/smb restart
```

13. **Try mounting the share by entering this command from the server:**

```
mount -t smbfs -o username=paul //cancun/cdrom /samba
```

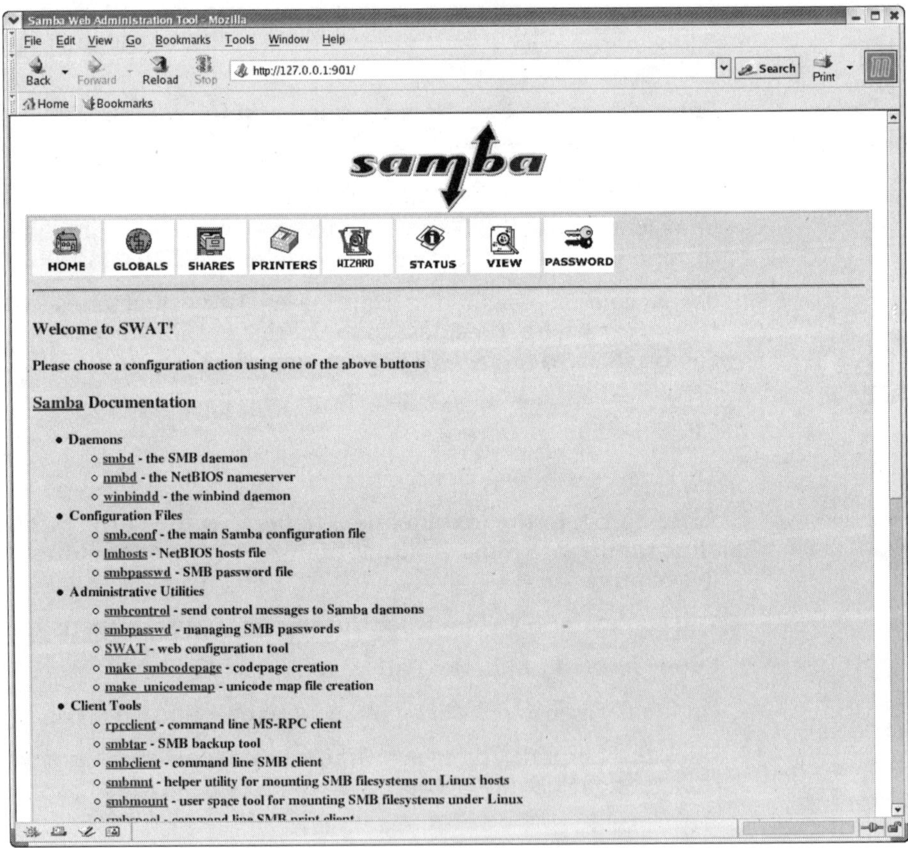

Figure 16-2: The SWAT configuration system.

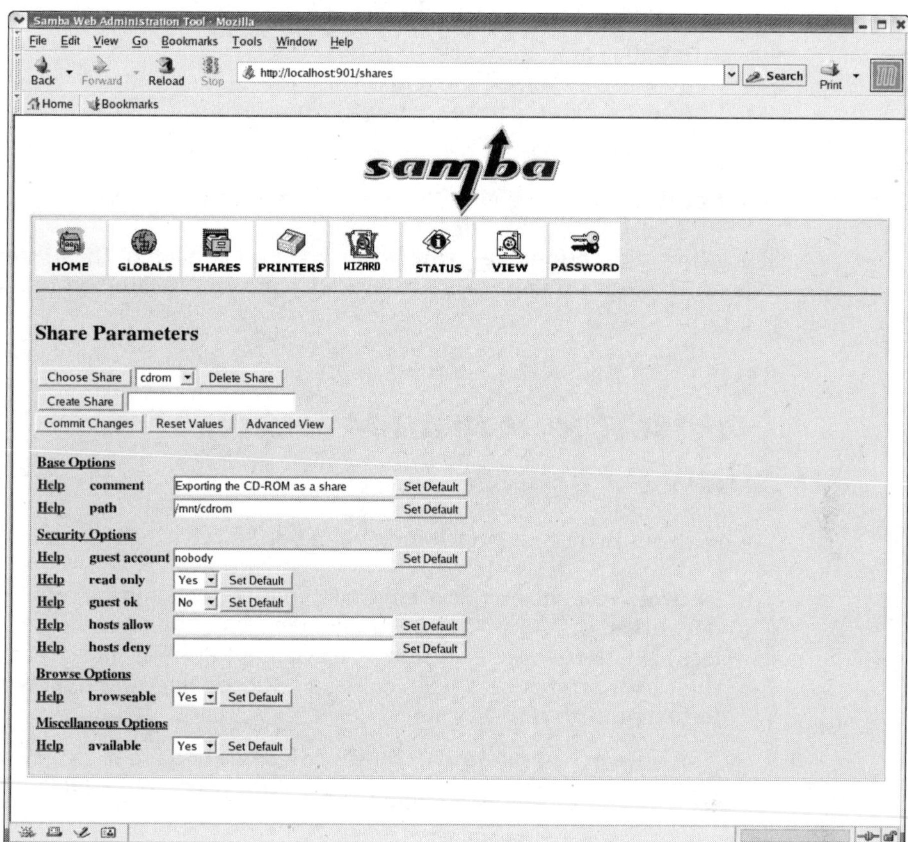

Figure 16-3: Configuring a new share.

14. **Enter your password and the share is mounted on the `/samba` directory.**

Note that when you mount a file system over an existing file system, only the newly mounted file system is visible. In this case, you mount the CD-ROM on `/mnt`, which covers over the initial CD-ROM mount.

Building a Print Server

Linux can share printers to other Linux (and Unix) computers without using Samba; you can select the Unix Style print queue to create a Linux print server. However, Windows doesn't speak Unix, and using Samba enables all Linux, Unix, and Windows computers to use the Linux print server.

You must complete these steps before your Linux computer acts as a print server to your entire network:

1. **Connect a printer to the Linux computer.**
2. **Configure the Linux print server to use the printer.**
3. **Configure a Linux client to print through the server.**

The following sections describe how to complete each of these steps so that every computer on your private network can print through your Linux print server.

Connecting a printer to your Linux computer

Choose from two types of printers when you're creating a print server:

- **Networked printers:** Printers that can be connected directly to a LAN are networked printers. They have their own Ethernet (and, in the future, wireless) NIC. Networked printers are divided between those that can act as their own print server (also called a *print spooler*) and the ones that need to be connected to a print server.
- **Non-networked printers:** Traditional printers have to be connected to a computer through a printer (parallel) or Universal Serial Bus (USB) port.

Non-networked printers outnumber networked printers because they cost less. Traditional printers are less flexible than networked printers because they must be connected to a computer; networked printers can be located anywhere that a network connection exists.

This section describes how to use non-networked computers because they're so common. The process is simple: You connect your printer to the Linux print server via the USB or parallel port. After you're connected, the Linux computer can be configured to send print jobs to the printer.

Using a parallel port requires no configuration of the Linux operating system. The USB connection, however, requires that Linux load a USB kernel module (essentially a driver, in Windows terminology). Loading the kernel module should be automatic. However, if you encounter problems, you can load the module manually:

1. **Log in as root.**
2. **Open a terminal emulator window (refer to Chapter 4).**
3. **Enter this command:**

```
modprobe printer
```

Linux loads the printer kernel module.

Configuring the Linux print server

After you connect a printer, you have to configure Linux to act as a print server. Red Hat provides an excellent print configuration utility. (Red Hat refers to its configuration systems as *utilities.*) Building a Linux print server requires you to configure the printer as a local device. However, every print server client — the computers on the LAN that send their print jobs to the print server — configure their print queues to use the Windows Printer type. The print server sees the printer directly through its USB or parallel port, but the print clients see the printer as a Samba (Windows) share on the server.

Red Hat Linux can handle five printer types. The printer configuration druid allows you to configure each type. This list describes the printer types:

- **Local Printer:** Use this type if your printer is connected directly to your computer. The print server is configured using this type because the printer is connected directly to it.
- **Unix Printer:** Use this type if you're creating a print server that only other Linux and Unix computers use. Windows computers can't use Unix printers. Unix printer queues don't require Samba in order to work.
- **Windows Printer:** Use this type if you're printing to a Windows print server. Samba makes the print server look like a Windows print server, and the clients on the private network use this setting.
- **Novell Printer:** Use this type if you're printing to a Novell print server.
- **JetDirect Printer:** Use this type if you're printing to a Hewlett-Packard (HP) JetDirect printer. The HP JetDirect interface is built into many HP and other printers. You can also purchase JetDirect print server devices that connect to non-networked, traditional printers. JetDirect print servers convert traditional printers into networked printers.

These steps describe how to configure an Epson Stylist printer because it's a good, inexpensive inkjet printer. The configuration utility can configure many different types of printers, so select the model that's appropriate for you:

1. **Log in to your Red Hat Linux print server.**
2. **Click the GNOME Menu button, choose System Settings⇨Printing, and enter the root password if you're prompted to do so. Click the New button and the Add a New Print Queue window opens.**
3. **Click the Forward button and you're prompted to enter a queue name and an optional description.**

   Figure 16-4 shows the Add a New Print Queue window.

   Enter in the Name text box the name you want to refer to the printer (the default is `printer`). You can enter any name you want for the queue name. For example, Epson777 clearly indicates that you're accessing an Epson Stylus 777 printer.
4. **Click the Forward button and the Queue Type dialog box opens.**

   Linux should detect the printer attached to either the USB or parallel port.

   You can configure the printer as a nonlocal device if you have a network printer. For example, if you have a high-end HP LaserJet with a JetDirect interface, select Networked Jet-Direct rather than Locally-Connected.

   Linux parallel (printer) ports correspond to Windows printer ports. Linux `lp0` is equivalent to LPT1 and `/dev/lp1` is equivalent to LPT2.
5. **Click the local printer device (typically, it should be listed as `/dev/lp0` or `/dev/lp1`) and click the Forward button.**

   The Printer model window pops up.
6. **Click the pull-down menu and select your printer's manufacturer. For example, select Epson. The manufacturer's model list appears. Scroll down the model list and select your printer model.**

   Some printers come with more than one driver. Select the driver that best suits your printer. Use trial-and-error if you don't know which driver is best.
7. **Click the Forward button.**
8. **Click the Finish button in the new window and the Question dialog box opens. Click the Yes button and you return to the Printer Configuration window.**
9. **Click the Apply button and the Linux print daemon, `lpd`, restarts and makes the new configuration active.**

The configuration utility sends a test page to the printer. If the page prints okay, click the Yes button in the Information dialog box.

10. **Close the configuration utility by choosing Action⇨Quit.**

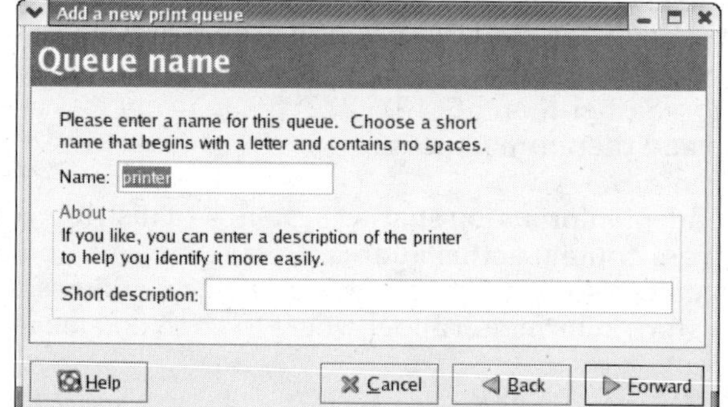

Figure 16-4: The Queue Name window.

The printer configuration druid allows you to go back and edit or delete a printer configuration.

Configuring a Linux client to print through the print server

Samba makes sharing a printer to Linux, Unix, and Windows computers easy because all those types can speak the Session Message Block (SMB) protocol; SMB is a Windows way of spreading the wealth (yeah, right).

Samba comes configured to automatically export the default Linux printer. Half the battle is won! You don't have to configure the server; you only have to configure each client.

Configure a Linux client to print through the Linux print server by repeating the steps in the preceding section. The steps are the same except that you select the Windows queue type rather than Local. You select the Windows type because the client is sending its jobs to the server via Samba; Samba makes the server act like it's a Windows queue type.

You can print a PostScript test page to test your printer configuration by choosing Test⇨US Letter PostScript Test Page in the Printer Configuration utility.

Building a DNS Server

Every device connected to the Internet, including your Red Hat Linux computer, requires an Internet Protocol (IP) address in order to communicate properly. IP addresses are unique numbers and are therefore difficult for us carbon-based humans to remember and use. The Domain Name System (DNS) solves that problem by converting numbers to names, making it possible to use names like `www.redhat.com` rather than `66.187.232.56`. In many ways, DNS makes the Internet usable and therefore popular.

DNS is an interdependent information-sharing system — a distributed database. No centralized servers contain actual addresses, such as `www.redhat.com`. Instead, DNS is structured so that local servers store local addresses, and a few centralized servers store information about where to go to find local addresses.

Introducing DNS components

The overall DNS system is a complex system that contains many components. But because we show you how to build a DNS server for your private network, you can use a more simple system. Building your DNS server requires understanding only a relative handful of DNS components.

This list outlines the basic DNS components:

- **Domains:** You're probably familiar with domains whether you realize it or not. *Domains* are the networks you access all the time on the Internet. For example, `redhat.com` is a domain (and `www.redhat.com` is the name of a server within the `redhat.com` domain).

  Domains can optionally be divided into subdomains. For example, Red Hat has a subdomain, `beta.redhat.com`, used for its beta software development.

  Domains themselves are divided into domains. The ubiquitous `.com`, `.edu`, and `.org` are all top-level domains. They organize the Internet into business, educational, and not-for-profit arenas, respectively.
- **Zones:** Domains are divided into zones. DNS servers service zones. A zone can map directly to a domain; multizones can service a domain too. The DNS server you're building in this section consists of a single domain that services the fictitious `paunchy.net` domain.
- **Authoritative name servers:** Every zone must have an authoritative name server. It holds the information for every host within the zone. You can

create primary and secondary authoritative name servers. The secondaries back up the primaries.

- **Non-authoritative name servers:** You can create name servers that don't necessarily provide the most up-to-date information.
- **Caching name server:** Name servers can be configured to look up addresses from other name servers and temporarily save, or *cache,* the information. Caching name servers helps spread out the load of servicing large domains.
- **Root name servers:** The authorities who control domain name registrations provide root name servers that hold the addresses of name servers for each domain. DNS queries go to root name servers to find out where to find authoritative name servers.

This list describes the parameters found in DNS configuration and zone files. The parameters are called resource records (RR):

- **A records:** Address (A) records map IP names to numeric addresses.
- **C records:** Canonical (C) records define aliases for A records.
- **MX records:** Mail exchange (MX) records specify the mail servers that service a domain.
- **NS records:** Name server (NS) records specify the name server for a zone.
- **SOA:** The start of authority (SOA) parameter creates a section that describes the generic properties of a zone file. The SOA configures parameters that set the serial number and various timeouts, plus the domain name of a zone.

Understanding how a DNS address request works

This section gives you a look at how your browser finds the Red Hat Linux Web page:

1. You open your browser and enter the URL `www.redhat.com`.
2. The browser asks Linux for the Web page's numeric address.
3. Linux looks in its `/etc/resolv.conf` configuration file and finds the address of a name server.

You can use any available DNS server on the Internet. For example, you can use Albuquerque's finest ISP Southwest Cyberport DNS server, `198.59.115.2`, from anywhere on the Internet. You should use your own ISP's servers because it has fewer routers, or *hops,* to go through, which results in better reliability and speed.

4. Linux requests the IP address for `www.redhat.com` from the name server.
5. If the name server doesn't know the IP address of `www.redhat.com`, it asks a root server for the address of an authoritative name server for the `redhat.com` domain.
6. The root server returns the address of the Red Hat authoritative name server, the first of which is `ns1.redhat.com` (`66.187.233.210`).
7. The name server asks `ns1.redhat.com` for the address of `www.redhat.com`.
8. The name server `ns1.redhat.com` returns the `www.redhat.com` address.
9. Using the numeric `www.redhat.com` IP address, your browser starts communicating with the web server.

Building a DNS server

It's time to build a server. The steps in this section describe how to build an authoritative name server for your private network. The server provides the addresses for the private, nonroutable private network we describe in Chapter 15. Therefore, you don't have to register the addresses with any authority. The DNS server is authoritative for your private domain, but that information isn't available outside your network.

The steps in this section show you how to install the DNS server software. You create the `/etc/named.conf`, `/var/named/local.zone`, `/var/named/paunchy.zone`, and `/var/named/1.168.192.zone` files.

Installing the DNS software

Start by installing the bind RPM that contains the named server software:

1. **Log in to your computer as root and insert this book's companion DVD-ROM.**
2. **Start a GNOME Terminal session.**
3. **Enter this command in the terminal emulator window:**

```
rpm -ivh /mnt/cdrom/Redhat/RPMS/bind-9*
```

Now you have to create the DNS configuration file, `/etc/named.conf`:

Creating the DNS configuration file

These steps describe how to create a basic `named.conf` file:

1. **Start the text editor by clicking the GNOME Menu button and choosing Accessories⇨Text Editor.**
2. **Enter this configuration in the Gedit window:**

```
options { directory "/var/named"; };

zone  "." {
        type hint;
        file  "named.ca";
};
zone  "localhost" {
        type master;
        file  "localhost.zone";
};
zone  "paunchy.net" {
        type master;
        file  "paunchy.zone";
};
zone  "1.168.192.in-addr.arpa" {
        type master;
        file  "1.168.192.zone";};
```

   This list describes the various parts of the `/var/named` file:

   - The `options` section defines the `/var/named` directory as the location of the database files. You can configure many more options. Enter the command **man named.conf** for more information.
   - The `named.ca` section defines the master name servers that serve the entire Internet.
   - The first zone section, `localhost`, defines the master server for the internal loopback interface.
   - The second zone section sets the master server for the `paunchy.net` domain or zone to be found in the file `/var/named/paunchy.zone`.
   - The third zone section defines the reverse lookup master server to be found in the `/var/named/1.168.192.in-addr.arpa` file.

3. **Save the configuration to `/etc/named.conf` by choosing File⇨Save As.**
4. **Enter** /etc/named.conf **in the Selection box and click OK.**

   Gedit saves your DNS configuration file.

Creating a localhost zone file

To create the `localhost.zone` file, follow these steps:

1. **From the Gedit text editor, choose File⇨New from the menu.**
2. **Enter the following configuration. (Of course, you can select the machine names you want. The names are arbitrary. In fact, the IP addresses are arbitrary too. You can select any nonroutable address space you want.)**

```
$TTL 86400
@        IN       SOA      @  root.localhost (
                           1 ; serial
                           28800 ; refresh
                           7200 ; retry
                           604800 ; expire
                           86400 ; ttl
                           )


@        IN       NS       localhost.


@        IN       A        127.0.0.1
```

Semicolons (;) indicate comments. All characters following a semicolon are treated as a comment and don't affect the operation of the DNS configuration files.

3. **Save the configuration by choosing File⇨Save As.**
4. **Enter /var/named/local.zone in the Selection box and click OK.**

Creating the private network zone file

Next, you create the `paunchy.zone` file, which serves the private network. This file contains the A and C records for all machines in your zone (in this case, the zone maps directly to the `paunchy.net` domain.)

1. **From the Gedit text editor, choose File⇨New from the menu.**
2. **Enter the following configuration. (Of course, you can select your own machine names. The names are arbitrary. In fact, the IP addresses are arbitrary too. You can select any nonroutable address space you want.)**

```
$TTL 86400
@                IN       SOA      paunchy.net.
         root.paunchy.net. (
                                   200112211
                                   10800
                                   3600
```

```
                                        3600000
                                        86400 )
                    IN        NS        ns.paunchy.net.
                    IN        A         192.168.1.254

; servers
veracruz              IN        A         192.168.1.254
www             CNAME               veracruz
ns              CNAME               veracruz
; workstations
chivas          IN        A         192.168.1.1   ; Linux
pumas           IN        A         192.168.1.2   ; Linux
tigres          IN        A         192.168.1.100 ; Windows
```

3. **Save the configuration by choosing File⇨Save As.**
4. **Enter** /var/named/paunchy.zone **in the Selection box and click OK.**

Creating the reverse zone file

The last step is to create a reverse DNS lookup file for your zone. This file is optional but quite useful. By providing reverse lookup capability to your network, you can specify a numeric IP address and get a name back:

1. **Back in the Gedit text editor, choose File⇨New from the menu.**
2. **Create the reverse DNS configuration file parameters:**

```
$TTL 86400
@       IN      SOA     paunchy.net     root.paunchy.net
        (
                        2002030801
                        28800
                        7200
                        604800
                        86400
                        )
@       IN      NS      paunchy.net.

;       servers
254     IN      PTR     veracruz

  Linux workstations
1      IN      PTR     cancun
2      IN      PTR     veracruz
;  Windows workstations
101      IN      PTR    cozumel
```

3. **Choose File⇨Save As.**
4. **Enter /var/named/1.168.192.zone in the Selection box and click OK.**

5. **Create the `rndc` configuration and key file. The rndc utility is used to control the name server. Enter this command to automatically create the configuration and key:**
6. **Open a GNOME Terminal window and create the `rndc` configuration and key file by entering this command:**

```
rndc-confgen
```

Again, the filename `1.168.192.zone` is arbitrary. You can call it `reverse.zone` or anything else you want as long as you match the name in the `/etc/named.conf` file — that is, `named.conf` would need to call the reverse IP address database `reverse.zone` rather than `1.168.192.zone`.

Starting your DNS server

After you have created the DNS configuration and zone files, you can start your server:

1. **Click the GNOME Menu and choose System Settings⇨Server Settings⇨Services.**
2. **Locate the named service and click its radio button.**

   This step selects the server to be started at boot time.
3. **Click the Restart button.**
4. **Click the OK button in the Information window that pops up.**

   You now have a DNS server.

Alternatively, you can start the DNS server by running this command: `/etc/init.d/named start`.

Configuring your DNS clients

To use your new DNS server, you have to configure the hosts on your LAN and modify the `/etc/resolv.conf` file on your Linux computers. Modify the network settings on your Windows machines.

Modify the `resolv.conf` file on Linux computers to look like this:

```
search paunchy.net
nameserver 192.168.1.254
```

You can specify as many as three name servers, so you may add your ISP's name server as an alternative:

```
search paunchy.net
nameserver 192.168.1.254
nameserver 198.59.115.2
```

Open a GNOME Terminal window and run this command.

```
host cancun
```

You see this result:

```
cancun.paunchy.net has address 192.168.1.121
```

The host command provides numerous options that provide more information about your query. For example, you can see information about where the host command gets its information. Add the verbose (`-v`) option to the preceding example and you see this information.

```
Trying "cancun.paunchy.net"
;; ->>HEADER<<- opcode: QUERY, status: NOERROR, id: 18016
;; flags: qr aa rd ra; QUERY: 1, ANSWER: 1, AUTHORITY: 1,
           ADDITIONAL: 0

;; QUESTION SECTION:
;cancun.paunchy.net.            IN      A

;; ANSWER SECTION:
cancun.paunchy.net.  86400   IN    A    192.168.1.1

;; AUTHORITY SECTION:
paunchy.net.         86400   IN    NS   ns.paunchy.net.1
Received 69 bytes from 192.168.1.120#53 in 263 ms
```

This list describes what the various sections in the preceding output mean.

- **Question section:** You see in the Question section that the query is `cancun.paunchy.net`. Note that we ask for only the address of `cancun` but that the search parameter in the `resolv.conf` file specifies that the `paunchy.net` domain be appended to `cancun`. You also see that an A record is part of the query — you're asking for an IP address.
- **Answer section:** This is the answer to your query. The answer includes the host name and domain — `cancun.sandia.gov` — and its numeric IP address. The Answer section also includes the time-to-live (TTL) value.

- **Authority section:** This data shows where the information was found in the preceding Answer section. You got the answer from the name server — `192.168.1.254` — that you just built.

All the computers on your network can use your DNS server. Your DNS supplies addresses for all internal machines. The server forwards requests for external addresses as necessary.

Chapter 17

Securing Your Future

In This Chapter

- Thinking security
- Preventing intruders
- Updating Red Hat Linux packages
- Deactivating services with chkconfig
- Using the Secure Shell client
- Configuring a Secure Shell server
- Securing your web server with SSL
- Reading logs
- Understanding the security process

Protecting your individual computers and collective network is an essential task in today's insecure world. Unfortunately, computer and network security is a big, complex job. This chapter boils down that job to some essential functions. We describe several straightforward methods and utilities that bring your security job down to size. Using these ideas makes both your computers and network safer.

This chapter describes security methods and systems. We have chosen several security tools and systems that should give you the most bang for your buck. This chapter provides a starting point for making your computers and network safer. We encourage you to continue learning and evolving your security system.

Thinking Security

Computer security is best thought of as an ongoing process. No single method, tool, or system — a silver bullet — can magically protect you from the wild-west Internet. Security, like exercise and diet, is just plain hard work.

Because no silver bullet exists, you have to use layers of security measures, called *defense in depth*. Each layer helps to protect the other layers and vice versa. If and when one layer fails, you fall back on the other. You can also add and remove layers as necessary.

Layered security systems and measures fall under three categories:

- **Prevention:** Tools, utilities, and methods prevent any attacks from succeeding. Tools such as passwords and the firewalls we describe in Chapter 8 are under this heading.
- **Detection:** Because not all attacks can be prevented, detecting them, if possible, is essential. Intrusion detection is still more of an art than a science.
- **Process:** Most computer users would prefer to construct a security system and then sit back and forget about it. However, the hacker world changes as fast as the rest of the world, and the systems that work now won't necessarily work tomorrow. Therefore, you must keep learning and use that knowledge to improve your security.

An Ounce of Protection: Preventing Intruders

We start by describing how to minimize your chances of being hacked. The following sections describe systems that increase your security:

- **Updating software:** The Red Hat up2date utility helps keep your computer's software up to date, which eliminates vulnerabilities as they are discovered.
- **Removing services:** Hackers can't take advantage of vulnerable software if you don't use it. Turning off unnecessary services reduces your exposure.
- **OpenSSH and SSL:** Except when viewing garden-variety, nonsecure Web pages, you should never communicate over the Internet (or wireless LANs) without using encryption. The open source SecureShell (SSH) and Secure Sockets Layer (SSL) provide effective encryption for your communications.

We describe each system in this section.

Reducing vulnerabilities by updating Red Hat Linux packages

Standard hacker operating procedure is simple: Find and then exploit vulnerabilities. The method, simple but effective, works like this: Joe Hacker walks around the Internet, rattling doorknobs and occasionally finding one that's open. When no door is unlocked, the hacker looks for easier locks to pick. Your job is to make sure that your doors and windows are locked and not easily picked. Running firewalls, shutting down unnecessary services, and using good passwords ensures that you don't leave anything unlocked. Making sure that your locks are not easily defeated requires constant supervision. Software is now powerful but complex. Complexity breeds bugs, and with bugs come vulnerabilities. Because the only certainties in life are death, taxes, and buggy software, the bugs have to be fixed whenever possible. Everyone needs to continually update software when errors are found and corrected.

Red Hat created an excellent method for updating its software: The Up-to-Date (up2date) system automatically detects new software and installs it for you. Next to using good passwords and firewalls, it's probably the most effective security system you can run.

The URL shown in the first text box is a server on the Red Hat Network (RHN). However, it's an artifact left over from the Red Hat Linux to Fedora Core conversion that doesn't control where up2date will search for updates. The configuration file `/etc/sysconfig/rhn/sources` contains the actual up2date server that Fedora will use.

The following steps describe how to configure up2date:

1. **Click the GNOME menu, choose System Tools⇨Red Hat Network, and enter your root password if you're prompted.**

   The Welcome to Red Hat Update Agent window, as shown in Figure 17-1, opens.

2. **Click the OK button and the Question dialog box opens.**

   You're told that your keyring doesn't contain the Red Hat public key. A *keyring* system helps maintain the public keys of places you need to securely communicate with. Because this is the first time you have tried to securely connect to the Red Hat Network, you don't have its public key.

Figure 17-1: The Red Hat Network Configuration window.

3. **Click Yes to accept the Red Hat public key.**

   The Welcome to Red Hat Update Agent window opens.

4. **Click the Forward button.**

   The Channels dialog box, shown in Figure 17-2, opens showing various options.

5. **The default options should be satisfactory, so click the Forward button.**

   Any updates that are available will be downloaded and you'll be prompted to install them.

6. **Click the OK button to install the updates (if available).**

   The updates are installed and an Information dialog box opens.

7. **Click the OK button and the up2date process finishes.**

You can skip having to manually click the up2date icon every time an update is available (oh, life is so hard). You can configure up2date to automatically update your system whenever it detects a new package.

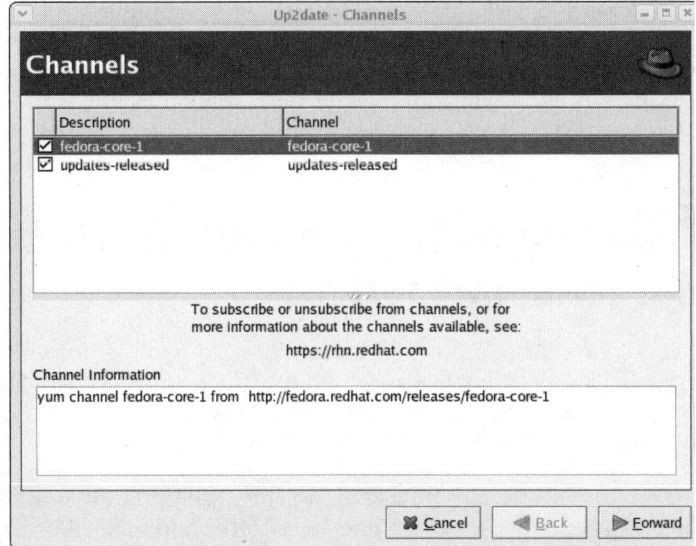

Figure 17-2: The Channels window

Your Red Hat Linux computer can now receive updates. The up2date icon is displayed on the right side of the GNOME Panel. When the icon is green, life is good. When the icon turns red, however, updates are available. (A yellow icon indicates that up2date doesn't know whether an update exists for your machine.) You want to click the icon so that it downloads and installs the updates.

You can automate the update process using the Linux cron facility. Run the `crontab -e` command and create a cron entry like this: `0 1 * * * up2date -u`. This example launches the up2date utility every day at 1 a.m. The `-u` option forces up2date to update any available Red Hat packages.

Red Hat provides summary and other information about your account at `rhn.redhat.com`. Go to that page and enter your username and password in the Sign In to RHN subwindow. You can view the status of your registered machine (or machines), modify your account, and read other important information.

Regularly updating your computer is an essential security measure. Many, many break-ins occur because of out-of-date software. With the help of RHN, you eliminate most vulnerabilities as they occur.

Red Hat permits you to register, for free, one computer for basic update service. Basic service allows you to download and install updated RPM packages. To update more machines, you have to purchase additional subscriptions at $60 per year. Note that you can register more machines under the Red Hat Network service, but they aren't eligible for updates.

Reducing your exposure: Removing and reducing services

Hackers look for computer vulnerabilities by probing for vulnerable network services. Network services — such as Apache, Samba, and DHCP — are, of course, designed to respond to network queries. Therefore, hackers can readily find out what services you run and then find which, if any, attacks to use.

We describe elsewhere how keeping software updated minimizes your vulnerability. However, you can go one step better and make a service invulnerable by turning it off. One simple security rule is "Keep it simple." The simple fact is that if you don't need to run a service, you shouldn't.

We describe in this section how to eliminate or reduce both network and non-network services. This section describes how to use the chkconfig utility to change the startup scripts that control when, how, and whether a network services starts at boot time:

1. **Click the GNOME Menu and choose System Settings⇨Server Settings⇨Services. Enter the root password if you're prompted.**

   The Service Configuration window opens.

2. **Select an unnecessary service and shut it off by clicking the Stop button.**
3. **Click the OK button when the confirmation window appears.**
4. **Click the check mark to the left of the service to remove the check mark.**

   Removing the check mark prevents the service from starting automatically at boot time.

5. **Repeat Steps 2–4 for each unnecessary service.**
6. **When you have turned off each unnecessary service, click the Save button.**
7. **Choose Quit from the File menu.**

Which services you turn off depends on your needs, of course. For example, if you're unintentionally running a web server, turn off the `httpd` service. You generally should be able to turn off these services:

- **The Advanced Power Management Daemon (APMD):** APMD is useful if you — like most people — regularly power-off your personal workstation or laptop. However, APMD is generally unnecessary on servers that run continuously. You want to keep APMD in the former case (workstation or laptop) and remove it in the latter (server).
- **GPM:** This service allows you to use a mouse when running in nongraphical mode. You're running in graphical mode, so turn it off.
- **The job queue daemon:** The atd daemon is used to schedule one-time cron-like jobs. If you need atd, you know it. Otherwise, turn it off.
- **Network File Sharing (NFS):** You need only services such as nfs, nfslock, portmap, and autofs when you're running an NFS server or client. The last thing you want to do is share files to the Internet, for example.
- **Print services:** Many people don't run the printer daemon on servers. Turn off cups or lpd whenever you don't need to print.
- **Samba:** Just like with NFS, you should turn off Samba if you don't need it.

The rest is up to you. Terminate services with a vengeance.

You can't modify a service when it isn't running. You can toggle off the check mark on a nonrunning service, but it doesn't have any effect if it's not running.

You can use the CLI-based chkconfig utility. Open a GNOME Terminal session and log in as root (**su -**):

- List the services by running the chkconfig `--list` command.
- List an individual service by specifying the service after the `--list` option: **chkconfig - - list *apmd***.
- Stop a service with the `--add` option: **chkconfig - - add *apmd***.
- Delete a service with the `--del` option: **chkconfig - - del *apmd***.

Using a Secure Shell client

You may be most familiar with graphical network communication applications, like the Mozilla web browser and Evolution e-mail clients. However, a world of text-based tools is available, such as Secure Shell, Telnet, and FTP. Those applications provide an interactive method for connecting to other computers across networks and the Internet using a command-line interface (CLI); refer to Chapter 4 for more information about CLIs.

Interactive communication is effective for performing tasks on remote machines. For example, the primary way to work on Linux machines originally was via the CLI. The CLI is often the best way to perform remote tasks.

CLI-based communication used to be primarily carried out over the insecure Telnet, FTP, and rsh connections. All services used unencrypted connections, and passwords were readily detected. The rsh service also used a system of intermachine trust. That trust allowed hackers, like the infamous Kevin Mitnik, to "own" a network by breaking into one machine and then logging in to additional ones without authentication.

Open Secure Shell (OpenSSH) provides an encrypted channel to perform all those tasks. Red Hat Linux bundles OpenSSH by default. We describe how first to use the OpenSSH client to communicate with other machines and, second, create an OpenSSH server.

You should (dare we say *must*?) use encrypted channels when you're communicating over the Internet and wireless networks. Both the Internet and Wi-Fi connections are inherently insecure, and you have to protect your communications.

Connecting to a Secure Shell server

Start by using OpenSSH as a client. Suppose that you want to log in to your ISP server, `ssh.myisp.com`, with OpenSSH:

1. **Open a GNOME Terminal session.**
2. **Enter this command:**

   ```
   ssh ssh.myisp.com
   ```

   Your mileage may vary, of course. You may have to use the `-l` option if, for example, your ISP user account name is different from your local computer. If your username on your local machine is `lidia`, but it's `lmaura` at your ISP, enter this line:

   ```
   ssh -l lmaura ssh.myisp.com
   ```

   The first time you connect to a remote server, you're prompted to accept the remote server's fingerprint.
3. **Enter** yes **when you're prompted.**
4. **Enter your password when you're prompted, and you're logged in.**

   For example, you can now use a text-based e-mail client, like pine, to read your messages. This program is useful if you want to read your e-mail securely but can't connect to your ISP with an SSL-enabled Mozilla or Evolution e-mail client.

Tunneling X across a network

That was a simple and useful way to use OpenSSH, but you can do more. The Red Hat OpenSSH client is automatically configured to forward 1X across its secure connection. While logged on to your ISP, you can run X Window client software and view it on your local machine:

1. **Log in to your ISP (or any machine running a Secure Shell server) as just described.**
2. **Run an X Window application, such as xclock.**

   The simple xclock window is displayed on your desktop.

   OpenSSH also bundles the file-transfer applications Secure Copy (scp) and Secure FTP (sftp). Secure Copy is non-interactive and copies files to and from a remote machine. Secure FTP is a secure version of FTP and is also interactive. This list describes how to copy files between two machines:

   - **Copy from a local machine to a remote one:** To transfer files from your local computer to a remote one, use Secure Copy (scp):

     ```
     scp abc myacct@remote.myisp.com
     ```

     This command copies the filename `abc` from the directory you're working in to the `myacct.myisp.com` home directory on the remote machine. You can specify either or both of the local and remote directories. For example, this command copies the file `abc` from the */tmp* directory on the local machine to the */var/tmp* directory on the remote machine and renames it to *xyz*:

     ```
     scp myaccount@remote.myisp.com:/tmp/abc /var/tmp/xyz
     ```

     The scp syntax is important. If you leave out the colon (:), your file isn't copied to the remote machine but rather is simply copied to a file named `myacct@remote.myisp.com` in your local directory.

   - **Copy from a remote to local machine:** Reverse the order of the parameters to copy from a remote machine. The following example copies the file `abc` from your home directory on the remote machine to your current working directory on the local machine:

     ```
     scp myacct@remote:abc
     ```

The sftp program works like the old standby FTP, but uses encryption, of course. Follow these steps to perform simple file transfers with sftp:

1. **Open a GNOME Terminal session.**
2. **Enter this command:**

   ```
   sftp ssh.myisp.com
   ```

3. **Enter your username and password.**
4. **Enter the help command at the `sftp` prompt.**

   You see a list of sftp commands. The ones you use most are `cd`, `lcd`, `dir`, `ls`, `get`, and `put`. These commands work in similar fashion to their Linux equivalents.

   Using `sftp` is self-explanatory. Use `get` to transfer a file, files, or directory from the remote to local machine; put transfers from local to remote.

Another cool feature of OpenSSH is its ability to tunnel any protocol. You can potentially display an entire X Window from a remote machine via X, for example. Consult the OpenSSH documentation for more information.

Configuring an OpenSSH server

Configuring an OpenSSH server is straightforward. You only have to modify the `/etc/ssh/sshd_config` file and run the `/etc/init.d/sshd` script. Let's look at the configuration file, the important parts of which are listed in these bullets:

- **Remove the older and faulty protocol version 1:** Version 1 is broken and should not be used (change the parameter Protocol 2,1 to Protocol 2, as shown in this example):

  ```
  Port 22
  Protocol 2
  # HostKeys for protocol version 2
  HostKey /etc/ssh/ssh_host_rsa_key
  HostKey /etc/ssh/ssh_host_dsa_key
  ```

- **Remove the comment from in front of the login grace-time parameter:** This action sets a limit on the length of time from when you start a login and the time you complete it:

  ```
  LoginGraceTime 600
  ```

- **Disallow root logins:** You should prevent users, including yourself, from logging in directly as root. Forcing users to first log in as a regular user and then "`su`-ing" to root provides an audit trail that can be used to see who did what as the root user; it also forces everyone to jump through two hoops before becoming the all-powerful root user:

  ```
  PermitRootLogin yes
  StrictModes yes
  ```

- **Uncomment these parameters to allow the various authentication modes:**

```
# rhosts authentication should not be used
RhostsAuthentication no
# Don't read the user's ~/.rhosts and ~/.shosts files
IgnoreRhosts yes
# For this to work you will also need host keys in
        /etc/ssh/ssh_known_hosts
RhostsRSAAuthentication no
# similar for protocol version 2
HostbasedAuthentication no
# Change to yes if you don't trust ~/.ssh/known_hosts for
 RhostsRSAAuthentication and HostbasedAuthentication
IgnoreUserKnownHosts no
```

- **Allow people to use password authentication, but don't allow unauthenticated access:**

```
# To disable tunneled clear text passwords, change to no
        here!
PasswordAuthentication yes
PermitEmptyPasswords no
```

To start the OpenSSH daemon, follow these steps:

1. **Make the changes and restart the Secure Shell daemon:**

   ```
   /etc/init.d/sshd restart
   ```

2. **If you're running a firewall, add this rule to your** `iptables`**-based firewall:**

   ```
   iptables -A INPUT  -p tcp --dport 22 -m state --state
           NEW,ESTABLISHED -j ACCEPT
   ```

3. **Save your new firewall:**

   ```
   iptables-save > /etc/sysconfig/iptables
   ```

4. **Restart the firewall:**

   ```
   /etc/init.d/iptables restart
   ```

Now you can use OpenSSH client and server to communicate to and from your Linux computer. Using the OpenSSH client, you can interactively log in to other computers, copy data between computers, and piggyback an arbitrary communication stream — such as X Window — with this puppy. You can reverse that process and communicate with your host Red Hat Linux computer. OpenSSH encrypts all your communication and prevents the exposure of your passwords and data to prying eyes.

Exchanging keys makes your life easier

You use OpenSSH by default to log in to a remote user account by using traditional passwords. However, OpenSSH can use a second authentication method that takes a little work to get started but saves work in the long run.

OpenSSH provides an authentication method called *public-key cryptography.* This system uses one public and one private key. You install the public key on the remote system and keep the private key on your computer. The public key can be shared with anyone — hey, it's public. The private key must be kept secret at all costs. In fact, OpenSSH encrypts the private key by default. You must use a pass phrase — essentially a password with spaces — to decrypt the private key before using it.

When you want to log in or communicate with the remote computer, the keys are used to negotiate the process. The public-private key system guarantees that your user account is authenticated and is also the initiating host; passwords only authenticate your login account, not the computer you're connecting from.

Setting up for a public-key cryptographic key exchange

To set up the key exchange, follow these steps:

1. **Log in to your user account on the local computer.**

   For example, log in as the user `rod` on `cancun`.

2. **Open a GNOME Terminal session.**
3. **Run this command:**

   ```
   ssh-keygen -t dsa
   ```

   This step starts the program that generates your public and private keys. Several encryption methods exist: DSA (Digital Signature Standard) and RSA (named after Ron *R*ivest, Adi *S*hamir, and Len *A*dleman) are the most popular. DSA is a nonproprietary algorithm, whereas RSA was until recently patented. Even though RSA is available for public use, we recommend using DSA.

   The program thinks for a moment and returns this output:

   ```
   Enter file in which to save the key
           (/home/rod/.ssh/id_dsa):
   ```

The keys are saved to the `.ssh` directory in your home directory. The default should be okay, so press the Return key.

4. **The ssh-keygen program asks you to enter a pass phrase that it uses to encrypt your private key:**

```
Enter passphrase (empty for no passphrase):
```

5. **Enter your pass phrase and ssh-keygen generates the keys.**

   Use a phrase peppered with numbers and other characters. For example, you may try a pass phrase like this:

```
Giv3 m3 @ bre@k!
```

6. **Verify the phrase by entering it a second time.**

The ssh-keygen program generates your public and private keys. Those keys are stored by default in the `.ssh` directory. The `.ssh` directory is stored by default in your home directory; `ssh-keygen` creates the `.ssh` directory, if necessary.

Copying your public key to the remote computer

You have to copy the public key to the computer you securely communicate with. This steps describe how to copy and configure them:

1. **Log in to your user account on the local computer.**

   For example, log in as the user `rod` on `cancun`.

2. **Open a GNOME Terminal window by clicking the GNOME Menu button and choosing System Tools➪Terminal.**

3. **Copy your public key to your account on the remote computer. For example, if your account on the remote computer cancun is `rod`, you can use the Open Secure Copy (`scp`):**

```
scp .ssh/id_dsa.pub rod@cancun:
```

   In this example, you're connecting back into the same computer you're already logged in to. This technique is the simplest way to test the OpenSSH server you're experimenting with — no other machines, or even a network, are needed.

4. **Enter your account password when you're prompted, and the DSA public key is copied to your home directory on Cancun.**

5. **Log in to the remote machine. For example, use `ssh`:**

```
ssh cancun
```

6. **Enter your password when you're prompted.**

   OpenSSH looks for public keys by default in the `authorized_keys` file in the `.ssh` directory (in your home directory).

7. **Use these commands to copy the public key into the `authorized_keys` file (remember that you should still be in your home directory):**

   ```
   cat id_dsa.pub >> .ssh/authorized_keys
   ```

   The `cat` command "concatenates" the contents of `id_dsa.pub` to the Linux standard output (that's generally your console, which is the GNOME Terminal, in this case). The double greater-than symbols (>>) append the standard output to the `authorized_keys` file in the `.ssh` directory. No preexisting keys are disturbed.

   The `authorized_keys` file must have the right permissions. (See Appendix B for more information about file permissions.) In this case, loose permissions sink ships, and OpenSSH doesn't work with, for example, read/-write/-execute group permissions.

8. **Ensure the correct permissions:**

   ```
   chmod 644 .ssh/authorized_keys
   ```

9. **Make sure that the OpenSSH server configuration allows key exchange. These options should be set in the `/etc/ssh/sshd_config` file:**

   ```
   RSAAuthentication yes
   PubkeyAuthentication yes
   AuthorizedKeysFile       .ssh/authorized_keys
   ```

10. **Restart the sshd daemon if you make any changes to the `sshd_config` file:**

    ```
    /etc/init.d/sshd restart
    ```

Connecting to the remote computer by using key exchange

Ready to use the key exchange authentication system? From the host (local) computer, try these steps:

1. **Log in to your user account on the local computer.**

   For example, log in as the user `rod` on `cancun`.

2. **Open a GNOME Terminal session.**

3. **Log in to the remote machine:**

   ```
   ssh cancun
   ```

4. **Enter the pass phrase you used to encrypt your private key.**

The remote computer authenticates you and your host computer. Voilà! You're in.

Making life even easier with ssh-agent

Red Hat automatically starts a system named `ssh-agent`. With `ssh-agent`, you enter your pass phrase and `ssh-agent` remembers it. You have to enter the pass phrase only once while logged in to your account. From then on, `ssh-agent` provides the OpenSSH clients with the pass phrase and you no longer have to enter a password or pass phrase. Life is easy.

Setting up `ssh-agent` is simple. Follow these steps:

1. **Log in to your user account on the local computer.**

   For example, log in as the user `rod` on `cancun`.

2. **Open a GNOME terminal by clicking the GNOME Menu and choosing System Tools⇨Terminal.**
3. **Enter this command:**

   ```
   ssh-add
   ```

4. **Enter your pass phrase when you're prompted.**
5. **Connect to the remote machine — for example, Cancun:**

   ```
   ssh cancun
   ```

You get logged in to your account on the remote machine without having to enter a password or pass phrase. This system works great.

Introducing encryption and security

Running a simple web server like the one introduced in Chapter 16 shouldn't require you to make heroic security measures. Serving up static text and graphics doesn't pique the interest of many hackers. However, when you start using the Web to do business or process sensitive information, you want to bump up your security. You build on the basic web server and create a secure web server.

Use the Secure Sockets Layer (SSL) protocol to construct a secure web server. SSL provides a mechanism that allows your web server to provide protected and authenticated connections. Using SSL with Apache allows the web server to prevent eavesdropping by encrypting the network communications to and from the web server and to identify itself to the client browser.

SSL provides encryption and ensures identification, which are described in the following two sections.

Encryption

The mathematical process *encryption* essentially garbles information so that only those with authorization can ungarble (and read) it; encryption prevents everyone whom you don't want to read your communications from reading it. The process of encryption and decryption requires the combination of the mathematical process named encryption algorithm and the mathematical entity cryptographic keys (keys, for short). A *key* is basically a very long number.

A description of the mathematical process of encryption is beyond the scope of this book, but suffice it to say that you need a key to encrypt information and a key to decrypt it. SSL uses a type of encryption named public-key encryption. Public-key encryption works by having the server keep a secret key and the client use a public key. The public key can be known and used by anyone and everyone; the private key must be kept secret and known only to the server.

Public-key encryption has an advantage over other encryption types because distributing public keys across a medium like the Internet is easy. It sounds counterintuitive, but public-key encryption does work.

Identification

All the encryption in the world is useless if you're tricked into connecting to the wrong web server. Suppose that you want to purchase a book from Amazon.com. You fire up Mozilla, connect to `www.amazon.com`, and happily enter your credit card number, expecting to receive your book the next day. It never comes.

In this scenario, some clever hacker has injected false DNS information into the Internet and your browser has even connected to `www.hackazon.com`. (Your web browser looked up the numeric IP address of Amazon.com but was deceived and received the address of the hacker's fraudulent web server.) In this case, encryption worked like it was supposed to and prevented other hackers from intercepting your credit card. However, it didn't ensure that the web server was the one you thought it was, and now the hacker is enjoying a wonderful vacation in Cancun, thanks to your credit card. D'oh!

SSL identification is based on the concept of a certificate. *Certificates* contain the public key you need to set up an encrypted connection and additional information used to verify the identity of the web server. The certificate also comes with information about who created it, when it was created, and how it was created. After you obtain a certificate from the web server you're connecting to, you're ready to safely conduct business. Huh? What good does that do if you're connecting to the hacker's web server? The certificate just ensures that you connect securely to the bad-boy site.

The problem is solved by using a go-between called a *certificate authority (CA)*. When you connect to a secure web server, it sends you its certificate. The web server also subscribes to a CA. The CA has investigated the subscribing web server and, if satisfied with its authenticity, vouches for its identity. If the CA is on your list of known CAs, you accept the certificate and use the public key to verify the server's identity and set up the encrypted connection.

Protecting your web server with SSL

A secure web server requires a certificate. The certificate is used to verify the web server to its clients. The instructions in this section describe how to create the certificate.

You can view the list of CAs your browser knows about. Follow these steps to view the CA list:

1. **Choose Mozilla Edit⇨Preferences.**

   The Preferences window opens.
2. **Expand the Privacy & Security menu by clicking the plus (+) sign immediately to the left of the menu option.**
3. **Click the Certificates menu.**

   The Certificates subwindow opens.
4. **Click the Manage Certificates button.**

   The Certificate Manager window opens behind the Preferences window.
5. **Click the upper margin of the Preferences window and move it so that you can see the Certificate Manager window.**
6. **Click the Authorities tab and you see a list of all CAs your browser knows about.**

Your browser automatically accepts the certificate from any secure web page you visit that subscribes to one of these CAs.

It costs time and money to subscribe to a CA, of course. However, you don't necessarily need to spend the money if you intend to use your secure web server for personal use or just to experiment. We show you how to construct a certificate and then use it without registering with a CA.

These steps outline the general process of creating a certificate:

1. **Install the SSL software.**
2. **Create your web server's private key.**
3. **Create your web server's certificate.**

   You can optionally register your certificate with a CA. For example, VeriSign, Inc., is one of the most widely known CAs. Go to `www.verisign.com` and click the SSL Certificates link to find out more about its service.
4. **Connect to the secure web server and accept the certificate; accepting the certificate is automatic if the server subscribes to a CA; otherwise, you have to accept the certificate manually.**

Just like Apache, the SSL software is included in the Red Hat Linux distribution. The following sections describe how to install, configure, and use SSL to create a secure web server.

Installing the SSL package

Follow these steps to install the SSL module package (we assume that you have already installed the Apache web server, as described in Chapter 16):

1. **Log in as root and open the GNOME Terminal session by clicking the GNOME Menu button and choosing System Tools⇨Terminal.**

   Apache needs an additional RPM package to provide SSL connections.
2. **Insert the companion DVD in the DVD/CD-ROM drive.**
3. **Enter this command to install the SSL package:**

   ```
   rpm -ivh /mnt/cdrom/RedHat/RPMS/mod_ssl*
   ```

Creating a private key

Recall that public-key encryption requires that the server use a private key. (Your web browser — the client — uses the public key.) We describe in this section how to generate a private key.

Generate your web server's private key by following these steps. Installing the Mod_ssl package created several directories in `/etc/httpd/conf` that contain generic keys and certificates. You have to remove those "dummy" files before you can create your own.

1. **Enter these commands to remove the generic key and certificate:**

   ```
   cd /etc/httpd/conf/ssl.key
   rm server.key ../ssl.crt/server.crt
   ```

2. **Press** y **each time you're prompted to remove the files.**
3. **Change to this directory, where the make file certificate is located:**

```
cd /usr/share/ssl/certs
```

4. **The makefile contains instructions for making the certificate. All you have to do is "run" the makefile and specify the action to take:**

```
make genkey
```

   This text is printed:

```
umask 77 ; \
/usr/bin/openssl genrsa -des3 1024 >
        /etc/httpd/conf/ssl.key/server.key
Generating RSA private key, 1024 bit long modulus
.....................++++++
....................++++++
e is 65537 (0x10001)
Enter pass phrase:
```

   Remember your pass phrase! You're asked to enter the pass phrase whenever you start your secure web server. You also have to manually start the web server and enter the pass phrase in order to start it.

5. **You have to enter a pass phrase. Like a password, a pass phrase protects your private key on the web server. Enter a good pass phrase.**

   For example, enter something like this:

```
hack me no more
```

   Note that spaces are allowed and are, in fact, encouraged.

6. **Enter the same phrase a second time when you're prompted.**

The Apache web server's private key is now in place. The key is readable by only the root user. Protect this key at all costs.

Certify yourself: Creating your own certificate

You need to generate a public key to use with the private one. Although the secure web server uses the private key, your web browser uses a public one. The browser uses the public key to verify the authenticity of the server; the server uses the public and private keys to create the encrypted connection.

Public keys are contained within a certificate.

Follow these steps to create your own certificate.

1. **Change to the directory where the certificate generating makefile is located:**

   ```
   cd /usr/share/ssl/certs
   ```

2. **Make the new certificate by entering this command:**

   ```
   make testcert
   ```

3. **You're prompted for the pass phrase you created in the preceding section. Enter the pass phrase when you're prompted.**

   You're prompted to enter information about your location, IP address, and other information that can help identify your certificate as valid. These steps outline the questions and what you need to enter.

4. **You're prompted to enter your country code.**

   For example, enter **US** if you live in the United States, **GB** for Great Britain, or **MX** for Mexico.

5. **Enter your state (for the United States) or province name. (Don't abbreviate the name.)**

   For example, enter **New Mexico**.

6. **Enter your city name.**

   In this example, enter Albuquerque.

7. **Enter your organization or company name if you have one.**

   For example, enter **Paunchy Heavy Industries, Ltd**.

8. **Optionally, enter your suborganization, if you have one.**

9. **Enter the full name of your web server.**

   For example, the sample web server is named Veracruz, and the network name is paunchy.net. Therefore, you enter **veracruz.paunchy.net**.

   The name of your server must match its DNS name (if you run your own DNS server). If the two don't match, you're prompted to access or reject the certificate every time you connect to the web server.

10. **Enter your e-mail address:**

    ```
    paul@paunchy.net
    ```

Your certificate is constructed. Restart your web server with this command:

```
/etc/init.d/httpd restart
```

Danger, Will Robinson! Detecting intruders

Everybody needs a loyal, vigilant robot to sound the alert when aliens, monsters, Dr. Smith, and hackers come at you. You can't have literal robots (or can you?), but you can have an intrusion-detection system (IDS).

Intrusion detection is the flip side of intrusion prevention. You can't depend on not getting hacked unless you turn off your computer and lock it in your panic room. Remember that no silver bullet exists in the world of computer security. You have to take measures to detect whether and when you get compromised.

Intrusion detection requires more on-going work than any of the security systems we discuss in this book. The other systems, such as firewalls and password protection, require some up-front work, but then run without much additional work. An IDS, however, requires some initial installation and configuration and then continual review. You have to monitor an IDS daily if you want it to be of any use to you.

Many IDSs — far too many to describe here — can give you extra security. We suggest two mature and relatively easy-to-use systems that provide good bang for your buck: Snort and Tripwire.

Snort is a network-based IDS. It looks for patterns in your network traffic that indicate hacker probes and break-in attempts. Snort isn't perfect and does report false positive alerts. You're going have to spend time identifying and eliminating false-positives if you want to use Snort. However, that will be time well spent because Snort is considered to be an excellent IDS by system administrators and security professionals. Go to www.snort.org to find more information.

Tripwire works by securely recording the fingerprints of files and directories and then comparing them to subsequent ones. Any differences between the current and original fingerprint indicates the file has changed and might have been compromised. The fingerprints are called checksums, which are unique mathematical values calculated from the contents of a file or directory. You can find Tripwire at `www.tripwire.com`.

Enter the pass phrase when you're prompted and your secure web server starts.

Connecting to your secure web server

After you have created the private key and certificate, you can connect to your secure web server.

These steps describe how the process of obtaining the server's certificate works:

1. **Log in to your Red Hat Linux computer and open Mozilla.**
2. **Click the GNOME Main Menu and choose Internet⇨Mozilla Web Browser.**

3. **Enter the URL of your secure web server.**

   For example, enter **https://cancun.paunchy.net** if that's where you installed the server. The `https`, which stands for Hyper Text Transport Protocol Secure, is used for secure browsing.

   Unless you have paid a CA to certify you, you're asked to accept the certificate. Every time you connect to a nonsubscribed (CA) secure web server from a browser for the first time, you're prompted to accept or reject the certificate. Because this secure web server is your own, you can accept the certificate and know that you're securely and authentically connected.

   A dialog box named Website Certified By an Unknown Authority opens.

4. **Click the Examine Certificate button and another dialog box opens.**

   The new window shows all the information you entered while creating the certificate.

5. **Click the Close button and you return to the preceding dialog box.**

   You're given three options: Accept the certificate temporarily, permanently, or not at all.

6. **Select the option that makes the most sense to you and then click the OK button.**

   For example, click the Accept This Certificate Temporarily for This Session button, and you're then allowed to view and interact with the secure web server. (You have to accept the certificate again the next time, however.)

7. **Right-click anywhere on the web page and choose View Page Info.**

   Another dialog box labeled Page Info opens. Click the Security tab. Information about your web site is displayed.

8. **Click the View button and you see the information about your certificate.**

9. **Click the Close button to leave the dialog box and return to viewing your Web page.**

After you have accepted the certificate, your browser coordinates with the web server and sets up an encrypted connection — also referred to as a *channel.* All your communication is hidden from eavesdropping.

You can view the certificate you just accepted by opening the Manage Certificate window from the Mozilla Preferences dialog box, as described earlier in this chapter.

Go to this site to find out how to create and register a certificate with a Certificate Authority (CA):

```
www.redhat.com/docs/manuals/linux/RHL-10-Manual/custom-
           guide/s1-secureserver-generatingkey.html
```

Modifying your firewall to allow SSL

You have to modify your Internet gateway or firewall to allow secure connections. You have to allow external web browsers to connect to Port 80 on your Apache server. The following rule allows SSL connections:

```
iptables -A INPUT -p tcp -m state --state NEW,ESTABLISHED -j
           -dport 443
```

If you're using a DSL modem like the one we describe in Chapter 6, you must modify the modem's network address translation (NAT) configuration. Many DSL modems are now on the market; describing how to configure them individually is beyond the scope of this book. Consult your modem's manual for configuration instructions: You have to allow external connections to Port 443.

Reading your logs

You are ultimately your best intrusion-detection system (IDS). Log files store information about nearly every one of your Red Hat Linux systems. Reading your logs lets you discover what has been happening on your computer and is one way to detect intrusions.

Unfortunately, exploring log files is somewhat akin to reading tea leaves. No mechanical method exists for sifting through log-file tea leaves. You have to look for unusual and suspicious occurrences. As you read more, you learn about what is usual and, of course, unusual. Experience counts for a great deal when you're an IDS.

Red Hat provides two good systems for viewing log files:

- **Logwatch:** The e-mail-based Logwatch log-alert system sifts through the log files in `/var/log` and e-mails the root user any alerts or errors. You can configure the Logwatch operational parameters to better fit your operation. However, the default works well at alerting you to the happenings on your computer.
- **Red Hat Logviewer:** The Logviewer graphical utility provides one-stop shopping for all standard log files. This manual tool helps you to remember which log files to look at.

Using Logwatch

Logwatch, installed by default during the Red Hat installation process, is a Perl script that's run nightly by `cron`. It reads through every log file in the `/var/log` directory and picks out items that it thinks are interesting.

The Logwatch Perl script is in `/etc/log.d/scripts/logwatch.pl`. The soft link, `00-logwatch`, in the `/etc/cron.daily` directory directs the `cron` system to run the script nightly.

Logwatch is controlled by the `/etc/log.d/conf/logwatch.conf` file. This file controls options like who is e-mailed the results. The `logwatch` configuration file is self documented and simple to configure.

Using Logviewer

Logviewer is a simple utility designed to display any of the standard Red Hat Linux log files in the `/var/log` directory. It displays by default the raw log information and leaves sifting out suspicious entries to your eyes. Logwatch can also perform simple filtering based on simple text strings.

Nothing is special about Logviewer other than helping you to access common log files and look at their data. Don't underestimate the value of that simple assistance, however. Although our busy lives makes reading log files a difficult task, it's one of those mind-numbing-but-necessary jobs. It's boring but essential!

Fending off modular root kits with a monolithic kernel

The Internet provides an ideal medium for finding and taking advantage of vulnerable computers. A hacker doesn't have to leave the comfort of home to attack your machine. However, you shouldn't consider the Internet as the only danger. You should also consider the physical vulnerability of your computer. If you work with other people, someone can potentially try to break in.

Understanding the Security Process

The best way to look at security is as a process. The more you think about it and the more you study it, the safer you are. You should use the security systems described in this chapter as the foundation for your security process. However, you should continue to build your security process to meet the needs of your own computer system and network.

This section outlines some additional building blocks you may consider adding to your process:

- **Making backups:** Backups are part of the security process? Yes! Backups are an essential security tool in the sense that you can never eliminate the possibility of getting hacked. If and when your security is breached, you may lose all sorts of information and configurations. For example, your computer may be completely erased or, worse, you may not know which files are good or bad. You must ensure your ability to recover from these types of catastrophes.

  One good backup method is to use the GNOME Toaster application, as we describe in Chapter 11. You can store your user account and configuration files on a CD-R/RW. It's reliable and should last forever. The only limitation is its ability to store only 700MB to 800MB; you can store more data with compression, however.

- **Security education:** Keeping up with security trends and topics helps you avoid getting bitten by new hacks. Knowing your adversaries and their techniques is essential.

  These URLs provide good security-based information; see Chapter 21 for some current top security holes:

  - `www.red.com/docs/manuals/linux/RHL-10-Manual/security-guide/`
  - `www.linuxsecurity.com`
  - `www.sans.org`
  - `www.nmap.org`
  - `www.securitytracker.com`
  - `www.infosyssec.com`
  - `www.cert.org`

- **Physical security:** We focus on network-based security in this book. We assume that your Red Hat Linux computer is running on your home network, in which case you have to worry most about Internet bad guys. However, in an office environment, you have to worry about physical security.

  Physical security involves preventing people from walking up and gaining unauthorized access to your computer. You should set a BIOS password to prevent anyone from booting your computer into single-user mode, totally avoiding your Linux passwords. You should lock your computer in your office, if possible, to prevent anyone from stealing your hard drive. Don't, under any circumstances, write your passwords in any accessible place (like on your desk or computer.)

You should also set the GNOME (or KDE) screen lock unless you want to log out every time you leave your desk. Choose GNOME Menu⇨Preferences⇨Screensaver and then select the Lock Screen After option. Select the amount time to wait before locking your screen and then click the Close button.

- **Boring consistency:** Good long-term security depends on consistency. Making your backups, reading security logs, and performing other, similar tasks all depend on your maintaining interest. It's just like staying in shape: You can't be good for a while and then forget about your exercise routine.

Chapter 18

Bringing In the Red Hat Linux Repair Man

In This Chapter

- Understanding the art of troubleshooting
- Gardening with the fault tree
- Diagnosing network problems

This book is perfect, and there's no way that anything we have written can ever go wrong — never, ever. You may be as lonely as the Maytag repairman if you expect trouble. As the "Pop Will Eat Itself" tune goes: The trouble is, trouble never happens. Errata (corrections) are as outdated as a bricks-and-mortar bookstore. This book makes setting up computers and networks so easy that you may wonder why other people have so many problems! Blah, blah, blah.

Maybe not. For example, this guy named Murphy (from Murphy's law) hangs out in both virtual and real bookstores in addition to all things mechanical and electronic. He's always jumping in just when things are starting to go well. The guy just can't keep his nose out of other people's business. This chapter is meant to smooth things out between you and Murphy in case he catches up with you.

One common problem involves getting your Red Hat Linux computer to work on a network. Sometimes, the best-laid plans go a little awry and Murphy comes to visit. This chapter is designed to help when networking problems pop up.

The Fix Is In: Troubleshooting Your Network

Your Red Hat Linux machine is the foundation of your network and must be set up correctly for anything to run. If it isn't working, or if you have an unusual setup (or if Murphy is in a bad mood), you can check for several different causes.

We use the Red Hat Linux network as the troubleshooting example in this chapter. The Red Hat Linux network is one of the more difficult things to set up correctly because it depends on not only your Linux computer but also other computers. Suppose that your Red Hat Linux network isn't working. Use the following sections of this chapter as a simple fault tree that you can follow to troubleshoot your network.

See Part V for insights into other problems. Chapter 17 describes how to find information about your Red Hat Linux computer. Chapter 20 also points out where you can get help and solve some simple, frequently encountered problems. Chapter 21 describes several security fixes.

Introducing Fault Trees

Troubleshooting is more of an art than a science. Sometimes, you can easily see what the problem is and how to fix it. At other times, that's not so easy. The degree of difficulty you have in fixing a problem depends on how complex the problem is and how well you know your stuff. Obviously, the better acquainted you are with computers and Linux, the better you are at troubleshooting.

Every problem has a solution. Computers are cause-and-effect-based machines. When something breaks or doesn't work, there's always a reason. The reason may not be easy to find, but it exists.

How do you find the cause? That's a million-dollar question. Getting a million bucks isn't easy unless you're willing to grind your teeth, plot against your fellow contestants for weeks on a remote island, purchase 10 million PowerBall tickets, or — believe it or not — work hard and work smart. Some people are willing to eat rats for the chance or are lucky enough to win the lottery, but most just have to work hard. Oh, well.

Working hard is conceptually easy, but how do you work smart? This concept is where the idea of the fault tree comes into play. The *fault tree* is a conceptual aid that helps you to eliminate all but the real cause of your problem. The fault tree looks like an upside-down tree, where the trunk of the tree represents the fault, or problem. The ends, or leaves, of the branches represent all the possible causes. After that's done, solving the problem is virtually guaranteed.

For example, Figure 18-1 shows part of a fault tree that points out which major subsystems you should examine. To find the solution to a problem, you have to systematically identify what's working. You work your way to what's not working and then when you find it, you usually solve your problem. The fault tree simply helps to formalize the process of problem solving.

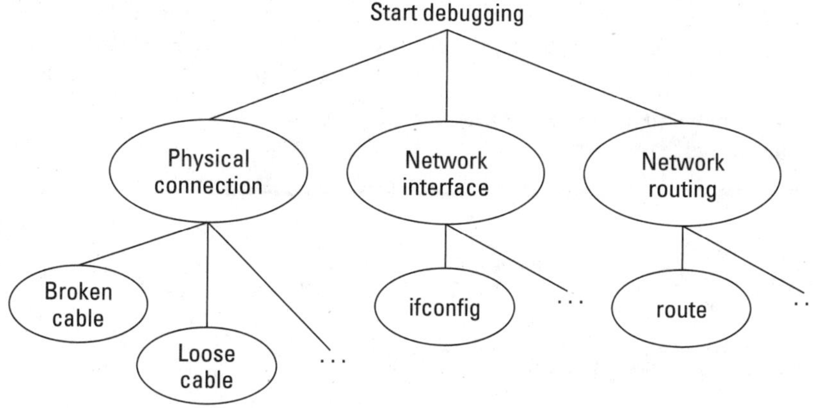

Figure 18-1: The fault tree.

Here are some possible faults:

- **The first branch on the left involves problems with the physical connection.** Do you have a network adapter? Is the cable connected properly to the adapter? Do you have a break in the cable? If so, you have to fix or replace the cable.
- **The second branch deals with the network interface configuration.** Have you configured the IP address for your Ethernet adapter correctly? If so, is the netmask correct?
- **The third branch helps you to decide whether the problem exists with the network routing.** Can your network packets be directed toward the correct network?

The fault tree helps you to break down any big problem into several simpler ones. By eliminating each simple problem one by one, you should eventually locate the root cause.

The blind leading the blind

Paul's colleague Ken Hatfield once said, "One of the side benefits from lots of troubleshooting comes from what I call 'the value of blind alleys.' Most often in troubleshooting, you go down blind alleys or, in your tree example, the wrong branches of the solution tree. But in doing so, you learn something. In the future, when you encounter a different problem, that previous blind alley may be the road to the solution." Well said.

Here's an example: Paul recently had a server that was having lots of problems. The `/var` file system had filled up, which caused some programs to fail. When space on `/var` was freed up, most of the programs started to do their jobs again. But one program didn't work. Paul spent a long time trying to figure out why it didn't work even after the problem was fixed. As it turned out, this particular program's real problem was that its license had expired. He had not only walked down a blind alley but also bumped into a wall and kept trying to go forward. D'oh!

Ticking through Your Linux Networking Checklist

We describe in this section some common network problems and symptoms. We start with simpler network problems and move on to more complex ones. After cataloging the problems, we look at one of the branches of the fault tree to solve a problem.

Is the power turned on?

First, verify that you turned on the power. It sounds simple, but, hey, sometimes the simplest things go wrong.

Is your network cable broken?

Make sure that your network cables aren't broken or cut. Check the connectors to make sure that they're okay. You should also make sure that you're using the correct network cable, which should be Category 5 (8-wire) straight-through cable.

Is your Ethernet hub or switch working?

Your Ethernet hub or switch should also be turned on. Ensure that the network cables are also connected securely.

If you're stuck in the Middle Ages (with us!) and are using that coaxial network cable named Thinnet — or 10Base-2, for geeks — you don't have to check an Ethernet switch or hub because you don't have one. Thinnet connects each NIC (computer and printer, for example) to every other NIC on the subnet. In other words, each computer that is on a Thinnet cable is connected electrically to all other computers in the network. Each computer sees all the network traffic on that cable. If any part of that bus is compromised, all traffic ceases. For example, if you disconnect the terminator at either end of the cable, all communication ends. The best way to troubleshoot that type of problem is to start at one end and work your way down the line. Try to get just two computers working together, and then three, and so on. Eventually, you find the problem.

Determining whether your network cable has been compromised requires you to address these issues:

- If you're using Thinnet, make sure that the BNCs (Bayonet Nut Connectors) are securely attached.
- Look at the interface between the cable and Ethernet switch or hub — or the BNC connector, if you're using Thinnet — to make sure that they're in good physical contact. Sometimes, the cable can pull out a little and break the connection.
- Look at the cable itself and make sure that it hasn't been cut or crushed.
- If you're using Thinnet, make sure that each end of the cable has a 50 ohm terminator attached to it. Thinnet must be terminated; otherwise, it doesn't work right, just as it doesn't work right if the cable is broken. The reason is that the radio frequency (RF) signal reflects from the unterminated end and interferes with the incoming signals. If you have a spare cable that you know is good, try substituting it. The idea is to eliminate as many segments that you're unsure about as possible. If you have just two computers in close proximity and you suspect a problem with the cable you're using, all you can do is try another cable. If the computers are far apart and rely on several segments or a long cable, try moving them closer together and using one short segment. If you have three or more computers, try getting just two of them working together. Then try adding another one. Proceed until you find the faulty segment.

Is your Ethernet adapter inserted correctly?

You have to have an Ethernet adapter to be connected to an Ethernet network. Make sure that your Ethernet adapter is plugged in to your computer's motherboard — snugly. Sometimes, you have to pull out the adapter and then reinsert it. The process of pulling out an adapter and then plugging it back in is called *reseating.*

Is your network adapter configured correctly?

Sometimes a startup script is misconfigured, which causes the startup screen to go by without your seeing an error message. If that happens, log in as root and from the shell prompt and type this command:

```
ifconfig
```

You see a listing of two different interfaces, as shown in the following code, or three interfaces if you have PPP configured. The `ifconfig` command tells the Linux kernel that you have a network adapter and gives it an IP address and network mask. This step is the first in connecting your Linux computer to your network:

```
eth0     Link encap:10Mbps Ethernet  HWaddr 00:A0:24:2F:30:69
           inet addr:192.168.1.1 Bcast:192.168.1.255
                         Mask:255.255.255.0
           UP BROADCAST RUNNING MULTICAST  MTU:1500  Metric:1
           RX packets:16010 errors:18 dropped:18 overruns:23
           TX packets:7075 errors:0 dropped:0 overruns:0
           Interrupt:10 Base address:0x300

lo        Link encap:Local Loopback
           inet addr:127.0.0.1  Bcast:127.255.255.255
                         Mask:255.0.0.0
           UP BROADCAST LOOPBACK RUNNING  MTU:3584  Metric:1
           RX packets:115 errors:0 dropped:0 overruns:0
           TX packets:115 errors:0 dropped:0 overruns:0
```

Checking your wireless NIC

Linux provides several tools to work with Wi-Fi network interfaces. Red Hat installs the wireless-tools RPM package by default. The tools include `iwconfig`, `iwspy`, and other utilities. We describe how to use `iwconfig` to examine your Wi-Fi interface configuration.

"I is an enganeer"

An experienced electrical engineer and Linux author once got really angry with a cable TV company. His cable service went dead in the middle of a Philadelphia Eagles game. It didn't matter that the Eagles were losing — he wanted to see the game because the Eagles don't appear on TV often in Albuquerque. The engineer called the cable company immediately. Blah! Blah! Blah! My connection — Blah! Blah! The nice support person guided the poor engineer step-by-step through his own fault tree. Step 1: Is your VCR or TV turned on? "Yes, of course." Step 2: Is the VCR button on your VCR toggled on? "Of course — ah, whoops, no, it isn't. Ah, yes, it works now, thank you very much. Goodbye." D'oh! What was five years of electrical engineering school good for?

Log in as root, open a GNOME Terminal window (refer to Chapter 4 for more information), and run the `iwconfig` command. If your NIC is configured correctly, you see output similar to this example:

```
lo        no wireless extensions.

eth0      IEEE 802.11-DS  ESSID:"linky" Nickname:"..."
          Mode:Ad-Hoc  Frequency:2.437GHz  Cell: "..."
          Bit Rate:11Mb/s   Tx-Power=15 dBm   Sensitivity:1/3
          Retry limit:4   RTS thr:off   Fragment thr:off
          Encryption key:A654-6277-43D6-ACC3-E6ED-1C12-98
          Power Management:off
          Link Quality:0  Signal level:0  Noise level:0
          Rx invalid nwid:0  Rx invalid crypt:0  Rx invalid ...
          Tx excessive retries:0  Invalid misc:0   Missed ...
```

These options are the important ones to examine:

- **Mode:** You have to set this value to `Ad-Hoc` when you're connecting to an ad hoc network. (Refer to Chapter 7 for more information about this method.) You can use the value `Any` when you're connecting to an infrastructure network. The `Any` value can work for an ad hoc network in some cases; however, a description of those cases is beyond the scope of this book, so use ad-hoc mode whenever necessary.
- **ESSID:** You have to use the same value on every machine connected to an ad hoc LAN. For example, every machine on the network is given the ESSID `linky`.
- **Encryption key:** You have to use the same encryption key on every machine connected to your wireless network. The key comes in two flavors: 40 bit and 128 bit. The 40-bit key is nearly useless because it can be readily cracked by hackers using widely available software.

Your wireless network should work as long as you set these parameters correctly and your computer is within range of the other devices on your LAN. The other parameters are either self generating or unimportant in getting the card to work.

Maybe the physical connections aren't set up right

If you don't see the line containing `lo`, which is the loopback interface, or `eth0`, which is your network adapter, your physical network connections aren't set up right. The loopback interface isn't a physical device; it's used for the network software's internal workings. The loopback interface must be present for the network adapter to be configured.

If the loopback interface isn't present, type this command:

```
ifconfig lo 127.0.0.1
```

If the network adapter — generally an Ethernet card — isn't present, type this command:

```
ifconfig eth0 192.168.1.1
```

Because this address is a class C network address, `ifconfig` automatically defaults to the `255.255.255.0` netmask. If you have an unusual netmask, which you shouldn't, type this command:

```
ifconfig eth0 192.168.1.1 netmask 255.255.255.0
```

Type **ifconfig** and your network adapter should be displayed correctly. If it's not, examine the manual page on `ifconfig`. You display this manual page by typing this command and then pressing Enter:

```
man ifconfig
```

You can page through the document in several ways: Press Enter to go line by line, press the spacebar to go forward one page at a time, press Ctrl+B to page backward, or press **Q** to quit. The `ifconfig` man page shows a great deal of information about what `ifconfig` is and how it works. If you're still having problems, look at the Linux startup information by running this command:

```
dmesg | more
```

Note that you pipe (use the | symbol) the output from `dmesg` to the `more` command. Linux pipes are used to transmit the output command to the input of another. After you run the preceding command, you see the information that was displayed during the boot process. The `more` command shows one page of information at a time; press the spacebar to display each subsequent page.

Maybe you have a hardware problem

If you don't see your Ethernet adapter, you may have a hardware problem. Check your adapter. *Reseat* it (take it out and put it back in) and see whether it works. If not, you probably need a new NIC. If you do see the NIC, look inside the Linux kernel and see which devices it has. Type this command to change to a special directory named /proc, where process information is located:

```
cat /proc/devices
```

You should see a line with your network adapter listed. If you don't, Linux doesn't know that it exists.

Try to run your Ethernet NIC again. If it still doesn't run, you have to find out more information.

Maybe you have an interrupt or address conflict

You may have an interrupt or address conflict. Look at the list of interrupts and then the I/O addresses of all the devices that the kernel knows about, by typing these commands:

```
cat /proc/interrupts
cat /proc/ioports
```

The I/O address is the location in memory where the device, such as the network adapter, is accessed by the microprocessor (for example, your Pentium chip). The interrupt communicates to the microprocessor that it should stop whatever it's doing in order to process information that has arrived at the device sending the interrupt.

When your Ethernet adapter receives a packet, it sends an interrupt to the microprocessor to signal that an event has occurred. Your Pentium stops what it's doing and processes the new information. The microprocessor even interacts with Linux to do the processing.

Type **cat /proc/interrupts** to show both the interrupts and the I/O addresses with which Red Hat Linux is familiar. The output should look like this example:

```
 0:    378425   timer
 1:      1120   keyboard
 2:         0   cascade
10:     16077   3c509
13:         1   math error
14:     63652 + ide0
```

This listing shows that Linux knows that the Ethernet NIC (3c509) exists. That's a good sign.

Typing `cat /proc/ioports` shows the input-output ports used by Red Hat Linux to interact with the computer's devices. This output shows the I/O ports used on this computer:

```
0000-001f : dma1
0020-003f : pic1
0040-005f : timer
0060-006f : keyboard
```

Look for your network adapter. In this case, it's `3c509`. If the adapter is working, you shouldn't have any conflicts. If the I/O ports of two devices overlap, a conflict exists and you have to reconfigure the adapter. Run your Ethernet NIC configuration program and set the adapter's parameters in its EEPROM. Older adapters may have jumpers or little switches, called *DIP switches,* to set. If you think that you have to do this, remember to write down all the other devices' interrupts and I/O addresses so that you don't end up conflicting with something else.

Perhaps you have a funky kernel

You also may be using a kernel that doesn't have networking installed. This situation is virtually impossible with Red Hat Linux 10 because the Linux kernel automatically loads networking — and other modules — on demand (it's mature technology). But go ahead and look at these files to gain an understanding of how Linux works.

Display the networking devices by typing this command:

```
cat /proc/net/dev
```

If you don't see the Ethernet interface, you may have an unsupported network adapter or a defective or misconfigured one. The Red Hat Linux kernel, by default, automatically loads modules as they're needed. You can look back at the results of your boot process by using the `dmesg` command. Look for a message that says `delaying eth0 configuration`. This message most likely means that Linux wasn't able to load the network adapter module or that the adapter isn't working.

Display the information about your devices by using the `cat /proc/net/dev` command.

The next step is to make sure that your network routing is configured correctly. This area is another spot where you can easily get confused. You don't have to set up routing outside your LAN yet, but Linux needs to know where to send packets on its own network. Look at your routing table by typing this command:

```
netstat -nr
```

You see a listing of your routing table.

This list briefly describes the elements in the routing table:

- The destination is the location — IP address — to where you want to send packets. For example, the address `192.168.1.0` refers to your local network.
- The gateway is the address (computer or router) where the packets have to be sent so that they can find their way to their destination. In the case where the destination is the local network, the address `0.0.0.0` means no gateway.
- The `genmask` is used to separate from the host number the parts of the IP address used for the network address.
- The flags are used to indicate various interface information, like *U* for *up* and *G* for *gateway.* The metric is used as a measure of how far a packet has to travel to its destination (a number greater than 32 is considered to be infinite). The next two flags — Ref and Use — aren't important for this discussion.
- The `Iface` field shows which network interface is being used. (`etho` refers to an Internet adapter, and `lo` refers to the loopback interface. The loopback interface is used internally by the Linux kernel, and you shouldn't have any need to use it directly.)

The information about each interface — the routing table — is displayed below the headings. For example, the first line tells Linux to send packets destined for the addresses `192.168.1.0` through `192.168.1.255` to the Ethernet adapter (`eth0`). The second line deals with the kernel's internal loopback interface. The third and last line, with the address `0.0.0.0`, is known as the default route. It defines where to send all packets not covered by a specific route.

If your table deviates from the example, you may have a routing problem. For example, if you don't have the default route — `0.0.0.0` — you can't communicate with any machines on your LAN or the Internet. If you lack a loopback — `127.0.0.1` — route, many internal processes are doomed to fail.

Defining a route to the loopback interface

You must have a route to the loopback interface (also referred to as `lo`), which is the `127.0.0.0` address. If you're missing either or both parameters, you must set them. To set the loopback device — which must be set for the network adapter to work — type this command:

```
route add -net 127.0.0.0
```

To set the route for the network adapter and your local network, type this command:

```
route add 192.168.1.0 dev eth0
```

This route is assigned automatically to your network adapter. You can assign the route to another NIC, if necessary; for example:

```
route add 192.168.1.0 dev eth1
```

Type **netstat -rn** to see your routing table. You should see entries for the loopback and the Ethernet. If you don't see a route to your network interface, try repeating the preceding steps. You may have to delete a route. To delete a route, type this command:

```
route del 192.168.1.0 dev eth0
```

Note that you use the network address rather than a host address here. The zero (`0`) designates the class C network address `192.168.1`.

Doing the ping thing

If the network adapter is configured correctly and the routing is correct, check the network. The best way to do it is to ping the loopback interface first and then the other computer. Type this command, let it run for a few seconds (one ping occurs per second), and stop it by pressing Ctrl+C:

```
ping 127.0.0.1
```

You should see a response like the one shown in the example in the preceding section.

Each line shows the number of bytes returned from the loopback interface, the sequence, and the round-trip time. The last lines comprise the summary, which shows whether any packets didn't make the trip. This is a working system, but if you don't see any returned packet, something is wrong with your setup and you should review the steps outlined in the preceding paragraphs.

Next, try pinging your Ethernet interface by typing this command:

```
ping 192.168.1.1
```

You should see a response like what's shown in this bit of code:

```
PING 192.168.1.1 (198.168.1.1): 56 data bytes
64 bytes from 198.168.1.1: icmp_seq=0 ttl=64 time=2.0 ms
64 bytes from 198.168.1.1: icmp_seq=1 ttl=64 time=1.2 ms
64 bytes from 198.168.1.1: icmp_seq=2 ttl=64 time=1.1 ms
64 bytes from 198.168.1.1: icmp_seq=3 ttl=64 time=1.1 ms
?
--- 198.168.1.1 ping statistics ---
4 packets transmitted, 4 packets received, 0% packet loss
           round-trip min/avg/max = 1.1/1.8/4.6 ms
```

Is there another computer or device to talk to?

Try to ping another computer — if one exists — on your network. Type the following command, let it run for 10 to 15 seconds, and stop it by pressing Ctrl+C:

```
ping 192.168.1.2
```

(This example assumes that another computer has the IP address `192.168.1.2`. Adjust the address you use to work with your network.)

You should see a response like what's shown in this bit of code:

```
PING 192.168.1.2 (192.168.1.2): 56 data bytes
64 bytes from 192.168.1.2: icmp_seq=0 ttl=32 time=3.1 ms
64 bytes from 192.168.1.2: icmp_seq=1 ttl=32 time=2.3 ms
64 bytes from 192.168.1.2: icmp_seq=2 ttl=32 time=2.5 ms
64 bytes from 192.168.1.2: icmp_seq=3 ttl=32 time=2.4 ms

--- 192.168.1.2 ping statistics ---
4 packets transmitted, 4 packets received, 0% packet loss
round-trip min/avg/max = 2.3/2.5/3.1 ms
```

If you get a continuous stream of returned packets and the packet loss is zero or very near zero, your network is working. If not, the problem may be in the other machine. Review the troubleshooting steps again in this chapter. Note that the ICMP is taking about 1 full millisecond (ms) longer to travel to the external computer than to the loopback device. The reason is that the loopback is completely internal to the Linux computer.

Chapter 19

Building a Streaming Audio Server

In This Chapter

- Introducing Ices2 and Icecast2 streaming audio servers
- Creating a music source
- Installing and configuring Ices2 and Icecast2
- Streaming audio to your private network

All work and no play makes Linux a dull boy. So let's play a little bit. This chapter describes how to play audio streams on your private network.

We show you in Chapter 12 how to use Linux applications like MPlayer and XMMS to listen to audio streams. In this chapter, we switch sides and show you how to serve up such streams. Again, the open source movement fills the bill with Ices2 and Icecast2.

Introducing Ices2 and Icecast2

You're most likely familiar with how audio streaming works from the desktop perspective. Chapter 12, for example, shows how to use XMMS and MPlayer to listen to Internet audio streams. (You can also use MPlayer to see video content.) However, many people consider it a mystery about how multimedia (audio, video and slide show) streams are created.

Feeding audio or visual data to a multimedia server, such as Icecast2, creates audio streams. (Shoutcast and RealServer, which are commercial servers, operate in a similar manner to Icecast2.) You can use Ices2 to feed audio information to Icecast2. A multimedia client then connects to the server. The server streams out the audio information to the client, and you can sit back and enjoy.

The original Icecast worked with MP3 streams. Icecast is still available, but is no longer being developed or supported. Because of possible copyright problems, Icecast has essentially been abandoned in favor of Icecast2, which works with the open source Ogg Vorbis format.

This list provides more detail on each component in the system:

- **Multimedia client:** The client connects to the multimedia server and plays the feed. For example, XMMS connects to Icecast2.
- **Multimedia server:** The server is responsible for accepting requests from a client and then streaming multimedia information to the client. The server also converts the original multimedia content into Internet Protocol (IP) packets in order to route it across a private network or the Internet.
- **Multimedia content:** Your multimedia server isn't very useful without a content source. Your source may be a music CD or a DJ — you, for example. Sources are either fixed or dynamic. For example, a music CD is a fixed source. If you decide to switch careers and become a DJ, you're a dynamic source. The Ices2 application reads from a fixed source and feeds it to Icecast2.

Creating a Music Source

Before you create your server, you have to create something to play. This section describes how to create an Ogg Vorbis file to play. We assume that you want to create a file from a commercial music CD. This practice is legal, and does not violate copyright law because you don't create a server that is broadcast on the Internet. Instead, you're creating a server that is broadcast to a private network (yours). As far as we know, you're still allowed to listen to your own CDs.

The Ogg Vorbis audio formatting system is similar in function to MP3. However, Ogg Vorbis — or Ogg, for short — is an open source format (also known as a codec) and, unlike MP3, doesn't have any proprietary algorithms or protocols. Ogg also provides higher fidelity than other formats. Ogg Vorbis is really two separate entities: Ogg is an audio compression format, and Vorbis is an encoding system.

Follow these steps to create an Ogg-Vorbis-formatted music file:

1. **Log in to your computer as any user and insert an audio CD.**
2. **Click the GNOME Menu button and choose Sound & Video⇨More Sound & Video Applications⇨Grip.**

   The Grip window opens and the CD's tracks are displayed in the initial Grip window.

3. **Click the Rip column (on the right side of the screen) of each track you want to use.**

   A check mark appears next to each track you select.

4. **Click the Config tab.**

   A subwindow opens, showing several additional tabs.

5. **Click the Encode tab in the subwindow.**

   Another subwindow opens that shows several configuration options.

6. **Click the Encoder pull-down menu (showing the default bladennc) and select oggenc.**

   Selecting oggenc tells Grip to create Ogg-encoded music files.

7. **Click the Rip tab at the top of the window (next to the Tracks tab).**

8. **Click the Rip+Encode button.**

   Grip rips the music from the CD to files on your computer. The files are stored in a subdirectory named `ogg` in your current working directory.

Grip doesn't do the CD ripping work. Grip does its thing by starting the cdparanoia program and feeding it the parameters you just selected. The tracks are ripped and initially saved in Wave format. After cdparanoia finishes, Grip starts the oggenc utility and coverts the Wave files to Ogg format.

You can convert from Wave to Ogg format by running this command in a terminal emulator: `oggenc *wav`. You can play Ogg-encoded files: `ogg123 xyz.wav`.

You now have one or more Ogg-Vorbis-formatted audio files. You have to install and configure Icecast2 and Ices2 to broadcast music to yourself.

Installing Ices2 and Icecast2

In this section, we tell you how to install other applications and services. Neither Ices2 or Icecast2 comes in RPM packages, so you have to build them from scratch.

Building from scratch in the Linux world requires that you follow these general steps:

1. **Configure.** The first step requires configuring the software. The configuration process builds dependency files. Several Linux systems are available that do this. The system used by Icecast2 and Ices2 is `autogen.sh`.

2. **Compile.** After the software is configured, you have to compile it. *Compiling* is a universal computer process that changes source code into

executable code. Source code is readable by human beings — well, at least the class of humans known as nerds. Compiling source code changes it into a form that computers can understand. All applications are compiled from source code.

3. **Install.** After the result is compiled, it must be installed. Linux uses default directories such as `/usr/bin`, `/usr/sbin`, `/usr/local/bin`, and `/usr/local/sbin` to store executable files (applications and services). Most software systems need to be placed in these types of locations to work correctly.

Programmers use systems like the open source Concurrent Versions System (CVS) to build and maintain large projects. Working with numerous people, who are also geographically separate, on a project like Icecast2 would be impossible without a system to keep everyone organized. CVS allows each individual to "check out" code, work on it, and then optionally reintegrate the modifications back into the system. This, plus other features, allows a group to keep from stepping on each other and keep the project efficiently moving forward.

Download Icecast2 and Ices2

Before you build Ices2 or Icecast2, you have to get it. This section describes how to download the software.

Many of you probably are familiar with compiling software. However, you may not have used the download system you're about to use in this section. You use the CVS.

By now, you know that Linux uses many names and acronyms, many of which are cryptic at best. So you probably didn't raise an eyebrow when you encountered the name Ogg Vorbis, Icecast2, or xiph.org. Ogg Vorbis is a science fiction character that its developers like. Icecast2 is a variation on the name Shoutcast, and Xihp is short for *Xiphophorus helleri,* a small swordtail fish popular in small aquariums.

These steps help you prepare your Red Hat Linux computer to start building the multimedia server:

1. **Log in to your computer as the root user.**

   Icecast2 depends on several libraries, most of which are already installed on your Red Hat Linux computer. One library, however, is not. Install the `xslt` library now.

2. **Insert the companion DVD-ROM into the DVD-ROM/CD-ROM drive and run these commands to install the extra software:**

```
rpm -ivh --nodeps /mnt/cdrom/RedHat/RPMS/libxslt*
rpm -ivh /mnt/cdrom/RedHat/RPMS/automake16*
```

If your computer doesn't have a DVD-ROM drive, you have to use the coupon in the back of this book to obtain Red Hat Linux on CD-ROMs. After you receive the CD-ROMs, use them to install the libxslt and automake packages.

Now you have to download the Icecast2 and Ices2 software from the Internet.

3. **Connect your computer to the Internet.**

   The method you use to connect to the Internet depends on the kind of service you subscribe to. Refer to Chapters 5, 6, and 7 for information about how to connect your computer to the Internet.

4. **Enter this command in a GNOME Terminal window:**

   ```
   export CVSROOT=:pserver:anoncvs@xiph.org:/usr/local/
           cvsroot
   ```

   This command sets up an *environmental variable* that CVS needs in order to complete its download. Environmental variables tell the shell you're working in — bash, in this case — where to find elements such as files and directories.

5. **Tell your CVS client to log in to the remote CVS server. Enter this command to log in to the remote system:**

   ```
   cvs login
   ```

6. **Enter** anoncvs **when you're prompted for the CVS server password.**

   After you have logged in, you can download — or *check out* (co), in CVS parlance — the software. Enter the first of the following commands in order (wait for each one to finish before continuing to the next one.)

7. **After you're logged in, you can download — check out (co), in CVS parlance — the software:**

   ```
   cvs co icecast
   cvs co ices
   cvs co libshout
   cvs co ogg
   ```

   You see the files displayed as they're downloaded, and the CVS checkout process is complete.

The following set of steps describes how to configure, compile, and install your multimedia server:

1. **Run the command in a terminal emulator:**

   ```
   export LD_LIBRARY_PATH=/lib:/usr/lib:/usr/local/lib
   ```

   This environmental variable is needed so that the compiler knows where to find several libraries.

2. **Configure, compile, and install the Shoutcast library. Enter this command in a terminal emulator:**

```
cd libshout
```

3. **Run this command to set up the compilation process:**

```
./autogen.sh
```

4. **Compile and link the software by running the** `make` **command:**

```
make
```

5. **Install the libraries:**

```
make install
```

6. **You create the Ogg software by repeating Steps 2–4. These commands summarize the steps:**

```
cd ../ogg
./autogen.sh
make
make install
```

7. **Create the Ices2 server by repeating Steps 2–4. These commands summarize the steps:**

```
cd ../ices
./autogen.sh
make
make install
```

8. **You can finish the process by compiling the Icecast2 server. These commands summarize the steps:**

```
cd ../icecast
./autogen.sh
make
make install
```

Your Ices2 and Icecast2 servers are now ready to broadcast. The following section describes how to configure both servers. After they're configured, you can serve up multimedia streams.

Configuring Icecast2

Ices2 gets its multimedia content from static files, such as music formatted in Ogg Vorbis. Ices2 then feeds the audio streams to the Icecast2 server. You can then connect to the Icecast2 serves with your client application to listen to the music. All these connections are made over IP networks.

Ices2 and Icecast2 use the loopback (`127.0.0.1`) interface to communicate. (The *loopback interface* is an internal network interface that doesn't use any physical device.) Using the loopback interface provides a simple method for testing your configuration.

Icecast2 uses Port 8000 to communicate with its stream source and Port 8001 for administration.

You begin by configuring Icecast2:

1. **Log in to your Red Hat Linux computer as the root user.**

   The Icecast2 configuration file was installed in the `/usr/local/etc` directory when you ran the `make install` command. Now, you have to make only some minor modifications to that file to set up your simple streaming server.

2. **Open the Gedit text editor by clicking the GNOME Menu and choosing Accessories➪Text Editor.**

   In the Gedit window, choose File➪Open.

3. **Enter** /usr/local/etc/icecast.xml **in the Selection text box and click OK.**

   The contents of `icecast.xml` are displayed in the text editor, as shown in Figure 19-1.

```
<icecast>
        <location>Jack's House</location>
        <admin>jack@icecast.org</admin>

        <limits>
                <clients>100</clients>
                <sources>2</sources>
                <threadpool>5</threadpool>
                <client-timeout>30</client-timeout>
                <header-timeout>15</header-timeout>
                <source-timeout>10</source-timeout>
        </limits>

        <source-password>hackme</source-password>
        <relay-password>hackme</relay-password>

        <directory>
                <touch-freq>5</touch-freq>
                <server>
                        <host>yp.icecast.org</host>
                        <touch-freq>15</touch-freq>
                </server>
        </directory>

        <hostname>i.cantcode.com</hostname>
```

Figure 19-1: The `icecast.xml` file.

4. **Find the part of the configuration file that defines the port number and bind address. Remove the comments from those parameters.**

   Comments encapsulate the configuration parameters with these character strings: `<!--` and `-->`.

5. **Remove the comments and the code should look like this:**

```
<!-- You can use these two if you only want a single
        listener -->
  <port>8000</port>
  <bind-address>127.0.0.1</bind-address>
```

   These parameters tell the Icecast2 server which port number and IP address to listen to. They also define the master server as the same machine.

6. **Find the Master Server section of the configuration and remove the comments. The configuration should look like this:**

```
  <master-server>127.0.0.1</master-server>
  <master-server-port>8001</master-server-port>
  <master-update-interval>120</master-update-interval>
  <master-password>hackme</master-password>
```

7. **Find the** `<logdir>` **parameter and change it to**

```
<logdir>/var/log/icecast</logdir>
```

   This location is where all the information about the running Icecast2 server is kept (in logs). Information about Icecast2 problems is placed there too.

8. **Find the** `<security>` **section. You should set the Icecast2 server to use the user and group identification number** `nobody`**:**

```
<security>
  <chroot>0</chroot>
  <!--
  <changeowner>
      <user>nobody</user>
      <group>nobody</group>
  </changeowner>
   -->
</security>
```

   Running the server as nobody reduces the security risk — breaking into your Icecast2 server doesn't provide a hacker with superuser privileges.

9. **Remove the comments from before the** `<changeowner>` **parameter and after the** `</changeowner>` **parameter:**

```
<security>
  <chroot>0</chroot>

  <changeowner>
      <user>nobody</user>
      <group>nobody</group>
  </changeowner>

</security>
```

Removing the comments allows the <user> and <group> directives to become active and force Icecast2 to run as user and group nobody. If you don't remove the comments, Icecast2 runs as the user and group of the process that starts it. Because you're logged in as root, Icecast2 runs as the root user when you start it in Step 10. Running a service as root can compromise your computer's security.

10. **Save your changes by clicking the Save button.**

    Choose File➪Quit and the Gedit window closes.

11. **Open a terminal emulator window by clicking the GNOME Menu and choosing System Tools➪Terminal.**
12. **Create an Icecast2 log file directory by entering this command:**

    ```
    mkdir /var/log/icecast
    ```

13. **Make the user** `nobody` **own the new directory:**

    ```
    chown nobody.nobody /var/log/icecast
    ```

14. **Enter this command to start the Icecast2 server:**

    ```
    icecast -c /usr/local/etc/icecast.xml &
    ```

You just started your multimedia server, but aren't transmitting anything. You have dead air now. Because you don't want to run afoul of the FCC, the next section describes how to configure and start the Ices2 server so that you can feed content to the Icecast2 server.

Configuring Ices2

Configuring Ices2 is similar to configuring Icecast2. Follow these steps to configure Ices2 and then feed an audio stream to Icecast2:

1. **Open a GNOME Terminal window.**

2. **Change to the** /usr/local/etc **directory and copy the sample Ices2 configuration file there:**

```
cd /usr/local/etc
cp ~/ices/conf/*.xml .
```

3. **Open the Gedit text editor by clicking the GNOME Menu and choosing Accessories➪Text Editor.**

4. **In the Gedit window, choose File➪Open.**

5. **Select** /usr/local/etc/ices.xml **and click OK.**

   The contents of icecast.xml are displayed in the text editor.

Ices2 can handle both static and live audio streams. The ices-live.xml configuration file deals with live streams, and the ices-playlist.xml configures static streams. However, providing live streams is more than we have space to describe in this book, so we leave it up to you to investigate that subject.

Ices2 uses a configuration file (a *playlist*) to provide static streams to Icecast2. Playlists define which audio files Ices2 provides to Icecast2.

6. **Use this command to create a simple playlist named** playlist**:**

```
echo "track1.ogg" > playlist.txt
```

7. **Modify the** ices-playlist.xml **file to work with your playlist file. Find the** <input> **module and modify the file parameter to point to your newly created playlist file:**

```
<input>
   <module>playlist</module>
   <param name="type">basic</param>
   <param name="file">/usr/local/etc/playlist.txt</param>
   <param name="random">0</param>
   <param name="once">0</param>
</input>
```

   The <input> and </input> delimiters tell Ices2 that these parameters are used to define the playlist:

   - <module> **and** </module>**:** These delimiters define the playlist boundary.
   - **Type:** This parameter defines the type of playlist you're using. In this case, it's a basic system.
   - **File:** The name of the file that contains the playlist is defined here.
   - **Random:** If this option is set to 1, the playlist tracks are played randomly.

- **Once:** If this parameter is set to 1, it tells Ices2 to play each track only once.

8. **Save your changes by clicking the Save button.**
9. **Choose File⇨Quit and the Gedit window closes.**
10. **Click the terminal emulator window and enter this command to start the Ices2 server:**

```
ices /usr/local/etc/ices-playlist.xml &
```

Ices2 starts streaming to the Icecast2 server the Ogg Vorbis file you created. You can start listening to your private streaming server. We describe how to do just that in the following section.

Putting It All Together: Streaming Music to Your Private Network

You can use a multimedia player like XMMS to connect to and listen to an audio stream. The steps in this section describe how to do that:

1. **Start XMMS and select the Play Location option by right-clicking anywhere on the XMMS window or pressing the Ctrl-L keystroke combination.**
2. **Enter the URL of your Icecast2 server. In this case, it's**

```
http://127.0.0.1:8000/track1.ogg.
```

That's it! You hear whatever music you ripped from your music CD.

You have little to gain by using Icecast2 to serve up music streams locally on your PC. Using the CD player described in Chapter 11 is much easier. However, listening to your multimedia streaming server is useful and interesting when it's done across a network.

Streaming on Your Private Network

The preceding section describes how to broadcast music on and to the computer you're sitting at. We extend that process in this section to encompass your private network. You create a jukebox of sorts that you can listen to from any computer on your LAN.

Understanding URLs

Have you ever wondered what the various parts of a URL mean? Using a URL like `http://localhost:8000/track1.ogg` to access a streaming audio server, we thought we should dissect what the various parts mean and do. This list describes the function of each URL element:

- **Protocol:** Icecast2 uses HyperText Transport Protocol — HTTP — packets to encapsulate audio streams. HTTP is a good choice because it's easy to configure your firewalls to allow HTTP connections.
- **Address:** The Icecast2 server's IP address. The address can either be a domain name or in numeric form. For example, you could replace localhost with its numeric address, `127.0.0.1`.
- **Port:** The port number Icecast2 uses to listen for TCP connection requests. Icecast2 uses port 8000 by default; you can easily change the port by modifying the Icecast2 configuration file.
- **MountPoint:** This component specifies the Icecast2 stream to which to connect. Icecast2 is capable of playing two streams. In this example, you use the content file `track1.ogg`, which you may have created in the preceding section.

These steps describe how to configure your Icecast2 server to broadcast over your private network.

1. **Log in as root and open the Gedit text editor by clicking the GNOME Menu and choosing Accessories⇨Text Editor.**
2. **In the Gedit window, choose File⇨Open.**
3. **Select `/usr/local/etc/icecast.xml` and click OK.**
4. **Change the loopback address, `127.0.0.1` — the IP address of your Icecast2 server. For example, if your server's IP address is `192.168.1.1`, modify the file as shown here; change the host name as appropriate too:**

   ```
   <hostname>veracruz</hostname>
   <port>8000</port>
   <bind-address>192.168.1.1</bind-address>
   <master-server>192.168.1.1</master-server>
   ```

   Note that the port number doesn't change.

5. **Change the passwords from their default values. Otherwise, anyone who downloads the Icecast2 package can determine your password:**

   ```
   <source-password>givememusic</source-password>
   <relay-password>givememusic</relay-password>
   ```

6. **Modify the e-mail and location information to match your network.**

   That gives any listeners an idea of who you are and where you're coming from.

   ```
   <location>Hi-Fi Paunchy</location>
   <admin>oldgomez@paunchy.net</admin>
   ```

7. **Save your changes by clicking the Save button and open the** `/usr/local/etc/ices-playlist.xml` **file in Gedit.**

8. **Modify the file so that Ices2 contacts the Icecast2 server:**

   ```
   <hostname>veracruz</hostname>
   <port>8000</port>
   <password>givememusic</password>
   <mount>/track1.ogg</mount>
   ```

9. **Save your changes and close the Gedit window.**

10. **Open a GNOME Terminal window and start the server:**

    ```
    killall -9 icecast ices
    icecast -c /usr/local/etc/icecast.xml &
    ices /usr/local/etc/ices-playlist.xml &
    ```

11. **Enter this command to start XMMS and connect to the newly configured Icecast2 stream:**

    ```
    xmms http://192.168.1.1:8000/track1.ogg
    ```

    You can also use MPlayer to listen to the stream, if you want:

    ```
    mplayer http://192.168.1.1:8000/track1.ogg
    ```

Part V
The Part of Tens

"We're here to clean the code."

In this part . . .

Ah, the part you find in every *For Dummies* book: The Part of Tens. Here, we get to rummage around and come up with ten of this and ten of that.

In Chapter 20, we list some frequently encountered problems (and their solutions).

Unfortunately, the world is still a dangerous place. Chapter 21 outlines ten computer security threats. We describe how to be a little safer in the Wild West, otherwise known as the Internet.

Chapter 20

Ten Problem Areas and Solutions

In This Chapter

- Finding information about Linux
- "I forgot my password"
- "I forgot my root password"
- "I need to break into my own computer!"
- "I want to change the GRUB boot order"
- "When I boot into Windows, I get the recovery process"
- "My network is working, yet not working"
- "I want to make an emergency boot disk"
- "I can't boot from my DVD"
- "Linux can't find a shell script (or a program)"
- "I don't know how to make the X Window System start at boot-time"
- "I never seem to have the correct time"

In any technical situation, people end up having problems and issues they need help with. This chapter is designed to help answer the most common problems people encounter when they're using Red Hat Linux.

In any technical situation, people end up having problems and issues they need help with. This chapter is designed to help answer the most common problems people encounter when they're using Red Hat Linux.

"Help! I Need Some Help!"

Before this chapter gets into solving specific problems, it first describes several sources of information. Because we cannot cover more than a few of the most common problems, we first point you in the direction where you can find more information and help.

Books and more books

When we were working with computers many years ago, the number of books about computers could fill little more than one bookshelf, and they were mostly about the electronics of the hardware itself. Networking books concentrated on such subjects as the probability of two Ethernet packets colliding and not on how to build simple networks. Hardly any books about computers were ever in the popular bookstores. Thousands of books about computers are available now; most describe the software and its interactions, with the hardware taking a back seat. Books such as the ones in the *For Dummies* series aren't just for bookstores any more. You can also find them in mass-market venues, such as your local superstore.

One great source for information about *For Dummies* books is the television series *The Simpsons.* That show loves *For Dummies* authors in particular and provides an amazingly accurate portrait of us. D'oh!

Perhaps you looked at other books before you bought this one and were intimidated by their use of technical terms. Or, you thought that the other books were too general for what you want to do and you want something more task oriented. You may want to look over those books again because your knowledge level should be higher after reading this book. TCP/IP networking, compiler design, operating system theory, formal language theory, computer graphics, and systems administration training are all topics you can study in greater depth when you have a Linux computer at your disposal.

Many books specifically about the Unix operating system are partially or completely applicable to Linux, such as books about Perl, a comprehensive interpreter. By getting one (or more) books about Perl and sitting down with your Linux system, you have both a new tool for doing your work and a new appreciation for a complete programming language. If you want to find out how to write Perl, you can just view the source code.

Linux HOWTOs and Red Hat manuals

Don't forget about the Linux HOWTOs, which come in the commercial version of Red Hat Linux. These excellent guides to Linux are covered under the Linux Documentation Project (LDP) *copyleft,* which means that you can print them.

Red Hat also provides online versions of the manuals you get when you purchase their full distribution. Look at `www.redhat.com/docs/manuals/linux/RHL-10-Manual` for information about nearly every aspect of Red Hat Linux.

School days

Another way to find out more information about Unix and Linux is to take a course, perhaps at a local community college. Many colleges offer courses in Unix, and some have started using Linux to teach their Unix courses. You can do your homework on your system at home, or, if you have a notebook (laptop computer), you can work anywhere. (Jon typed text for the first edition of this book in a hotel in Auckland, New Zealand, and updated text for the second edition in the United Airlines lounge in Chicago.) What we would have given during college for the chance to do computer projects while sitting in the comfort of our own pub — er, dorm rooms. Instead, we had to sit in a room with a bunch of punch-card machines — well, never mind. We would have been much more comfortable and productive with a Linux system.

In the news

You can obtain additional information about the Linux operating system from mailing lists and newsgroups on the Internet. In fact, one of the first popular uses of the Internet was the Usenet information-sharing system. Usenet is similar to the World Wide Web in that it uses a set of protocols to perform a special type of communication over the general-purpose Internet. Usenet provides the capability to let people participate in discussions via e-mail. People post messages to a specific interest group that anyone can view and respond to.

Newsgroups and mailing lists are dedicated to specific topics: technological and any topic that two or more people (or one person with multiple personalities) are interested in. Dozens of newsgroups and mailing lists are devoted to Linux topics. Searching these groups often provides laser-like answers to your questions. That's because someone else is quite likely to have encountered your problem and found a solution to it. You can also post your questions to newsgroups when necessary.

You can search for newsgroups at, for example, `www.dejanews.com` and `www.mailgate.org`. Google also provides an excellent mechanism to search groups, named Google Groups, at `www.google.com/advanced_group_search`.

Don't neglect to check out the Red Hat mailing lists directly, at `https://listman.redhat.com/mailmain/listinfo`. This Web page provides a summary of all Red Hat groups.

User groups

User groups are springing up all over the country. Some are more active than others, but most hold meetings at least once a month. Some groups are Linux only; others are connected to a larger computer group — either Unix or a more general computer users' association. User groups offer a great opportunity to ask questions. User groups also tend to stimulate new ideas and ways of doing tasks.

You can find out whether a Linux user group is in your area by checking with GLUE (Groups of Linux Users Everywhere), a service run by Specialized Systems Consultants, Inc. (SSC), which publishes *Linux Journal.* You can find GLUE, an automated map of user groups, at `www.ssc.com`.

When you arrive at the site, click the Resources link, which takes you to the *Linux Journal* site. Then check out the Resources area there, to find out where the user group closest to you meets.

No user group in your area? Post a message at your local university or community college saying that you want to start one; other people in your area may decide to join you. Terrified at the thought of trying to start a user group? User group leaders often aren't the most technically knowledgeable members but are simply good planners. They organize the meeting space, find (or hound) speakers, send out meeting notices, locate sponsors, arrange refreshments (usually beer), and perform other organizational tasks. Sometimes, being the leader seems like a thankless job, but when a meeting goes really well, it makes all the work worthwhile. So, as a newbie to Linux, you may not know a grep from an awk, but you still may make a good chairperson.

Fixing Common Problems

This section describes how to fix several common problems. Each of the following sections outlines the problem and then describes the solution.

"I forgot my password"

Problem: You have to remember a zillion passwords at work and home. Unfortunately, you can't remember your Linux password.

Solution: The solution is simple if you have forgotten a user account password but still remember the root password. In that case, simply log in as root and reset the user password. For example, if your user name is `rod`, run the command **passwd rod** and enter the new password (for example) ***likes coffee***.

The solution is more difficult when you forget the root password. You have to become a hacker and break in to your computer to fix the problem. Fortunately, Red Hat provides two possible solutions: Either boot into single-user mode via GRUB or boot from the first Red Hat installation disc.

"I forgot my root password!"

You can't reset a regular user's password if you can't log in as the root (superuser). However, you can easily circumvent having to log in as the root user by booting your Red Hat Linux computer into Single User mode.

Turn on or restart your computer and use the cursor keys to select the Linux operation system when the GRUB boot screen appears; Linux is selected automatically if you're not using a dual-boot system (you installed only Linux). Next, press the **e** key to edit the GRUB configuration. You see three lines, the middle of which starts with the word *kernel*. Select the `kernel` line with the cursor keys when the 3-line menu appears. Press the **e** key again, press the spacebar, and then enter the number **1** at the end of the line. Press the Enter key and you return to the original GRUB window. Finally, press the **b** key to boot your system into single-user mode.

You can tell Linux to boot into nongraphical — rather than single-user — mode by substituting **3** for `1` when you're editing the GRUB boot mechanism.

"I need to break into my own computer!"

Power on or reset your computer. Change your BIOS to boot from CD-ROM, if necessary. Before your computer starts the GRUB boot system, insert the companion DVD in the DVD/CD-ROM drive. When the Red Hat installation process starts, type **linux rescue** at the `boot:` prompt.

Red Hat boots into single-user mode and mounts your Linux partitions. You can access and use your computer's root file system by entering this command:

```
chroot /mnt/sysimage
```

You now have complete control over your computer. For example, you can reset the root password:

```
passwd
```

Enter the new password when prompted. Note that anyone who has physical access to your computer can use this method to break into it! If you use your computer in public or semipublic places, you should set your BIOS password. Setting a BIOS password doesn't make using this method to break in impossible, but it does make it harder.

"I want to change the GRUB boot order"

Problem: You created a dual-boot computer with Red Hat Linux and Windows, and you want to change which one boots by default.

Solution: Modify the `/etc/grub/grub.conf` file on your Linux computer. The `grub.conf` should look similar to this example:

```
default=0
timeout=10
splashimage=(hd0,0)/grub/splash.xpm.gz
title Red Hat Linux (2.4.20-20.1)
        root (hd0,1)
        kernel /vmlinuz-2.4.20-20.1 ro root=LABEL=/1 hdb=ide-
           scsi
        initrd /initrd-2.4.20-20.1.img
title DOS
         rootnoverify (hd0,0)
default=0

timeout=10
splashimage=(hd0,0)/grub/splash.xpm.gz
title Red Hat Linux (2.4.x)
        root (hd0,1)
        kernel /vmlinuz-2.4.x ro root=/dev/hda7 hdb=ide-scsi
        initrd /initrd-2.4.x.img
title Windows 2000
        chainloader +1
        rootnoverify (hd0,0)        chainloader +1
```

In this case, Linux is the operating system that boots by default, unless you select otherwise; `default = 0` corresponds to the first operating system in the list — the first Title line. To change the order, simply change the default value from `0` to `1`:

```
default=1
timeout=10
splashimage=(hd0,0)/grub/splash.xpm.gz
title Red Hat Linux (2.4.20-20.1)
        root (hd0,1)
```

```
        kernel /vmlinuz-2.4.20-20.1 ro root=LABEL=/1 hdb=ide-
           scsi
        initrd /initrd-2.4.20-20.1.img
title DOS
         rootnoverify (hd0,0)        chainloader +1
```

The next time you boot your computer, your Windows operating system (the DOS line) automatically boots.

"When I boot into Windows, I get the recovery process"

Problem: You have a dual-boot computer with Microsoft Windows as the alternative operating system. When you boot into Windows, you get the Windows recovery screen. "Help, I'm scared!"

Solution: Relax — you probably haven't lost your mind or your Windows partition. What happened is that the Red Hat Linux installation process mistakenly selected the recovery partition from which to boot Windows. Most computers now come with a preinstalled Windows recovery partition (rather than a recovery CD-ROM), so Red Hat Linux sees at least two Windows partitions when configuring GRUB, and it made the wrong choice. For example, you have `hda1` and `hda2`, and GRUB thinks that `hda1` is the Windows partition; `hda1` is the recovery partition, however, and `hda2` is the Windows C: drive.

You have to reconfigure GRUB to point to the correct Windows partition to make it work correctly. You may have this `/etc/grub/grub.conf` file for example:

```
default=0
timeout=10
splashimage=(hd0,0)/grub/splash.xpm.gz
title Red Hat Linux (2.4.20-20.1)
        root (hd0,1)
        kernel /vmlinuz-2.4.20-20.1 ro root=LABEL=/1 hdb=ide-
           scsi
        initrd /initrd-2.4.20-20.1.img
title DOS
         rootnoverify (hd0,0)
         chainloader +1
```

Change the `rootnoverify (hd0,0)` parameter to `rootnoverify (hd0,1)` and reboot your computer. This technique should fix your problem.

"My network is working, yet not working"

Problem: You have configured and checked your network connection, and it appears to be okay. But you can't connect to some or all of the machines or network services you want. You're perplexed.

Solution: Check your Iptables-based firewall. Red Hat configures two different levels of firewalls during the installation. This book describes several different Iptables firewall configurations too. If your firewall isn't configured correctly, it prevents some or all network communications. Even if your firewall is configured correctly, it may be designed, in many cases, to block the type of communications you want.

Turn off your firewall with this command:

```
/etc/init.d/iptables stop
```

If your network connection instantaneously works, your firewall was most likely the culprit. In that case, you have to go modify your firewall to make it work for your needs. Don't forget to turn your firewall back on as soon as you fix the problem:

```
/etc/init.d/iptables start
```

A description of how to customize an Iptables firewall is beyond the scope of this book. However, the firewalls we show you how to construct in this book may work for you and also be easier to understand and modify. Refer to Chapter 8 for more information about Iptables-based firewalls.

"I want to make an emergency boot floppy disk"

Problem: You skipped making an emergency boot disk when you installed Red Hat Linux and want one now.

Solution: All is not lost if you read Chapter 3 and skipped making a boot disk. Nothing is lost because it's easy, in fact, to make one. Log in to your computer as root and insert a floppy disk that you don't mind erasing (losing everything on that disk). Run this command:

```
uname -r
```

This command returns information about the version of Linux you're running. The output looks similar to this:

```
2.4.21-20.1
```

Use that number to run this command:

```
mkbootdisk 2.4.21-20.1
```

You have a Red Hat Linux boot floppy when the process finishes writing to the disk. Restart your computer and press the Enter key at the `boot:` prompt. You computer then starts Red Hat Linux.

"I can't boot from my DVD"

Problem: Sometimes, you get a DVD (or CD-ROM) disc that you can't boot from. The disc may otherwise be perfectly good, but for some reason it just doesn't work for booting.

Solution: You can get around this problem by using the boot image supplied with the companion DVD in the back of this book to create a bootable floppy disk. (This disc is different from the emergency boot floppy disk you have the option of creating in Chapter 3.)

Log in to your Red Hat Linux computer as root and mount the first companion CD:

```
mount /mnt/cdrom
```

Change to the `images` directory on the CD-ROM:

```
cd /mnt/cdrom/images
```

Insert a disk into the floppy drive and run this command:

```
dd if=bootdisk.img of=/dev/fd0
```

A boot image is written to the disk, from which you can boot your computer.

You can also create a bootable CD-ROM if you have a CD-R drive. Insert a writable CD-ROM (CD-R or CD-R/W) and run this command:

```
cdrecord -isosize boot.iso
```

"Linux can't find a shell script (or a program)"

Problem: You type a command name, but Linux can't find the command, even if it's in the current directory.

Solution: When you type a shell or binary command name, Linux looks for the name in specific places and in a specific order. To find out which directories Linux looks in, and in which order, type this command:

```
echo $PATH
```

You see a stream similar to this one:

```
/bin:/usr/bin:/usr/local/bin
```

Linux looks at these directories to find the command, program, or shell you want to execute. You may see more directories depending on your distribution or how your system administrator (if you have one) set up your system.

Suppose that you create a shell or a program named `bark` and want to execute it (and assuming that you have set the permission bits to make `bark` executable by you). You have a couple of choices (although you have more than two choices, we list the safest ones). One choice is to type this line on the command line:

```
./bark
```

This line tells Linux to look in this directory (`./`) and execute `bark`.

Your second choice is to move `bark` to one of the directories shown in the PATH variable, such as `/usr/local/bin`, and then enter **bark** at the prompt again.

"I don't know how to make the X Window System start at boot time"

Problem: You don't want to log in to a command-line mode (such as DOS) and then type **startx**. Instead, you want to log in through the X Window System.

Solution: If you like to see a graphical interface from the beginning, change this line in the /etc/inittab file:

```
id:3:initdefault:
```

to this:

```
id:5:initdefault:
```

Save your changes and reboot. X starts at the end of the boot process, and you can then log in through the graphical interface. To go back to the old way of booting, change the line in the /etc/inittab file back to this:

```
id:3:initdefault:
```

and reboot your machine.

"I never seem to have the correct time"

Problem: When you boot Linux, the time is wrong, so you set it with the date command. Then you boot Windows and its time is wrong, so you reset it. When you reboot Linux, its time is wrong again.

Solution: Most Unix systems keep their time by using Universal Time (also known as Greenwich Mean Time, or GMT), but Microsoft systems keep their time as local time. When you set the time in either system, you set the CPU clock to that version of the time. Then, when you boot the other system, it interprets differently what is in the CPU clock and reports a different time.

Linux enables you to use either GMT or your local time. You make this choice when you install the system. To change your choice, follow these steps:

1. **Log in as root and type** timeconfig**.**

   The Configure Timezone dialog box appears.

2. **Select the GMT option.**

   Highlight the option by pressing the Tab key, if necessary. (You should already be there when you activate the timeconfig command.)

3. **Press the spacebar to deselect the option. Press the Tab key until you reach the OK button and then press Enter.**

4. **Reset the time to the proper value by using the** ntpdate **command.**

   You have to point the `ntpdate` command at a Network Time Protocol (NTP) time server. For example, you can run the command `ntpdate clock.redhat.com`. Some ISPs maintain their own NTP server, so you may be able run the command, like this:

   ```
   ntpdate clock.redhat.com
   ```

Chapter 21

Ten Security Vulnerabilities

In This Chapter

- Simplifying your system
- Encrypting your communications
- Using firewalls
- Updating your software
- Backing up your data
- Introducing buffer overflows
- Getting social
- Using good passwords
- Scanning the horizon
- Keeping track of your logs

They're here! The monster is under the bed. That big wooden horse is full of Greeks. Here's Johnny! Come into the light. And so on, and so on. However you say it, one thing's for sure: The bad guys are out to get you.

Do you want the good news or the bad news first? The good news is, the Internet has changed the world for the better and continues to do so in more and unforeseen ways. And the speed of change will only accelerate. The bad news is, because the Internet is constantly changing, the number of ways that someone can use the Internet to hurt you is always growing. This chapter outlines some of the more dangerous spooks that lurk out on that poorly lit electronic street.

Our purpose in this chapter is to point you in the right direction so that you can gain a general awareness of computer security. Computer security is, unfortunately, a complex subject. Because of the complexity of the topic of security, we cannot hope to do any more here than touch on some important aspects. We just try to give you the most bang for your buck by adding a few simple but effective security measures to your new Red Hat Linux computer.

This chapter introduces ten important security topics. You can use them as a starting point to increase your computer security.

How Many Daemons Can Dance on the Head of the Linux Process Table?

Every commercial operating system company wants to make its operating systems easy to install and use. Operating systems are inherently complex animals, and Linux is no exception. (Of course, we're not biased when we say that Linux is, overall, a simpler system than Windows, whether you measure simplicity by the number of lines of code or the transparency — the open source concept — of its design.) Companies walk the tightrope of making systems easy to use and also making them reasonably secure — they sell more copies when they make it simple but buy your wrath when you get hacked.

Ease of use and security often don't get along. Your operating system is much easier to use, for example, if you install and activate every software package and option. On the other hand, running every software package means that you have more potential vulnerabilities. Entering your own house is a breeze if you install 10 doors and 20 windows, but that number of entrances also provides burglars with more opportunities to break in. The same logic applies to your computer's operating system: The more software you install, the more chances someone has of getting inside your computer.

We can't think of a cure-all for this dilemma. The best answer from a security viewpoint is to not provide intruders with any openings: Place your computer in a locked room with no network or external connections and turn it off. You then have a truly safe system whose only job is to hold the floor down.

As with most things in life, the best answer is to use your best judgment and balance security with ease of use. Run only the services you need. For example, don't run the Samba file system service if you don't want to use your Red Hat Linux computer as a (Windows) file system server. Don't run the text-based gpm mouse program if you use the graphical X Window mode on your computer. The list is endless and is beyond the scope of this book to discuss in detail. You can find more info from these sources:

- **Web sites:** Both `www.sans.org` and `www.usenix.org` deal with security issues.
- **HOWTOs:** Go to the site `www.redhat.com/docs/manuals/linux/RHL-10.0-Manual` and open the *Customization Guide* and *Reference* documents to access security advice.
- **Books covering security:** Browse through your local bookstore to find Linux books that discuss how to reduce services. Some good books are *Red Hat Linux Security and Optimization,* by Mohammed J. Kabir, and *Linux Security Toolkit,* by David A. Bandel, both published by Wiley Publishing, Inc.

Hide Your Communications with OpenSSH

You may find it difficult to trust communication media that you don't completely control — such as university LANs, wireless home networks, and the Internet. Our point: Trust no one!

Any public network is potentially dangerous, especially the Internet. One way to protect yourself is to use encryption for all communication. You use encryption when you conduct credit card transactions or read remote e-mail. Secure Socket Layer (SSL) communication is the standard encryption mechanism for secure Internet browsing and e-commerce transactions.

The *Secure Shell (SSH)* protocol is used to conduct encrypted CLI (command-line interface) terminal sessions and file transfers. Red Hat bundles the open source version of SSH called OpenSSH with its distributions. When you install Red Hat Linux, you automatically get the OpenSSH client. You can use OpenSSH from a terminal session by entering the command `ssh` *`destination`*. The destination is the computer you want to communicate with. You can get information about OpenSSH from `www.openssh.org`.

Using encryption is essential when you use wireless networking. Wi-Fi (also known as 802.11b) wireless networks can use built-in encryption based on the WEP protocol. WEP does have some significant security vulnerabilities, though. The only long-term answer is either to wait until the next standard comes along to fix the problem or to use OpenSSH to provide your own encryption. You're much safer if you use OpenSSH and SSL for as much of your communication as possible.

Aha! No Firewall — Very, Very Good

Broadband connections give you a quantum leap in speed and convenience when you're connecting to the Internet. The two most popular choices for a broadband connection are DSL and cable modems. After you start using them, you may never go back to slow, Stone Age telephone-based modems.

But every silver lining implies a dark cloud. Broadband connections give you not only fast Internet connections but also continuous ones. With a telephone-based modem, a hacker can attack only your home computer and private network while you're connected to the Internet. Using a 24/7 broadband connection means that every hacker on the Internet — that means every hacker in the world — can constantly bang on your computer and private network. That's lots of vulnerability.

Firewalls provide your number-one protection from Internet-based attacks. The modern Netfilter/Iptables packet-filtering firewall system gives you excellent protection when it's properly configured. The Red Hat installation process installs a good Iptables-based firewall by default, and Chapter 8 describes how to configure an even better one. You should never, ever connect to the Internet without first configuring your personal firewall.

We don't mean to imply that you're invulnerable to attack if you use a telephone-based modem to connect to the Internet. Traditional modem connections are just as vulnerable as continuous broadband connections *when they're active.* What we mean is that an unconnected modem is a safe modem.

Keeping Up with the Software Joneses

Nobody's perfect, and that goes for operating system vendors. Even open source Linux developers and excellent companies like Red Hat make mistakes. Vulnerabilities are found in software systems all the time and have to be fixed.

Red Hat provides a way to keep up-to-date with current problem and security fixes through its Web site. Go to `ftp.redhat.com/pub/redhat` to find the newest and safest versions of all your system's RPM packages. You can also find out how to use the Red Hat Linux Network, at `rhn.redhat.com`, so that it updates itself automatically — see Chapter 17 for details.

"Backups? I Don't Need No Stinking Backups!"

If you don't regularly make backups of your computer's contents, you face a security vulnerability, plain and simple. You may lose some or all of your valuable information if your computer is compromised. You should back up your data as frequently as possible.

You can use one of many techniques and software for making backups, but that's stuff we couldn't possibly begin to cover in this book. We wouldn't be able to cover Red Hat Linux if we even began to go into detail.

So keep it simple: Archiving your home directory and copying it to another location is a simple and effective backup mechanism.

For example, the following commands use the ubiquitous Linux tape archive (tar) command to create an archive of your home directory. You can then use the OpenSSH `scp` command to securely copy the archive to another location, such as your ISP account or another computer you have access to. Follow these steps to create an archive of your home directory:

1. **Log in to your user account.**
2. **Run this `tar` command:**

   ```
   tar czf mybackup.tgz .
   ```

   In this case, the `c` option means to use `tar` to copy the specified files and directories. The `z` option tells `tar` to compress the data. The `f` option defines the text that follows it — *`mybackup`*`.tgz` — as the file to copy the files to. The single dot (`.`) says to copy to the archive all files in the current working directory.
3. **Use OpenSSH to copy the `tar` archive to another location:**

   ```
   scp mybackup.tgz myloginaccount@myisp.com
   ```

   This command securely copies the `tar` archive to the account *`myloginaccount`* at the ISP *`myisp.com`*.

My Buffer Overflow-eth

One of the most popular methods that hackers use to break in to computers is via buffer overflows. The buffer overflow technique attempts to feed crazy streams of data to programs in order to make them behave in ways their designers never intended. (A detailed description of what a queue does is beyond the scope of this book. Suffice it to say that Linux uses a queue to store instructions and addresses for later use.) The result of the buffer overflow is that sometimes the program provides the hacker with a shell or other open door when it fails.

The shell created by a buffer overflow is an open door to your computer. Sometimes, the shell has root (superuser) privileges, and then the hacker owns your system.

Here are some simple techniques you can use to minimize buffer overflows:

- **The first line of defense is simply to minimize the number of services you run.** You run zero risk of compromise from a buffer overflow vulnerability in Service A if you don't run that service.

  For example, the Lion worm wreaked havoc in spring 2001. Lion exercised vulnerability in the Linux sendmail and lpd printer services. Computers that didn't run those services weren't vulnerable to the Lion worm.

- **The second line of defense is to update your Red Hat Linux computer as often as possible.** Red Hat posts package updates, as they become available, that fix vulnerabilities. Buffer overflow fixes comprise many of the package updates. Updating your system fixes many buffer overflow vulnerabilities.

Social Engineering 1010101010

Hackers don't have to discover supertechnical tricks to break into your computer. Many smart hackers aren't deterred when they encounter a well-protected computer or network. What does a poor hacker in these security-aware times have to do to break into your system?

Some hacker techniques don't rely on technological means. One such technique is *social engineering,* which is a fancy way of saying "I plan to trick you or your associates into giving me information to use against you."

Social engineering can be as simple as a hacker calling you to see whether you're at home or in the office. If you're not physically present, the hacker or burglar can drop by, break in and steal the computer or its disks. After someone gains physical possession of your computer, most security precautions you take can be easily defeated.

Another social engineering technique hackers employ is to call a corporation's help desk and pretend to be a VIP. The poor minimum-wage employee can often be bullied or cajoled into giving out a password or other important information.

The moral of the story is to exercise good security hygiene and be careful of strangers. Don't give out information unless it's essential and you can verify the authenticity of the request.

Bad Passwords

Probably the easiest to avoid, and most often abused, vulnerability is poor or non-existent passwords. Passwords are your first line of defense. If your password is easily guessed or — even worse — blank, someone will break in.

Bad passwords are easy to fix. Start by assigning a password to every account you create — *especially* root. Then make it a habit to use "good" passwords. Passwords can be cracked by brute force because computers have become very fast. Because you connect to the Internet, hackers can steal your `/etc/passwd` file, which contains the encrypted version of your text-based passwords and then use a computer to crack them.

Use passwords that don't use any word found in a dictionary. Simple words of any language are extremely easy to crack. For example, don't use the password *redhat80*. Instead, you can change the *e* in *red* to *3* and the *a* in *hat* to @. Your password becomes *r3dh@t80*, which means that the cracking software has to use brute force, rather than a mere dictionary search, to discover it.

Scan Me

Information is king when it comes to people hacking into systems and keeping them out. Hackers use knowledge about your computer and network to break into your systems. One common and powerful tool for gaining information about which type of operating system you have and the services it runs is nmap. This port-scanning tool can discover a wealth of information about individual computers and networks.

Nmap is included in the Red Hat Linux distribution. Install it by logging in as root, mounting the DVD (insert the DVD into the DVD/CD-ROM drive), and entering this command:

```
rpm -ivh /mnt/cdrom/RedHat/RPMS/nmap*
```

You can then scan yourself, or any computer on your private network (if you have one). If you're logged into `cancun`, for example, you can run this command:

```
nmap localhost
```

The `nmap` command probes your internal loop-back network interface — `lo`, for example — and returns a list of services you're running. This list shows a sample result:

```
Starting nmap 3.27 ( www.insecure.org/nmap/ ) at 2003-07-05


Interesting ports on localhost.localdomain (127.0.0.1):
(The 1616 ports scanned but not shown below are in state:
           closed)
Port       State        Service
22/tcp     open         ssh
25/tcp     open         smtp
80/tcp     open         http
111/tcp    open         sunrpc
443/tcp    open         https
631/tcp    open         ipp
6000/tcp   open         X11

Nmap run completed -- 1 IP address (1 host up) scanned in
           0.385 seconds
```

If you're a hacker, this information is good stuff. By knowing that the machine is running certain services, you can try to find vulnerabilities to exploit.

Another good test to run is to log in to your ISP account and scan the Internet connection your computer or private network is attached to. If your firewall is running correctly, the scan shows little or nothing. That's good. If the scan displays information about your computer and network, either your firewall isn't running correctly or it's not running at all.

You can use that information to your advantage. Seeing what the hackers see gives you the ability to plug your security holes.

I Know Where You Logged In Last Summer

Linux is good at keeping a diary. Red Hat is configured at installation to keep logs of every user login and other technical information. Examining logs is more of an art than a science, however. We don't have any explicit techniques for determining whether your system is being attacked or has been broken into. Sorry.

Experience counts for a great deal when you're examining logs for discrepancies. The more you keep track of your system, the more you recognize its idiosyncrasies and general behavior. Red Hat checks its general-purpose logs in the `/var/log` directory. Check your logs frequently.

Part VI
Appendixes

In this part . . .

This part is the area of every book where you find things that just didn't fit into the flow of the chapters: the fun and exciting appendixes.

Appendix A outlines the Red Hat Linux systems administration utilities. Appendix B shows how to figure out what stuff your computer is made of. Appendixes C and D describe the Linux file system and how to use it. In Appendix E, you find out all about RPM, the Red Hat Package Manager. Finally, the contents of the companion DVD are described in Appendix F.

Appendix A

Red Hat Linux Administration Utilities

In This Appendix

- The Red Hat system settings
- The Red Hat server settings
- The Red Hat system tools

Red Hat, Inc., does what many other Linux distributions do: It packages the Linux kernel with GNU utilities and other applications to make using Linux easy and convenient. Some distributions, like SELinux, customize Linux to perform specific tasks, such as provide a secure platform. Most distributions, however (like Red Hat) provide general-purpose Linux configurations you can use to create servers or desktop workstations.

Red Hat tries to set itself apart from the pack by creating utilities to make your job easier. For example, it has created numerous systems administration utilities that are integrated, easy to use, and quite powerful. These utilities are one reason that Red Hat wins the market share competition. This appendix outlines the Red Hat Linux configuration utilities.

The lists throughout this section describe each of the utilities available on a Red Hat Linux computer. The lists are organized according to the menu on which you find them.

Not all utilities listed in this appendix are installed by default. Many are installed only if you install their respective services. For example, you can use the Apache configuration utility only if you install the Apache web server package. We tell you when a utility isn't installed as part of the Workstation installation type (refer to Chapter 3).

System Settings

These utilities are on the GNOME System Settings menu, which you find by using the GNOME Menu or the Start Here window:

- **Add/Remove Applications:** Adds and deletes RPM packages. See Appendix E for more information.
- **Authentication:** Deals with all forms of Linux user account authentication. The default settings should satisfy most people's needs.
- **Date & Time:** Sets the date, time, and time zone of your Linux computer. You can also configure the automatic time synchronizer — the Network Time Protocol (NTP) — daemon.
- **Display:** Allows you to configure both your video driver and monitor. Refer to Chapter 4 for more information.
- **Keyboard:** Lets you choose the nationality of your keyboard.
- **Language:** Helps you choose the default language of your computer.
- **Login Screen:** Lets you configure the look and feel, and other aspects, of your login screen.
- **Mouse:** Configures your mouse.
- **Network:** Configures your network interfaces. You can also use it to turn network devices on and off. Refer to Chapters 5, 6, and 7 for examples of how to use this tool.
- **Printing:** Configures a printer. Chapter 16 provides an example that uses this utility.
- **Root Password:** Sets the root password.
- **Security Level:** Configures your workstation's IP filtering firewall (using Iptables) with this system. You may recall that you were given three standard firewall configuration options during the Red Hat Linux installation described in Chapter 3. This tool allows you to duplicate those settings and then customize them.
- **Soundcard Detection:** Detects and configures your sound card. Chapter 11 has further instructions.
- **Users and Groups:** Creates new users and groups. You can also modify existing ones. Chapter 4 shows how to use this utility.

Server Settings

You display the Server Settings menu by choosing the GNOME Main Menu⇨System Settings command. It contains, by default, only the Service

Configuration utility. This list describes the service utilities you can install by choice (the first four utilities listed aren't installed as part of the Workstation installation type):

- Apache Configuration
- Domain Name Service
- NFS Server Configuration
- Samba Server Configuration
- Service Configuration

These utilities are in packages that start with the name `redhat-config`. To install the Apache Configuration utility, for example, insert the companion DVD-ROM and run the command `rpm -ivh /mnt/cdrom/RedHat/RPMS/redhat-config-httpd*`.

System Tools

Choose GNOME Main Menu⇨System Tools to find these tools:

- **Disk Management:** Mounts, dismounts, and formats file systems and devices with this system.
- **Floppy Formatter:** Formats floppy disks.
- **Hardware Browser:** Displays information about your computer's hardware subsystems. See Appendix B for more information about this tool.
- **Internet Configuration Wizard:** Lets you create network interfaces. Refer to Chapters 5, 6, and 7 for examples of how to work with this tool.
- **Kickstart:** Helps you automate and customize Red Hat Linux installations. You can use this tool to record and customize the settings that created your current Red Hat installation. You then use that template to create new installations.
- **Network Device Control:** Turns your network devices on and off.
- **Printing Notification Icon**: Notifies you of print jobs.
- **Print Manager:** Helps you maintain and modify your printer settings.
- **Red Hat Network:** Connects to the Red Hat Network (RHN). You use the RHN to keep your Red Hat Linux computer updated.
- **Red Hat Network Alert Icon:** Alerts you whenever RHN updates are available.

- **System Logs:** Shows the contents of your system logs. Refer to Chapter 21 for more information about this tool.
- **System Monitor:** Displays information about your computer's running processes. This utility also shows the recent history of your computer's processor and memory use.

More System Tools

You see the More System Tools submenu whenever you open the System Tools menu. Several administrative tools listed are in this location, as described in this list:

- **Desktop Switcher:** Red Hat includes the popular GNOME and KDE desktop environments in their distributions.
- **Kernel Tuning:** Your Linux kernel comes preconfigured to work in a wide variety of situations. The default configuration works well for both workstations and general-purpose servers. However, you can use this utility to modify the kernel parameters if the default doesn't fit your needs.
- **Mail Transport Agent Switcher:** Red Hat Linux installs the ubiquitous sendmail mail transport agent (MTA). You can install the newer alternative, Postfix MTA, and use this utility to switch between them.

Appendix B

Discovering Your Hardware

In This Appendix

- PC hardware subsystems
- Hard drive controllers
- Computer memory
- Hardware identification on Windows NT, Windows 2000, and Windows XP computers
- Hardware identification on Windows 9*x* and Windows Me computers

You should know as much about your computer as possible before installing Red Hat Linux. This appendix introduces the basic systems that make up a computer. We also show you how to discover information about those parts.

Knowing your hardware can be useful at parties: "My processor is faster than your processor!" In addition to letting you brag at parties, this knowledge can be helpful if you have problems installing Red Hat Linux in Chapter 3. Understanding the bits and pieces that comprise your computer can help you install Red Hat Linux. That information also lets you know better what your new Linux computer is capable of. This appendix helps you get started on your path to self discovery.

Linux runs on Intel processors from the venerable 386 on up to the Digital Equipment Corporation (DEC) Alpha, Sun SPARC, and other systems. However, the version of Red Hat Linux included with this book works on only Intel 386-, 486-, and Pentium-based computers. That shouldn't be a problem because it seems that 99.9 percent (well, maybe not quite that many) of the world's computers use Intel.

Breaking Down Your Computer

No, we don't want you to break your computer. But we do want to describe the computer subsystems. Computers may seem mysterious when you first use them, but the truth is that they're not terribly complex. When you break down the parts that make up a PC, you see that each part performs a specific task. The sum of the parts equals a computer. This list outlines the subsystems that comprise a computer:

- **Central processing unit (CPU):** The CPU, or microprocessor, is often referred to as the brains of a computer because the CPU controls, in minute detail, everything the computer does. CPUs are controlled by software that is essentially a recipe for doing tasks as simple as detecting keyboard input or as complex as communicating across networks to display pictures in a web browser.

  The most common CPUs are now Intel Pentiums, which you're using to run your PC. Generally, the faster the CPU, the faster your computer. CPU speed is measured in *megahertz* (MHz), which means millions of cycles per second. To perform complex tasks such as sending e-mail, a CPU has to perform many simple tasks, or instructions, in order to complete the larger one. Although the simplest instructions require a single CPU cycle, most require several cycles. However, the MHz measurement is a reasonably good measure of how fast a microprocessor runs.

- **Hard disks:** Hard disks — also referred to as hard drives — store all the permanent information on a computer. Hard disks are metal platters that store bits and bytes in tiny magnetic domains (spots). The disk spins, and a magnetic head that floats on a cushion of air reads and writes from the disk. The spinning disk allows the head to quickly access any location on the disk and also creates the air cushion.

- **Disk controllers:** The disk controller connects the drive to the computer's microprocessor. Several types of controllers are commonly used: IDE, USB, FireWire, and SCSI. Most PCs come with IDE internal hard drives. However, high-performance computers tend to use SCSI–based drives because they're faster (and more expensive). IDE controllers can connect as many as four drives.

- **CD-ROM:** CD-ROMs store information like hard drives do, but in optical rather than magnetic form. Most PCs use IDE-based CD-ROMs. SCSI CD-ROMs are faster, just like SCSI hard disks. Because the prices of USB and FireWire CD-ROMS are dropping fast, they're becoming more common.

- **RAM, or Random Access Memory:** RAM is much faster than hard disks and CD-ROMs. Because RAM is used to store temporary information, programs, data, and other types of information are stored in RAM — it "forgets" everything when power to the computer is turned off. RAM is measured in megabytes (MB). A megabyte is roughly one million bytes.

- **Mouse:** Which type of mouse do you have — bus, PS/2, or serial? How many buttons does it have? If you have a serial mouse, which COM port is it attached to, and which protocol (Microsoft or Logitech) does it use?

- **Monitor/flat panel display:** What are the make and model of the monitor or flat panel display? What are its vertical and horizontal refresh rates? You need this information only if you plan to use the X Window System, the graphical portion of Linux. Monitors and flat panel displays perform exactly the same function, but with different technologies. Monitors are the ubiquitous television-like, glass vacuum tube devices that are heavy and quickly being replaced by flat panel displays. Flat panels use liquid crystal display (LCD) technology, which uses less power and space.
- **Video card:** What are the make and model number of the video card or video chip set, and what is the amount of video RAM?
- **Network interface card (NIC):** If you have a network connection, what are the make and model number of the network interface card?

That's the rundown of computer subsystems. Each one performs a specific function; buttoned up inside a computer chassis (desktop style or laptop), they work together to create the computer you're familiar with. The next two sections describe hard drives and memory in more detail.

Understanding Hard Drive Controllers

The two main types of hard drives are IDE and SCSI, and each type has its own controller. IDE is more common in PCs, and newer PCs usually have two IDE controllers rather than one. For each IDE controller, your system can have only two hard drives: a master and a slave. Therefore, a PC with two IDE controllers can have as many as four hard drives. You should know which hard drive is which. Also, if you have a Windows system you want to preserve, you should know on which hard drive it resides. The following list shows a normal configuration on a Windows system:

- The first controller's master drive is named C.
- The next hard drive, named D, is the slave drive on the first controller.
- The next hard drive, E, is the master drive on the second controller.
- The last hard drive, F, is the slave drive on the second controller.

Windows is normally located on your C drive, and data is on your other drives. This lettering scheme is one possibility; your hard drives may be set up differently and may include CD-ROMs as drives on your IDE controllers.

Some high-end PCs have SCSI controllers on their motherboards or on separate SCSI controller boards, either in addition to or instead of the IDE controllers. Older SCSI controllers can have as many as 8 devices on them, numbered from 0 to 7, including the controller. Newer SCSI controllers (known as *wide controllers*) can have as many as 16 devices, including the controller itself.

If all you have is a SCSI hard drive, Drive 0 or Drive 1 is usually your C drive, and others follow in order.

If you have a mixture of IDE and SCSI controllers, your C drive could be on any of them. The sections "Discovering Your Windows 9*x* or Windows Me Hardware" and "Discovering Your Windows NT, Windows 2000, or Windows XP Hardware," later in this appendix, show how to identify how many hard drives you have, what type they are, and which controllers they're attached to.

Consider putting Red Hat Linux on a separate hard drive, for a couple of reasons. First, you can now find 80GB hard drives for much less than $100 (U.S.). Second, the task of shrinking MS-DOS and Windows to be small enough to allow Red Hat Linux to reside in its full glory on an existing hard drive is difficult at best and impossible at worst. Also, although splitting the Red Hat Linux distribution across hard drives is possible, doing so makes updating the distribution difficult later.

A Bit about Memory Bytes

Memory is the most important factor in determining how fast your computer runs. Computers use Random Access Memory (RAM) to store and access the operating system, programs, and data. The Intel processor usually has the following amounts of RAM (main memory):

- Linux can run on a surprisingly small amount of memory. With some work and no graphics, you can squeeze Linux on an old PC with only 16MB of memory; 32MB makes life much easier and your computer significantly faster. Many people use old PCs with small amounts of memory as simple network servers.
- If you want to run Linux with graphics, however, you need 64MB.
- With 128MB, Red Hat Linux runs multiple graphical programs, like OpenOffice, with ease.
- You need 256MB or more (many PCs now come standard with 512MB) for hard-core computing. Using big applications, such as VMware, make having enough memory essential.

VMware virtual computers need their own RAM to operate at a reasonable speed; for example, you should allocate a minimum of 128MB of memory to run a Windows 2000 virtual computer. Plan to use 512MB if you want to run multiple instances of VMware virtual computers.

You can install Red Hat Linux on most laptop computers by using the notebook's built-in CD-ROM drive, or a PCMCIA, USB, or proprietary CD-ROM drive. If you don't have any of these items, you can try to get a PCMCIA Ethernet controller and do a network installation, as long as another Linux system on the network has a CD-ROM drive installed. If that is the course you take, consult the Red Hat installation documentation at `www.redhat.com/support`. You also need a video card that Red Hat understands. Red Hat Linux supports most video cards, and usually the only problems result from bleeding-edge notebook computers that use the latest and greatest video hardware. You can use the generic VGA, XGA, or SVGA drivers that Red Hat supplies if you can't find the specific driver.

Discovering Your Windows 9x or Windows Me Hardware

You don't have to go to Hollywood to be discovered if you're a piece of computer hardware. Windows provides the tools to use to discover your bits and pieces right at home. This section describes how to use Windows 9*x* or Windows Me for the discovery process.

If you have a Windows 9*x* or Windows Me computer, use this section to discover and display information about your computer. We use the ubiquitous Control Panel. Start your Windows computer and follow these instructions:

1. **Click the Start button and choose Settings⇨Control Panel. Double-click the System icon and select the Device Manager tab.**
2. **At the top of the screen, select View Devices by Connection. This step shows all components and how they relate to each other.**
3. **On the Device Manager tab (from the Control Panel) in the System Properties dialog box, select the View Devices by Type option.**

   On the list, notice how a plus (+) or minus (–) sign precedes some icons. A plus sign indicates that the entry is collapsed. A minus sign indicates that the entry is expanded to show all subentries.
4. **Click the plus (+) sign to expand the list.**

   Expanding the list shows each computer subsystem. Every device that makes up your computer is shown. Right-click a device and choose the Properties option to display information about a particular device.

You can use the Web to find out about your computer. Computer companies provide detailed information about their products on their Web sites. Go to the manufacturer's Web page and look up your computer's model number. When you get to your page, look for the Specification (or Specs) link.

Discovering Your Windows NT, Windows 2000, or Windows XP Hardware

Discovering information about Windows NT, Windows 2000, and Windows XP is similar to discovering it about Windows 9*x* and Windows Me. The process is the same, although getting there is a little different:

On Windows NT and Windows 2000 computers

1. **Click the Start button and choose Settings⇨Control Panel. Then, double-click the System icon in the Control Panel window.**
2. **Click the Hardware tab when the Systems Properties window opens. Then, click the Device Manager button to open the Device Manager window.**
3. **Click the plus sign of any hardware subsystem you want to examine.**

   A submenu opens, showing all devices of a particular type.
4. **Right-click any hardware subsystem and choose Properties.**

   The Properties option shows information about that particular device.

On Windows XP computers

1. **Click the Start button and choose the My Computer option.**
2. **Double-click the Control Panel icon.**
3. **Double-click the System icon, select the Hardware tab, and then double-click the Device Manager button. The Device Manager window opens.**
4. **Click the plus (+) sign to display the devices within a subsystem.**
5. **Right-click a device to open a menu from which you can choose the Properties option. The Properties window opens and shows information about the device.**

Appendix C
Filing Your Life Away

In This Appendix

- Finding out all about Linux files and directories
- Finding your way through the Linux file system
- Creating, moving, copying, and destroying directories and files
- Changing file ownership and permissions

In this appendix, you take your first steps through the Linux file and directory structure. Don't worry: Linux may live a structured life, but it's flexible. With a little bit of introduction, you begin to understand the Linux way of life.

We also introduce you to file types, subdirectories, and the root (which is not evil at all) directory. You're also shown the way home — to your home directory. After you're oriented to the Linux files-and-directories structure, we show you how to make some changes, such as how to copy and move files and directories and how to — eeek! — destroy them.

Getting Linux File Facts Straight

Linux files are similar to Unix, DOS, Windows, and Macintosh files. All operating systems use files to store information. Files allow you to organize your stuff and keep them separate. For example, the text that comprises this appendix is stored in a file; all other book elements are stored in their own files. Follow the bouncing prompt as we make short work of long files.

Storing files

We assume that you know that a *file* is a collection of information identified by a filename and that Linux can store multiple files in directories as long as the files have different names. Linux stores files with the same name in different directories.

Wonderful or not, Linux filenames can be as long as 256 characters. The filenames can contain uppercase and lowercase letters (also known as *mixed case*), numbers, and special characters, such as underscores (_), dots (.), and hyphens (-). Because filenames can be composed of mixed-case names, and because each name is distinct, these names are *case sensitive.* For example, the names *FILENAME, filename,* and *FiLeNaMe* are unique filenames of different files, but they're the same filename.

Although filenames technically can contain wildcard characters, such as asterisks (*) and question marks (?), using them isn't a good idea. Various command interpreters, or *shells,* use wildcards to match several filenames at one time. If your filenames contain wildcard characters, you have trouble specifying only those files. We recommend that you create filenames that don't contain spaces or other characters that have meaning to shells. In this way, Linux filenames are different from DOS and Windows filenames.

Sorting through file types

Linux files can contain all sorts of information. In fact, Linux sees as a file every device (disks, display, or keyboard, for example) except for a network interface. These five categories of files eventually become the most familiar to you:

- **User data files:** Contain information you create. User data files, sometimes known as *flat files,* usually contain the simplest data, consisting of plain text and numbers. More complex user data files, such as graphics or spreadsheet files, must be interpreted and used by special programs. These files are mostly illegible if you look at them with a text editor because the contents of these files aren't always ASCII text. Changing these files generally affects only the user who owns the files.
- **System data files:** Are used by the system to keep track of users on the system, logins, and passwords, for example. As system administrator, you may be required to view or edit these files. As a regular user, you don't need to be concerned with system data files except, perhaps, the ones you use as examples for your own, private startup files.
- **Directory files:** Hold the names of files — and other directories — that belong to them. These files and directories are called *children.* Directories in Linux (and Unix) are just another type of file. If you're in a directory, the directory above you is the *parent.* Isn't that homey?

  When you list files with the `ls -l` command, it displays a list of files and directories. Directory files begin with the letter *d;* for example:

  ```
  [lidia@cancun lidia]$ ls -l
  drwxr-xr-x 5 lidia lidia 1024 Jul 3  2002 Desktop
  drwx------ 2 lidia lidia 1024 Jul 10 2002 nsmail
  ```

- **Special files:** Represent either hardware devices (such as disk drives, tape drives, or keyboards) or some type of placeholder that the operating system uses. The `/dev` directory holds many of these special files. You can see this directory by running this command at a command prompt:

  ```
  ls -l /dev
  ```

- **Executable files:** Contain instructions (usually called *programs* or *shell scripts*) for your computer. When you type the name of one of these files, you're telling the operating system to *execute* the instructions. Some executable files look like gibberish, and others look like long lists of computer commands. Many of these executable files are located in `/bin`, `/usr/bin`, `/sbin`, and `/usr/sbin`.

Understanding files and directories

If you live in the Windows world, you can think of a Linux file system as one huge file folder that contains files and other file folders, which in turn contain files and other file folders, which in turn contain files and — well, you get the point. In fact, the Linux file system is generally organized in this way. One big directory contains files and other directories, and all the other directories in turn contain files and directories.

Directories and subdirectories

A directory contained, or *nested,* in another directory is a *subdirectory.* For example, the directory named `/mother` may contain a subdirectory named `/child`. The relationship between the two is referred to as parent and child. The full name of the subdirectory is `/mother/child`, which would make a good place to keep a file named `/mother/child/reunion` that contains information about a family reunion.

The root directory

In the tree directory structure of Linux, DOS, and Unix, the big directory at the bottom of the tree is the *root* directory. The root directory is the parent of all other directories (the poor guy must be exhausted) and is represented by a single / symbol (pronounced "slash"). From the root directory, the whole directory structure grows like a tree, with directories and subdirectories branching off like limbs.

If you could turn the tree over so that the trunk is in the air and the branches are toward the ground, you would have an *inverted tree* — which is how the Linux file system is normally drawn and represented (with the root at the top). If we were talking about Mother Nature, you would soon have a dead tree. Because the subject is computer technology, however, you have something that looks like an ever-growing, upside-down tree.

What's in a name?

You name directories in the same way as you name files, following the same rules. Almost the only way you can tell whether a name is a filename or a directory name is the way the slash character (/) is used to show directories nested in other directories. For example, `usr/local` means that `local` is in the `usr` directory. You know that `usr` is a directory because the trailing slash character tells you so; however, you don't know whether `local` is a file or a directory.

If you issue the `ls` command with the `-f` option, Linux lists directories with a slash character at the end, as in `local/`, so you know that local is a directory.

The simplest way to tell whether the slash character indicates the root directory or separate directories, or directories and files, is to see whether anything appears before the slash character in the directory path specification. If nothing appears before the slash, you have the root directory. For example, you know that `/usr` is a subdirectory or a file in the root directory because it has only a single slash character in front of it.

Home again

Linux systems have a directory named `/home`, which contains the user's home directory, where she can

- Store files
- Create more subdirectories
- Move, delete, and modify subdirectories and files

Linux system files and files belonging to other users are never in a user's `/home` directory. Linux decides where the `/home` directory is placed, and that location can be changed only by a superuser (root), and not by general users. Linux is dictatorial because it has to maintain order and keep a handle on security.

Moving Around the File System with pwd and cd

You can navigate the Linux file system without a map or the Global Positioning System (GPS). All you need to know are two commands: `pwd` and `cd`. (You run these commands from the command line.) However, you also need to know where to start; hence, the usefulness of the next section.

Figuring out where you are

Log in to your Red Hat Linux computer and open a GNOME Terminal session. In this case, you log in as the example user `lidia`. To find out where you are in the Linux file system, simply type **pwd** at the command prompt:

```
[lidia@cancun lidia]$pwd
```

You receive this response:

```
/home/lidia
[lidia@cancun lidia]$
```

This response indicates that you're logged in as `lidia` and are in the `/home/lidia` directory. Unless your alter ego is out there, you should be logged in as *yourself* and be in the `/home/`*`yourself`* directory, where *yourself* is your login name.

The `pwd` command stands for *p*rint *w*orking *d*irectory. Your *working directory* is the default directory where Linux commands perform their actions; the working directory is where you are in the file system when you type a command. When you type the `ls(1)` command, for example, Linux shows you the files in your working directory. Any file actions on your part occur in your working directory unless you are root. For security reasons that we don't go into here, the root user isn't configured by default to be able to work on the current working directory. You can change this setting, but the root user generally must explicitly specify the working directory. For example, if you are root and are in the `/etc` directory and you want to indicate the `hosts` file, you must type **cat ./hosts** rather than just **cat hosts**.

Type this command:

```
ls -la
```

You see only the files in your working directory. If you want to specify a file that isn't in your working directory, you have to specify the name of the directory that contains the file in addition to the name of the file. For example, this command lists the `passwd` file in the `/etc` directory:

```
ls -la /etc/passwd
```

Specifying the directory path

If the file you want to read is in a subdirectory of the directory you're in, you can reach the file by typing a relative filename. *Relative filenames* specify the location of files relative to where you are.

In addition to what we discuss earlier in this appendix about specifying directory paths, you need to know these three rules:

- One dot (.) always stands for your current directory.
- Two dots (..) specify the parent directory of the directory you're in.
- All directory paths that include (.) or (..) are relative directory paths.

You can see these files by using the `-a` option of the `ls(1)` command. Without the `-a` option, the `ls(1)` command doesn't bother to list the . or .. files, or any filename beginning with a period. This statement may seem strange, but the creators of Unix thought that having some files that are normally hidden keeps the directory structure cleaner. Therefore, filenames that are always present (. and ..) and special-purpose files are hidden. The types of files that should be hidden are those a user normally doesn't need to see in every listing of the directory structure (files used to tailor applications to the user's preferences, for example).

Specify a pathname relative to where you are; for example:

```
[lidia@cancun lidia]$pwd
/home/lidia
[lidia@cancun lidia]$ ls -la ../../etc/passwd
```

The last line indicates that in order to find the `passwd` file, you move up two directory levels (`../../`) and then down to `/etc`.

If you want to see the login accounts on your system, you can issue this command from your home directory:

```
[lidia@cancun lidia]$ ls -la ..
```

This command lists the parent directory. Because the parent directory (`/home`) has all the login directories of the people on your system, this command shows the names of their login directories.

You have been looking at relative pathnames, which are relative to where you are in the file system. Filenames that are valid from anywhere in the file system are *absolute filenames.* These filenames always begin with the slash character (/), which signifies the root:

```
ls -la /etc/passwd
```

Changing your working directory

You occasionally (often?) want to change your working directory. Why? We're glad you asked — because changing it enables you to work with shorter relative pathnames. To do so, you simply use the `cd` (for *c*hange *d*irectory) command.

To change from your working directory to the `/usr` directory, for example, type this command:

```
cd /usr
```

Going home

If you type **cd** by itself, without any directory name, you return to your home directory. Just knowing that you can easily get back to familiar territory is comforting. There's no place like home.

You can also use `cd` with a *relative* specification; for example:

```
cd ..
```

If you're in the directory `/usr/bin` and type the preceding command, Linux takes you to the parent directory named `/usr`:

```
[lidia@cancun lidia]$ cd /usr/bin
[lidia@cancun bin]$ cd ..
[lidia@cancun usr]$
```

Here are a couple of tricks: If you type **cd ~**, you go to your home directory (the tilde symbol (~) is synonymous with `/home/username`). If you type **cd ~<*username*>**, you can go to that user's home directory. On very large systems, this command is useful because it eliminates the need for you to remember — and type — large directory specifications.

This list describes the shell redirection symbols:

- > is known as *redirect standard output.* When you use it, you tell the computer "Capture the information that normally goes to the screen, create a file, and put the information in it."
- >> is known as *append standard output.* When you use this symbol, you tell the computer "Capture the information that would normally go to the screen and append the information to an existing file. If the file doesn't exist, create it."
- < tells the computer, "Feed the information from the specified file to *standard in* (also known as *standard input*), acting as though the information is coming from the keyboard."

Manipulating Files and Directories

Linux has many ways to create, move, copy, and delete files and directories. Some features are so easy to use that you need to be careful: Unlike other operating systems, Linux doesn't tell you that you're about to overwrite a file — it just follows your orders and overwrites!

We have said it elsewhere in this book, and we'll say it again: Make sure that you're *not* logged in as root when you read through these sections. You can unintentionally harm your computer when you're logged in as root. As root, or the superuser, you can erase any file or directory — regardless of which permissions are set. Be careful!

Creating directories

To create a new directory in Linux, you use the `mkdir` command (just like in MS-DOS). The command looks like this:

```
[lidia@cancun lidia]$mkdir newdirectory
```

This command creates a subdirectory under your current or working directory. If you want the subdirectory under another directory, change to that directory first and then create the new subdirectory.

Create a new directory named `cancun`. Go ahead — do it:

```
mkdir cancun
```

(Can you tell where we would rather be right now?)

Create another directory named `vacation`:

```
mkdir veracruz
```

Then, change the directory to put yourself in the `cancun` directory:

```
cd cancun
```

Now verify that you're in the directory `cancun`:

```
pwd
```

Moving and copying files and directories

The commands for moving and copying directories and files are `mv` for move and `cp` for copy. If you want to rename a file, you can use the `mv` command. No, you're not really moving the file, but in Linux (and Unix), the developers realized that renaming something was much like moving it. The format of the move command is

```
mv source destination
```

Create a file that you can practice moving. The `touch` command updates the time stamp on an existing file or creates an empty file if it doesn't exist. In this case, the file `test` doesn't exist and will be created by `touch`:

```
touch go
```

Move the new file:

```
mv go to
```

This command leaves the file in the same directory and changes its name to `to`. The file wasn't really moved — just renamed.

Now try moving the `to` file to the `veracruz` directory. To do that, you have to first move the file up and then move it into the `veracruz` directory. You can do it with one command:

```
mv to ../veracruz
```

The destination file uses the double-dot (..) designation; every directory contains a double-dot directory that points to the parent directory. This command tells Linux to go up one directory level and look for a directory named `veracruz` and then put the file into that directory with the name `newgoto` because you didn't specify any other name. If you do this instead:

```
mv go ../veracruz/now
```

the `go` file moves to the `veracruz` directory named `now`. Note that in both cases (with the file maintaining its name of `go` or taking the new name `now`), your current directory is still `cancun` and all your filenames are relative to that directory.

Strictly speaking, the file still hasn't really moved. The data bits are still on the same part of the disk where they were originally. The *file specification* (the directory path plus the filename) you use to talk about the file is different, so it appears to have moved.

Removing files and directories

The command for removing, or deleting, a file is `rm`. Using `rm` is straightforward. Create a dummy file to erase:

```
touch junk
```

You can delete the file with this command:

```
rm junk
```

You have removed the dummy file from the current directory. To remove a file from another directory, you need to provide a relative filename or an absolute filename. For example, if you want to expunge `now` from the `veracruz` directory, you type this line:

```
rm ../veracruz/now
```

You can use metacharacters (similar in many ways to Windows wildcards) with `rm`, but *be very careful* if you do so! When files are removed in Linux, they are gone forever — kaput, vanished — and can't be recovered.

This command removes *everything* in the current directory and all the directories under it that you have permission to remove:

```
[lidia@cancun lidia]$rm -r *
```

Do *not* give this command as root (the superuser)! You should always be careful when running any command as root, but be especially careful with commands that can erase entire directories and file systems.

To decrease the danger of removing lots of files inadvertently when you use metacharacters, be sure to use the `-i` option with `rm`, `cp`, `mv`, and various other commands. The `-i` option, which means *interactive,* lists each filename to be removed (with the `rm` command) or overwritten (with the `mv` or `cp` command). If you answer either **y** or **Y** to the question, the file is removed or overwritten, respectively. If you answer anything else, Linux leaves the file alone.

You can remove not only files but also directories. Suppose that you have an old directory, `/tmp/junk`, that you don't need any more. You can remove it and all its contents:

```
[lidia@cancun lidia]$rm -rf /tmp/junk
```

Giving the `rm` command these options (`r` and `f`) removes the `/tmp/junk` directory and all files and directories under it. The `r` option means to remove *recursively;* in recursion, the command works through every subdirectory in the parent directory. The `f` option issues the command *forcefully.* No prompts are given.

Changing File Ownership and Granting Permissions

All Linux files and directories have owners and are assigned a list of permissions. This system of *ownership* and *permissions* forms the basis for restricting and allowing users' access to files. File permissions can also be used to specify whether a file is executable as a command and to determine who can use the file or command.

Files and directories are owned by user accounts. User accounts are defined in the `/etc/passwd` file. For example, you created the root (superuser) user account when you installed Red Hat Linux in Chapter 3, and the installation system created the superuser home directory, `/root`, plus several configuration files (for example, `.bashrc`). The root user owns all those files and directories. If you created a regular user account — for example, `lidia` — that user's home directory and configuration files are all owned by `lidia`. Users can access and modify any files or directories they own.

Files and directories all have group ownership in addition to user ownership. Groups are defined by the `/etc/group` file and provide a secondary level of access. For example, you can assign group ownership to files you own and allow other users who belong to the group to access those files.

Files and directories are assigned permissions that permit or deny read, write, and execute access. Permissions are assigned to the owner, group, or non-owner of the file or directory. Non-owners are referred to as "other." The owner, group, or other permissions are independent of each other.

Using the `ls` command with the `-l` option allows you to see the file's permissions along with other relevant information, such as who owns the file, which group of people have permission to access or modify the file, the size of the file or directory, the last time the file was modified, and its name.

First, create a file and then list it:

```
[lidia@cancun lidia]$ touch gotowork
[lidia@cancun lidia]$ ls -l gotowork
-rw-rw-r-- owner group 0 Feb 3  16:00 gotowork
```

The `-rw-rw-r--` characters are the permissions for the `gotowork` file: The owner is you, and the group is probably you, but may be someone or something else, depending on how your system is set up and administered.

You may be wondering how you can become an owner of a file. You're automatically the owner of any file you create, which makes sense. As the owner, you can change the default file permissions — and even the ownership. If you change the file ownership, however, *you* lose ownership privileges.

To change the ownership of a file or a directory, use the chown command. (Get it? chown — *ch*ange *own*ership.) You generally have to be root to do this.

Suppose that you have decided to settle down and lead a more contemplative life, one more in line with a new profession of haiku writing. Someone else will have to plan the weekend sprees and all-night bashes. So you give up ownership of the gotowork file:

```
[lidia@cancun lidia]$chown root gotowork
```

This command changes the ownership of gotowork to root. To change it back, you can use the chown command, but you have to do it as root.

Files and users all belong to *groups*. In the gotowork example, the group consists of users. Having groups enables you to give large numbers of users — but not all users — access to files. Group permissions and ownership are handy for making sure that the members of a special project or workgroup have access to files needed by the entire group.

To see which groups are available to you on your system, take a look at the /etc/group file. To do so, use the more command. You see a file that looks somewhat like this:

```
root::0:root
bin::1:root,bin,daemon
...
nobody::99:
users::100:
floppy:x:19:
.....
your_user_name::500:your_user_name
```

where *your_user_name* is the login name you use for your account. Remember that the file doesn't look exactly like this — just similar. The names at the beginning of the line are the group names. The names at the end of the line (such as root, bin, and daemon) are user-group names that can belong to the user-group list.

To change the group the file belongs to, log in as root and use the chgrp command. Its syntax is the same as that of the chown command. For example, to change the group that gotowork belongs to, you issue this command:

```
[lidia@cancun lidia]$chgrp newgroupname gotowork
```

Red Hat assigns a unique group to each user. For example, when you add the first user to your system, that user gets the user ID and group ID of 500. The next user receives the user ID and group ID of 501, and so on. This system gives you lots of control over who gets what access to your files.

Making Your Own Rules

You, as the owner of a file, can specify permissions for reading, writing to, or executing a file. You can also determine who (yourself, a group of people, or everyone in general) can do these actions on a file. What do these permissions mean? Read on (you have our permission):

- **Read permission:** You can read the file. For a directory, read permission allows the `ls` command to list the names of the files in the directory. You must also have execute permission for the directory name to use the `-l` option of the `ls` command or to change to that directory.
- **Write permission:** You can modify the file. For a directory, you can create or delete files inside that directory.
- **Execute permission:** You can type the name of the file and execute it. You can't view or copy the file unless you also have read permission. Files containing executable Linux commands, called *shell scripts,* must therefore be both executable and readable by the person executing them. Programs written in a compiled language, such as C, however, must have only executable permissions, to protect them from being copied where they shouldn't be copied.

  For a directory, execute permission means that you can change to that directory (with `cd`). Unless you also have read permission for the directory, `ls -l` doesn't work. You can list directories and files in that directory, but you can't see additional information about the files or directories by using just an `ls -l` command. This arrangement may seem strange, but it's useful for security.

The first character of a file permission is a hyphen (-) if it's a file; the first character of a directory is `d`. The nine other characters are read, write, and execute positions for each of the three categories of file permissions:

- Owner (also known as the user)
- Group
- Others

Your `gotowork` file, for example, may show these permissions when listed with the `ls -l gotowork` command:

```
-rw-rw-r--
```

The hyphen (-) in the first position indicates that it's a regular file (not a directory or other special file). The next characters (`rw-`) are the owner's permissions. The owner can read and write to the file, but can't execute it.

The next three characters (`rw-`) are the group's permissions. The group also has read-write access to the file. The last three characters (`r--`) are the others' permissions, which are read-only.

`[-][rw-][rw-][r--]` illustrates the four parts of the permissions: the file type followed by three sets of triplets, indicating the read, write, and execute permissions for the owner, group, and *other* users of the file (meaning *everyone else*).

You can specify most file permissions by using only six letters:

- **ugo** stands for — no, not a car — user (or owner), group, and other.
- **rwx** stands for *r*ead, *w*rite, and e*x*ecute.

These six letters, and some symbols, such as the equal sign (=) and commas, are put together into a specification of how you want to set the file's permissions.

The command for changing permissions is `chmod`. Here's its syntax:

```
chmod specification filename
```

Change the mode of `gotowork` to give users the ability to read, write, and execute a file:

```
chmod u=rwx gotowork
```

That was easy enough. What if you want to give the group permission to only read and execute the file? You execute this command:

```
chmod g=rx gotowork
```

This command doesn't affect the permissions for owner or other — just the group's permissions. You can set the permission bits in other ways. But because this way is so simple, why use any other?

Appendix D

Becoming a Suit: Managing the Red Hat Linux File System

In This Appendix

- Mounting and unmounting a file system
- Increasing disk space with a new drive or memory stick

Managing the Linux file system isn't a complex job, but it's an important one. You have the responsibility of managing the Linux file system and ensuring that users (even if you're the only user) have access to secure, uncorrupted data. You're the manager (yes, — gag — a *suit*) of your file system.

This chapter introduces you to managing your Linux file system. Consider yourself a management trainee. When you're done reading this chapter, feel free to take a nice, long, expensive lunch.

Mounting and Unmounting a File System

Red Hat Linux and other Unix-like operating systems use files in different ways from MS-DOS, Windows, and Macintosh operating systems. In Linux, *everything* is stored as files in predictable locations in the directory structure; Linux even stores commands as files. Like other modern operating systems, it has a tree-structured, hierarchical directory organization: the *file system.*

All user-available disk space is combined in a single directory tree. The base of this system is the *root directory* (not to be confused with the root user), designated with a slash (/). A file system's contents are made available to Linux by using the mounting process. *Mounting* a file system makes Linux aware of the files and directories it contains. This process is just like mounting a horse — except that no horse is involved.

Unlike in the Windows world, Linux file systems, except for `/root`, must be explicitly *mounted* or *unmounted,* which means that file systems can be connected to or disconnected from the directory tree.

Mounting Windows files from a floppy disk

File system mounting and unmounting provide a good example of the difference between Linux and Windows. If you use a floppy disk or CD with Windows, you just insert it into the drive and you have immediate access to it. With Linux, you must insert the floppy disk into the drive and then explicitly mount it. Sound complicated? Not really.

You can mount a Windows hard drive partition or floppy on your Linux computer. You can read and write to FAT or FAT32 but can only read from NTFS file systems. These steps show you how to mount a Windows floppy:

1. **Insert a Windows MS–DOS-formatted floppy disk into the drive, click the GNOME Menu button, and choose System Tools⇨Disk Management. Enter the root password if requested.**
2. **Select the floppy disk and click the Mount button.**

   You know that the floppy disk has mounted successfully when a floppy disk icon is displayed on the left side of the screen.

   You can now read and write to the floppy disk (unless the read-only tab on the disk is set).
3. **Click the Exit button to close the utility.**

Red Hat Linux and GNOME are configured to automatically start the process that mounts your floppy disk or CD when you insert it into the drive. We use the manual method here to show you how the process works. To manually mount the floppy in the command-line interface, log in as root, open the terminal window, and run this command:

```
mount _t msdos /dev/fd0 /mnt/floppy
```

Unmounting file systems

Unmounting a Linux file system is a little simpler than mounting one. Because the file system is already mounted, you don't have to specify any options or other information. You just have to tell the Red Hat disk management druid to unmount the file system. Follow these steps:

1. **Click the Main Menu button and choose System Tools⇨Disk Management. Enter the root password if prompted.**
2. **When the User Mount Tool window appears, click the button to the right of the file system in which you're interested.**

The button indicates whether the file system is mounted or unmounted. After a few seconds, the button changes from Unmount to Mount to show that it has been unmounted.

3. **Click the Exit button to close the utility.**

   The file system is unmounted. If the file system is a removable type, such as a floppy disk or CD, you can remove it. Otherwise, the file system is simply not available for use until you remount it.

You can run the `eject` command from a `bash` shell to eject a CD. You have to unmount the CD first and then enter the `eject` command. Otherwise, to eject a CD, you must unmount it and then press the eject button on the CD-ROM drive. In either case, you can't eject the CD until you have unmounted it.

Adding a Disk Drive

Sooner or later, life catches up with us and you're likely to need or want a bigger house or car or diamond in your tooth, or whatever. The same goes for disk space, in which case you want to add another disk drive.

The first step to increasing your drive space is to add a new storage device. It can be a hard drive (IDE or SCSI), but also a USB or FireWire memory stick. These steps describe the general process of adding a storage device and then formatting and mounting it:

1. **Install the hard drive or insert the USB or FireWire device.**

   If the device is an IDE or SCSI hard drive, turn off the power to your computer and monitor. Unplug the power cable and open the computer case. (Don't cut yourself on the sometimes sharp metal edges when reaching into the computer.) Use the antistatic strap that comes with the hard drive; follow the instructions included with the strap.

   Most PCs use IDE controllers. SCSI-based PCs are more expensive and aren't commonly found in consumer PCs; these types are more common in the commercial realm. IDE-based PCs have two IDE controllers. Each device can control as many as two IDE devices. Ribbon cables connect the controller to the devices.

   You have to configure your new disk to function as a slave device if it's connected to a ribbon cable or IDE controller that already has another device (hard drive or CD-ROM) attached.

   If the device is a USB or FireWire memory stick, skip to Step 3.

2. **Reboot your computer and run the `dmesg` command from a GNOME Terminal window.**

If you added an IDE drive, look for the mention of an `hdx` device, where *x* is replaced with the letter *b, c, d,* or *e.* This information tells you that your kernel "saw" the new hard drive as it booted:

```
hdb: HITACHI_DK227A-50, 4789MB w/512KB
        Cache,CHS=610/255/63
```

If you added a SCSI drive, the general device type is `sdx`.

3. **Partition the new drive.**

   Run this command for an IDE drive:

   ```
   fdisk /dev/hdb
   ```

   Use the command `fdisk /dev/sda` for a USB or FireWire memory stick. The memory stick appears as a SCSI device, such as `/dev/sda`, `/dev/sdb`, or `/dev/sdc`, depending on your computer's configuration.

   You can find out more information about *fdisk* at `www.redhat.com/docs/manuals/linux/RHL-10-Manual/install-guide/`.

4. **Create a file system on the new partition (change the devices as appropriate).**

   When using an IDE or SCSI drive, for example, enter this command:

   ```
   mkfs /dev/hdb
   ```

   For a USB memory stick, enter this command:

   ```
   mkfs /dev/sdc
   ```

5. **Create a new directory in which to mount the new device:**

   ```
   mkdir /space
   ```

6. **Mount the newly formatted drive by using the appropriate command:**

   ```
   mount /dev/hdb /space
   ```

   or

   ```
   mount /dev/sdc /space
   ```

Your drive has been physically added to your system and partitioned, and you have added file systems. The drive is ready to join the rest of the file system.

Appendix E

Revving Up RPM

In This Appendix

- RPM explained
- What RPM does
- The Red Hat Package Manager
- Manually using RPM

This appendix introduces you to the Red Hat Package Manager (RPM). Red Hat, Inc., developed RPM in conjunction with another Linux distributor, Caldera Systems. RPM makes a grand effort to reduce the amount of work you have to do when you install software. In other words, RPM makes installing, updating, and removing software an automatic process. Woo-hoo!

Although other package managers are available, RPM has become the most popular system for installing, modifying, and transporting Linux software. This handy-dandy tool is a big reason that Red Hat is the de facto Linux distribution leader. Motor through this chapter to find out everything you need to know about RPM.

Introducing RPM

One of the primary reasons that the Red Hat Linux distribution became popular was that it added value for its customers with technologies such as Red Hat Package Manager (RPM).

All the software that was installed during the Red Hat installation process is stored in RPM's giving format, called packages. *Packages* are a collection of individual software (applications, libraries, and documentation, for example) contained in one file.

The package-management concept has been around for quite a while, with all the major Unix vendors supplying their own systems. The idea is to distribute software in a single file and have a package manager do the work of installing, or uninstalling, and managing the individual files. The Linux world has benefited greatly from this system, which simplifies the distribution and use of software.

You *can* install software without RPM, but we're not sure why you would want to — the RPM package contains everything you need to install and run an application. For example, if you didn't have the RPM package, installing Mozilla would work a little something like this: You would have to install the individual pieces that make up the Mozilla system, which can require dozens or more steps. You can also install, update, or uninstall RPM software (see the following section for details).

We remember, back in the day, when we used the Linux operating system for the first time. We had to install all the software using the dreaded tape archive system (tar). Trust us: Installing, maintaining, and upgrading Linux with tar was a difficult task. RPM has made life easy.

The `/mnt/cdrom/RedHat/RPMS` directory contains all the RPM packages.

Taking a Look at What RPM Does

RPM performs three basic functions: It installs, upgrades, and removes packages. In addition to these functions, it can find out all sorts of information about installed and yet-to-be-installed packages. (All this, and it washes windows too.) Here's a brief rundown of each function:

- **Installing packages:** RPM installs software. Software systems, such as Mozilla, have files of all types that must be put into certain locations in order to work properly. For example, under Red Hat, some (but not all) of the Mozilla files need to go into the `/usr/bin` directory. RPM performs this organizational stuff automatically, without any fuss or muss.

  RPM not only installs files in their proper directories but also performs tasks such as creating the directories and running scripts to do the things that need to be done. (It's such a tidy and organized little scamp.)

- **Upgrading packages:** Gone are the days when updating a system was worse than going to the dentist. RPM acts like the personal Linux assistant you wish you had by updating existing software packages for you. RPM also keeps track of, in a database of its own, all the packages you have installed. When you upgrade a package, RPM does all the bookkeeping chores and replaces only the files that need to be replaced. It also saves the configuration files it replaces.

- **Removing packages:** The package database the RPM keeps is also useful in removing packages. To put it simply, RPM takes out the trash. (Housekeeping was never so easy.) RPM goes to each file and uninstalls it. Directories belonging to the package are also removed when no files from other packages occupy them.

- **Querying packages and files:** RPM can also give you a great deal of information about a package and its files. You can use the query function to find out the function of a package and which files belong to it. RPM can also work on the RPM packages themselves, regardless of whether they have been installed.
- **Verifying packages:** RPM can validate an installed package against a `checksum` (a computer fingerprint) to see whether and how it has been changed. This feature is useful for security reasons. If you suspect that a file or system has been hacked, you can use RPM to find out how it has changed.

RPM packages often include configuration files as part of their installation. If you erase an RPM package, those configuration files are *not* deleted but instead are renamed by appending the suffix `.rpmsave` to the end of the original filename. For example, removing the Kerberos package, `krbafs`, saves the configuration file by renaming `/etc/krb.conf` to `/etc/krb.conf.rpmsave`.

When you remove a package, RPM removes the associated files and directories. RPM cleans up after itself — what Martha Stewart would definitely call "a good thing."

Using the Red Hat Package Manager

Red Hat Linux provides a tool named Red Hat Package Manager for working with RPM packages. The package manager graphical tool provides all the functions for managing RPMs. It's like putting an automatic transmission on a car: The Package Manger does the shifting for you.

Okay, the package manager does the shifting for you, but you still have to drive it. The package manager provides easy access to RPM functions, such as install, upgrade, uninstall, query, and verify. This section describes how to use the package manager to rev up your RPM.

To start the package manager, click the GNOME Menu button and choose System Settings⇨Add/Remove Applications. If you aren't logged in as root, type the root password in the Input window when you're prompted. A progress window appears briefly while the package manager determines which packages you have installed. After "thinking," the Package Management window appears.

The package manager displays all the Red Hat package groups installed by default on your system. Individual packages are organized into groups, such as the X Window System and GNOME. When the check box to the left of a group is active, designated by a plus sign (+), one or more packages from that group is installed. The number to the right of the package group shows how many packages of the total number in that group are installed.

Clicking the Details option opens the GNOME Desktop Environment Package Details window, which shows all the base and optional packages in the group; short, one-line descriptions of each package are also displayed next to each package. Base packages are always installed with a package group. Optional packages are, well, optionally installed.

This may be a *For Dummies* book, but you, of course, are no dummy. It's obvious what the GNOME RPM buttons, displayed along the top of the GNOME RPM window, are used for. This section describes how to use them for their intended functions.

Installing an RPM package from a CD-ROM

When you install your Red Hat Linux system, all the software that is copied to your hard drive from the CD-ROM comes from RPM packages. When you want to add software from the companion DVD or an RPM repository, such as `www.freshmeat.net`, or from Red Hat, at `www.redhat.com`, you can do so by using the Install button. To install an RPM package from a CD-ROM, follow these steps:

1. **Start the package manager: Choose System Tools⇨Add/Remove Packages.**

   Enter the root password in the Information window if you're prompted.

2. **When the Add and Remove Software window opens, select the package group you want to install.**

   For example, if you want to install the Mozilla e-mail client, you have to do some exploring first. Scroll down to the Graphical Internet package group. The short description next to the package group says "This group includes graphical e-mail, Web, and chat clients," which indicates that you're on the right path.

3. **Click the Details button to find out the details of the package you're installing.**

   For example, select the Graphical Internet group and the Graphical Internet Package Details window opens. You see that the Mozilla mail client is included.

4. **Select the radio button next to the menu option.**

5. **Click the Close button to return to the Package Management window.**

6. **Click the Install button and the Preparing Systems Update window opens.**

The package manager determines which additional packages are needed by the package you're installing. After the dependencies are determined, the Completed System Preparation window displays the number of packages to be installed and how much disk space they require.

7. **Click the Continue button.**

   The Information window opens and you're prompted to insert the DVD.

8. **Insert the CD and click OK.**

   The System Update Progress Installing window shows a progress meter.

9. **Insert additional CDs, if prompted, and click the OK button in the Information window.**

10. **After the installation process is finished, the System Update Process window shows the Update Complete message.**

11. **Click the OK button to return to the Add and Remove Software window.**

Using Nautilus to install a package

You can use the Nautilus file manager to install packages too. Nautilus acts as a front end to Red Hat Package Manager. You use Nautilus to select the packages you want to manipulate and the rest is taken care of for you.

These instructions describe how to use Nautilus to install an RPM package or packages from a CD-ROM:

1. **Insert a CD containing the RPM packages you want to install.**

   You can install a package from your hard disk too. If you have a package stored, for example, in your home directory, skip to Step 3.

2. **Insert the CD-ROM and a Nautilus window showing the CD opens.**

3. **Find the package you want to install and double-click the package you want to install.**

   If you're not logged in as root, you're prompted to enter the root password. Enter the password if and when you're prompted.

4. **Click the Continue button when the Completed System Preparation window opens.**

   If the package to be installed requires other packages, they're displayed in the Completed System Preparation window; they get installed too. You can also see more information about the packages to be installed by clicking the Details button.

5. **The Updating system window opens and shows the progress of the package-installation process.**

Red Hat installs the package for you, and the Updating System window closes. You're prompted to insert other CD-ROMs if necessary.

Until the advent of the RPM (and the Debian package manager on Debian Linux systems), Linux software was distributed only by tar archives, which are sometimes referred to as *tarballs,* or more descriptively, *hairballs.* The tar file storage mechanism stores one or more files in a single file in a tar format. A tar file has the `.tar` file suffix; if the tar file is compressed, it has a suffix like `.tgz` or `.tar.gz`. Using the tar-based distribution system is sufficient if your software doesn't change often and you're young. But when you need to upgrade or change software or work with complex software systems, tar becomes quite difficult to work with. Rather than spend your life spitting up hairballs, use systems such as RPM to greatly simplify your life.

Removing an RPM package

You can remove Red Hat packages as easily as you install them. Use the RPM erase (`-e`) function, which is the opposite of the install (`-i`) function. The package manager removes a package when you unselect an installed package. These steps describe how to remove a package:

1. **Click the GNOME Menu button and choose System Settings⇨Add/Remove Packages.**
2. **Enter the root password in the Information window, if you're prompted.**

   The Package Management window opens.
3. **Click the Remove Software button to open the Remove Package Groups menu.**
4. **Click the Remove button to select the package group that contains the package you want to remove.**

   For example, to remove a package in the Mail Server group, select the option to the left of the Mail Server group, if it's blank. (Leave the radio button alone if it's already selected.)
5. **Select the radio button to the left of the package you want to remove.**

   The check mark disappears.
6. **Click the Remove Packages button.**

   The Preparing System Update dialog box opens briefly, and you return to the Completed System Preparation window.
7. **Click the Continue button.**

   The package (or packages) is removed
8. **Click the Continue button in the Completed System Preparation window.**

   The package (or packages) is removed.
9. **After the package-removal process is finished, click the OK button.**

   You return to the Add or Remove Software window.

Be sure that you really want to get rid of the package because when you remove a package, it's gone — as in *gone.* Okay, okay, maybe we're being a little dramatic. You can always go online to a site like `www.freshmeat.net` or `www.redhat.com`. From there, you can download more packages to install. We recommend that you do so. Some new tool is always coming out that can help optimize your Red Hat Linux computing experience.

Manual Shifting with RPM

The first part of this chapter concentrates on using Red Hat Package Manager to install and remove packages. But you also have the option using the `rpm` command. It provides additional features for installation and removal functions. You can use `rpm` to install, update, remove, and query packages. This section provides examples of how to use the manual `rpm` command.

Manually installing and upgrading packages

The `RPM -i` parameter indicates that an installation will take place. You can add Verbose mode (which provides additional information) by using the `-v` option. (You can combine options into a single group; for example, `-i -v` can become `-iv`.) Follow these instructions to install and upgrade packages:

1. **Log in as root.**
2. **Open a terminal emulator window by clicking the terminal icon in the GNOME Panel (refer to Chapter 4 for instructions).**

   The GNOME Terminal emulator window opens.
3. **To add the package, type this command from a terminal window:**

   ```
   rpm -iv /mnt/cdrom/RedHat/RPMS/mozilla-mail*
   ```

Alternatively, you can upgrade a package that has already been installed on your system. Substitute the RPM upgrade option, `-U`, in place of the install option, `-i`. For example, this command updates the Mozilla e-mail client package:

```
rpm -Uv /mnt/cdrom/RedHat/RPMS/mozilla-mail*
```

The files that constitute the newer Mozilla-mail package overwrite the older version. Existing configurations, however, are saved by adding the `.rpmsave` suffix to the configuration file.

Manually removing packages

RPM packages are good residents on your computer because they lend themselves to easy removal. The `rpm` command permits you to remove packages via the erase (`-e`) function.

Suppose that you're not so fond of the Mozilla e-mail client because you like the Evolution client better. No problem: Go ahead and remove the Mozilla mail package. To remove an RPM package, follow these steps:

1. **Log in as root and open a terminal emulator window.**

   The GNOME Terminal window opens.

2. **Enter this command to find the name of the package to remove:**

   ```
   rpm -qa | grep mozilla
   ```

   You should see these results:

   ```
   mozilla-nss-1.0.1-10
   mozilla-1.0.1-10
   mozilla-nspr-1.0.1-10
   mozilla-psm-1.0.1-10
   mozilla-mail-1.0.1-10
   ```

   You need to know the name of the package before you can remove it. We use this step to display all installed Mozilla packages to find the name of the package.

3. **You can also find out about the package by using this command:**

   ```
   rpm -qi mozilla-mail
   ```

   Alternatively, you can display a list of all installed packages by using the `rpm -qa` command. Run the `man rpm` command to find query options.

4. **Enter this command to remove the Mozilla e-mail client:**

   ```
   rpm -e mozilla-mail
   ```

Appendix F

About the DVD

The DVD-ROM that comes with this book contains the full Red Hat Linux 10 (now named Fedora Core) distribution. This appendix describes the minimum computer configuration you need in order to install Red Hat Linux and also some of what you get on the companion DVD-ROM.

If your computer isn't capable of reading DVD-ROMs, you can get the Red Hat Linux 10 (Fedora Core) distribution on CD-ROMs by sending in the coupon in the back of this book.

Although the DVD-ROM contains the Linux kernel and supporting GNU programs and applications, it doesn't carry some applications described in this book. You must download from the Internet applications such as Wine and Icecast2. We describe where and how to download all the applications we discuss in this book that aren't on the companion DVD-ROM.

System Requirements

Make sure that your computer meets the minimum system requirements listed here and in Chapter 3. More resources are needed for a graphical workstation. If your computer doesn't match up to most of these requirements, you may have problems installing and running Red Hat Linux:

- A Pentium-class PC with a 133MHz or faster processor is recommended.
- For reasonable graphics performance using the X Window System, we recommend at least 64MB, and preferably 256MB, of main memory. You can never have too much memory, and these numbers are the least amount you should have.
- You can run Linux on less than 128MB of memory if you don't want graphics. Nongraphical Linux systems are typically used as servers.

- Red Hat provides several installation classes that install different bundles of software. The various classes take up different amounts of space, of course. The basic installation, Personal Desktop, takes 2.1GB of disk space. The Workstation installation that we use in Chapter 3 consumes roughly 2.6GB. We recommend that your computer have a minimum of 3GB so that you have some room to play with after you install Linux.
- A DVD-ROM drive, (and, optionally, a 3¼-inch floppy disk drive plus a blank 3¼-inch disk), a multisync monitor, an internal IDE or SCSI hard drive, a keyboard, and a mouse.

The instructions for installing the Red Hat Linux operating system from the DVD-ROM are detailed in Part I. After you install the software, return the DVD-ROM to its plastic jacket, or another appropriate place, for safekeeping.

What You Find

You can download the installation manual from the Red Hat Web site (`www.redhat.com/support`).

You can view much of the documentation on this DVD-ROM through an HTML viewer, such as Mozilla, which is also included on the DVD-ROM; or you can print it. You can also view most of the documentation from other operating systems, such as DOS, Windows, or Unix.

The DVD-ROM has a full implementation of Linux, and to list all the accompanying tools and utilities would take too much room. The DVD-ROM includes, briefly, most of the software so that you can

- Access the Internet
- Write programs in several computer languages
- Create and manipulate images
- Create, manipulate, and play back sounds (if you have a sound card)
- Play certain games
- Work with electrical design

For more information about Red Hat Linux agreements and installation, see the pages at the end of this book following the index.

If You Have Problems (Of the DVD Kind)

We tried our best to test various computers with the minimum system requirements. Alas, your computer may differ, and Linux may not install or work as stated.

The two likeliest problems are that you don't have enough RAM for the programs you want to use or you have some hardware that Linux doesn't support. Luckily, the latter problem occurs less frequently each day as more hardware is supported by Linux.

You may also have one or more FireWire, USB, or SCSI hard drives that use a driver (called a *kernel module* in Linux parlance) not supported by Linux or a controller that is simply too new for the Linux development team to have given it the proper support at the time the DVD-ROM was pressed.

If you still have trouble with the DVD-ROM, call the Wiley Product Technical Support phone number: 800-762-2974. Outside the United States, call 1-317-572-3994. You can also contact Wiley Product Technical Support on the Internet, at `www.wiley.com/techsupport`. Wiley Publishing, Inc., provides technical support for only installation and other general quality-control items; for technical support for the applications themselves, consult the program's vendor or author.

To place additional orders or to request information about other Wiley products, call 800-225-5945.

Index

• A •

• B •

• C •

• D •

• E •

• F •

• G •

• H •

• I •

• N •

• O •

• P •

• T •

• U •

Notes

Notes

Notes

Notes

FOR DUMMIES®

A world of resources to help you grow

TRAVEL

0-7645-5453-0

0-7645-5438-7

0-7645-5444-1

Also available:

America's National Parks For Dummies (0-7645-6204-5)
Caribbean For Dummies (0-7645-5445-X)
Cruise Vacations For Dummies 2003 (0-7645-5459-X)
Europe For Dummies (0-7645-5456-5)
Ireland For Dummies (0-7645-6199-5)
France For Dummies (0-7645-6292-4)
Las Vegas For Dummi (0-7645-5448-4)
London For Dummies (0-7645-5416-6)
Mexico's Beach Resor For Dummies (0-7645-6262-2)
Paris For Dummies (0-7645-5494-8)
RV Vacations For Dur (0-7645-5443-3)

EDUCATION & TEST PREPARATION

0-7645-5194-9

0-7645-5325-9

0-7645-5249-X

Also available:

The ACT For Dummies (0-7645-5210-4)
Chemistry For Dummies (0-7645-5430-1)
English Grammar For Dummies (0-7645-5322-4)
French For Dummies (0-7645-5193-0)
GMAT For Dummies (0-7645-5251-1)
Inglés Para Dummies (0-7645-5427-1)
Italian For Dummies (0-7645-5196-5)
Research Papers For D (0-7645-5426-3)
SAT I For Dummies (0-7645-5472-7)
U.S. History For Dumr (0-7645-5249-X)
World History For Du (0-7645-5242-2)

HEALTH, SELF-HELP & SPIRITUALITY

0-7645-5154-X

0-7645-5302-X

0-7645-5418-2

Also available:

The Bible For Dummies (0-7645-5296-1)
Controlling Cholesterol For Dummies (0-7645-5440-9)
Dating For Dummies (0-7645-5072-1)
Dieting For Dummies (0-7645-5126-4)
High Blood Pressure For Dummies (0-7645-5424-7)
Judaism For Dummies (0-7645-5299-6)
Menopause For Dum (0-7645-5458-1)
Nutrition For Dummi (0-7645-5180-9)
Potty Training For Du (0-7645-5417-4)
Pregnancy For Dumr (0-7645-5074-8)
Rekindling Romance Dummies (0-7645-5303-8)
Religion For Dummie (0-7645-5264-3)

Available wherever books are sold. Go to www.dummies.com or call 1-877-762-2974 to order direc

GNU General Public License

Version 2, June 1991

Preamble

The licenses for most software are designed to take away your freedom to share and change it. By contrast, the GNU General Public License is intended to guarantee your freedom to share and change free software—to make sure the software is free for all its users. This General Public License applies to most of the Free Software Foundation's software and to any other program whose authors commit to using it. (Some other Free Software Foundation software is covered by the GNU Library General Public License instead.) You can apply it to your programs, too.

When we speak of free software, we are referring to freedom, not price. Our General Public Licenses are designed to make sure that you have the freedom to distribute copies of free software (and charge for this service if you wish), that you receive source code or can get it if you want it, that you can change the software or use pieces of it in new free programs; and that you know you can do these things.

To protect your rights, we need to make restrictions that forbid anyone to deny you these rights or to ask you to surrender the rights. These restrictions translate to certain responsibilities for you if you distribute copies of the software, or if you modify it.

For example, if you distribute copies of such a program, whether gratis or for a fee, you must give the recipients all the rights that you have. You must make sure that they, too, receive or can get the source code. And you must show them these terms so they know their rights.

We protect your rights with two steps: (1) copyright the software, and (2) offer you this license which gives you legal permission to copy, distribute and/or modify the software.

Also, for each author's protection and ours, we want to make certain that everyone understands that there is no warranty for this free software. If the software is modified by someone else and passed on, we want its recipients to know that what they have is not the original, so that any problems introduced by others will not reflect on the original authors' reputations.

Finally, any free program is threatened constantly by software patents. We wish to avoid the danger that redistributors of a free program will individually obtain patent licenses, in effect making the program proprietary. To prevent this, we have made it clear that any patent must be licensed for everyone's free use or not licensed at all.

The precise terms and conditions for copying, distribution and modification follow.

Terms and Conditions for Copying, Distribution, and Modification

0. This License applies to any program or other work which contains a notice placed by the copyright holder saying it may be distributed under the terms of this General Public License. The "Program", below, refers to any such program or work, and a "work based on the Program" means either the Program or any derivative work under copyright law: that is to say, a work containing the Program or a portion of it, either verbatim or with modifications and/or translated into another language. (Hereinafter, translation is included without limitation in the term "modification".) Each licensee is addressed as "you".

   Activities other than copying, distribution and modification are not covered by this License; they are outside its scope. The act of running the Program is not restricted, and the output from the Program is covered only if its contents constitute a work based on the Program (independent of having been made by running the Program). Whether that is true depends on what the Program does.

1. You may copy and distribute verbatim copies of the Program's source code as you receive it, in any medium, provided that you conspicuously and appropriately publish on each copy an appropriate copyright notice and disclaimer of warranty; keep intact all the notices that refer to this License and to the absence of any warranty; and give any other recipients of the Program a copy of this License along with the Program.

   You may charge a fee for the physical act of transferring a copy, and you may at your option offer warranty protection in exchange for a fee.

2. You may modify your copy or copies of the Program or any portion of it, thus forming a work based on the Program, and copy and distribute such modifications or work under the terms of Section 1 above, provided that you also meet all of these conditions:

   a) You must cause the modified files to carry prominent notices stating that you changed the files and the date of any change.

   b) You must cause any work that you distribute or publish, that in whole or in part contains or is derived from the Program or any part thereof, to be licensed as a whole at no charge to all third parties under the terms of this License.

   c) If the modified program normally reads commands interactively when run, you must cause it, when started running for such interactive use in the most ordinary way, to print or display an announcement including an appropriate copyright notice and a notice that there is no warranty (or else, saying that you provide a warranty) and that users may redistribute the program under these conditions, and telling the user how to view a copy of this License. (Exception: if the Program itself is interactive but does not normally print such an announcement, your work based on the Program is not required to print an announcement.)

   These requirements apply to the modified work as a whole. If identifiable sections of that work are not derived from the Program, and can be reasonably considered independent and separate works in themselves, then this License, and its terms, do not apply to those sections when you distribute them as separate works. But when you distribute the same sections as part of a whole which is a work based on the Program, the distribution of the whole must be on the terms of this License, whose permissions for other licensees extend to the entire whole, and thus to each and every part regardless of who wrote it.

   Thus, it is not the intent of this section to claim rights or contest your rights to work written entirely by you; rather, the intent is to exercise the right to control the distribution of derivative or collective works based on the Program.

In addition, mere aggregation of another work not based on the Program with the Program (or with a work based on the Program) on a volume of a storage or distribution medium does not bring the other work under the scope of this License.

3. You may copy and distribute the Program (or a work based on it, under Section 2) in object code or executable form under the terms of Sections 1 and 2 above provided that you also do one of the following:

   a) Accompany it with the complete corresponding machine-readable source code, which must be distributed under the terms of Sections 1 and 2 above on a medium customarily used for software interchange; or,

   b) Accompany it with a written offer, valid for at least three years, to give any third party, for a charge no more than your cost of physically performing source distribution, a complete machine-readable copy of the corresponding source code, to be distributed under the terms of Sections 1 and 2 above on a medium customarily used for software interchange; or,

   c) Accompany it with the information you received as to the offer to distribute corresponding source code. (This alternative is allowed only for noncommercial distribution and only if you received the program in object code or executable form with such an offer, in accord with Subsection b above.)

   The source code for a work means the preferred form of the work for making modifications to it. For an executable work, complete source code means all the source code for all modules it contains, plus any associated interface definition files, plus the scripts used to control compilation and installation of the executable. However, as a special exception, the source code distributed need not include anything that is normally distributed (in either source or binary form) with the major components (compiler, kernel, and so on) of the operating system on which the executable runs, unless that component itself accompanies the executable.

   If distribution of executable or object code is made by offering access to copy from a designated place, then offering equivalent access to copy the source code from the same place counts as distribution of the source code, even though third parties are not compelled to copy the source along with the object code.

4. You may not copy, modify, sublicense, or distribute the Program except as expressly provided under this License. Any attempt otherwise to copy, modify, sublicense or distribute the Program is void, and will automatically terminate your rights under this License. However, parties who have received copies, or rights, from you under this License will not have their licenses terminated so long as such parties remain in full compliance.

5. You are not required to accept this License, since you have not signed it. However, nothing else grants you permission to modify or distribute the Program or its derivative works. These actions are prohibited by law if you do not accept this License. Therefore, by modifying or distributing the Program (or any work based on the Program), you indicate your acceptance of this License to do so, and all its terms and conditions for copying, distributing or modifying the Program or works based on it.

6. Each time you redistribute the Program (or any work based on the Program), the recipient automatically receives a license from the original licensor to copy, distribute or modify the Program subject to these terms and conditions. You may not impose any further restrictions on the recipients' exercise of the rights granted herein. You are not responsible for enforcing compliance by third parties to this License.

7. If, as a consequence of a court judgment or allegation of patent infringement or for any other reason (not limited to patent issues), conditions are imposed on you (whether by court order, agreement or otherwise) that contradict the conditions of this License, they do not excuse you from the conditions of this License. If you cannot distribute so as to satisfy simultaneously your obligations under this License and any other pertinent obligations, then as a consequence you may not distribute the Program at all. For example, if a patent license would not permit royalty-free redistribution of the Program by all those who receive copies directly or indirectly through you, then the only way you could satisfy both it and this License would be to refrain entirely from distribution of the Program.

   If any portion of this section is held invalid or unenforceable under any particular circumstance, the balance of the section is intended to apply and the section as a whole is intended to apply in other circumstances.

   It is not the purpose of this section to induce you to infringe any patents or other property right claims or to contest validity of any such claims; this section has the sole purpose of protecting the integrity of the free software distribution system, which is implemented by public license practices. Many people have made generous contributions to the wide range of software distributed through that system in reliance on consistent application of that system; it is up to the author/donor to decide if he or she is willing to distribute software through any other system and a licensee cannot impose that choice.

   This section is intended to make thoroughly clear what is believed to be a consequence of the rest of this License.

8. If the distribution and/or use of the Program is restricted in certain countries either by patents or by copyrighted interfaces, the original copyright holder who places the Program under this License may add an explicit geographical distribution limitation excluding those countries, so that distribution is permitted only in or among countries not thus excluded. In such case, this License incorporates the limitation as if written in the body of this License.

9. The Free Software Foundation may publish revised and/or new versions of the General Public License from time to time. Such new versions will be similar in spirit to the present version, but may differ in detail to address new problems or concerns.

   Each version is given a distinguishing version number. If the Program specifies a version number of this License which applies to it and "any later version", you have the option of following the terms and conditions either of that version or of any later version published by the Free Software Foundation. If the Program does not specify a version number of this License, you may choose any version ever published by the Free Software Foundation.

10. If you wish to incorporate parts of the Program into other free programs whose distribution conditions are different, write to the author to ask for permission. For software which is copyrighted by the Free Software Foundation, write to the Free Software Foundation; we sometimes make exceptions for this. Our decision will be guided by the two goals of preserving the free status of all derivatives of our free software and of promoting the sharing and reuse of software generally.

NO WARRANTY

11. BECAUSE THE PROGRAM IS LICENSED FREE OF CHARGE, THERE IS NO WARRANTY FOR THE PROGRAM, TO THE EXTENT PERMITTED BY APPLICABLE LAW. EXCEPT WHEN OTHERWISE STATED IN WRITING THE COPYRIGHT HOLDERS AND/OR OTHER PARTIES PROVIDE THE PROGRAM "AS IS" WITHOUT WARRANTY OF ANY KIND, EITHER EXPRESSED OR IMPLIED, INCLUDING, BUT NOT LIMITED TO, THE IMPLIED WARRANTIES OF MERCHANTABILITY AND FITNESS FOR A PARTICULAR PURPOSE. THE ENTIRE RISK AS TO THE QUALITY AND PERFORMANCE OF THE PROGRAM IS WITH YOU. SHOULD THE PROGRAM PROVE DEFECTIVE, YOU ASSUME THE COST OF ALL NECESSARY SERVICING, REPAIR OR CORRECTION.

12. IN NO EVENT UNLESS REQUIRED BY APPLICABLE LAW OR AGREED TO IN WRITING WILL ANY COPYRIGHT HOLDER, OR ANY OTHER PARTY WHO MAY MODIFY AND/OR REDISTRIBUTE THE PROGRAM AS PERMITTED ABOVE, BE LIABLE TO YOU FOR DAMAGES, INCLUDING ANY GENERAL, SPECIAL, INCIDENTAL OR CONSEQUENTIAL DAMAGES ARISING OUT OF THE USE OR INABILITY TO USE THE PROGRAM (INCLUDING BUT NOT LIMITED TO LOSS OF DATA OR DATA BEING RENDERED INACCURATE OR LOSSES SUSTAINED BY YOU OR THIRD PARTIES OR A FAILURE OF THE PROGRAM TO OPERATE WITH ANY OTHER PROGRAMS), EVEN IF SUCH HOLDER OR OTHER PARTY HAS BEEN ADVISED OF THE POSSIBILITY OF SUCH DAMAGES.

End of Terms and Conditions

Wiley Publishing, Inc.
Linux CD Mail-In Coupon

If you do not have access to a PC with a DVD drive, we are offering the complete set on CD-ROMs for a nominal shipping-and-materials fee. If you'd like the CDs sent to you, please:

1. Complete the coupon.
2. Include where you purchased the book and the date purchased.
3. Include a check or money order for $12 (U.S. funds) for orders shipping within the U.S. or $20 (U.S. funds) for orders outside the U.S.
4. Send it to us at the address listed at the bottom of the coupon.

Name ______________________________

Company ______________________________

Address ______________________________

City ______________ State ________ Postal Code ________

Country ______________________________

E-mail ______________________________

Telephone ______________________________

Return this coupon with the appropriate US funds to:
Attn: Media Development
076454232X Red Hat Linux Fedora Fulfillment
Wiley Publishing, Inc.
10475 Crosspoint Blvd.
Indianapolis, IN 46256

Terms: Void where prohibited or restricted by law. Allow 2-4 weeks for delivery. Wiley is not responsible for lost, stolen, late, or illegible orders. For questions regarding this fulfillment offer, please e-mail us at MediaDev@wiley.com.